"Whatever I got from my days representing organized crime is not enough to compensate me for what happened to me."

—Defense attorney John Fitzgerald, Jr., whose right leg was blown off by a car-bomb blast in retaliation for his representation of Boston hit-man-turned-informant Joseph "the Animal" Barboza.

⁊ ⁊ ⁊

"'*The United States of America versus Anthony Spilotro.*' Now what kind of odds are those?"

—Chicago mobster Anthony "Tough Tony" Spilotro, a suspect in at least 22 murders. Never convicted.

⁊ ⁊ ⁊

"I'd rather have my daughter date Tony Spilotro than an FBI agent."

—Oscar B. Goodman

⁊ ⁊ ⁊

"Thank God for Oscar Goodman!"

—Multimillion-dollar drug trafficker Jimmy Chagra, after beating the rap for the murder of federal Judge "Maximum" John Wood.

⁊ ⁊ ⁊

"There is no mob."

—Oscar B. Goodman, to anyone who would listen.

⁊ ⁊ ⁊

"The biggest lie of the 20th century: There is no mob."

—Message on souvenir T-shirts distributed to hundreds of guests at the black-tie 25th anniversary celebration of Oscar B. Goodman's law practice specializing in criminal defense of reputed members of organized crime.

⁊ ⁊ ⁊

"If I am not for myself, who will be for me? Yet if I am for myself only, what am I?"

—Hillel

Of Rats and Men

Of Rats and Men

Oscar Goodman's Life From Mob Mouthpiece to Mayor of Las Vegas

by John L. Smith

HUNTINGTON PRESS

LAS VEGAS, NEVADA

Of Rats and Men: Oscar Goodman's Life From Mob Mouthpiece to Mayor of Las Vegas

Published by
   Huntington Press
   3687 South Procyon Avenue
   Las Vegas, Nevada 89103
   Phone (702) 252-0655
   e-mail: books@huntingtonpress.com

ISBN: 0-929712-98-6

Cover Design: Bethany Coffey Rihel & Laurie Shaw
Interior Design & Production: Laurie Shaw

Photo Credits: Photos obtained from the archives of the *Las Vegas Review-Journal* and private collections. Photo of Bob Martin by Howard Schwartz. Front cover photo by Jeff Scheid.

Library of Congress Cataloging-in-Publication Data

Smith, John L., 1960-
   Of rats and men : Oscar Goodman's life from mob mouthpiece to mayor of Las Vegas / by John L. Smith.
      p. cm.
Includes bibliographical references (p.) and index.
   ISBN 0-929712-98-6 (Hard Cover)
   1. Goodman, Oscar Baylin, 1939- 2. Mayors—Nevada—Las Vegas—Biography. 3. Las Vegas (Nev.)—Politics and government. 4. Lawyers—Nevada—Las Vegas—Biography. 5. Organized crime—United States—History—20th century. I. Title.
F849.L35 S588 2003
979.3'135033'092—dc22

2003017606

Contents

Dedication

For four stand-up women: Laura Goodman,
Carolyn Goodman, Janet Smith, and Tricia Smith.

Acknowledgments

For a man who has lived much of his professional life in the media spotlight, tracking Oscar Goodman's incredible legal career provided a genuine challenge that was assisted by a variety of people. Those who provided insight into Goodman's character were often glad to do so on the condition they not be identified. I came to believe that this had far less to do with Goodman's reputation as a tough mob lawyer than it had to do with his meteoric political success. In a juice town, most attorneys and business owners would rather have Tony Spilotro mad at them than City Hall's mercurial chief enforcer.

Off and on throughout the long process of researching this book, Goodman sat for many hours of interviews and allowed me to glimpse his heavily guarded personal life. That access is greatly appreciated.

Thanks are due to Carolyn Goodman, a class act who provided insight into her husband and their impressively successful and surprisingly well-adjusted children, Oscar Jr., Ross, Eric, and Cara. There is no doubt Carolyn is the real power behind the Goodmans. Thanks also to Oscar's mother, Laura Baylin Goodman, an artist and charmer who agreed to be interviewed for this project. It's obvious that Oscar got his sense of humor and flair for the dramatic from his mother. Lona

Livingston, Oscar's sister, was also kind enough to grant an interview.

Next come the attorneys, business operators, law-enforcement investigators, former reporters, and underworld characters who shared their knowledge of the subject: Pete Beckman, Donald Campbell, Bill Cassidy, David Chesnoff, Harry Claiborne, Dick Crane, Joey Cusumano, Tom Dillard, Jim Ferrence, Mark Fierro, Byron Fox, Dominic Gentile, Brad Jerbic, Marty Keach, Tom Letizia, Don Logan, Gary Peck, Frank Rosenthal, Steve Stein, Loren Stevens, Michael Stuhff, Howard Stutz, Alan Tobin, Billy Vassiliadis, Gerald Werksman, and three dozen sources who spoke on the condition of anonymity.

Oscar Goodman has been good copy for journalists for more than three decades and, as Las Vegas mayor, shows no signs of slowing down in the media and self-promotion departments. The work of the following reporters, columnists, and authors was insightful: Warren Bates, Connie Bruck, Jeff Burbank, Gary Cartwright, Juliet V. Casey, Norm Clarke, Donald Cox, Jim Day, Steve Friess, Frank Geary, Jeff German, John Kerr, George Knapp, Ed Koch, Glen Meek, Thomas Mitchell, Mike Miller, Jan Moller, Jane Ann Morrison, Erin Neff, Matt O'Brien, Peter O'Connell, Glenn Puit, Jon Ralston, Joe Schoenmann, Geoff Schumacher, Steve Sebelius, Vin Suprynowicz, and Mike Zapler. The work of Ned Day, late mob aficionado, continues to resound more than 15 years after his death.

When others faltered, Anthony Curtis of Huntington Press saw the potential in this project and showed great patience in ushering it into existence. The next editorial sitdown at the Tap House is on me, A. C. Editors Deke Castleman and Wendy Y. Tucker worked wonders with the manuscript and kept it on course through considerable tumult. Thanks also are due Huntington Press' Bethany Coffey Rihel, Len Cipkins, Laurie Shaw, and Doug Meyer, as well as Jackie Joniec for her early contributions.

Thanks once again to *Review-Journal* publisher Sherman Frederick and editor Tom Mitchell, who give me the freedom to pursue writing outside my daily column.

Finally, I am grateful to my wife, Tricia, and daughter, Amelia, for enduring the numerous ups and downs associated with taking this project from concept to publication. With the two of you at my side, I'm the luckiest mug to ever play Las Vegas.

Prologue

Living In The House
the Mob Built

A nd it came to pass in the new Las Vegas at the
twilight of the 20th century that all the most notorious mobsters—at least those with the snappy
monikers and blood-soaked resumés who lacked Ivy League
MBAs and vast stock portfolios—were either infirm, incarcer-
ated, interred, or had assumed new identities in the Federal
Witness Protection Program.

This state of affairs suited the corporate image of a city
built by Meyer Lansky and Benny Siegel, Moe Dalitz and the
recalcitrant killers behind the Teamsters Central States Pension Fund. But it was no fun at all for criminal defense attorney Oscar B. Goodman, whose marble-floored law office at
520 South Fourth Street in downtown Las Vegas was known
nationally as "the House the Mob Built." Not that Goodman
was complaining loudly. He'd grown rich and infamous representing a rogue's gallery of reputed members of organized
crime—a felonious fraternity whose very existence he'd denied throughout most of his 35-year legal career. If the Mafia
was a myth, it certainly paid exceedingly well and often in
cash.

Goodman had become a name in the American justice system. He was among the nation's premier criminal defense attorneys. He'd argued on the floor of the U.S. Senate, served as

president of the National Association of Criminal Defense Attorneys, was named one of America's "Best Trial Lawyers" by the *National Law Journal*, generated a seven-figure annual income, and attracted a legion of clients to his plush office lobby. Accused killers and racketeers lined up to see the lawyer who'd spent his life zealously and successfully defending the rights of such dangerous men in hostile courtrooms across the nation. His winning percentage was as enviable as his client list was disreputable. His in-your-face taunts sizzled in the psyches of Organized Crime Strike Force attorneys.

Whenever the latter-day history of gangsterism was considered, Goodman the Mob Mouthpiece was prominently mentioned. Here was a man whose image was so synonymous with organized crime that he appeared as himself in Martin Scorsese's Las Vegas mobster epic *Casino*, a man whose life was so intriguing it was the subject of the feature-length documentary *Mob Law: The True Story of Oscar Goodman*. Here was a man some organized-crime experts believed was juiced in to Las Vegas at a pivotal time in the city's dark history through a mysterious connection from Philadelphia, as well as Lansky, the financial titan of the underworld whom he'd one day represent but would never meet. Here was a man without a criminal record, but a record of criminal representation that made him Public Enemy Number One among federal mob prosecutors.

In his shadowy netherworld, Oscar Goodman was a celebrity.

But what about the rest of the world?

As he sat in his office near the turn of the millennium, crafting his cases like Balzac with his endless manuscripts, a question formed in the morning light: If Las Vegas, America's most tawdry and notorious city, could lose its five-o'clock shadow, dress up in a corporate collar, and merge with mainstream society as a sort of Mickey Cohen-meets-Mickey Mouse resort-destination mecca, might it not also be possible for a man of Oscar Goodman's reputation to change his pinstripes and write a fresh ending to his life story?

The odds were long, but then Las Vegas is the land of long odds. Of all the mobsters who gave Las Vegas its reputation as a bastion of the broken-nose set, eventually it was their mouthpiece who came to symbolize all that was notorious about Las Vegas. Chicago hitman Tony Spilotro wasn't quoted in the newspapers more than a handful of times in his life; Oscar Goodman talked tough for him. Most FBI agents couldn't have picked Kansas City boss Nick Civella out of a lineup, but they could see Oscar Goodman's hawk's beak, piercing eyes, and perpetual sneer coming from a mile away. Goodman paraded his dangerous clients past a line of television cameras and print reporters. He was one-part lion tamer one-part bodyguard, and he played the role to perfection.

After Spilotro's grisly murder by his Outfit bosses in 1986, Goodman's professional life began to change. His wiseguy worldview was altered forever.

Like Olivier rendering *Hamlet* for the ten thousandth time, Goodman wore the character of the mob mouthpiece like the Prince of Denmark's cape. He began to grow tired of metaphorically holding up the bullet-pierced skull of his client's victim and decrying, "Alas, poor Yorick! We never knew him, Your Honor, and we've got alibi witnesses." With so much attention paid to Oscar the Mouthpiece, there was little recognition of the other Oscar, the fiercely loyal husband and father of four who privately cared more about the academic success of his kids than the succession of the Chicago mob or the Gambino crime family.

An actor at heart, he'd spent a career courting the spotlight like a Broadway hoofer. That high profile was great for business, but he gradually became identified more with his clients than with his practice of jurisprudence. There came a time early in his career when Goodman was no longer simply considered a skilled attorney, but was widely known as a mob lawyer. In at least a segment of the government's view, he was a mobster with a juris doctorate. FBI men and local police investigators whispered that he was quite likely a *consigliere* to La Cosa Nostra, a man whose advice was sought by the mob's top hoodlums, killers, and bosses.

Was Goodman really connected by more than the attorney-client relationship?

It had happened many times with other criminal defense attorneys who had stepped out of their roles and stood too close to the fire. Chicago had Sidney Korshak, the dynamo long suspected of playing a senior role in Outfit business. Boston had John Fitzgerald, who'd lost a leg and nearly his life when his car exploded. Philadelphia had Goodman's old college friend Bobby Simone, who took a federal tax fall after being identified as a trusted confidant of Philadelphia mob boss Nicky Scarfo.

Whether a mobster lawyer or, as he'd long argued, a lawyer who represented reputed mobsters, Goodman was sorely in need of the kind of character rehabilitation that Las Vegas seemed able to provide. For generations, the city had been the place a fellow hamstrung by felonious repute could come to change his luck, or at least his name, and start life anew. If even Oscar Goodman could redefine his persona, then Las Vegas truly was a magical place, a neon River Jordan capable of making any man reborn.

The odds were far longer than the chances of the traditional mob making a comeback in the new Las Vegas. Then again, Oscar Goodman had faced long odds throughout his legal career.

? ? ?

From behind a desk in an expansive office lined with photographs of the celebrated and inglorious people in his life, Goodman leaned forward in his chair for emphasis and started to explain how the mob had been a figment of the government's imagination.

Then the phone rang.

It was Vinny Ferrara calling from Terminal Island, the federal penitentiary in California. The underboss of New England's most powerful Mafia family was in prison after a murder and racketeering conviction, but was still fighting for his freedom, and he called his attorney regularly from inside for updates on his long-shot appeal.

A few minutes later, the phone rang again. This time it was Natale "Big Chris" Richichi calling from the hospital at a federal prison in Springfield, Missouri. A Gambino crime-family capo, Richichi was best known as "Dapper Don," John Gotti's confidant. With criminal activity dating to the FDR administration, Richichi was considered one of the last great

dinosaur mobsters in a nation that had seen traditional organized crime either merge with Corporate America or hover on
the edge of extinction. "To the public, these are bad men,"
Goodman explained after hanging up. "I know a different side
of them. They may be bad men, but they are men, not animals,
no matter what nickname the police may label them with."

The first irony. Oscar Goodman hears more from the clients he has failed to keep out of prison than from those for
whom he's won freedom. Ferrara and Richichi weren't going
anywhere soon, and Goodman knew it. But they faithfully
called their man in Vegas. The winners? They rarely write, and
never call.

A few of the remaining old-schoolers who were still on the
street, however, appeared to appreciate Goodman's role in their
lives and found time to visit. Take Charles Panarella.

With Goodman in his corner, the Colombo crime-family
capo had won a split decision on money-laundering charges.
He waited in the outer office and chatted with Goodman's legal assistant, Vinny Montalto. Although crippled by arthritis,
at 75 years old Panarella still possessed an ironworker's hand-
shake — and one of the underworld's great monikers, "Charlie
Moose." Those who know him recommend that strangers not
bring up the legendary underworld story about the time Charlie Moose cut off the testicles of an offending hoodlum before
delivering the kill shot.

Montalto, a slender gray-haired New York transplant
known on the street as "Skinny Vinny," entered stage-left-style
through the office door. Like a character out of a David Mamet
play, Montalto talked naturally out of the side of his mouth,
handing Goodman the latest betting line, spouting one-liners
like a street-wise Yogi Berra. When he wasn't providing Goodman with gambling information, Vinny interpreted the voluminous Title III federal wiretaps the firm's clients invariably
generated. Lord knows he knew the lingo.

؟ ؟ ؟

The walls of Oscar Goodman's gaudy inner sanctum were
festooned with photographs of clients and advertisements for
himself. Snapshots captured Goodman being interviewed by

Mike Wallace, Dick Cavett, and Geraldo Rivera. On one wall, life imitated art with stills of Goodman portraying himself in *Casino* with Robert DeNiro, Joe Pesci, and Sharon Stone. With clients ranging from Mike Tyson to LaToya Jackson, Goodman was no stranger to tabloid celebrity. Photographers also captured Goodman on the courthouse steps with Spilotro, Philadelphia mob boss "Little Nicky" Scarfo, and his underboss "Crazy Phil" Leonetti, collectively suspected in as many as 50 murders. Artist's courtroom renderings depicted drug-trafficking kingpin Jamiel "Jimmy" Chagra, the focal point of one of the most expensive investigations in FBI history — the murder of federal judge John Wood.

If those walls could talk, a vaudevillian might say, half the underworld murders in America might be solved. The fact that he'd basked in the spotlight while representing clients whose lives depended on their maintaining a code of silence was the second irony about the federal Organized Crime Strike Force's biggest nemesis and greatest critic.

Goodman wore his reputation as a courtroom hitman with pride, bristling at government prosecutors and newspaper reporters who questioned his win-loss record. In conversation, he sounded more like Jake LaMotta arguing about his greatest fights than America's best mob attorney reminiscing about his cases.

"I'm not like Gerry Spence who says he's never lost a case," Goodman cracked. "The man who's never lost a case hasn't tried too many of them. The people who say that are just talking off the top of their head. First of all, I never lost a case for Anthony Spilotro. You start off with that premise. The last major case I tried was the government against show producer Jeff Kutash, a dead-bang case of bribery against a public official, in this case a District Court Judge. Kutash: not guilty. There's the Maximum John Wood murder case against my client, Jimmy Chagra. He walked on the murder. Chris Petti was the government's choice to assume the head of all Mafia activity in Southern California. They had him nailed on a stack of cases. I wrapped them up and instead of receiving two hundred years, he got seven; I consider that a victory. There's Leonardo Contreras Subias. All he faced was something like fifteen thousand years in prison. I persuaded the court to give him a ten-year sentence to run concurrent with a sentence he was serving in another case. In other words, he got nothing. It's a win. I represented a man involved in a two-hundred-thirty-seven-million-dollar fraud. I got him probation. The government can crow all it wants about getting a conviction. But probation for a two-hundred-thirty-seven-million-dollar fraud is not a loss.

"But there's no question that I do lose cases. That's because I try cases."

The photograph of Harry Claiborne, for example. Rail slim with a coyote grin, as a criminal defense attorney Claiborne was as smooth as single-malt scotch. He dined daily with Horseshoe Casino patriarch and former Dallas rackets king Lester "Benny" Binion. When Claiborne became a federal judge, he was immediately targeted by the FBI on suspicion of corruption. He was eventually tried and convicted of tax evasion, becoming the first federal judge in a century to be impeached. The case originated with a sweetheart deal and cooperation from Mustang Ranch whoremaster Joe Conforte.

Mention Conforte and Goodman still bares his teeth. Rats earn the utmost derision from Goodman. Through the years, he railed relentlessly against government informants, such as Aladena "Jimmy the Weasel" Fratianno, Frank Cullotta, even the young killer he once thought might grow up to be the boss of all bosses, Philip Leonetti. And with good reason. Mob historians know that the government's real success against organized crime came not only with the liberalization of the telephone-wiretap statutes, but with the steady parade of defectors. Pretty soon, there will be more mob guys on the government payroll than there are on the streets. Ever aware that today's standup guy might be tomorrow's star witness for the prosecution, Goodman no longer engaged in casual conversations with his new clients.

"It's taken a lot of the fun out of the game," he said.

Fun? Out of representing some of the most notorious criminals in the history of the American justice system? The third irony.

In a justice system turned upside down, in which dark is light and the government uses admitted killers to convict suspected ones, high-wire criminal defense is the final mind-bend-ing frontier. When professional hitmen retain your services, it's not how you play the game, but whether you win or lose. This is a story of rats and men, of how a scrawny Jewish kid from Philadelphia grew up to be called the powerhouse *consigliere* to La Cosa Nostra and still managed to keep his scalp, raise a family in Las Vegas, put down daily bets on the ballgames, and get elected the mayor of the whole damn town.

This is that most improbable of Las Vegas long-shot stories: the one in which the high roller, after making a highly unlikely comeback, decides to quit while he's ahead. He takes what he's learned in his previous existence and goes legit without entirely changing his stripes.

It's a far-fetched plot line. But if ever a city needed a fearless advocate at the twilight of the 20th century, it was Las Vegas.

And what better preparation for a political career than representing the mob?

1

From West Philadelphia to West of Arizona

Like so many immigrants before him, Rudolph Guterman survived the long arduous ocean journey from Eastern Europe to the United States and managed to endure all the indignities of Ellis Island with everything but his name intact. Upon entering the country from Lodz, Poland, the Guterman name became Americanized as Goodman. After moving to Philadelphia, Rudolph worked as a bartender and eventually owned a shot-and-a-beer joint at Third and Lombard streets at a time bootleggers associated with Meyer Lansky ran the city's liquor racket. Philadelphia's working-class army marched on Prohibition whiskey and bathtub gin. The hootch not only quenched the thirst of a suppressed nation, but funded the rise of organized crime as a force in society.

Rudolph's bar was a narrow dimly lit room where working men could forget their troubles with a boilermaker, a shot of whiskey dropped into a glass of draft beer. Rudolph's young family lived in an apartment above the bar. He watched as another branch of the Goodman family grew wealthy after opening a bathhouse. People from miles around went there to take a *schvitz* in the hot steamy waters. In future generations, family members distinguished each side as either the "bath-house Goodmans" or the "saloon Goodmans."

Somewhere in that milieu, Rudolph Goodman realized his American Dream. This immigrant owned his own business, but decided his young son, Allan, was destined for greater things. Though Allan Goodman displayed a strong work ethic, pickling eggs and sweeping the floor of the bar after hours, he focused most on his education. Thanks to a father who sacrificed and saved, the saloonkeeper's boy attended academically exclusive Central High School, the University of Pennsylvania Law School, and the Wharton School of Business. At that time, few Jews managed to be admitted to prestigious Wharton.

Allan Goodman married Laura Baylin on June 15, 1933. His bride's family had come to America the previous generation from Mongolia. Laura's father started in the new world with a pickle barrel and had turned kosher dills into a small fortune before losing lock, stock, and barrel in the crash of '29. Laura was a modern woman, two generations ahead of her time. Far from submissive, she was an artist and actress who spoke her mind and challenged her husband. Allan realized early in his adult life that he would be nowhere without his education and his Laura. Their marriage, although at times tempestuous, would provide a strong example for their own children.

The Goodman name might have been only one generation old in America, but Allan was determined to ensure it was respected. He took a job in the Philadelphia District Attorney's office and focused his energies on the law and raising his family.

Oscar Baylin Goodman was born on July 26, 1939, to doting parents. Family photographs depict a cherubic infant with curly blond hair and bright eyes. Allan and Laura would have two more children, Lona in 1942 and Erica in 1945, but their first-born son was their golden child. Oscar seemed to have been born with an innate ability to work a crowd: Years later his mother recalled neighbors being drawn to him not long after he learned to walk.

In those early years, the Goodman family lived in a tough working-class section of West Philadelphia, first on Catherine Street, then two blocks away on Christian Street. Their house on Christian Street was a narrow brick building with a front stoop leading to a small entry. Many years later, when he re-visited the neighborhood as part of a documentary on his life as a Mafia attorney, Goodman required a police escort. (He was overcome by a sense of nostalgia at the diminutive home that held such a large place in his memory.)

Christian Street near 61st was a crossroad in ethnically stratified Philadelphia. A Jewish kid learned young that he was different — not only from the blacks who lived a few blocks away, but from the Irish who lived just down the street. The taunts started early. His Jewishness was as plain as the nose on his face. Goodman's schnoz and typically Jewish surname made him an easy target for bigots and bullies. So did his slight frame and bookish appearance.

Goodman prospered inside his family circle, but when he ventured outside he faced the reality that being a Jew set him apart from other children. Anti-Semitism manifested in many ways. First, in the loss of childhood innocence.

Laura Goodman remembered the first time her son came home with the painful question: "What's a dirty Jew?"

The epithets stung less than the shoving and battering at the hands of bullies, but they had an effect on young Oscar. They made him angry and street tough. His nose was blood-ied often and broken several times on the street and ballfields, but in time, the scuffles with the scrawny kid ceased. No bully likes a victim who won't back down. In light of the schoolyard fights and anti-Semitic catcalls on the street, it's no wonder that, years later, his few fond memories of public school were of classmates with names like Glickman and Gladstone, Jew-ish boys who were next to him through the grace of an alpha-betical seating chart. Although young Oscar was not afraid to mix it up on the street, the only gang he joined was the Boy Scouts.

"When we lived in West Philadelphia as youngsters and my father was an assistant district attorney, it wasn't a good neighborhood," Lona Goodman Livingston recalled. "We had friends outside the family, but we were closest with family."

In fact, there was little time for outsiders. Laura had four sisters in Philadelphia and Allan had two; their children had cousins galore. The large extended family kept the Goodmans somewhat insulated even in their own neighborhood. Religious holidays were observed with the extended family in crowded celebrations teeming with children.

Although Oscar at times had difficulty taking his education seriously, learning was stressed to the extreme in the Goodman household. Oscar and Lona attended school together for a short time at William Cullen Bryant Elementary. They were accompanied by their grandmother Elizabeth Baylin, an immigrant who learned to speak English by sitting in a classroom with first-graders. With such an example set for them, how could the children of Allan and Laura Goodman not succeed in school?

The pressure to succeed was great and young Oscar wasn't always successful. When he received an unsatisfactory citizenship notice in music class, he was so ashamed he marched home, went into his bedroom, and decided to take his own life. Lacking a pistol, sharp knife, or noose, he attempted to poison himself by eating a mothball, which only made him sick and incurred the wrath of his mother, who despite her diminutive size gave him the beating of his young life. For years he wondered whether it was for the poor grade or the amateurish suicide attempt.

As a boy, Oscar Goodman toyed with the idea of becoming a rabbi, doctor, or artist. The dream of becoming a doctor ended when he failed organic chemistry and art was replaced by more mainstream pursuits. The law, however, scriptural and societal, was almost as much a part of his young life as breathing. Although he would remain close to his faith throughout his life, one day becoming president of Temple Beth Sholom in Las Vegas, he eventually gravitated toward the work of his father.

Allan Goodman set a daily example of how a professional comported himself. He was respected by his peers and admired by his neighbors.

"I'd walk down the street with him in Philadelphia," Oscar Goodman said. "It stayed with me forever. Everybody would say, 'Good morning, counselor.' 'Hello, counselor.' And they said it with love and affection. Because he cared. He was a very caring guy. As a DA for many years back there, he used to take me on Sunday down to the police station and to see him in court. And he didn't get his just due. I think that's part of the reason I have no respect for the system. Because hard work and being a good person don't necessarily add up to success."

A dignified conservative man who voted Republican, the elder Goodman kept abreast of city politics and was a stalwart deputy prosecutor. Although his personality was suited for the law, not the caprice of politics and the Philadelphia DA's office, he was exposed to both. He eventually went into private practice, where he dreamed of one day teaming up with his son.

After entering private practice, Allan Goodman successfully defended Billie Holiday, the singing legend, on a charge of heroin possession. In later years, he garnered headlines for saving a mentally ill woman who suffered from nightmares of the Holocaust, whether asleep or awake. Her family wanted to have her lobotomized.

At one point, the family story goes, Allan Goodman refused to grease the wheels of the system by paying a cash tribute to local powerbrokers in order to obtain a coveted federal judgeship that his son angrily declares would have cut his stress and added years to his life. The elder Goodman felt entitled to the judgeship, and he'd been a good Republican party man, but the powerbrokers still insisted on a payoff. But Allan had something money couldn't buy. The respect of common men.

It was a kind of respect Oscar Goodman would crave in years to come.

※ ※ ※

"We were very very typically Jewish," Lona Livingston recalled. "Education was important and there was never a question of not going to college and becoming a professional person. Our family was also, and still is to this very moment, mother-centered. At the same time, she raised us to be extremely independent. Her relationship with Oscar was always very special, and I don't remember one day being jealous of it."

As a youngster, Lona Goodman worshiped her big brother. She remembered how protective he was of her—and that he began developing his persuasive skills at an early age. Once, she was hit in the mouth by a rollerskate during a skirmish with a neighbor girl. Oscar the dealmaker went into action, extorting comic books from area children as a get-well tribute to his sister.

"I must have had fifty comic books," she recalled. "I became queen for a moment, had my fifteen minutes, and I think it was the only time in my life I had the attention of the entire neighborhood. We weren't allowed to have comic books in the house. We read them, of course, but we had to sneak them. And suddenly, thanks to Oscar, I had dozens."

An excellent student, Lona was afforded the opportunity to skip a grade. But her parents were out of town when the paperwork arrived. With the deadline looming, her big brother again came through, providing passable forgeries.

In 1952 at William L. Sayre Junior High at 58th Avenue and Walnut Street, Goodman made such an impression on his eighth-grade history teacher, Joseph Pollock, that nearly 50 years later the two remained in contact. Goodman's impersonation of General Douglas MacArthur's "Old Soldiers Never Die" speech during a mock political convention remains fresh in Pollock's mind. Goodman worked his audience even then.

"If I were to pick the ten best kids I ever met, Oscar would be in that group," Pollock said. "He was always warm and outgoing."

After Sayre, Goodman was one of hundreds of teenage boys who traveled from all over the city to attend Central High, a public school with a reputation for producing college graduates. Allan Goodman had attended Central at a time when Greek and Latin were prerequisites for graduation, and the curriculum had grown only slightly softer with the passing years. If parents couldn't afford to send their budding scholar to a private college-preparatory academy, Central was the next best choice. Prospective students had to take a test before gaining admission to the all-boys' school where doctorate degrees commonly appeared on teachers' resumés.

Goodman used every form of Philadelphia's public transit system to get from West Philadelphia to Central High, which was located in the northwestern part of the city. He walked a block, hopped a trolley to the Frankfort Elevated train, connected to the subway, then caught a bus to the campus gate. The commute was more than an hour each way, on a good day. On afternoons when he played football after school, he didn't get home until after 8 p.m.

When he arrived as a freshman in 1953, Goodman took his seat next to Edward Glickman.

"We were both cut-ups and delighted in making fun of the teachers, most of the time behind their backs," Glickman recalled. "One of our favorite targets was a teacher we called Dancing Dave Newmark, who sort of pirouetted while he lectured. He was a wonderful teacher, though. There was a lot of joking around, but people at Central were for the most part very motivated."

Glickman was the more dedicated student, Goodman the more polished wit, but both boys were sports crazy. Although they lived far apart, they managed to get together for schoolyard basketball, pinball at a neighborhood arcade, and to watch Philadelphia Warriors games in person at the arena or on the Goodman family television.

"Everyone who went to Central at that time was going to become a doctor, a lawyer, or a nuclear physicist," said Glickman, a Philadelphia attorney. " I remember that if I hadn't helped him, Oscar would have flunked Algebra One with Mr. Shock."

Glickman wasn't Oscar's only tutor. Allan Goodman and his son spent countless hours in the basement of the family home at a large chalkboard, practicing his schoolwork until the results were flawless. Algebra equations went up on the board time after time until they were solved. Essays were written in chalk first, the grammar checked and re-checked, before pen was set to paper. It was in no small part through the help of his father, not his conventional teachers despite their expertise, that Oscar Goodman became a top student.

"Hour after hour we would work on my homework," Goodman recalled many years later. "I not only became more accomplished, I also had a chance to be with my father, who in those days took my education more seriously than I did. It was tougher getting through my father than it was getting through the teachers. We couldn't go to school unless our homework was perfect. I wasn't a motivated student, but I didn't have to be. I got my education at home."

In the front yard, Allan and Oscar threw the football, but

as with everything else it was not just a simple game of catch. Oscar crouched at center and Allan played quarterback, calling out math problems while the boy listened closely for the right answer.

"He would say, for instance, forty-three. Six times one times three-and-a-half times two plus one.' When it added up to forty-three, that's when I snapped the ball. He was a remarkable man. And that's also how I became a center on the football team."

After a year, Goodman transferred to Haverford School, a private college preparatory. Glickman said, "I remember being very disappointed and upset when Oscar decided not to return to Central. I remember visiting with him and his parents with my parents at the end of the first year and expressing real regret. He was a great friend who I wasn't going to see. He was having some academic problems, wasn't doing very well, and his parents may have felt he would be better served at the Haverford School. It also might have been a matter of geography. Haverford was a lot closer to his house than Central."

Haverford not only was a prestigious and expensive school—tuition cut deeply into the Goodman family's budget—but it also shortened the commute time by half. Haverford, which required students to wear a jacket and tie to class, had an even more serious atmosphere than Central. Goodman's grades improved and he made the football team despite his slight frame.

"Oscar was anything but conservative," recalled Haverford School classmate William Frankel. "He was just different. The way he dressed, his mannerisms. He was always very smart, but he wasn't always very serious. He had a good sense of humor. But if somebody had said he'd become a good criminal lawyer, I don't know if anyone would have believed it. He just didn't have the seriousness at that age."

Goodman managed to receive above-average grades without carrying a book, a habit his mother noticed and decided to investigate.

"I found out the secret," he told her candidly. "You don't say a word. You listen and watch the teacher. You find out what the teacher wants and you give it to him."

8

His tailored approach to learning did not, however, impress Haverford School's dean, who warned Goodman's parents of their son's unfulfilled academic potential.

To the high school girls, on the other hand, nothing about Oscar's potential seemed to falter. Although hardly a handsome lad, he was not only the life of the classroom, but he was articulate, charming, and had a reputation as a schoolyard scrapper. Whatever the reason, girls were drawn to Goodman, who showed more interest in football than females.

The schoolwork came easily, but not from an abundance of effort. His father's daily drilling at home had honed Oscar's ability to recall facts and recite texts nearly line for line. He received good grades without breaking much of a sweat, but they still weren't quite good enough to transfer from Haverford Prep to Haverford College.

During the summer after his senior year, sister Lona recalled, Oscar lobbied to enter the college, by dropping by the admissions office regularly to apply his gifts of personality and persuasion. In the end, he was accepted, and he entered as a freshman in 1957. He graduated with a bachelor's degree in 1961 with grades sufficient to gain entrance into the University of Pennsylvania Law School, where he would receive his juris doctorate in 1964.

"He pretty much charmed his way into a fine school," Lona said. "And he did well once he got there."

At Haverford, Goodman grew interested in the arts and creative writing. He was a gifted illustrator who penned his own comic strips and cartoons, including some with rather pointed references to the caliber of beauty present at nearby Bryn Mawr College.

Goodman fell in love at Haverford, but not with learning. His greatest challenge was fitting academics into his burgeoning social calendar. Most courses failed to challenge him. There was an outline to follow, a system to synchronize. He understood what professors wanted and he gave it to them—all the while knowing that he'd never encounter a tougher taskmaster than his father.

Finding time for all his extracurricular activities presented a greater challenge. Although not even by his own sense of hyperbole a gifted athlete, he insisted on turning out for the football team and managed to get into a few games as a backup center — all 160 pounds of him — before suffering a concussion. He was cut out more for the bench than the breach.

During a summer break in the heart of the Beat era made famous by Jack Kerouac's memoir *On the Road*, Goodman and a buddy bummed their way across country and stopped off in Las Vegas, where the gambling-crazed Oscar walked into the Dunes with a nearly foolproof system to beat the house. There was only one fool he hadn't planned for.

"I was up!" he recalled. "I saw myself paying for my college education, buying a car to drive back home, gifts for my folks, the whole works. I went bust, of course."

From there he limped on alone to the Bay Area, where he enjoyed a few Bohemian comforts before drifting down to Venice Beach. At the beach, he sold sketches for food money and marveled at the openly alternative lifestyles.

Flat busted once more, he floated farther south, where in Encinitas he charmed a generous older couple, the Appletons, into taking him into their home. He ate well, enjoyed riding in their Cadillac, and was impressed by their home's ocean view.

"They lived the way I had never seen people live before," Goodman later recalled. "It was the first time I'd seen the good life, and I liked what I saw."

With the Appletons' help, Oscar the beatnik beat it back to Philadelphia.

On weekends, he took the train to New York to watch performances of the Actors Studio led by Lee Strasberg. He watched a young Marlon Brando perform scenes and one-act plays.

"I would go up there and watch all the plays and hang around with all the people," Goodman recalled. "I thought I was an expert on the theater. I got invited to a reading of a play. I think John Facenda, who was best known as the 'Voice of God' on the NFL highlight films, did the reading."

He joined in with the theater crowd, was invited to cast parties, and at one point was offered an opportunity to invest in a play that was just coming together off-Broadway. The playwright called it *Come Blow Your Horn*, and Goodman bluffed his way into receiving a reading script. If he liked it, he could buy 10% for $50,000. Although he had little more than the change in his pocket, his father could swing such a deal. What's more, he was told that if it lasted even seven days on Broadway, chances were good it would be made into a movie.

But Oscar Goodman the college man was no fool, or so he thought. He'd done a little acting and creative writing and fancied himself a young aficionado of the stage. He knew quality when he saw it and *Come Blow Your Horn* wasn't it. He hated the script and advised his father against making such an imprudent investment.

Somehow the playwright, Neil Simon, managed to get over Oscar's rejection. The play generated plenty of interest from other investors. *Come Blow Your Horn* was a hit and later a movie starring Frank Sinatra.

"It made nothing but money, and of course the genius here said it wouldn't run two days," Goodman laughed. "From then on my father stopped listening to me about anything."

？？？

What prowess Goodman lacked on the playing field, he made up for while playing the field of college girls at Bryn Mawr. He developed a reputation as a love-'em-and-dump-'em Lothario who rarely traveled without his entourage of characters in their herringbone jackets and Vitalis. When he wasn't on a date, he was drinking whiskey shots and beer with the boys or gambling his spare change on a ballgame or the ponies. As early as his college years, Goodman's taste for liquor and sports betting was well-established. He kept campus bookmakers hopping and even placed bets with the wiseguys who used the city's delis as their offices.

Then he met Carolyn Goldmark who, after a fashion, stopped him cold. She was a tall, progressive, secular Jewish girl from New York related on her mother's side to the Seligman family. In the social registry, the "saloon Goodmans" were not the sort of people who could expect much contact from the Seligman-Goldmark crowd. In Stephen Birmingham's remarkable study, *Our Crowd: The Great Jewish Families of New York*, he captured the essence of the tradition that light-hearted Oscar Goodman faced. Edwin Seligman, a Columbia University economics professor and a confidant of President Theodore Roosevelt, once wrote, "My father was the most tolerant of men. But he was also very intolerant of anything not quite up to standard, sometimes being a little unfair to stupid people." Stupid included anyone who did not appear serious — as the family defined the term.

Had he known what he was up against, he might have moved on, but Oscar Goodman was blissfully ignorant and soon became hopelessly smitten.

Near the rise of the civil-rights movement, "Carol" Goldmark, as she was known, roomed with one of Bryn Mawr's few African-American students. It was this roommate who searched throughout sophomore year to find a nice Jewish boy for Carol to date and came up with a wisecracking junior from Haverford College named Oscar Goodman. Whoever said first impressions are lasting ones didn't have those two in mind.

"My roommate Jan Douglass said, 'You've got to meet this guy,'" Carolyn recalled. "Unfortunately, he was known as a ladies' man on our campus. He came in with four or five of what I call his henchmen, and Oscar was in the middle of them. My roommate stopped him as he came in, saying, 'I'd like you to meet my roommate Carol Goldmark.' I said hello and he said hello, and it really fell flat. And I said to Jan, 'Yech.' Later, I found out that he said the same thing about me to his friends. So that was the end of that. Or so I thought."

Oscar returned to his dating marathon and Carol had no shortage of suitors. Both ran for student council of their respective colleges. She was elected council president. He lost his bid.

"He was always running for office," she recalled. "He was always 'on.' That's part of his soul. Oscar was very arrogant, very swaggering, and overstuffed with himself. He had his guys around him and everything, but during a study hall, he kept coming over to my table. He was a little too attentive, but I thought he was sort of cute."

"She had the best legs, the best legs in the world," Goodman said. "Still does."

A series of late-night calls to her dorm ensued and after two more false starts, he finally asked her out — much to the chagrin of her fellow dorm dwellers, several of whom had had brief encounters with the young man Carolyn affectionately described as "that idiot Oscar."

"When he came to pick me up, he stunk of whatever he'd been drinking, which I found out later was a scotch-and-beer combination called a boilermaker. His face and ears were really red. He picked me up in a black four-door Oldsmobile that belonged to his parents. I was thinking, 'Hey, not bad. Maybe he's got a little money.' We got in the car and he said he had to go home, but on the way we stopped at this little bar on City Line Avenue. We went inside and he ordered a shot and a beer for both of us. I didn't even know what to do with it. But that was the way we started, with a shot and a beer."

Later, at Oscar's house, Carolyn met his sister Erica and realized that the tough-guy persona was all an act. He came from a good family—even if the automobile was leased and the house was rented. That night they went to a party and she was reluctantly impressed by the way Oscar was greeted when he entered the house. With a wave of the hand he had the host remove a record by the foul-mouthed comedienne, Belle Barth, from the turntable so as not to offend his date's delicate sensibilities. In the backyard, they talked for hours before her curfew, then he drove her back to the dorm. On the way, he had to admit that he'd lost his glasses back in the yard and couldn't see well at night. She sat close and helped steer the Oldsmobile. She spurned his playful advances at the door, quipping, "I don't kiss drunks."

Meeting Carolyn Goldmark changed his life. For her part, Carolyn was drawn to Goodman's sense of humor and his unabashed enthusiasm. What he lacked in classic physical features—a hawk nose dominated his face and made his chin look weak, and he stood barely five feet ten inches—was overcome by an irrepressible personality.

The relentless salesmanship revealed itself yet again when he took a Christmas-holiday job selling electric shavers at a department store and Fuller Brush products door to door. Goodman was a successful shaver salesman, but was compelled to quit when he found himself being able to so easily make a sale to older customers. His Fuller Brush work was also a moneymaker, but he turned in his suitcase as soon as he realized the point of the job was to sell to people who really didn't need the product he was pushing.

In the summer between junior and senior terms, Goodman

followed Carolyn to New York City, where she was employed as a switchboard operator at the Manhattanville Community Center in Harlem at 125th and Amsterdam. It was a world away from life at Bryn Mawr and Haverford College. Goodman worked there as a janitor.

"I cleaned out the restrooms of the lowest economic group of people, perhaps, in the United States," he recalled. "If other people cleaned toilets the way I did, you would never go to the bathroom in a public place. There was more Lysol in that room than any place in the history of the world."

But the experience broadened his worldview. The Goodmans lived in middle-class comfort and in terms of helping his understanding of people, one summer in Harlem was worth four years at Haverford. Even then, Carolyn acted as his better angel, steering the cocky young Oscar toward a kind of self-awareness not learned in law books or from self-important professors.

With their undergraduate work nearing an end, the young couple decided it was time to get married. They didn't anticipate the absolute lack of encouragement from Carolyn's parents.

"We knew we were right for each other," Carolyn recalled. "My parents took a little convincing. My father was the consummate professional OB/GYN who'd been president of both the New York City Medical Society and the New York State Medical Society. He thought Oscar was 'not good enough' for his daughter—too young, one hundred percent unproven, no plans, no profession, absolutely green. He thought Oscar had a lot of *chutzpah* to be asking to marry his daughter."

Rich—and not quite so Jewish. The Goldmarks had made every attempt to assimilate into New York society, downplaying their heritage and refraining from attending synagogue. As a result, the Goldmarks considered themselves only technically Jewish. Carolyn had grown up without being subjected to anti-Semitism—or to the rich Jewish religious and cultural traditions. As a child, she'd spent part of each summer at a private camp on the Connecticut River near Dartmouth University. An adolescent discussion once turned to religion. "I'd been with these same girls every summer since I was five years old," she recalled. "When the discussion got around to me, I said, 'I'm Jewish.' It was like every head spun around and looked at me. I thought, 'What's wrong with being Jewish?' I thought, 'This is weird. What is this?' It was that moment that finally brought home a sense of Jewishness to me. I had heard about the Holocaust, but it wasn't part of me. I had never been in a synagogue. My parents were Ethical Culturalists. We celebrated Christmas at my uncle's house. It wasn't that they hated Jews, but they would have preferred that we marry non-Jews."

"Her father was suspicious of me," Goodman recalled. "Her mother grew to like me after Carolyn and I were married, but her father took longer to warm up to me."

"They were Jewish people who hated being known as Jews. They'd been a part of New York society through the Seligman family. They were related to Edwin Robert Anderson Seligman on her mother's side. Her grandfather, a good friend of Theodore Roosevelt, was a prime mover in establishing the income tax. He was friends with Gandhi, and the lawyers in the family were members of the same law firm as John Foster Dulles. Branches of the Seligman family helped establish towns in the west, including eastern Arizona and what would later be called White Pine County in Nevada.

"Her father wanted her to marry a gentile. It broke their hearts when she fell in love with me. They would have paid a billion dollars for her to marry someone other than me. Carolyn made me—made me—ask for her hand, because I don't come from that kind of background. She listened from the other room.

"Her father said, 'How are you going to support Carol?' I said, 'We're going to work our way through law school.' Then he said, 'You better keep her in the style to which she is accustomed or I'll kick your ass from here to Seventy-Sixth Street.' I said, 'If you're big enough.'"

On that night, one that ought to have been special, Carl Goldmark struck a desperate compromise. He persuaded the young couple to wait a year while she attended secretarial school and he focused on his first year of law school. She would remain in New York. He would live and attend class in Philadelphia.

Although it had been expected that Oscar Goodman would go to law school, he entertained a number of career options—from writing novels and painting in Venice, California, to becoming a rabbi in Philadelphia. Carl and Hazel Goldmark might have gone into cardiac arrest had they only known. Oscar didn't know precisely what he would do, but he knew he wanted it to be big. He was determined that no one would for long be able to say that the son of Allan Goodman, of the Saloon Goodmans, wasn't good enough.

❧ ❧ ❧

Some things hadn't changed. As always, Goodman found the classroom less than stimulating. He was destined for an undistinguished career at the University of Pennsylvania School of Law. Philadelphia attorney Hank Gladstone sat next to Goodman that first year.

"The first year of law school, no matter how good your credentials coming in, is extremely stressful unless you're an extraordinary person," Gladstone said. "There's an anxiety that penetrates the whole first year. I had aspirations of being at the top of the class. I don't think that Oscar would say that. Oscar was a very laid-back understated kind of guy who I don't think really had aspirations of being at the top of the class. He just wanted to become a lawyer."

Indeed, Oscar Goodman had more important things on his mind. He had found the love of his life. She was smart, beautiful, and most of all, focused. Oscar and Carolyn were married after his first year of law school.

On the day of the wedding in New York, Carl Goldmark drove his daughter to the hotel for the ceremony. "Are you sure?" he asked, scowling. "You don't have to do this."

A photo taken that day captures Carl Goldmark as cheery as Julius Rosenberg as he and his daughter arrive for the wedding. Oscar Goodman and Carolyn Goldmark were wed by a rabbi and an Ethical Culturalist official on June 6, 1962, in New York City.

"It was the anniversary of D-Day," Carolyn said. "I thought that would help him remember."

The Goldmarks never smiled once and even Carolyn cried tears of anxiety. She noted years later that the two men were vying for her affection.

The Goodmans were on their honeymoon in Europe when Oscar's grades came back. Upon returning, Goodman found he had received a 70.1, a reed-slim one-tenth percent above the minimum passing grade.

? ? ?

Back in Philadelphia, Oscar dreamed of producing documentaries of the city's once-proud neighborhoods, streets with houses dating to the early 1700s that he ached to redevelop.

"I had an interest in doing two things when I went to law school," he said. "Law wasn't on the list. I had an interest in producing movies about the city. I had a great desire to make a movie about the inner city. It's funny, because as mayor of Las Vegas I'm trying to redevelop an inner city. And I wanted to buy and renovate the old Federalist homes down in Philadelphia in a terrible neighborhood, but they were these classic little brick homes that the colonists lived in. My father had lived there as a boy. I went to my dad to see whether or not he'd be interested in fronting me. He had a mental block about it. He left that neighborhood and wasn't ever going back and couldn't see the potential. Today, it's known as Society Hill and it's incredibly beautiful. I guess I was a little ahead of my time."

The next two years, his grades improved more by chance than by application. The newlyweds lived in a tiny third-floor apartment at 4039 Chestnut Street in Philadelphia, a crime-riddled neighborhood a few blocks from the law school. Carolyn worked as a secretary at Sun Oil and assisted Allan Goodman by typing for him pro bono. Carolyn's paying secretarial duties brought $72 a week into their lives at a much-needed time.

Meanwhile, Oscar's dislike of the classroom grew stronger. The minute he completed his day at the law school, he ran directly to City Hall, where he held a full-time job with then-Assistant District Attorney Arlen Specter, the future United States Senator. Goodman's job clerking for Specter provided him with a working laboratory in which he began to see how the law really worked, how its great weight was sometimes applied in the system unequally.

"Working for Specter in the District Attorney's office was important for me," Goodman said. "I realized the difference between law school and the law. I grew to love the law, but I hated law school."

Hank Gladstone recalled, "What sticks out in my mind the most is there were a lot of us who were very focused on getting a job with a law firm in the summer between the second and third year. A good law-firm job in the summer might mean you'd get invited back and be asked to join the firm or it could be used as currency to pursue other jobs. I didn't have a clue what Oscar did in that second summer. All I know is that at the beginning of the third year, I remember him saying, 'You know, I think I'd like to get into a DA's office somewhere. I'm going to write a whole bunch of district attorneys and see what happens.' He wrote, I think, one hundred and fifty to two hundred letters to district attorneys and one day said, 'I got this interesting response from Las Vegas. They'd like to talk to me.' It was all sort of accidental. His path to Las Vegas was like being in Las Vegas and spinning the wheel. It could have been the same letter from Houston and that might have been where he ended up."

Hank Gladstone finished fifth in his class, Oscar Goodman closer to fifth from the bottom. Although Goodman had an opportunity to work for Philadelphia's respected Bernstein & Bernstein law firm, he had other places to go.

"I couldn't wait to get out and see the world," he said. "Most of the students were, quite understandably, interested in doing well in order to make a lot of money and land a good position with a major hometown firm. They don't move two blocks from where they were born. They go to the same country clubs their parents did, send their kids to the same private schools they attended, have a summer house at Beach Haven. They were fine people, but they were the most incestuous bunch of people you'd ever meet. I wasn't interested in making money or working at a prestigious firm. I was interested in helping people. It was only a matter of luck that I made a lot of money helping people."

But those who observed Oscar Goodman in early adulthood agree it was his young wife Carolyn who inspired him to be more than a class clown and slacker. In his expansive Las Vegas law office years later, Goodman would gaze at the large portrait of his wife, which hung on a nearby wall and joke, "There she is, always watching, whispering for me to get back to work. Telling me, 'Earn, baby, earn.'" Then he would add, "Without Carolyn, I'd be nothing."

"Carolyn and Oscar have a partnership that is in many ways enviable," Lona Livingston said. "She is largely responsible for his success. She is a strong personality who supports him in many ways. Together they're an extremely strong couple."

Carolyn had many talents and great potential to excel in a career of her own. But after graduating from Bryn Mawr College with a bachelor's degree in 1961 — she later received a master's degree in counseling from the University of Nevada-Las Vegas — she focused not on her own career, but on her husband's professional success. By delaying her personal work goals, she enabled Oscar to thrive.

Oscar and Carolyn started their life together with ample good luck. Goodman, by then an avid gambler, recalled winning a $100 bet on Sherluck, a 35-to-1 longshot in the Belmont Stakes. Where a struggling law student might have come up with $100 to place on an astronomical outsider remains a mystery.

? ? ?

When the letter came from Clark County District Attorney Ted Marshall inviting Goodman to Las Vegas for the purpose of accepting employment, he jumped at the opportunity. The Las Vegas he was about to see in the summer of 1964 was far different from the city that exists today. The nine resort-casinos on the fledgling Strip were all low-rise motor inns — even the 1,000-room Stardust, which was touted as one of the largest hotels in the world. Only the nine-story Riviera could be called a tower. The Mint downtown, at 15 stories, was the tallest building in the state. Many of the city's casinos, the Hotel Last Frontier on the Strip and the Fremont and Golden Nugget downtown, were Western-themed. Others such as the Sahara, Sands, and Dunes, reflected the Vegas version of an Arabian Nights fantasy. Themes for the rest, including the Riviera, Flamingo and Tropicana, were lifted from the city's connection to Miami Beach.

The community was segregated and still known as the "Mississippi of the West" for its backward treatment of African-Americans and other minorities. Sammy Davis Jr., then a member of the Will Mastin Trio, headlined on the Strip, but for years had been forced by custom to sleep in the predominantly black West Side of Las Vegas. Such treatment of black celebrities was common. Black educators weren't allowed to teach outside the West Side and jobs for minorities, for the most part, were limited to menial service positions. Women — white, of course — were encouraged to work semi-nude in the showroom chorus line, but they weren't allowed to deal cards in the casino.

In short, Las Vegas was a dream come true for white male chauvinists. Just beneath a placid surface, it was also a mecca for the mob.

The gambling business was regulated by a cozy county licensing process and a convenient two-tiered state system that grandfathered in many notorious characters straight out of Murder, Inc. In simplest terms, as long as an operator kept up appearances, Nevada's casino cops practiced a policy of see no evil, hear no evil, speak no evil. Governor Grant Sawyer expressed Nevada's libertarian nature when he said, "Our attitude toward life, save under the most urgent provocation, is relaxed, tolerant, and mindful that if others are allowed to go on their way unmolested, a man stands a chance of getting through the world himself with a minimum of irritation."

Although gambling was legalized in 1931, the state didn't begin attempting to regulate casinos until 1945, with the creation of the Nevada Tax Commission. Before then, gambling in Nevada was regulated, if one can call it that, by readily corruptible county officials. The Tax Commission's first role was to peek under the tent and collect a small tax. It wasn't until 1957 — six years after Tennessee Senator Estes Kefauver had exposed so many of Nevada's ties to racket bosses across America — that the state Legislature got around to establishing the two-tiered system that exists today. The three-member Gaming Control Board, consisting of an accountant, lawyer, and former member of law enforcement, was charged with investigations and licensing recommendations. The five-member Gaming Commission voted on the Board's recommendations.

It was a novel structure, enabling the state not only to regulate gambling, but to argue to outsiders that it had ensured propitious behavior on the part of the industry. In reality, the governor was responsible for all appointments to the Control Board and Commission. Since his political fortunes rose or fell largely on whether he remained in the good graces of the casino industry, only rarely were appointees unsympathetic to Nevada's thirst for gambling revenues and the contradictions inherent in the business. Appointees acknowledged that whatever ills it might invite to the Silver State, casino dollars kept Nevada growing. They also came to understand that often all that separated a solid citizen from a notorious racketeer was that Nevada license.

The Gaming Control Board became not only a watchdog of, but also a guard dog for, the industry. License revocations were extremely rare. Regulation effectively buffered the gambling bosses, and the true owners of the casinos, from troublesome federal scrutiny in an era in which Attorney General Robert Kennedy declared war on the hoodlum and gambler element. The system of state regulation was in place as a vehicle to collect taxes, allay public suspicion about the propriety of the games, and ensure that the joints themselves weren't privately owned by the mob.

Trouble was, the system didn't work. It managed to keep the obvious thugs, such as Marshall Caifano and John Rosselli, out of the front offices of such places as the Stardust, Desert Inn, and Riviera, but it didn't prevent the mob from maintaining its holdings. Truth told, without the involvement of such men as Meyer Lansky, Moe Dalitz, Anthony Accardo, Vincent Alo, and Tony Salerno, by 1964 Las Vegas would have had tumbleweeds rolling down Main Street. For all the notoriety the hoodlum element brought the community, it also put the neon in the city.

Despite the best efforts of the agents of the Gaming Control Board, most of the casinos were mobbed up from the crap pit to the penthouse. The Dunes, Stardust, Riviera, Hacienda, Aladdin, Flamingo, Fremont, Frontier, and Tropicana all had either hidden ownerships or were being skimmed in the casino. The rest had either been built with mob money or, like Jay Sarno's Caesars Palace, were being constructed thanks to La Cosa Nostra-connected loans from the Teamsters Central States Pension Fund.

Meyer Lansky was suspected of having a piece of everything that moved on the Strip. Lansky had held an interest in
several downtown casinos, the El Cortez and Fremont among
them, and was known as a secret owner of the Flamingo, the
carpet joint his late pal Ben Siegel had opened. Lansky's influence was not so far beneath the surface that he was unable to
take phone calls on the property. "Meyer owns more in Vegas
than anybody—than all of ours put together," Genovese family soldier Ray DeCarlo once told Anthony "Little Pussy"
Russo. "He's got a piece of every joint in Vegas."

Jake Lansky, Meyer's brother, had a stake in the Sahara
and the Thunderbird. Dalitz, the Cleveland bootlegger and
racket boss who'd made a monkey out of Kefauver's organized-
crime investigation, publicly owned with several partners the
Desert Inn and Stardust casinos and, thanks to his influence
with the Teamsters, helped develop the community's first private hospital.

? ? ?

Oscar Goodman was a young boy when most of America
became mesmerized by the televised coverage of the U.S. Senate Rackets Committee led by the self-promoting Estes
Kefauver in 1950 and '51. Goodman had been fascinated by
the highly publicized Kefauver Committee to Investigate Organized Crime, with its proceedings shown not only on television, but in movie theaters as well. With his father often at his
side, Goodman soaked in the proceedings and years later recalled being intrigued by the hard-hitting interrogators, cagey
Mafia men, and professional gamblers. He was also intrigued
by the publicity that followed the mob in Philadelphia, a city
with a rich organized-crime tradition.

During Prohibition, about the time Rudolph Goodman was
serving beer out of the first floor of the family home, the arrogant Waxey Gordon rose to power in Philadelphia as a key
figure in the Syndicate's liquor production. With Max "Boo-
Boo" Hoff and Harry Stromberg, Gordon was responsible for
producing domestic whiskey and rebottling imported goods.
But Gordon invited his own demise when he cheated his senior business partner, Meyer Lansky. Ever willing to use guile

in place of guns, Lansky secretly reported Gordon to the Internal Revenue Service. Not only had Gordon been cheating his partners in crime, he'd been short-changing Uncle Sam by more than $2 million a year. Waxey Gordon was hit with a 10-year sentence and became a historical footnote in Philadelphia's racket history.

From that point forward, Lansky worked through Stromberg to control the traditional rackets, while mob figures such as Joe Ida, Frankie Carbo, Angelo Bruno, and eventually Nicky Scarfo held positions of power on the streets of Philadelphia.

Were the Kefauver spectacle and the legends of Waxey Gordon and Meyer Lansky the initial stirrings of Goodman's life path? Whatever his level of interest in the underworld, Goodman was being drawn closer to the mob's gambling paradise.

Still, family ties were strong. Many of the people closest to him were shocked when they learned that he and Carolyn wanted to move to far-off Las Vegas, the notorious Sin City, not exactly known for the presence of Philadelphia lawyers.

Lona Livingston observed, "The family was upset when Oscar decided to move west. I remember some of the relatives saying to him, 'How can you leave when your father is dying?' My father had a series of medical problems, including a bad heart. He'd been dying for sixteen or seventeen years. I just don't think they wanted Oscar and Carolyn to go. They liked Oscar and Carolyn."

Allan Goodman lived until August 1979, a month before his 76th birthday. He and Laura eventually came to accept the fact that their son and daughter-in-law lived in Las Vegas, a place where the Mafia ran everything. To them, and a majority of other Americans in the early 1960s, Las Vegas wasn't a city, it was a disease.

"When I decided to come out here, my father, may his soul rest in peace, refused to accept that his son was going to live in Las Vegas," Goodman recalled. "It was just so foreign to him, and Las Vegas had a stigma. Respectable people didn't move there. When Carolyn and I moved out, everyone we knew gave us copies of *The Green Felt Jungle* as going-away presents. When someone would ask my father where I was moving, he would say, 'Arizona.' He was trying to will it."

On a scouting trip before the big move, the young Oscar

found the small town of Las Vegas, with its western sensibility and casinos full of men who had made their bones in gambling dens from Miami to Portland, appealing to him. There was opportunity there. The lawyers and few judges Goodman met on his foray were cordial and responded sincerely when he asked whether there was enough work in town for one more lawyer. In Philadelphia, they'd have told him to go drive a cab, or worse.

"The first problem was going to be persuading Carolyn to come out to Las Vegas and give the town a chance," Goodman remembered. "We booked a gambling junket from Philadelphia with the idea that once she saw Las Vegas, she would warm up to the place. She had mononucleosis, so she wasn't exactly feeling like gambling and stayed in the room at the Flamingo most of the time, but she was a good sport and we made the best of it.

"I went downtown on a Saturday and it was the version of downtown you can only see in black-and-white photographs. There were none of the tall buildings that exist today. I went from law office to law office. I still remember who I spoke to. There was Tom Purcell, Tom O'Donnell, Don Wadsworth, and some others. I asked them, naively, whether Las Vegas might be a good place to practice law. Now, if I'd posed that same question to lawyers in Philadelphia, they would have said, 'You're nuts.' But standing downtown, everybody said it was a great place.

"On the plane ride back, Carolyn was sleeping and I struck up a conversation with a guy named Jerry Rosenberg. He asked whether I'd had a good time, and in the course of conversation I told him who I was and why I'd come out. I told him I was ready to graduate from the University of Pennsylvania Law School and was thinking about moving out to Las Vegas to practice. Out of the blue he said to me, 'I like what I hear and I really want to look you up.' He was from New York, but was associated somehow with the junket. I gave him my address and he promised he'd be in touch with me.

"I didn't think anything of it, but not long after we got back to Philadelphia, he called and flew in. He came up to our apartment with gifts, a very expensive light brown suede jacket for me and something equally expensive for my wife. He said he wanted to say hello and we immediately thought it was weird, but we didn't want to look a gift horse in the mouth, either, because at the time I couldn't have afforded a suede jacket with a month's pay. We made small talk and shook hands, then said our goodbyes.

"The next week I got another call from Rosenberg, who again appeared in Philadelphia with more gifts. I truly didn't know what this guy wanted from us.

"Then he made his pitch. He literally tried to make an offer I couldn't refuse. We were living in an eighty-five-dollar-a-month apartment at the time. It was in a neighborhood where gunshots were regularly heard. He could tell we didn't have two cents. He said he could offer us the kind of lifestyle we'd only be able to dream about. He represented people who needed good lawyers who were loyal. It was a job for life and he made it very clear that I'd be part of an organization whose bosses and members I couldn't talk about. It was a scene out of *The Godfather*, only this guy wasn't play-acting.

"It would make a much better story, but, contrary to popular belief in law enforcement, I respectfully declined his offer. Even gave him back the jacket, if I remember correctly."

"Jerry Rosenberg said that if Oscar came to work for the company, he would have a year, but at the end of the year if he decided to stay on he'd never get out," Carolyn recalled. "This was before *The Godfather*. All the things you've seen in the movies he alluded to before those movies were made. Our eyes were as wide as saucers.

"We were given a chance to sell ourselves to the devil. Anything we wanted. Here were two kids finishing up law school. We were nothing people with no money. We started soul-searching discussions. It took us about two months and he kept bothering us. But when Oscar and I talked about it, we always came back to the same thing: How can you not be a man of your word, and let somebody else have control of you? We were both young, but we realized there was nothing in this world we would sell ourselves for. We came to Las Vegas with eighty-seven dollars in our pockets, thirty-seven boxes of books, and a bedroom set. We were either going to be poor or we weren't going to be poor, but we were going to do it ourselves."

The Jerry Rosenberg story would appear to dispel the long-time law-enforcement conjecture that Goodman not only was a trusted counselor to the mob, but enjoyed a broad range of connections, from Civella's Kansas City to Lansky's Miami Beach. One former federal Organized Crime Strike Force attorney, who was interviewed on the condition of anonymity, said the Justice Department and FBI believed Oscar Goodman had been duked in to Las Vegas by associates of the Philadelphia mob and Meyer Lansky. Their problem was, their information never rose higher than the level of street rumor, and in all the thousands of hours of recorded Mafia surveillance, Goodman's supposed mystery benefactor was never authenticated.

"I think Oscar had to have been introduced to people in Las Vegas," the Strike Force lawyer said. "They weren't going to let an outsider get that close to them. But by the same token I don't believe he got a free ride. He was juiced in, but it's a juice town. That doesn't mean it was handed to him. He worked hard and was a formidable adversary. He represented his clients and didn't cross the line."

What members of law enforcement would never note, however, is the uncanny similarity between the name of Goodman's fondly remembered mystery man, "Jerry Rosenberg," and the name of Lansky's man in Philadelphia, Harry Stromberg, who was known as Nig Rosen in the City of Brotherly Love and placed his daffy brother, Wilbur Stromberg, in the casino at Las Vegas' Caesars Palace at a time when Carolyn Goodman worked there as an executive secretary. It was such coincidences that created suspicions among the police and FBI that would last more than three decades.

Just west of Arizona, in 1964 Oscar Goodman found himself in Las Vegas and was about to become a member of the bar in good standing.

2

The Green Felt Jungle on $87

In September 1964, with the promise of employment in the Clark County District Attorney's office, Oscar and Carolyn Goodman left Philadelphia for Las Vegas with $87 between them.

Oscar had already fallen in love with the town and its western neon sensibility, but the move was a culture shock for Carolyn. Southern Nevada wasn't exactly bustling with Bryn Mawr graduates. She'd spent her only previous trip to Las Vegas sick in bed and the town she had agreed to move to, even months later, left her somewhat queasy.

"I finally got a good look at Las Vegas when we moved there, and there was nothing as far as the eye could see," Carolyn recalled. "I thought, 'My dad was right. I did marry an idiot. Why did I do this? I'm doomed here.' But once we got settled into a little place at the Palms Apartments, we became comfortable. All kinds of different people with every variety of job lived there. And we all got together and threw parties. There was Del Webb's secretary, a single father and his son, a prostitute. Who cared? I thought, 'This is either the realest place in the world or the most unreal.' That was what was so unusual and I think wonderful about Las Vegas. Unlike where we'd come from, there were no status symbols, no class structure, to speak of."

With a population of 75,000, Las Vegas in 1964 had fewer residents than some neighborhoods in Philadelphia. And with the exception of a few Strip casinos and the Mint and Fremont downtown, Sin City was pancake flat.

By day Las Vegas was a homely burgh dotted with stucco tract homes and one-horse ranchettes on the edge of town. By night Las Vegas transformed itself into a dazzling suburb of Hollywood with movie stars and millionaires awash in green felt and neon. The Rat Pack was at the Sands. The ultimate pleasure dome called Caesars Palace was set to open in a few months. The muted maunderings of the Gaming Control Board aside, Mob influence coursed through the count rooms of every major joint in the city and few imagined it would ever be otherwise. Men such as Miami Beach's Lansky, Chicago's Sam Giancana, New York's Vincent Alo, Jerry Catena, and Anthony Salerno, Detroit's Joseph Zerilli, and St. Louis' Tony Giordano all held a piece of the desert dream.

Oscar Goodman entered that maelstrom not as a slick-talking mouthpiece, but as a clerk studying to pass the Nevada Bar exam in the employ of District Attorney Ted Marshall. He lasted 18 months in the prosecutor's office and had to struggle every day against his own anti-establishment nature. As time passed, he grew tired of bringing the weight of the system to bear against suspected criminals who were either too poor or too unsophisticated to discern justice from punishment. And after a year and a half on the prosecution side of the law, he quit.

The young clerk, meanwhile, managed to make a few contacts of his own.

Of the many gifts Allan Goodman imparted to his son, one of the best was the $25 a week he sent the couple in the early months of their lives together. They were told to spend it unwisely on entertainment. That $25 enabled them to move more easily in the cash-oriented Las Vegas casino and lounge subculture. In a few months, they became regulars at Villa D'Este, owned by Sam Giancana's pal Joe Pignatello, and the popular Luigi's Ristorante. They also got to know their way around a blackjack table, with Carolyn taking advantage of a gift for memorizing cards. After a steak one night at the Hacienda, she sat down at one of the tables. Oscar stood behind, acting as chaperone.

"After dinner Carolyn would take ten dollars or twenty dollars or whatever we had saved up and go to the blackjack tables," Goodman said. "She was a phenomenal blackjack player. She'd go there and invariably win twenty dollars, put it in her purse, then play the rest of the night with the house's money. I would stand behind her and chat with the dealer. In those days dealers didn't get fired for exchanging pleasantries with customers. And I struck up a conversation with a dealer named Bob Butler. Butler had a little legal matter and I filled out the court paperwork for him. I wrote it out by hand and didn't charge him anything. I thought nothing of it, really, but Bob Butler remembered."

In the mid-1960s, the Southern Nevada legal community was small and close-knit, but its attorneys were by no means bumpkins. A young attorney hungry to observe front-line law-yering had his pick of splendid legal minds and courtroom magicians. Goodman immediately gravitated toward them. He became friends almost immediately with criminal defense at-torneys Harry Claiborne, George Foley, and Morton Galane. He was impressed with the intellect of District Judge Thomas J. O'Donnell and Foley's eldest brother, Federal District Judge Roger Foley. In these men, he found the kindred spirits he'd lacked in Philadelphia.

"He was nothing like he is now," Harry Claiborne recalled. "He was quiet, feeling his way in the practice. I saw him in the courtroom a number of times when I was trying cases. I don't want to sound egotistical, but for a long time here I was the only show in town. The courtrooms were always filled. I dis-tinctly remember him. He came over to shake hands with me during recess and then one day he walked into the office and asked me if he could sit in with me on some cases. He wanted to sit in with me on a murder case. He told me that he wanted to be a criminal lawyer.

"I tried to talk him out of it because I told him there was no money in it. The money was in civil trial work, but that didn't deter him. That's what he wanted to do. That's what appealed to him. That's what he did and he became very good at what he did."

Goodman breezed through the 1964 Nevada bar exam, but his early clients were, to say the least, eclectic. Operating out of Morton Galane's cramped office on Carson Street, he accepted anyone who came through his door and worked the courthouse halls and legal-community watering holes to generate business. He paid the rent by accepting court-appointed criminal cases. The pay was low, but the work was steady.

Court-appointed clients were indigent and often blacks from the West Side. Many had previous criminal records and knew the system better than the inexperienced lawyers assigned to defend them. It was through a court appointment that Goodman met the man perhaps most responsible for setting the tone of his legal career: accused shotgun killer Lewis Crockett.

۶ ۶ ۶

On the morning of May 16, 1967, Lewis Crockett was a few hours from being arraigned on narcotics-trafficking charges. Known to police as the black community's up-and-coming drug kingpin, Crockett hailed from an entrenched West Las Vegas family. He was a star on the street, but he faced more than a decade in prison. Curtis Wheeler, a driver for Dot's Dry Cleaners, stood in his way. Wheeler, facing separate felony charges, had agreed to cooperate as a witness against Crockett.

Shortly before 10 that morning, Wheeler arrived at a North Las Vegas apartment to pick up some dry cleaning and instead was greeted at the door by shotgun blasts. Eyewitness David Bingham, a blond-haired Mormon man, observed a black man fitting Lewis Crockett's description run from the apartment, cross a parking lot, and drive away.

Lewis Crockett was later arrested for the murder of Wheeler. After a first trial resulted in a hung jury, Oscar Goodman was assigned to the case by the court. His fee was $900.

If young attorney Goodman had had difficulty concentrating on his classwork in college and his casework in the District Attorney's office, the time had come for him to focus. Without an uncommon effort to impugn the eyewitness account, his client was headed for Death Row.

"Crockett was my first big case. I was representing a black

kid who was charged with killing an informant in a drug case. The Crockett case had all the ingredients of what criminal law is all about," Goodman recalled. "It had informants, a dogged prosecutor, even racial overtones. This guy Bingham, who was painting a sign outside the complex, was a white Mormon fella, and the defendant was black. Bingham swore he'd seen somebody run out of a window with a shotgun and get into a car. He made his identification from a total of twelve seconds. Twelve seconds isn't a long time. Crockett's life hung on those twelve seconds.

"I saw Crockett in custody. He was always in custody. He didn't make bail. He had already gone through one trial in which the jury came back eleven to one to convict. He was saved when a woman changed her mind about being a juror, locked herself in a bathroom, and refused to vote on the case. I had never seen him without his jailhouse-issue clothes. But when he came to court, they let him wear a suit, street clothes instead of jail garb. He was very pleasant, always smiling. In those days, his family was known to be very powerful on the West Side."

Patriarch Johnny Crockett had a barbershop, but law enforcement believed the family gained its real power from its connections to major drug traffickers. In the years before street gangs proliferated in the poor neighborhoods, a few violent men ruled the traditional vice rackets, earning more in a few scores than their neighbors would in a lifetime toiling as maids and kitchen workers in the casino-hotels.

Lewis Crockett swore to Goodman that his running mate, Floyd Hamlet, could clear him of the murder charge. But Hamlet was also implicated in the Wheeler murder and was being held incommunicado; Goodman was denied any access to him. Meanwhile, a friend of Hamlet's, Clifford Epperson, gave a taped statement to the district attorney in which he cleared Crockett. Epperson accused Hamlet of firing the shotgun, but the recording was of poor quality and was not fully analyzed.

Then Hamlet was briefly let out of jail on his own recognizance by the district attorney. When he disappeared into the West Side (although he was eventually returned to custody), it meant only one thing: The government was attempting to hide him from the defense.

"The West Side was an interesting place in those days,"

Goodman said. "It was very hierarchical, even clannish. And there were places a young lawyer had to be if he wanted to make the scene and, more importantly, become acquainted with current and future clients. These people were constantly being arrested by the Sheriff's Office, which had a Jim Crow-type attitude toward blacks.

"So blacks became our training ground. And Crockett was a big case. It was well-publicized, because at that time there wasn't a great deal of violence in the small community."

District Court Judge Thomas O'Donnell, a devout Catholic, was personally opposed to the death penalty. Unlike many judges then and now, he didn't see himself as the second prosecutor in the courtroom. He put the government through its paces and brought an uncommon credibility to the bench.

Goodman tried what few tricks he knew. Proving his law-school experience hadn't been entirely wasted, he used a contact at the University of Pennsylvania to bring in John Bitterman, a renowned expert on cross-racial identification.

"Bitterman testified that the prosecution's key witness, David Bingham, especially being a Mormon, would have tremendous difficulty in identifying a black who was running in the manner in which Crockett was supposedly running for a period of twelve seconds because of the cross-racial identification and the characteristics."

Based on Bitterman's testimony, Goodman tore into Bingham, whose family had been respected members of the Southern Nevada community for generations. Jurors reported they were unimpressed with Bingham by the time Goodman finished with him, but the weight of evidence was against Crockett.

The jury returned on Thursday night with Carolyn Goodman in the gallery. The verdict: guilty, with the first death sentence issued in Southern Nevada in 25 years.

"I went back to see Crockett after the verdict while Carolyn stood outside the door," Oscar said.

"I heard loud sobs coming from the other room," Carolyn remembers. "And when Oscar returned I asked him whether Crockett had taken it hard. He said, 'That was *me* crying.'"

Crockett maintained his innocence, but was headed for Death Row.

❢ ❢ ❢

Angry tears rose to his eyes. Try as he might, he couldn't get the ringing of District Judge O'Donnell's gavel out of his ears.

It was Friday, and most of the attorneys had already started their weekends. But Goodman was at the law library, burying himself in the Nevada Revised Statutes and volume after volume of case law.

"I was distraught," he says. "I was devastated by these jurors and that's the reason I locked myself up in the library. I was there for three days with the water from the drinking fountain, and that's about it. No food. Just trying to get this concept where the judge could overrule the jury, because I knew that O'Donnell was a very religious man, a real practicing devout Catholic, who really did not want to impose the death penalty. And by law he would have to do it. And I was looking for a way he could get out of it because, at the time, there hadn't been a death penalty case in Nevada for twenty-five years. There really wasn't any law on it."

If the trial had gone poorly, Goodman's first interview with a reporter went even worse. *Las Vegas Sun* reporter Jerry Ralya, himself an attorney, questioned Goodman after the jury verdict, then misread his own notes. The result was mortifying.

"I told Jerry, 'My client is gutsy,'" Goodman recalled. "In the newspaper the next day, I was quoted saying, 'My client is guilty.' I couldn't believe it. I was insane about it. I went down to the county jail and saw Crockett. I half expected him to hurt me, but I talked to him and he understood. He said, 'I knew you wouldn't say something like that. I'm glad you're here. I want you to talk to somebody.'

"About what?" Goodman asked.

Crockett then introduced to Goodman the man who could have been the defendant's twin.

"This is the guy that was carrying the gun," he said.

The man's name was Floyd Hamlet.

Goodman moved quickly, calling in a court stenographer on a Sunday. Within minutes he took Hamlet's statement, who said he didn't shoot Wheeler, but he did climb out the window holding the gun.

The next morning, Goodman filed a motion for a new trial based on newly discovered evidence. Shortly thereafter, Judge O'Donnell made his own trip to the jail where he also confused Hamlet with Crockett.

"He said, 'Hi Brown,' which was Crockett's nickname," Goodman remembered. "That sewed it up as far as whether my motion was going to be granted."

O'Donnell granted Goodman's motion, which survived a prosecution appeal to the Nevada Supreme Court by a 3-to-2 decision.

"It was then I saw Lewis Crockett believed that I could save him, even though he was a longshot to ever see daylight again," Goodman said. "At that moment I made up my mind. I wanted to be a lawyer."

A new trial was good news, but Goodman knew the score. A white jury was highly unlikely to go against the District Attorney's office in the prosecution of a black defendant.

District Attorney George Franklin was outraged that any lawyer, much less a former prosecutor who was under 30, would upstage not only his own office, but the police department as well. Franklin, given to fits of bombast despite the fact that he never attended law school or read for the bar, demanded a new trial and vowed to make Crockett pay for the crime, whether or not he'd actually committed it.

Goodman volunteered his client for a polygraph examination—but not one conducted by the hand-picked locals who made their living off the DA's office. Someone independent.

Franklin chose Leonard Harrelson, one of the top polygraph examiners in the United States. Harrelson interviewed Crockett at the Fremont Hotel. Crockett passed without difficulty.

"I said, 'Okay, he passed,'" Goodman recalled. "Franklin wouldn't acknowledge the truth. He said, 'Well, we don't believe he didn't do it.' I was stunned. They don't teach you these things in law school. So now I was facing a turning point: Go quietly, knowing that my client would never get a fair shake in court, or lash out and risk the consequences of angering the district attorney.

"I took a deep breath and let him have it. I called him every single name in the book. And I was lucky. At the time I was having this discussion with him, the National Association of District Attorneys was meeting in Las Vegas. It was the first time they were ever out here, and Franklin was very prominent. I told Franklin that unless he kept his word and accepted the polygraph, I'd hold a press conference and embarrass him. I'd tell everyone he was a liar and a cheat, even though it would have ruined me locally. Instead of kicking me out of his office, he got quiet. He said, 'Okay.' It took that kind of threat to get justice for Lewis Crockett. I had never run into that kind of deception before. I didn't know the ways of evil men and politics and power. These were all eye-openers to me. I was right and I prevailed, but only because he didn't want the heat.

"That night, I called O'Donnell and said, 'Let me buy you a drink.' We had a huge meal at Al Mengarelli's place and drank, drank, drank. Then it was on to the Moulin Rouge, with Carolyn driving. Carolyn and I were living at the Palms Apartments then and O'Donnell and I—I don't know how we got there—ended up passed out on the floor. Carolyn came out in the morning and found us. She gave us more beer so we could sober up, then cooked us the biggest breakfast. Corned beef hash, scrambled eggs, toast, and coffee. And from that point on there was a real terrific bonding with O'Donnell."

The two became such good friends that Goodman later recalled the Crockett case while making a public endorsement of O'Donnell's bid for re-election.

"If it hadn't been for Judge O'Donnell's courage, an innocent man would have been put to death," Goodman wrote in a full-page political advertisement printed in the local newspapers. "Judge Tom O'Donnell would not bend to public pressure when he knew he was right."

"Crockett was a big case for me for many reasons, one of which was the fact that it gave me entrée into the West Side as a credible criminal lawyer. I was hardly the only lawyer who dropped by the Cove, the New Town Tavern, or the Moulin Rouge for a drink to meet a client. Although I didn't make a habit of it, it was the way things were done then.

"Years later I learned that Crockett got into trouble again. He was told he could buy himself out of the problem if he tried to set me up. He called me and asked me for money. I told him I wasn't in a position to help him out. Had I given him the money, it would have been some kind of a drug deal. I can't blame him for trying, but that's the game I found myself in."

After the Crockett victory, the cases poured in for Goodman. He became a name on the West Side and started to generate income.

In the following months, Goodman represented Hamlet, who was then on the police department's hit list for failing to remain quiet in the Crockett case.

? ? ?

In Las Vegas, participants in the casino subculture were always in need of a good attorney, so when he wasn't working felony criminal cases, Goodman began picking up civil work — a divorce case here, a contract dispute there. It was good for business and circulated his name among potential paying clients.

At night, there were restaurants to go to, shows arranged by Carolyn's contacts to attend. And always a little blackjack to be played at any of a number of clubs. Their favorite was the Hacienda, where Oscar's acquaintance Bob Butler worked as a dealer. Goodman had helped Butler and now the dealer wanted to do him a favor.

"One day Butler's dealing and a phone call comes into the pit. The caller asks, 'Who's the best criminal lawyer in Las Vegas?' Bob Butler hears the Hacienda's old-school pit boss, who's cupping the phone, ask the question out loud. Butler says, 'I don't know whether he does any criminal work, but Oscar Goodman's a helluva guy.' So the boss gets back on the phone and says, 'The best lawyer in Las Vegas is Oscar Goodman.' That's the way it happened."

Legend to the contrary and the suspicions of a generation of skeptical FBI agents and Strike Force attorneys aside, that's how Oscar Goodman swears he became married to the Mob.

3

The Sporting Life

That fateful phone call to the Hacienda pit wasn't from just any inquiring hoodlum. It was from an international-organized-crime figure named Mel Horowitz, whose wayward stepbrother had been arrested with another man in Las Vegas on a charge of violating the federal Dyer Act, better known as interstate transportation of a stolen vehicle. Though the stepbrother was a criminal nebbish, Mel Horowitz was a force to be reckoned with.

Born in Canada and schooled in Boston, New York, and Miami Beach, Horowitz was one of the reigning princes of pornography trafficking in North America in the years before that racket went corporate. Through associations with crime figures such as Raymond Patriarca, Meyer Lansky, and "Fat Tony" Salerno, Horowitz also operated one of the largest illegal bookmaking offices in the United States out of his Miami Beach headquarters.

The Dyer Act was put in place largely as a means of solving jurisdictional issues in car-theft cases. As such, it was nearly impossible to defend against. A prosecutor had only to prove that a car was stolen and that it was transported across state lines by the defendant. Barring a miracle, Horowitz's stepbrother was sunk.

Not that Oscar Goodman says he knew that initially. In fact, he didn't even know what the Dyer Act was and had to look it up.

"Mel Horowitz said he was going to retain me and told me to go to a home on South Fifteenth Street and knock on the door and they'd have something for me," Goodman later recalled. "Here I was a young kid and the only temptation I'd had before was that Jerry Rosenberg situation. So I go up to the door and I meet Bob Martin."

Born in Brooklyn, Martin was the gravelly voiced brain of all brains in the sports handicapping business. He all but invented modern sports wagering as it's practiced today by putting up a solid betting line inside Las Vegas sports books. He was also well-acquainted with the nation's vast network of mobsters and illegal bookmakers. Although famous for his biting sense of humor — Martin once asked a spouse-abusing Jake LaMotta, "Jake, which one of your wives took the best punch?" — Martin was a gruff-sounding character with a mile-deep voice scarred by cigarettes, alcohol, and late nights. Goodman was scared senseless.

"I didn't know him from Adam," he said. "He answered the door and handed me an envelope. He growled, 'Here's three dimes, kid. You better win it.' I went around the corner. I was sweating. I didn't know what three dimes was. I opened up the envelope and it was the first time I ever saw thirty one-hundred-dollar bills all together. I said 'Wow.'"

Then the work began. Goodman managed to find the federal courthouse on Stewart Avenue and arranged bail for his client.

"The day before the trial is supposed to start, on Valentine's Day, I meet Mel, who'd flown into town. He came down to the office with Bob. He said, 'You better win this. He's my brother.' I said, 'No problem.'

"I didn't know you couldn't win a Dyer Act case. Nobody won those.

"I dressed the kid up like an Ivy Leaguer, made him wear khakis, loafers, and a tie, button-down collar, the whole works. Dressed up his buddy the same way. I said I'd meet them down at the office. The night before, I went home sweating. The bed was soaking wet.

"The morning of trial, I got down to court early, ran into Carol Fitzgerald, the clerk of the court, and I said, 'Mrs. Fitzgerald, I think we should waive a jury on this case.' I didn't know how to pick a federal jury. I didn't realize that the judge in those days did all the selection. I thought this was a matter of great legal issues and I was going to win it on the legal issues. I was more than naive. She said, 'I'll talk to the judge.' She came back a few minutes later and said, 'The judge has already summoned the jury. You're going to have a jury trial.' I barely made it outside before vomiting on the courthouse steps."

Nearly 40 years later, as mayor of Las Vegas, Goodman would lobby to take custody of the old Stewart Avenue federal courthouse for use as a possible arts center and public park. It was the least he could do for defacing it that February morning.

On Valentine's Day, the jury's mind was obviously not on the simple theft case, but on hearts and flowers and the whims of Cupid. Goodman did something he would rarely do in the coming 30 years: He called his client and co-defendant to the witness stand. They'd concocted a lame excuse for borrowing the vehicle, and Goodman's cross-examination of the government's two witnesses, the offended car owner and the arresting officer, was half-baked and brief.

During his closing argument, Goodman implored the jurors to probe their hearts before finding fault with the defendant. His best Olivier touched not only the jurors, but affected the Assistant U.S. Attorney assigned to the case. The prosecutor, Bob Linnell, told the jurors, "Justice is not done by a determination of guilt. Justice is served by whatever your decision is."

"After the jury went out, we walked back to my office," Goodman recalled. "On the way back, Mel said, 'The faster the verdict, the better.' And I said, 'No, no, no, in my experience' — and what I'd just watched in the courtroom was about the sum total of my federal experience — 'the longer they're out the better.' We walked into the office and the phone was ringing. The jury had the verdict. I thought, 'Oh my God. I'm a dead man.' Mel said, 'That's very good.' We returned to the courthouse and the jury came back with a verdict of not guilty.

"I could have tried the case a thousand times, with all the experience I gained over the years, and I would have lost it nine hundred ninety-nine times. I couldn't have won it. But I did win it and that was my big break. That case resulted in other cases coming my way."

Oscar Goodman had become a name, albeit a small one, with the kind of people who were seldom not in need of a good lawyer. In the underworld of illegal bookmakers of that era, a man's word held Herculean weight. The only thing more important was his reputation, and the name of Oscar Goodman, the tough young lawyer from Las Vegas, was mentioned in such circles. Of such talk legends are made.

? ? ?

Months later, Goodman was busy managing a series of small cases when he received a call from a Golden Nugget bartender named John DePasquale, who'd been charged in a sweeping federal indictment, the first of many following the passage of the Omnibus Crime Bill of 1968, which expanded the nation's controversial and little-used federal wiretap statute. DePasquale was accused of transmitting sports wagering information in the form of the morning betting line to a formidable group of illegal bookmakers.

"The wiretap statute was enacted in 1968 and Little Marty Sklaroff was the first one to be wiretapped," Goodman said. "Sklaroff was a big-time bookmaker who followed in his father Jesse's footsteps. They were partial focus of a big investigation and the feds tapped the phone he used at the Miami airport. Little Marty was getting the line information from John DePasquale, who got indicted with Sklaroff. It was the first legal wiretap case in the history of the United States. They hired me as a result of my victory on behalf of Mel Horowitz's stepbrother. Mel Horowitz told Sklaroff that DePasquale had better hire Goodman.

"I went down to Florida and represented John and I argued for severance. My client was not being mentioned in all the government's evidence. He was a long way from the key players in the case and I thought severing his trial from the rest was his only real chance. Finally, I got the severance, and

DePasquale went home. Sklaroff says, 'Why don't you stick around. I'll pay you. You can be a little help to us.'"

Very little, as it turned out. All the defendants but one were convicted. The wiretap prosecution had been a resounding success, but in the government's zeal it had neglected to pursue one defendant — lowly John DePasquale, the Golden Nugget bartender with the confidential underworld connections. Goodman had won by forfeit.

But such details were quickly forgotten. On the street, Goodman became known as the lawyer with the only client to walk on a wiretap case.

"Word goes out that the only guy who beat the case was Goodman's client," he said. "The only guy who wasn't convicted was my client. That's the way it happened. The other defendants had some darn good attorneys representing them, but I got lucky and won the severance.

"All of a sudden, I was getting calls from all over the country. Could I come to Chicago? Was I interested in working in Cleveland? Overnight my career shifted gears.

"Then I met Marty Kane."

Kane, who'd been booking bets since childhood and was a former journalism student at the University of Alabama, was at the center of the investigation. It was no secret that "Marty the Jew" was one of a small group of men who operated America's biggest illegal bookmaking network. He'd been a trusted associate of Gil "the Brain" Beckley, Anthony "Fat Tony" Salerno, Frank "Lefty" Rosenthal, Bob Martin, and Chicago Outfit oddsmaker Donald "the Wizard of Odds" Angelini. These men were responsible for making America's sports-betting line. The fact that it was illegal for Americans to bet ballgames hadn't cost them any sleep.

A lengthy indictment filed in Nassau County, New York, however, did interfere with peaceful slumber. The lawsuit linked Kane to a $100-million-a-year illegal bookmaking empire. With a bookmaking-related wiretap victory to his credit, Goodman was a logical choice for Kane, who at the time was living in a house on Desert Inn Road in Las Vegas.

Faced with felony charges that could put him away for as much as a decade, Kane grew suddenly allergic to New York. Goodman fought extradition for two years. If New York authorities wanted to glimpse more than a Polaroid of Kane, they'd have to offer him more than jailhouse pajamas. Forget about a felony. Never mind a gross misdemeanor. As the months clicked off and their case lost its punch in the headlines, prosecutors became more amenable to making a deal. In time, New York authorities had heard enough from Goodman on behalf of Martin Paul Kane.

"They were literally sick of hearing my voice," he recalled. "They finally said, 'All right. Here's the New York penal code. Pick a crime. Whatever you want your client to plead to, we'll accept it. I looked at it and laughed a little. I chose walking a dog without a leash on the streets of New York."

And Marty Kane didn't even own a dog.

? ? ?

On December 12, 1970, the FBI executed search warrants in 26 cities in 11 states and shattered a nationwide illegal-bookmaking operation with ties to organized crime. Attorney General John Mitchell called it "the largest coordinated gambling raids ever." Dozens of arrests were made. Oscar Goodman, fresh from the Kane victory, became the attorney of record in 19 of the 26 cases.

In Las Vegas, federal investigators arrested Marty Kane's friend Frank Rosenthal, Patriarca crime-family associate Elliot Paul Price, and Genovese front man Jerry Zarowitz. Price was employed at the Churchill Downs Race Book and Zarowitz was one of the original owners of Caesars Palace. The raid had uncovered more than $1.5 million in cash in Zarowitz's casino and sportsbook safe-deposit boxes. Zarowitz fought to maintain his status. But Price was fired after the raid and lost his sheriff's-department work card. Later, it was mysteriously returned to him so he could accept a job at Circus Circus. Gaming Control Board member Shannon Bybee demanded that Price's card be confiscated. (Subsequently, testifying before a U.S. Senate subcommittee on mob activity in the gaming industry, Bybee was asked his personal definition of organized crime. He replied, "Anybody that Oscar Goodman represents.")

Price, Zarowitz, and "Lefty" Rosenthal, then employed at

the Stardust Hotel, came to Goodman through Kane, who was well aware of the interest the federal government had taken in illegal bookmaking and sports betting generally. Kane had just learned of the disappearance of his old friend Gil Beckley, who'd had a falling out with Salerno; Fat Tony had been threatened by talk that Beckley was cooperating with federal prosecutors. Kane also worked with Rosenthal, a respected handicapper and the rising star when it came to setting the so-called Las Vegas line. Kane placed a call to his young attorney.

"Marty Kane knew everyone in the city who was anyone in the sporting crowd," Goodman recalled. "He was best friends with Bob Martin. I loved to bet so I knew how to speak their language. The case was potentially devastating to all the defendants, whom the government considered mobsters. But most of them were bookmakers, the kind of people who get exploited by the tough guys. The case hinged on wiretap information, which solidly established the multi-state connections and the activity of the group. In short, they were dead."

In the cases of Price, Zarowitz, and Rosenthal, the criminal charges not only imperiled their freedom, but stood to bust them out of legalized gaming. In Nevada, casino employees must pass a criminal background check before obtaining a sheriff's work card. In the following months, Goodman would fight successfully on Price's behalf to have his work card returned, arguing that authorities were not allowed to take it without due process. That fight would result in the *O'Callaghan v. Eighth Judicial District* decision, which mandated for the first time in Nevada history that possession of a work card was a "property interest" and as such, could not be taken without affording due process.

For Goodman it was a victory — and the first of many battles with state regulatory authorities.

Even with the facts stacked against his clients, Goodman launched a highly visible attack against the federal and state governments. In time, this speech would become as much a part of Goodman's defense as his lucky briefcase and courtroom charm. During a Nevada Gaming Commission hearing, Goodman said, "Unless we are told what specific charges there are here, this hearing is like a grand inquisition of the type held in Spain, the Kremlin, and Nazi Germany."

The script that both the defense and prosecution would follow had been written. Goodman immediately became a lightning rod for the storm of criticism leveled by the Control Board's Shannon Bybee and all those who followed him.

But for the present time, Goodman focused on the federal gambling indictment.

"The more I studied the documents, including the wiretap affidavits and authorization, the more something didn't look right," he recalled. "It was the signatures of John Mitchell, who was the Attorney General then. The affidavit was in order, except for the signatures, which to my eyes didn't match at all. If John Mitchell's top assistant signed the paperwork, he did it with two different hands.

"At one point I told one of the other attorneys on the case, 'You know, these two signatures don't look alike.' He said, 'Don't bother me. I'm working.' Then he took a closer look at the signatures and said, 'Wait a second, they really don't look alike.'

"It was from that observation that I took the Attorney General's deposition. It wasn't Mitchell's signature. It was Will Wilson's signature. Wilson was Mitchell's Assistant Attorney General in charge of the Criminal Division, and he had signed it on behalf of his boss, which is commonly done, but isn't legal. He had never been authorized to do so, and Mitchell knew it. Then we took the deposition of Sol Lindenbaum, who was Wilson's assistant, and got to the bottom of it. The signature wasn't authentic and he admitted it. We moved to dismiss and we won."

On November 5, 1975, after nearly four years of legal wrangling, U.S. District Judge Roger Foley dismissed the charges against the defendants, citing the government's failure to exhaust its normal investigative avenues and the inconsistent signatures of John Mitchell. Every defendant walked away without a scratch from the biggest federal assault on the national bookmaking syndicate since the Roaring '20s. They had Oscar Goodman to thank. And they did so by recommending his services to all their pals.

Although Kane was eventually added to Nevada's Black Book of people banned from entering the state's casinos, that didn't prevent him from continuing to lay off the high bets for illegal bookmakers and high-stakes sports bettors until his death in 1990. Kane remained Goodman's friend and unpaid agent the rest of his life.

In the early 1970s, in his early thirties, Goodman found himself intoxicated by his success and the colorful characters who surrounded him. It was a world in which everyone seemed to have a nickname. There was the Hat and the Hunchback, Crippled Julius and Bobby the Midget. Diminutive Bobby Kaye, a syndicate bookmaker from New York who worked in Las Vegas for Rosenthal, became Goodman's good-luck charm.

"Bobby Kaye was so short he had a hard time making a call from a pay phone. He had to jump up to put the dime in the right slot. He worked out of the Churchill Downs, one of the old stand-alone sports books on the Strip. When Bobby got in some trouble and was subpoenaed to appear before a grand jury, he called me. As with all my clients, I was very specific with him. I insist, even though prosecutors and grand juries hate me for it, that they come out after each question and seek my advice as to whether or not they should answer the question or take the Fifth. And let's be honest, most of the time they're taking the Fifth. I've never seen anybody help themselves by testifying before the grand jury. They usually pick up a perjury charge as a result of doing it.

"Little Bobby Kaye is not dumb. In terms of street smarts and in bookmaking and handicapping, he's a very sharp guy. But he wasn't used to testifying in front of any grand juries and the fact is he's a talkative guy by nature. He's no rat, but nobody would share a secret with Bobby.

"So we're outside the jury room and I had just gone over everything with him again. I said, 'Bobby, you've got to come out after every question. Every single question. Promise me you'll do it.' He promised. So I sat there outside the grand jury room and waited. Two minutes went by, then ten, then twenty. After twenty-five minutes he came back out. I was steaming. I said, 'You hired me and paid me to come over here with you. You pay me to give you advice, but you don't listen to my advice. I told you to take the Fifth.'

"He says, "Don't worry about it. I couldn't reach the Fifth, so I took the two-and-a-half to every question.'"

Goodman's life was filled with so many characters that he

began to lose his sense of himself. He continued to bet sports, drink hard, seek the wisdom of his friends in the sports-betting world, and hang out with the overgrown Dead-End Kids.

After a few months, Carolyn had seen enough of the Lemon Drop Kid routine that she felt compelled to remind her husband one of the most important lessons of his young career: Lawyers are not their clients.

"I learned early on, and my wife taught me this, that my credibility with the court was critically important and could be jeopardized by what I did outside the courtroom," Goodman recalled. "If people think I'm a pea in a pod with my client, then I'm no better than my client to the court. But it also works with my client. I don't want my clients to look at me as though I'm better than they are, but as though I'm different than they are. I think they appreciate that. Because I'm their mouthpiece. I'm able to speak on their behalf and not be tainted by the perception that I am them. It's very important.

"I used to love to go out with these guys. It was Damon Runyonesque night after night. I was a pig in mud. I loved everything about it. You ate well, drank well. Bob Martin would tell his stories and jokes. For a young kid, it was the best. But I had to balance that. Thanks to Carolyn, I realized that I was weakening my position as far as helping these guys if I kept hanging out with them."

It was always tempting to want to pass a few hours sipping martinis and listening to Bob Martin regale a room with tales of taking bets from Joseph Kennedy or smarting off to Jake La Motta. But in the end, Goodman tried to limit his encounters with clients to his own law office.

And then they were beating a path to his door.

One of them was the Little Man, Meyer Lansky.

4

Meeting the
Little Man—Almost

Thanks to Martin Scorsese's 1995 movie *Casino*, which was based on the dangerous friendship between Anthony Spilotro and Frank Rosenthal, it would be easy to assume Lefty and the Ant were Oscar Goodman's most infamous clients.

They weren't.

The Little Man, Meyer Lansky, held that distinction.

Known as the financial wizard of organized crime, Lansky had played a major role in the development of Las Vegas following the legalization of gambling in 1931. Although he's most remembered as one of Ben Siegel's partners in the completion of the Flamingo, Lansky and his associates held percentages in many Las Vegas casinos, as well as gambling operations in Kentucky, Florida, Cuba, the Bahamas, and London. Although his personal fortune in the 1960s was estimated, if never officially measured, at more than $300 million and he reportedly once described the syndicate's financial empire as "bigger than U.S. Steel," for many years Lansky lived modestly with his second wife Teddy and dog Bruzzer in an apartment on Collins Avenue in Miami Beach.

By 1970, Lansky's personal wealth was the stuff of legend. But all the money in the world couldn't buy him a new start.

With the FBI, Justice Department, and a federal grand jury investigating his link to the Flamingo, Lansky left the United States in an attempt to find asylum and citizenship in Israel, a country to which he'd contributed heavily from its inception. Israeli officials, mindful of Lansky's status in the United States as Public Enemy Number One, decided against alienating its biggest ally. The FBI developed intelligence reports linking Lansky to rumored bribes of high-ranking Israeli officials, and in the end the Little Man was shut out.

Then came the bad news.

On February 24, 1972, Lansky and six other men were indicted on charges that from 1960 to 1967, they skimmed $4.5 million annually, or $36 million in all, in untaxed casino profits from the Flamingo in Las Vegas. Lansky, whom law-enforcement agencies worldwide considered organized-crime's financial wizard, was accused of profiting first from the $10.6 million sale of the Flamingo in 1960 by Albert Parvin and a group of lesser investors to Miami Beach hotel operators and Lansky intimates Sam Cohen, Morris Lansburgh, and Daniel Lifter. As the story goes, Lansky introduced Parvin to Cohen and Lansburgh in exchange for a 2% finder's fee. Then, in 1967, with the eyes of the government scrutinizing every move, Cohen and Lansburgh sold the Flamingo to Kirk Kerkorian. The $200,000 Lansky received for putting that deal together became his official connection to the skim.

When Lansky's Florida attorney, E. David Rosen, went searching for Las Vegas counsel for his client, he found Oscar Goodman. Whether he received Goodman's name through Mel Horowitz or someone associated with the 26-city bookmaking case, Goodman can't recall.

But what is apparent is the fact that representing Lansky forever changed Goodman's status in the eyes of the government. After Lansky, Goodman would always be known as a mob attorney.

Lansky fled to Israel, but was denied citizenship and returned after political pressure from the United States authorities. Lansky briefly attempted to relocate to South America, but in November 1972, he flew back to Miami and the increasingly impatient arms of the FBI. Lansky was charged with contempt after he refused to return to the United States during the grand jury proceeding in the Flamingo case. Although the charge stuck, the conviction was overturned on appeal. Lansky also managed to beat a flimsy tax charge.

But the Flamingo case held a genuine threat of incarceration. For the first time in decades of trying, it appeared the FBI was going to nail the man commonly called the Chairman of the Board of organized crime. Others indicted in the case, perhaps sensing the elephantine battle commencing, scrambled to settle their differences. Steve Delmont, Jerry Gordon, Harry Goldberg, and Sam Ziegman pled out to lesser charges and served minimal jail time. Lansburgh and Cohen pleaded guilty to conspiracy charges and received one-year sentences.

Little-remembered is Goodman's representation of Cohen and Lansburgh. Goodman's timely sentence-reduction motion filed on their behalf resulted in Cohen and Lansburgh serving just four months of their sentences. If the government was correct in its contention that $36 million had been skimmed from the Flamingo, Cohen and Lansburgh surely were comforted to know they were serving time at a compensated rate of approximately $300,000 per day.

There's also a common assumption, as deftly noted in Robert Lacey's *Little Man: Meyer Lansky and the Gangster Life*, that someone must have managed to corrupt federal Judge Roger D. Foley for him to dismiss felony charges against the Chairman. That someone would have to have been Lansky's Las Vegas counsel, Oscar Goodman. Goodman had a personal relationship with Foley. It was a friendship groomed over the better part of the previous decade. In addition, Goodman had succeeded in getting the massive 26-city bookmaking indictment tossed on a technicality in Foley's court. In fact, Foley had sat on many of Goodman's most compelling and controversial federal cases and the two had several friends in common, including Clark County District Judge Thomas J. O'Donnell and future federal judge Harry Claiborne.

In light of Goodman's reputation for representing members and associates of organized crime and America's loosely assembled illegal bookmaking syndicate, through the years, police investigators and FBI agents have scoffed at the propriety of him being named by David Rosen as Lansky's Las Vegas lawyer.

"The judge discovered that government counsel might have been justified in its lack of courage when he finally decided to take matters into his own hands, and to dismiss the case against Lansky in September 1976," Lacey writes. "Making no mention of the dozen stalemated hearings, newspaper accounts managed to make the judge sound like Lansky's dupe or lackey — and today the dark opinion persists in certain law enforcement circles that someone, somehow, 'got to' Judge Foley in 1976, and that his final decision to end the Lansky case after more than four years of deadlock represented not exasperation, or justice, or a bureaucratic wish to clear his court calendar, but a good old-fashioned fix."

Although he was laughed at in law-enforcement circles thereafter, Foley wasn't the first judge to take note of Lansky's medical condition. In fact, the judges who presided over Lansky's previous tax and contempt cases also remarked about his fragile health. But the suspicions shadowed Foley the rest of his career.

The contempt charges had been heard in Miami. Lansky was convicted for failing to return to the United States to face the grand jury. And although his sentence was eventually overturned, it's interesting to note that the U.S. District Judge in the case, James Lawrence King, upon sentencing recommended the ailing Lansky be placed in the Medical Center for Federal Prisoners in Springfield, Missouri.

Lansky's tax-evasion case had been based almost entirely on the shaky statements of government informant Vincent Teresa, who claimed that during his years as a New England Mafia hoodlum he had paid Lansky a percentage of gambling junkets from Boston to the Colony Club in London. Teresa, whose street monikers "Fat Vinnie" and "Fatty Arbuckle" offered proof of the lack of respect he received from members of the underworld in Boston, became a big man once he began cooperating with the government. He offered no physical evidence to substantiate his claim, but Teresa's word resulted in Lansky's indictment. Before a jury acquitted Lansky of the charges based on the lack of evidence, federal Judge Joseph Eaton noted that he was conscious of Lansky's heart problems and other medical maladies: "The government has a right to try this man," Eaton said. "But we don't want to kill him."

When the time came for Lansky to face the government in

the Flamingo skim case, his medical problems were well-documented. He suffered from stomach ulcers, clogged coronary valves, and general deterioration of his heart.

Defendants in the Flamingo case began cutting their deals early. The trial that would finally bring Meyer Lansky and his pals to their knees never materialized. Rumors have persisted, mostly promoted by retired FBI agents and Justice Department prosecutors, but no evidence has ever been made public linking Goodman or Foley to anything untoward in the Lansky dismissal.

What's more, Lansky was not Goodman's only client before Foley at the time. Only a month before the Little Man won his dismissal, Goodman represented Las Vegan John Peter Perri in Foley's court. Perri, a reputed member of the Buffalo mob, was convicted of selling 100 unused Pan American airline tickets to an undercover agent for $5,000. In July 1974, Perri was bludgeoned with a 10-year sentence for the minor white-collar crime.

"This may shock you, but I'm doing so because I'm satisfied this defendant has been recently identified as a representative of organized crime in this community," Foley pronounced. "When I'm satisfied that a defendant is associated with organized crime, I'll impose the maximum sentence."

The judge was nowhere as harsh with Lansky.

No one doubted Lansky had medical problems; the question was one of their severity. Judge Foley ruled Lansky was too ill to stand trial in August 1974. He died January 15, 1983, fully eight and a half years later.

Federal judges are appointed for life, so Foley didn't fear reprisal from the government. No matter how much prosecutors and FBI agents might hate him, as long as he was clean they couldn't touch him. But Foley invited speculation as to his impartiality when he lashed out against the Justice Department and announced that the case against the 74-year-old Lansky would never proceed to trial.

"… It is almost a certainty that this elderly and seriously ill defendant will never be well enough to undergo the rigors of the trial of this complex case. There is a serious question as to this defendant's ability now and in the future to effectively assist his counsel in his defense. His memory is impaired now and probably will worsen. … This court is tempted to dismiss the case regardless of the rules and statutes since it is convinced that the entry of an order of dismissal is in the interest of justice."

Justice Department prosecutors were stunned. Several lengthy delays managed to put the government on the wrong side of a fiery Irishman who reveled in his independence on the federal bench. Foley would go to his grave being suspected by the FBI of doing illicit business with Meyer Lansky.

"Obviously, Judge Foley was a lawyer and not a doctor," one long-time mob-watcher said. "No matter how square Roger Foley might have been, the time between Lansky's dismissal and death became a cynical joke in federal law-enforcement circles. Foley was the butt of that joke."

Foley incurred the limitless wrath of Strike Force prosecutors such as Mike DeFeo, who believed the judge was on the take. The decision also provided fodder for future Las Vegas FBI Special Agent in Charge Joseph Yablonsky, who believed the judge was "doing business" on behalf of Lansky and his allies.

For his part, Oscar Goodman could barely contain himself. Years later Goodman said, "First Foley kicked Lansky out of town, then he kicked the government out of town."

The representation of Lansky stoked Goodman's growing reputation as an intimate of the mob at the highest levels. Where the Chairman of the Board was concerned, there was only one problem with that perception: Although when interviewed Oscar Goodman would admit he'd been casual friends for years with Miami attorney Alvin Malnik, the man FBI experts believe was the Little Man's successor, he never met Meyer Lansky.

"I worked hard to make sure Lansky never had to make an appearance in Las Vegas," Goodman said. "As a result, I never met him. Although it would make a better story if I had, I don't remember ever even speaking to him. There was no need to. I was his lawyer, not his friend."

ʔ ʔ ʔ

The importance of landing Lansky as a client cannot be understated, believes Dominic Gentile, a nationally recognized criminal defense attorney.

"Probably the thing that really brought him into the center of attention with mob clients was the fact that Meyer Lansky chose him," Gentile said. "Once he had Lansky, there's a 'Guys and Dolls' attitude that made others want to emulate Lansky and go to Lansky's lawyer. So Oscar came to be identified with those people."

In the meantime, Goodman was representing not only Lansky, but Sam Cohen and Morris Lansburgh as well on conspiracy charges in the Flamingo sale.

In Miami Beach, Cohen was the owner of the Fontainebleau Hotel. In the early 1960s, the Fontainebleau was a haven for mobsters and movie stars ranging from Genovese crime-family capo Vincent "Jimmy Blue Eyes" Alo to Frank Sinatra. But for all of Cohen's worldly associations, his greatest concern was in preventing his elderly mother from discovering that her favorite son was in trouble with the law. Cohen was a son who never missed celebrating Passover with his mother.

Although being associated with Lansky made him part of a worldwide story and the Flamingo casino skim case was major news in Miami Beach where she lived, somehow Cohen kept his mother from reading the papers and watching the television news. But when he was convicted and sentenced to a year, not even resourceful Sam Cohen could figure a way around missing a Passover seder with his mother.

Oscar Goodman could. While Judge Foley was still infuriated at the government's recalcitrance in refusing to dismiss the charges against Lansky, Goodman filed a series of motions. The first request was for a sentence reduction for Cohen and Lansburgh. Foley granted it. The two men wound up serving four months of their one-year sentences.

Then came the truly difficult part: Getting Sam Cohen out of federal prison temporarily so he could be with his mother for the Jewish holiday.

"The lady never knew her son was charged with anything," Goodman recalls. "We went through the entire proceeding without her knowing. After Sam was sentenced, I got a letter from him explaining his problem. He felt that his mother was so frail that she wouldn't be able to live with the news that her son was in prison. Judge Foley granted my motion and Cohen was released on a furlough to see his mother, then returned to custody. She never knew he was in prison."

But if Foley was suspected of coddling Lansky and even fixing the Flamingo case, the favor he did for Cohen ensured his name would be ridiculed in every FBI and Organized Crime Strike Force Office in the country. It's important to note that from the early 1960s forward, Foley believed his phones were tapped.

"Judge Foley was a good man who knew what justice really meant," Goodman responds. "It means being fair and impartial to the defense as well as the prosecution. It doesn't mean being the second prosecutor in the courtroom or someone who allows sloppy work and transparent evidence to be submitted on the part of the government. As a judge in Nevada, for years Foley had seen the way the federal government treated Nevadans. For a while, there were more IRS agents assigned to Las Vegas than anywhere else in the country. The citizens of the community, and not just the notorious ones, were Public Enemy Number One. Foley made sure that everyone got a fair shake in his courtroom. And if anything, he was harder than other judges on defendants with real mob connections.

"I never met Meyer Lansky, but the one thing I did get from him was a check. I'll never forget it. It was for seven-thousand five-hundred dollars as local counsel. And I never even spoke to him. I wish I'd been called by him and that we'd shared some intriguing confidences, but the truth is we didn't. The money came in handy, however."

5

Lefty and
the Little Guy

B y the time he needed Oscar Goodman's help, Frank Rosenthal had already carved out a personal legend as a Chicago Outfit bookmaker and handicapper. To the police from Miami to Las Vegas, he was "Lefty," one of the top brains in the national illegal-bookmaking syndicate. To his intimates, he was "Crazy," the brilliant but volatile gambler who wasn't shy about puffing out his chest. Not only was he a gifted handicapper, but he held status as a supreme earner and a friend of Outfit underbosses Fiori "Fifi" Buccieri and "Milwaukee Phil" Alderisio. Though both men were fighting incarceration and infirmity, they allowed part of their street-racket activity to be supervised by Anthony Spilotro, Rosenthal's life-long friend.

Rosenthal was born on June 12, 1929, and raised in the heart of Chicago's West Side. Rosenthal's father was a produce wholesaler, but young Frank wasn't interested in the price of Red Delicious apples. He grew up reading the Racing Form and hanging around his father's small stable of horses. Rosenthal alternated between the track and Comiskey Park, then at 19 gravitated to Miami Beach and took a job as a clerk with Bill Kaplan of the Angel-Kaplan Sports Service. In Florida, Rosenthal prospered under Kaplan's tutelage and the influence of mob bookmakers Donald Angelini and Gil Beckley.

In September 1961, at the request of Attorney General Robert Kennedy, U.S. Senator John McClellan focused the Permanent Subcommittee on Investigations on the nation's gambling syndicate. Rosenthal was called before the McClellan committee and questioned about his knowledge of illegal bookmaking and college football and basketball fixes. He invoked his Fifth Amendment right 37 times.

As Kennedy's attack on the mob and all its ancillary activities increased, even slow-moving FBI Director J. Edgar Hoover, himself an avid horse bettor with his own underworld associations, was moved to take action. Only months after the McClellan hearings, Rosenthal was arrested along with hundreds of other gamblers, bookies, and hoodlums as part of an unprecedented FBI crackdown on racket activity. The Florida State Racing Commission added insult by banning him from all the state's racetracks and jai-alai frontons. At the age of 32, Rosenthal suddenly found himself being regularly arrested for bookmaking by police officers who had condoned, and even profited from, his activity for years. Thanks to a high profile and a notorious circle of friends, Rosenthal was rapidly busting out of Miami.

Then real trouble hit. Rosenthal was indicted in 1962 for attempting to bribe a New York University basketball player named Ray Paprocky. After a lengthy delay in the proceedings, during which time Rosenthal protested his innocence, he pleaded no contest.

By that time, Anthony Spilotro had made his bones as a proficient killer and was a rising star with the Chicago Outfit.

Born May 19, 1938, not far from Lefty Rosenthal's West Side home, Anthony John Spilotro was the fourth of six boys brought into the world by Patsy and Antoinette Spilotro. The Italian immigrant settled his family into a two-story bungalow on North Melvina and spent the rest of his life breaking his back to operate his own restaurant, Patsy's, at the corner of Grand and Ogden avenues. Although Patsy's became a hangout for Outfit guys, Patsy himself was never accused of being part of the mob.

Young Anthony's fascination with street life was evident from an early age. Although diminutive at barely five-feet-five, Tony was a heavyweight troublemaker. By the time he was a teenager, he was regularly boosting cars and robbing store owners in nearby neighborhoods. He gained a reputation as a schoolyard brawler and extortionist before he'd even completed puberty. He dropped out of high school, was arrested for the first time at age 16, and by 18 had gained the attention of Chicago's big-league hoodlums, especially bloody 42 Gang alumnus "Mad Sam" DeStefano. Although young Anthony showed promise as a jewel thief — on his European honeymoon, he was deported from Belgium for possession of burglary tools — it was his knowledge of bookmaking and propensity for violence that raised his stock with the Outfit.

Spilotro followed Rosenthal to Florida in 1964 in an attempt to escape the heat that followed a string of murders linked to him and his early career supervisor, the icepick-wielding DeStefano. The most notable homicides were the grisly Outfit hits of petty criminals Jimmy Miraglia and Billy McCarthy on May 15, 1962. Miraglia and McCarthy had committed the fatal sin of killing connected guys named Frankie and Ronnie Scalvo. Chicago police dubbed the crimes "the M&M murders," which were perhaps most memorable for the way McCarthy was tortured — his scrotum was icepicked and his head was placed in a vice and squeezed until one eye popped out — to give up the name of his partner. The cops found the stiffs stuffed into the trunk of a car. Police suspicions immediately focused on DeStefano, Charles Nicoletti, Phil Alderisio, and their violent young protégé, Tony Spilotro. A few months later, the body of DeStefano's estranged loansharking partner, Leo Foreman, was found in the trunk of another car, riddled with icepick and bullet wounds.

Spilotro's presence in Florida only increased Rosenthal's high profile. Rosenthal battled Florida authorities until 1966, when he finally got smart and decided to move to a place sports betting was legal and bookmakers were respected: Las Vegas. But Lefty had barely unpacked his bags before finding himself in the company of the mob cops of the Clark County Sheriff's Office Task Force. Though his criminal record was spotty, his reputation as a trusted associate of Buccieri, Alderisio, and Chicago Outfit lieutenants Jackie Cerone and Turk Torello preceded him.

Frank Rosenthal had become a name. He was reminded of

that fact by police harassment shortly after he opened the Rose Bowl Sports Book in 1966 and when he gravitated toward the mobbed-up Stardust after managing to acquire a sheriff's work card, and again when he was indicted in the 1970 26-city bookmaking dragnet. If Rosenthal was attempting to go legitimate, he was having a helluva time proving it.

As if his indictment in the bookmaking case weren't trouble enough, in early 1971 he was joined in Las Vegas by Anthony Spilotro, his violent old pal from Chicago. Spilotro was immediately targeted by police.

He wasn't hard to find. For a short guy, Tony Spilotro was never good at keeping his head down. Instead of remaining part of the scenery in Southern Nevada, he began showing up at almost all the local casinos. He drove a brand new chocolate-brown Mark IV Lincoln Continental and spent money like a sailor on holiday. In June 1971, Spilotro was arrested in Las Vegas by Clark County Sheriff's deputies and charged with vagrancy. Although he could show "no visible means of support," he drove a new car and carried a fat bankroll. The charges were later dropped, but Spilotro was on notice. The misdemeanor charge and thinly veiled police harassment reverberated from Las Vegas to Chicago, where Spilotro's arrest made headlines in the *Chicago Sun-Times*.

That sort of treatment continued for the next few months until the Task Force received a genuine excuse to pick up Spilotro: He was arrested on charges stemming from the 1963 Leo Foreman murder. Jailed in Las Vegas, he needed someone to vouch for his character in order to make bail. The only man who could do so was Frank Rosenthal, who at the time was trying to persuade authorities he had shaken off his notorious past in an attempt to land a coveted state gaming license. In a rare break, neither the police nor the press took notice; Spilotro was eventually acquitted of the Foreman murder and Rosenthal managed to keep from being burned by his pal Tony's intense notoriety. Goodman, the attorney for both men, thought little of it.

It wasn't until March 1974 that Goodman recalls beginning to recognize with certainty the depth of Rosenthal's relationship with Spilotro. Spilotro had been arrested for the June 23, 1973, murder of William "Red" Klim, a Caesars Palace casino employee who had been shot Outfit style — two bullets behind the ear and one in the chest — in the parking lot of the Churchill Downs Race Book. Was Klim cooperating with authorities in the federal gambling investigation of Price, Zarowitz, Rosenthal, and the rest of the wiseguys involved in the mob's bookmaking syndicate? Did Klim have information damaging to Spilotro, who was then under investigation for defrauding the Teamsters Central States Pension Fund of $1.4 million for loans to a Deming, New Mexico, plastics factory?

Or was Klim, as some knowledgeable Las Vegans believe, a loanshark who refused to pay tribute to Rosenthal and Spilotro?

Goodman says he never learned of the motive for Klim's murder. But he surprised many observers when he used Rosenthal, still embroiled in his own battles with state gaming authorities, to vouch for the accused killer's character before Justice of the Peace Robert Legakes. Not long after, Legakes would be suspected by the FBI of doing business for the Chicago Outfit.

"I don't see things the way other people see them," Goodman said. "I see them through my looking glass, my rose-colored glasses. And perhaps my gin-soaked brain cells. I was there, and I went back and certainly I used Rosenthal as a character witness. This may have been a mistake, but I didn't know that. If I had a crystal ball and could have seen what was ahead — or what the truth was — I wouldn't have done a lot of things. But in my naiveté, when Tony was arrested for Red Klim's murder on a Sunday, I had Ray Jeffers come down in front of Bob Legakes, who was the justice of the peace, to have a bail hearing. Who did I call as Tony's character witness? The guy who introduced him to me: Frank Rosenthal. And Frank said, 'Yeah, Tony and I are buddies. We go back all the way to our childhood in Chicago.' I didn't give it a second thought, mixing the two of them together.

"It was right there. And if I knew that these guys were who they turned out to be, and I was part of trying to maintain the secret of who they were, I certainly wouldn't have put them together.

"At the time — and I know this will sound unbelievable — I didn't know they were all that friendly with each other. The business they were in isn't as it's portrayed on television and in the movies. There are very few instances in which all the principal parties involved in a massive conspiracy are in the same room. And, perhaps with one or two exceptions, they'd never allow an outsider to sit in and listen. And again, this will sound like a line, but I was an outsider.

"I had a certain knowledge and I'd had the kind of success in cases these men understood. But I wasn't a *consigliere*. In fact, I was like a lot of other people in those days. I didn't know Chicago and Kansas City and whoever else had the Stardust and all those other casinos. Remember, the owners were always licensed by the Gaming Control Board and the politicians were fond of being quoted at length in the press about how legitimate Nevada gambling was. Well, a lot of people knew it wasn't as lily white as the politicians claimed, but no one was going around naming names."

The silence on the street, anyway, was due to Spilotro's reputation for violence. During those years, whenever a gambler was found shot in the head, Spilotro or one of his cronies immediately became a suspect. Whether it was the demise of Red Klim and illegal bookmaker Jerry Dellmann, the disappearance of casino host Johnny Pappas, or the murders of nearly two dozen others, for more than a decade, Spilotro was the target. For a street guy to talk about the Outfit's business in Las Vegas behind the Little Guy's back was to put himself in serious harm's way.

Harry Claiborne recalled trying unsuccessfully to school Goodman against representing organized crime.

"I have all my life steered away from the mob guys in my practice and I had numerous opportunities," Claiborne said. "I guess the only one I ever had was Doc Stacher. I simply always had a feeling that there was no way you could represent one of those guys without pretty soon learning too much, and when you learned too much about their activities you were expendable, in my opinion. And I just wanted to live a long time. That was my sole reason.

"I told Oscar something, but by this time Oscar had gone money crazy. His lifestyle changed. His requirement for money was great. He began to focus mainly on fees. He reached a point where his ability began to be recognized and his fee schedule increased accordingly. That's not a knock. I think all lawyers do it, but he was looking for clients who could pay large fees and they were looking for good counsel. It was kind of a natural progression of things."

Goodman's denial is all the more intriguing given the fact that, by 1973, Rosenthal's underworld connections were widely known. Although he was primarily a gambler, his association with mobsters in Chicago and Florida and his connection with two major sports scandals were the stuff of Chicago Crime Commission reports and Senate subcommittee records. But it's also important to remember that few casino men or high-rolling gamblers were without some connection to the mob. Frank Rosenthal's colorful background was far from unique.

Goodman had little difficulty beating the charges on behalf of his client in the Klim murder case. Although Klim was shot less than 100 feet from the front door of the Churchill Downs, witnesses appeared unable or unwilling to step forward to describe the killer.

? ? ?

At 64, Marvin Krause was a Caesars Palace slot supervisor with a 71-year-old wife, Hilda, and a passion for cards, ponies, and a buxom babe named Rosalie Maxwell, who worked cocktails at Caesars and eventually rose to supervisor. Krause was connected. When he wasn't looking after his shadowy friends' slot proceeds, he kept an eye on Rosalie. She, in turn, kept handsome young stud Frank LaPena on the side. LaPena ran a few working girls as a Hacienda Hotel bell captain and in his spare time pulled robberies and collected personal debts. LaPena's circle of friends was a veritable police lineup of drug-addled thugs, broken-down boxers, and wanna-be hoodlums, people who qualify as colorful characters in Las Vegas. One of those mutts was Gerald "Jerry" Weakland.

In the predawn hours of January 14, 1974, Jerry Weakland pulled a mask over his face and entered the Las Vegas Country Club home of Marvin Krause while his wife lay sleeping. Hilda awoke during the robbery and Weakland overpowered her, tying her to a chair with an electrical extension cord. According to his statement to police, Marvin entered his garage to find a masked gunman waiting for him. He, too, was taken to a bedroom and tied to a chair. He was hit over the back of the head and knocked nearly unconscious, although he later said he managed to untie his hands.

Weakland burglarized the home, picking up cash and a few items he could trade quickly for drugs, but left many expensive items alone, then returned outside to his vehicle, where former professional football player Thomas Boutwell sat. Weakland hesitated, then told his friend he had some unfinished business inside.

Upon re-entering the house, Weakland took a butcher knife from the kitchen and slashed the throat of Hilda Krause. He stabbed her several times and left the knife in her back.

Two weeks later, Weakland was picked up on murder charges. During his interrogation he named his friends Frank LaPena and Rosalie Maxwell as co-conspirators and agreed to testify against them in exchange for a reduced sentence that might allow him to leave prison in just five years. As part of his deal, charges against him in a separate robbery and attempted-murder case, one in which he admitted shooting a Hacienda Hotel manager in the kneecaps, were dropped. Weakland implicated LaPena in the kneecapping case as well.

Professing their innocence, LaPena and Maxwell hired Oscar Goodman, who would eventually be forced to choose between the two. At the time, Goodman was juggling the murder case, representing Lansky in the Flamingo casino skimming case, and attempting to keep Buffalo mob figure John Perri out of prison on the charge of selling Pan Am tickets to a cop. In addition, Goodman was in the midst of defending multiple federal illegal-bookmaking cases. He also took on the Jay Sarno-Stanley Mallin IRS bribe case, at the time the largest tax-related case in state history. In addition, Goodman's successful argument before the Nevada Supreme Court saved accused teen killers Douglas and Clinton Hanks from being tried on capital murder charges that would have led to the gas chamber by postponing the brothers' trial dates for several months, a delay that proved fortuitous when the state Supreme Court struck down the death penalty.

With few exceptions, every major criminal case in Las Vegas went to either Oscar Goodman or his friend Harry Claiborne.

By October 1974, after the longest preliminary hearing in the history of the Southern Nevada court system, LaPena and Maxwell learned that they faced the death penalty for the murder of Hilda Krause, largely on the purchased testimony of Weakland. Despite all his obvious motives for wanting his wife out of the picture, Marvin Krause remained uncharged.

Before being forced to continue as only LaPena's attorney because of the possibility of conflict between LaPena and Maxwell, Goodman filed a series of motions pointing out numerous leaps of faith in the government's case against the defendants. First, Goodman questioned how Weakland's testimony might be corroborated when, by his own admission, only LaPena and Maxwell knew of the plan to rob and murder Hilda Krause to take advantage of Marvin's money. With no other witnesses available — even the ex-jock Boutwell hadn't heard of any conspiracy or seen a crime take place — the police were depending on unreliable jailhouse snitches for much of their information.

But the most egregious move of all was the deal handed Weakland. A street thug and gym-sparring partner, in a more candid moment Weakland had told police, "I took a knife and I sliced her throat." Now he was telling them that Frank LaPena and Rosalie Maxwell put him up to it for $1,000 down and $9,000 once their plan came together. With the help of Goodman's motions, the trials of Maxwell and LaPena were severed.

Marvin Krause, meanwhile, was only briefly considered a suspect in the conspiracy. In his police statement, Krause said he had no way of identifying his masked assailant.

At Maxwell's trial, Weakland's elaborate conspiracy changed again. He admitted LaPena helped plan the attack, but denied Maxwell had knowledge of it. Maxwell was acquitted.

At LaPena's trial, Weakland claimed he couldn't remember anything associated with the Krause murder. Prosecutors produced Weakland's prior testimony for the jury, which convicted LaPena of murder. Despite a lack of evidence connecting him to the crime, in 1976 LaPena was sentenced to life in prison without the possibility of parole. Weakland was hit with a 20-year sentence for perjury. LaPena maintained his innocence for the next 25 years as he fought for a second and eventually a third trial.

"I don't know whether Frank LaPena had anything to do with Hilda Krause's murder, but I do know something about defendants, and his actions have been those of a man who was innocent," Goodman said. "He passed up opportunities to get out of prison if he'd only admit his role in the murder. But he's refused. And to my knowledge he's been a model prisoner."

♪ ♪ ♪

Jay Sarno was the greatest big-idea man in the history of Las Vegas. He envisioned Caesars Palace, a plush casino with a Roman theme, and saw it built in 1966. He then came up with the idea for Circus Circus, the city's first true family resort, which not only featured a sprawling carnival midway, but also a trapeze above the casino floor, and lived to see his dream come true in 1968.

Sarno's connections fueled his visions and plans. He knew representatives of the Teamsters Central States Pension Fund, which saw fit to make millions in loans for Caesars Palace and Circus Circus. He also knew the representatives of the Chicago Outfit, including Tough Tony Spilotro. Sarno leased space to Spilotro for a gift shop at Circus Circus under the name Anthony Stuart.

Due to Sarno's connections, he was a prime target for federal investigators, and his sloppy income-tax returns made him easy pickings for the Internal Revenue Service. Sarno's personal and corporate tax returns for the years 1968 through 1971 were a mess and in the early '70s, Sarno and his associate, local businessman Leo Crutchfield, began receiving calls and visits from IRS agents.

By September 1973, Sarno was getting desperate. He owed the government big and needed time to pay. In conversations with IRS agents, Crutchfield and Sarno began offering them cash. When Sarno, Circus Circus executive Stanley Mallin, and Crutchfield were indicted for conspiring to bribe an Internal Revenue Service agent, the case wound up in U.S. District Judge Roger Foley's courtroom. Goodman represented Sarno, Harry Claiborne defended Mallin, and Crutchfield was severed after he began cooperating with the government.

The trial began in February 1975 and lasted nearly a month.

Justice Department prosecutor James Duff guided jurors through a series of alleged events in which Sarno and Crutchfield, and to a lesser extent Mallin, attempted to find a way to securely bribe one of the IRS agents. At one point, according to Duff, Sarno attempted to induce the agent to meet with him in the steamroom at Circus Circus. Without clothes, there would be no way to bug the conversation.

Goodman and Claiborne countered with an elaborate and persuasive defense, contending that the defendants were innocent men with no predisposition to commit such a crime. Rather, they were the victims of entrapment by greedy government agents.

There was plenty of damning evidence against the defendants. A reasonable mind might have wondered at one point whether men as sharp as Sarno and Mallin had known that bribing an IRS agent was perhaps not the normal course of doing business. But the government had done sloppy work as well and several phone conversations made it appear the agents not only solicited bribes, but even held out for more money.

During trial, Goodman had a chance to marvel up close at his gifted co-counsel, Claiborne, the Arkansas native son who had the ability to create thunder and lightning in the courtroom. When Claiborne took umbrage with the government's outrageous conduct, the jury listened closely.

Goodman couldn't reasonably deny that a bribe had been discussed by Sarno. So he didn't try to hide it. While Claiborne reminded jurors of the bad intentions of the IRS, Goodman explained his client's behavior.

"The hardest thing for me to do is stand before twelve people and tell them my client did a misdeed and expect them to acquit him," Goodman told the jury during his opening statement. "But that's what I'm doing."

While government prosecutors claimed that Sarno and Mallin had practiced despicable behavior worthy of lengthy prison sentences, Goodman and Claiborne created the image of an IRS watchdog that was off its leash. Then Mallin and Sarno took the stand and told of being afraid of the IRS agents. If those government agents were corrupt, Goodman asked, who could Sarno and Mallin be expected to run to?

"We were stupid, we were idiotic, and we were wrong,"

Sarno pleaded to the jury. "But we were scared. We saw how they could be. We were frightened of the IRS. I was paying him not to frame me and put me in the can."

Goodman and the flamboyant Sarno almost parted ways during the trial. Claiborne was calling character witnesses for Mallin, a mild-mannered fellow, and Sarno began to chafe. Before court, Sarno demanded that Goodman also put on character witnesses. Goodman refused, reminding the casino man that the government would then be able to show the jury a stack of damning magazine articles and newspaper clippings. Sarno said, "You're fired," but Goodman replied, "I'll see you in court."

At trial, Claiborne called a university chancellor and asked a series of standard questions: "Do you know my client? How long have you known him? Do you have an opinion about his character traits of honesty and integrity?"

The chancellor answered the final question, "Excellent."

Sarno's face turned scarlet. Another witness, a noted local physician, was called by Claiborne. The standard questions were asked.

The physician answered the final question, "Excellent."

Sarno's toupee began to turn. He jabbed Goodman in the ribs. "Stanley's going to win and I won't," he sneered.

The next witness resulted in another "Excellent" opinion of Mallin's character.

The last witness was known to both defendants and Sarno said, "He's a friend. Ask him about me."

Goodman shrugged, stood before the court and asked Judge Foley for a few words with the witness. "Go ahead, Mr. Goodman," Foley said.

"Do you know my client, Jay Sarno?" Goodman asked. "How long? In what capacity? Do you have an opinion as to his character trait of honesty and integrity? Please tell the jury."

"Fair," the witness answered.

Goodman slumped back to his chair. The prosecutor, Richard Wright, stood up holding a box of critical magazine articles outlining Sarno's nefarious associations. Goodman rose and interrupted with, "Your honor, the prosecutor is going to ask questions out of *Reader's Digest*."

Sensing he was being insulted, Foley replied, "Not in my court."

A catastrophe had been narrowly averted.

At one point, Goodman used an elaborate chain-of-events chart as a visual aid. Although such props are commonly used now, they were novel in the mid-1970s.

"I use demonstrative evidence more than scientific evidence and I learned that from Jay Sarno," Goodman said. "During his bribery trial, I had this huge chart in front of the jury, 'Government Entrapment Efforts,' and the government didn't object. At one point, after I finished my closing argument, one of the jurors corrected a mistake I'd made. He said, 'Excuse me, but August has thirty-one days, not thirty.' That really sunk in—the jury studied the chart. It was pretty impressive. Sarno gave me the idea. He said, 'You can't just go out there and talk. You have to show these people these things. You have to make things visual to them.' It was another great idea from Jay Sarno. He really was a genius.

"Sarno also taught me a lot about the incredible anxiety a defendant goes through. It was while representing Sarno that I realized my clients needed to be defended not only in the courtroom, but in the press as well. Some people will call that ego, but in my estimation it's very important. It violates a rule of procedure, but it's a rule that's made to be broken. I will not take the initiative, but when the prosecutors send out their press releases, which they do in just about every case I'm involved in, and I see the press release in black and white and it goes way over the line, I feel my function is more than just to get a not guilty or to resolve the case in my client's favor. I think my function really is as their spokesperson. Because as Jay Sarno said when he was indicted, 'This indictment is a ninety-nine-percent conviction. I haven't even gone to trial, but I've lost all my friends. I don't have any access to money anymore; my funding has dried up. I'm through unless I win.' For someone like Jay Sarno, the mere charge was enough to kill him."

Nevadans have traditionally been mistrustful of the federal government—only 14% of the state is owned by interests other than the feds—but with the Watergate scandal still fresh in the public's mind, it was an especially bad time to be connected to any institution from Washington, D.C. Goodman seized the moment and enlisted his client, Sarno, to do the same.

"I am incensed and enraged by the Gestapo-type tactics that were used against these men," Goodman said. "It is not the role of government to embark on a horrendous scheme to put these men in a situation where they are forced to bribe a federal agent. ... The same thing that happened in Watergate must end right here and now."

In the end, the jury was unable to reach a verdict. Foley declared a mistrial, then quickly granted a defense motion for acquittal.

When the government appealed the acquittal in Foley's court, Goodman was prepared: "The government is completely out of line and is like a baby crying over spilt milk. They are engaging in a rotten tactic that can bear them no success, but in their efforts to harass Sarno they're subjecting him to embarrassment, expense, ordeal, and compelling him to live in a constant state of anxiety."

The prosecutors were eventually forced to admit defeat.

When his travails had ended, Sarno said, "These men saved our lives. I'm grateful we had a learned judge and two fine attorneys."

"I don't think Harry Claiborne ever charged a big fee before he met me," Goodman recalled. "I think I taught him how to charge a big fee. When I represented Sarno, I charged a lot of money and Claiborne followed suit. Before that, he loved what he did so much, he couldn't have cared less about the money."

Interviewed years later, Claiborne observed, "I think money was very important to Oscar. He was a fine attorney, but he was very focused on making a lot of money."

For many years, IRS criminal investigators suspected that Sarno had all three in his pocket. But Oscar Goodman had no time to defend himself. He had his hands full with the pressing legal affairs of Tough Tony Spilotro, Frank "Lefty" Rosenthal, and one Joe Agosto.

§ § §

Like so many things in Las Vegas, Joseph Vincent Agosto's appearance was deceiving. Originally known as Vincenzo Pianetti, he was born in 1927 in Italy or Cleveland, depending on which story one preferred to believe. Agosto was either born in Cleveland and taken to Sicily by his mother as a young boy, where he was educated and became a practicing lawyer before returning to the United States, or he was born in Sicily and slipped into America from Canada, where he borrowed the identity of a deceased hoodlum from Cleveland named Agosto. Either way, he ended up in Seattle, where he first attracted the attention of the FBI.

By the mid-1970s, Agosto occupied a small office at the Tropicana Hotel. His job title: manager of the *Folies Bergére* production show.

The unassuming Agosto—who spoke in heavily accented English and was fond of wearing a short-brimmed cap favored by so many Italian immigrants—was arrested by the U.S. Immigration Service in April 1975 as an illegal alien. He became a law-enforcement curiosity when it was discovered he kept an office at the Tropicana, but was not employed by the hotel. He also denied owning any part of the *Folies Bergére*, but was merely a manager for the Production Leasing Company. In various interviews, Agosto claimed to have ties to Ohio, Alaska, and Washington.

After being arrested by the INS, Joe Agosto called Oscar Goodman. By the time Agosto made bail, the state Gaming Control Board announced it was scrutinizing his association with the Tropicana and its part-owners, brothers Edward and Fred Doumani. At the time, the Doumanis also owned two prime Strip motels and a large percentage of the Golden Nugget downtown. The gaming regulatory inquiry came in the wake of an ongoing federal investigation into potential hidden ownership and skimming at the Tropicana by Kansas City's Civella crime family. In time, Agosto would be suspected of watching the skim at the Tropicana on behalf of the Civellas.

"In the beginning," Goodman recalled, "Joe came up with a story. The story as I recall it was that he was born in Cleveland and his mother sent him to live with an aunt in Italy. And when he came back from Italy, they were trying to deport him. That's what he says was the truth and we won the immigration case. We prevailed as far as that was concerned.

"He was an extraordinary human being. The reason I didn't think there was a mob was in large part because of Joe Agosto.

He would wear one of those little hats like the guy in the Mario Puzo story, *The Sicilian*, almost like a *yarmulke*, a round rectangular one. A stupid hat with a little brim.

"And he looked like what I thought he was, and that was a cab driver. I thought he was a driver. And I thought all this stuff about him owning rights to the *Folies* was just a bunch of hype. And he would come up here just about every day. And when I found out he was connected with Tony Civella and was Kansas City's man, I said, 'Well, I really don't know what's happening.' I was amazed."

Later, Agosto continued to surprise his friends and allies by agreeing to become a prosecution witness against crime boss Nick Civella, along with his family and allies. But in 1975, Agosto was as loyal to his friends as he was subdued.

The Kansas City investigation promised trouble for the Civella family, but for the present, Goodman's priority remained keeping Spilotro out of jail and the casino-owning Argent Corporation running.

6

The Trouble with Tony

Not long after Anthony Spilotro followed Frank Rosenthal to Las Vegas, a strange thing began happening to local gamblers, casino wiseguys, illegal bookmakers, and loansharks. They began suffering violent deaths. The weapon used — a .22 High Standard pistol with a silencer — was wickedly consistent. Someone was sending a message that there was a new street boss in town, one who demanded not only respect, but also tribute. Although no one ever seemed to see anything, the Little Guy was said to be responsible for the lengthy list of murders.

But beyond his long-standing friendship with Rosenthal, the question was: Did Spilotro and his superiors in the Chicago mob have real connections to Argent Corporation Chief Executive Officer Allen R. Glick and his Las Vegas casinos?

Law-enforcement authorities thought they had the answer in the summer of 1975 when Caesars Palace pit boss Marty Buccieri was found shot to death. Buccieri wasn't just another Strip scuffler. In addition to being an accomplished hand in the casino business, he was also a distant relative of Fifi Buccieri and the men who manipulated the Teamsters Central States Pension Fund.

Marty Buccieri appeared to know everyone who was anyone in Las Vegas. Among his many local contacts was Allen Glick, the CEO of Argent Corporation, which with $62.75 million in Teamsters Central States Pension Fund loans had purchased the Stardust, Hacienda, Fremont, and Marina casinos. Law enforcement had learned through confidential sources that shortly before his death, Buccieri had been arguing with Glick about a finder's fee for helping to secure the Teamsters loans. Buccieri had often bragged to friends of helping land Glick his financing. He thought he deserved a $30,000 fee and at one point reportedly physically threatened Glick.

Days later, Marty Buccieri was murdered.

Witnesses said they saw two shadowy figures approach Buccieri and pump him full of slugs.

Although law enforcement blamed Spilotro for the Buccieri murder, according to Nicholas Pileggi's *Casino*, the hit was carried out by two assassins from out of town. Careful observers noted that Buccieri had been murdered by a 25-caliber handgun, not Spilotro's signature 22-caliber.

It was obvious to local police that it was unhealthy to argue with Glick, a Vietnam veteran born in Pittsburgh with no apparent ties to Las Vegas. Although his name was as prominent as his executive office and job title on the door at the Stardust, Glick wasn't the man in charge of the casino company. Behind the scenes, the decisions were being made by Frank Rosenthal. It was Glick, according to *Casino*, who told Rosenthal of the problem with Buccieri.

Essential to understanding Goodman's life is an appreciation that 1975 was a tumultuous turning point for the Outfit. Earlier that year, Spilotro, Joseph "Joey the Clown" Lombardo, and Allen Dorfman faced long prison sentences in a Teamsters loan-scam case, until key witness Dan Seifert was murdered by shotgun-wielding hit men. On June 19, Chicago mob boss Sam Giancana was murdered in the basement of his home in a Chicago suburb, the murder weapon a silenced 22-caliber pistol. A few months later the body of John Rosselli, who had shepherded the Outfit's Las Vegas and Hollywood interests for many years, was found stuffed in an oil drum and floating in Dumfoundling Bay near Miami.

Someone from Chicago was apparently sewing up loose

ends and silencing potential witnesses.

When Tamara Rand was murdered on November 9 at her home in the San Diego suburb of Mission Hills, law enforcement saw Spilotro's role in Las Vegas in a whole new light. In California, Rand had been Allen Glick's friend, business associate, and real-estate partner. Although she had no gaming experience, Rand had invested $2 million with Glick in the Las Vegas casinos and had signed a contract as a consultant with the Hacienda for $100,000 a year.

She had also sued Glick for breach of contract and fraud and she'd had a bitter argument with him only days before her husband discovered her body. She'd been shot in the back of the head at close range with a silenced 22-caliber pistol — Tony Spilotro's calling card.

But Spilotro had a curious alibi for the day of the murder provided by FBI agent Duncan Everette, who for some inexplicable reason had flown from Chicago to Las Vegas to casually visit one of the most notorious hit men in America. Everette was later chastised for his actions, which he called an act of "investigative initiative," but Spilotro had made a patsy out of the politically sensitive FBI. Tough Tony was laughing at the most powerful law-enforcement agency in the United States.

Allen Glick was feeling so much heat from media from across the nation pursuing the story that by Thanksgiving, he was forced to make a public statement denying not only any connection with the Rand murder, but any Argent connection to organized crime.

"To associate me or any department or employee of my company with so-called 'organized crime' is false," Glick said in a prepared statement. "The truth is I have never been convicted of a crime greater than a traffic violation. The truth is that Argent operated three Las Vegas hotels and four casinos. The truth is that I was unanimously approved for licensing to operate these hotel casinos after an exhaustive and extensive investigation. ... Instead of recognizing these truths, there have been continuous distortions by certain members of the news media. ... I have no newspaper, magazine, or television station to openly use in a response to combat these false allegations, but I do have one fact on my side which cannot be distorted, maligned, nor falsified when it be known — that is the truth that Allen R. Glick has never, nor will ever be, associated with anything other than what is lawful."

With that statement, Glick sealed his fate as a local laughingstock and the most consciously naive man in the history of Las Vegas. Glick had been only too happy to accept the largesse of the Teamsters Central States Pension Fund, which for decades had been linked to organized crime. He'd chosen to assume the reins of a casino empire in Las Vegas, which for all intents had been built by the mob. He had even found it in his heart to hire and attempt to protect the job status of long-time Chicago mob associate Frank Rosenthal, who in turn saw to it that an inordinate number of his friends and associates were employed at the Stardust.

Glick's admission made him one of the only men in Las Vegas who didn't know something shady was going on at the Stardust, which, despite a substantial increase in gross revenues, had managed a net loss of $7.5 million in fiscal year 1974.

Goodman might have been one of the only other men who didn't know. Publicly, he betrayed no knowledge of an association between the licensed Glick and Spilotro, Public Enemy Number One.

"My client categorically and emphatically denies any connection with the Argent Corporation!" Goodman roared to the press.

But it was too late.

With wiretaps up in Chicago, Las Vegas, and Kansas City, the FBI, IRS, and Justice Department's Organized Crime Strike Force were assembling an unprecedented case, which linked Spilotro to Glick and connected the Stardust, Hacienda, Marina, Fremont, and Tropicana casinos to mob families in Chicago, Milwaukee, Cleveland, and Kansas City. Many of the suspects had one attorney in common, Oscar Goodman, who somehow managed to hold the complex matrix of developing cases and characters in his head — while continuing to maintain that there was no connection among them at all.

Glick was under investigation in connection with a slot-machine skimming operation at his casinos that had generated millions in untaxed profits. Federal investigators were busy tracing those dollars to the pockets of Milwaukee mob boss Frank Balistrieri and the Chicago Outfit. Argent was in trouble, Glick was fresh meat, and Goodman tried to keep the wolves at bay.

Always in the public eye, Goodman's reputation as a capable representative of organized crime was rarely in doubt. One story holds that at one point, the Chicago Outfit became dissatisfied with him and sent attorney Dominic Gentile to Las Vegas as a reinforcement against the federal investigative onslaught. The tale, believed by police and FBI agents, was refuted by Gentile in Alan Balboni's book, *Beyond the Mafia: Italian Americans and the Development of Las Vegas*. "Gentile did not let these bizarre stories bother him," Balboni wrote. "… Gentile did not challenge Goodman's role; indeed, the two defense attorneys occasionally cooperated." Both were dedicated to defending Spilotro.

"I learned it a couple of years later," Gentile recalled. "There really was no truth to it at all. In fact, when I found out about it, I was really kind of angry, because I'd had all this burden that I didn't know about and none of the benefit that should have gone with it if it were true.

"If Oscar says he was lucky, I think he's right, at least from the standpoint of timing," Gentile added, commenting on Goodman's early career. "His arrival in Las Vegas coincided with a stepping up of federal organized-crime enforcement activity. If you think about it, he got here right about the time Attorney General Bobby Kennedy and Bob Blakely, the creator of the RICO statute, were most active. It was right at the time the immunity law was put into effect. It was right at the time when the new federal wiretap statute went into effect. All these federal laws were created and no one knew about them, because they were brand new. Any time you have new laws, you have unlimited potential for creativity and God knows Oscar does not lack for creativity. He happened to be in the right place at the right time and he made the most of it. Oscar was right there at the most propitious moment."

But that opportunity was double-edged.

"The FBI figured Oscar couldn't represent all these people without in some way being used by them for illegal purposes," Harry Claiborne said. "Even though they had no proof of it and I'm sure it didn't exist, it didn't have to exist in order for them to be certain that it was occurring. And pretty soon they didn't distinguish between criminal activity and legal services. Nor did they try to."

Goodman, Claiborne believes, became victimized by his legal associations.

"I'm sure that's what happened to Oscar," he said. "It would be very difficult to convince any of the law-enforcement agents at work in the mob investigations that all of Oscar's activities were without criminality. In other words, they would believe that any lawyer who represented those people more than once was one of them. It wouldn't have made any difference who it was."

Goodman, of course, compounded his image problem by relentlessly ripping at the character of the FBI and Department of Justice.

§ § §

On the street, while the FBI worked undercover and used court-authorized wiretaps, Metro's Intelligence Bureau kept Spilotro and his associates under 24-hour surveillance.

Plainclothes detectives in unmarked cars stopped Spilotro and his men night after night, a practice that eventually led to the fatal shooting of Michael Bluestein, a Chicago mob associate and the son of Culinary Union business agent Steve Bluestein, by police detectives Gene Smith and David Groover. After a lengthy civil litigation, the police were eventually cleared in the suspicious shooting death.

"Gene Clark, who was one of the toughest cops on the force, had been leaning on Tony and his associates, pulling them over, harassing them, violating their rights every day," Goodman said. "Clark leaned on the attorney Neil Beller, who was pulled over, taken out of his car, and searched. It was the kind of stuff that caused Bluestein to be killed. The bullshit stops, the roust, and then the blasting away, and Tony had had it up to here. He even filed a lawsuit to stop the harassment of him and his friends. He didn't really care about himself — he'd lived that way all his life — but for his friends. It embarrassed Tony and made him mad.

"Eventually, they wanted to take his deposition [in the

harassment lawsuit], knowing he wasn't going to let them. I couldn't prevent them from taking Tony's deposition. Tony never said boo to law enforcement, so I wasn't about to expose him and the case was dismissed. But the rousting went on and Tony decided he was going to, you know, settle it in his own way at that point. Outside the Coachman's Inn, Tony challenged Clark to a shootout, in effect. And Tony was the kind of guy who would have been happy to accommodate him. Clark backed off."

Tensions continued to escalate after police veteran Joe Blasko was found to have shared classified information with Spilotro and his associates. Blasko was fired and other cops were transferred in the wake of the incident. Blasko was later tried and convicted as one of Spilotro's Hole-in-the-Wall Gang of burglars. For his part, Gene Clark invited suspicion by retiring after 28 years on the force and accepting loans totaling $150,000 from Allen Glick for casino investments.

¿ ¿ ¿

Despite his $2.5 million long-term contract with the Stardust, Frank Rosenthal had a problem. As the inside man at the casino, his importance to the operation, not to mention his livelihood, hinged on his ability to fly under the radar of the authorities. In Nevada, all prospective casino employees must first obtain a sheriff's work card before getting hired. Without a work card, which under Nevada law can be revoked for cause, Rosenthal couldn't run Argent and advise Glick. His ruse of posing as the Stardust's entertainment director worked for a short time, but when the Gaming Control Board called him forward for a suitability hearing as a casino key employee, his facade of legitimacy began to crack.

Unlike Spilotro, who appeared to have no allies in political circles, Rosenthal's persistent lobbying efforts had made several inroads with important gaming regulators. Nevada Governor Bob List was clearly a fan of Lefty. So was Gaming Control Board Chairman Phil Hannifan, who, though known as a tough regulator, for some reason went out of his way to show respect for Rosenthal. Hannifan chided curious gaming agents who dropped by the increasingly shaky Stardust to attempt to define Rosenthal's actual role at the casino. While his latest business cards listed him as an assistant to publicity director and former news columnist Dick Odessky, Rosenthal was clearly a key figure in the operation of the casino.

But Hannifan's friendship alone was useless in Nevada's two-tiered system of gaming regulation. After a two-day hearing, on January 15, 1976, the Control Board with Hannifan present voted unanimously to recommend denial of Rosenthal's application for status as a key employee. The Gaming Commission made it official by endorsing the Control Board's recommendation. Rosenthal was finished in an official capacity as a casino executive.

Still, Lefty managed to hold onto his lucrative contract, while Oscar Goodman went to work hammering away at Nevada's casino work regulations. In January 1978, District Judge Carl Christensen ruled that the Gaming Commission lacked jurisdiction in denying Rosenthal's right to work on property at the Stardust. He could be prevented from working in the casino, but not at the resort in another capacity.

It was as if he'd never left the building. In no time Frank Rosenthal re-emerged as the Stardust's entertainment director. Some local observers considered Rosenthal's move to be tactical, but it did nothing to endear him to gaming regulators and only increased the already-intense scrutiny of Glick's Stardust operations. Although Goodman fought losing battles, he bought time for Rosenthal and the mob. He also proved once again that he wasn't afraid of challenging authority, at one point suing Governor Mike O'Callaghan on Rosenthal's behalf. Ultimately, Goodman became the consummate legal authority on Nevada work-card and key-employee law. Years later, his name would be closely linked to nearly every major case on the subject. And why not? At one time or another, he represented almost every major player to be challenged by state gaming regulators.

¶ ¶ ¶

"Nobody will ever believe this, but I never had any idea that Chicago and Kansas City and Milwaukee were running the Stardust, Fremont, Marina, and Hacienda," Goodman said.

"I didn't know that. I knew that Glick was there and I thought that he was the boss. And I knew that Rosenthal exercised some influence, but I never knew to what degree. I knew that Rosenthal had known Spilotro, but I never really thought that Rosenthal was part of Chicago. I mean, I knew he had associates back then, Wizard Angelini was his friend, but I never saw him having that close of a relationship with Spilotro. Over the years, I've come to find out that it was a lot closer than I thought it was. Had I known then what I know now, instead of making $12,000 a month from him, I would have made $120,000. I didn't realize what it was all about. I was on the up and up. I was a square guy who was doing everything as though I thought it was all legit."

But Goodman's protestations seem laughable in the face of the facts.

In March 1978, the IRS announced it was inquiring into the tax records and financial status not only of Anthony Spilotro, but of Oscar Goodman as well. Though those financial documents were generated by officers at First National Bank, Valley Bank, and Grand Resorts, Inc., bank officials refused to turn them over to IRS investigators. They refused even in the face of Spilotro's public links to organized crime through a devastating *Time* magazine article, which called him the supervisor of the Mafia's Las Vegas gambling operations and a close associate of Felix "Milwaukee Phil" Alderesio. After a one-day hearing, U.S. District Judge Roger Foley—in a move that surely disappointed those who believed he had an improper relationship with Goodman and his clients—ordered that the information be turned over to the IRS. The best Goodman could manage was a lengthy oral battering of IRS Agent Leo Halper.

"I think they'd rather get the lawyer than the client," Goodman told a *National Law Journal* reporter. "The newspapers are running blaring headlines and the prosecutors are holding press conferences, and it's very difficult to shadowbox with dime-store-novel allegations."

Of course, there were plenty of people in federal law enforcement who believed the lawyer was worth getting.

"Well, if he wasn't a *consigliere*, he was the closest goddamn thing to it," said one ex-Strike Force attorney interviewed under the condition he remain anonymous. "I'll say this for Oscar, I think he's one of the best attorneys I've ever seen argue a motion. He's not half the trial lawyer he's said to be, but he argued a motion as well as anyone I've ever seen."

❡ ❡ ❡

Meanwhile, the mob was angry with Allen Glick. He'd been pulling large sums of money out of the Stardust's revenue stream for his own use. Worse, Glick appeared to be denying the reality, obvious to everyone but him, that he wasn't the man in charge of the corporation. Before resorting to eliminating him in the traditional manner, Kansas City boss Nick Civella thought it prudent to give him a chance to leave the company while still breathing. A buyout proposal was broached, through Rosenthal, for Glick to part ways with Argent for $10 million. When Glick turned down the offer, it set in motion a frenzy of meetings between representatives of the Midwestern mob families and Frank Rosenthal. After some discussion, a meeting was arranged with Glick for April 25. Kansas City underboss Carl DeLuna flew to Las Vegas to give Glick the news from Nick Civella.

The meeting took place in Oscar Goodman's law office. Without Goodman present, DeLuna, Glick, and Rosenthal had a sitdown.

"I entered Mr. Goodman's office and behind Mr. Goodman's desk with his feet up was Mr. DeLuna," Glick testified in the Kansas City case years later. "... Mr. DeLuna, in a gruff voice, using graphic terms, told me to sit down. With that he pulled out a piece of paper from his pocket ... and he looked down at the paper for a few seconds. Then he informed me he was sent to deliver one final message from his partners. And he began reading the paper. ... He said he and his partners were finally sick of having to deal with me and having me around and that I could no longer be tolerated. ... He informed me that it was their desire to have me sell Argent Corporation immediately and I was to announce that sale as soon as I left Mr. Goodman's office that day. He said he realized that the threats I received perhaps may not have been taken by me to be as serious as they were given to me. And he said that since

I perhaps find my life expendable, he was certain I wouldn't find my children's lives expendable. With that he looked down on his piece of paper and he gave me the names and ages of each one of my sons."

It was painfully obvious from the DeLuna-Rosenthal-Glick meeting that Goodman's law office was being used to evade surveillance under the guise of the attorney-client privilege. At various times, all three men's legal interests were represented by Oscar Goodman.

"DeLuna's meeting, which took place without my knowledge, was in keeping with a longstanding Kansas City tradition," Goodman said. "Nick Civella would use his Kansas City attorney Jim Quinn's office. Nick knew Quinn loved to play golf. Every time there was a warm sunny day, he knew Quinn would be on the golf course, thinking that the government would never put a bug in Quinn's office and that they would be immune from any kind of government overhear. In those days we were up in the Valley Bank building on the sixteenth floor. You had to be buzzed into the office. They couldn't have just walked in. They had to be buzzed in. I certainly didn't give these people permission to go in there, but obviously someone buzzed them in."

Less than two months after the meeting in Goodman's office, Glick publicly announced his intention to sell Argent Corporation. By then, bug and telephone-wiretap surveillance had captured Kansas City mob figures discussing in code the impending sale of the Stardust and the skim at the Tropicana. The seemingly innocuous Joe Agosto was identified as part of the operation, as was trusted Nevada casino executive Carl Thomas, who was in the process of leaving the Tropicana and joining the Stardust as the head of casino operations in place of Rosenthal. Privately, Thomas was preparing to take over the skim on behalf of his mob benefactors.

Not that Oscar Goodman has ever admitted knowing anything about that, either.

※ ※ ※

Oscar Goodman continued to practice criminal defense for numerous other clients. He also served as president of Temple

Beth Sholom, and of course participated in the lives of his four young children. But he devoted an enormous amount of time attempting to keep Spilotro out of jail and Rosenthal in the gaming industry.

During the late 1970s, Spilotro was simultaneously the focus of investigations by the FBI, IRS, Las Vegas police, and state Gaming Control Board. At the same time, Rosenthal found himself in the cross-hairs of the FBI, local cops, and Gaming Control. Goodman was also counsel for Argent Corporation, which invited scrutiny into his professional and personal life, but was festooned with perquisites: a $12,000 monthly retainer, full complimentary privileges at the casinos, even use of the corporate jet. Although Goodman was not listed as an owner or investor, he was long suspected of being offered a percentage not only of the Stardust, but of the Bingo Palace (which later became Palace Station), as well. He has publicly denied this.

The multiple investigations pursued by one law-enforcement agency after another had an effect on Goodman, who increasingly became disenchanted with what he saw as lawlessness on the part of the government. Where he had once picked his battles carefully, he began lashing out almost daily against the IRS, FBI, Justice Department, Gaming Control Board, and especially Las Vegas Metro's Intelligence Bureau detectives.

Finally, in defense of so many suspected outlaws, he and they became one in the eyes of the government.

FBI agents began investigating Goodman and his law partners, Jay Brown and Mike Singer, as associates of organized crime. Law enforcement suspected Brown of acting as a political conduit and bag man between mob interests and Southern Nevada politicians, including his long-time friend, then Nevada Gaming Commission Chairman Harry Reid. But it was Reid who eventually helped drive Rosenthal from the gaming industry for good.

"The government won't shut me up," Goodman told a reporter. "When a man doesn't do anything wrong, he has nothing to worry about. I'm going to represent whomever I want. I'm not going to be intimidated by anyone. If the government doesn't like it, that's their tough luck. It's a shame what's happening in this country. The government's aggressiveness exceeds the bounds of fair play. My role is to make sure the gov-

ernment plays its role properly. And I intend to continue doing that.

"They can't violate the attorney-client privilege. The clients' interests must come first. I'm just trying to protect my
clients' rights the best I know how. If they're able to shut me
up, then individual rights in this country won't be worth two
cents. Somebody has to be willing to speak out against government excess."

❡ ❡ ❡

As busy as he was, Goodman made time to represent controversial high-profile defendants who fell outside the massive Argent case files.

One of those was rotund candy and ice-cream magnate
Lawrence Arvey, who was accused by Las Vegas prostitute
Nancy Pipkin of committing lewd acts with her nine-year-old
daughter. Arvey, known locally as "the Candyman," wore a
gray wig and beard during the pretrial proceedings in a failed
attempt to discourage public scrutiny. He went without the
disguise during trial. Arvey was eventually convicted and sentenced to life in prison, but was released on $100,000 bail pend-
ing appeal. His potential to win the appeal improved dramatically after Pipkin was found beaten and near death on a San
Diego beach in June 1978.

The Arvey case gave Goodman the opportunity to work
again with Harry Claiborne. Their teamwork was not lost on
local reporters, who sat entranced as Goodman and Claiborne
took over the courtroom. A *Valley Times* columnist wrote, "Because of his low-key presentation, Claiborne automatically
scores points for his side, simply by being the nice guy. His
record in gaining acquittals is held in envy by attorneys across
the country. ... Oscar Goodman, on the other hand, is a fighter,
pure and simple. He will go toe-to-toe with the best of them
and usually comes out a winner. When an attorney is as brilliant as Goodman, there is always the possibility that he will
even win acquittal for a guilty party. But when that does oc-
cur, the prosecution can be blamed for not doing their job as
well as they should."

The two attorneys succeeded in gaining a bail release for

Arvey, who vanished from Las Vegas three days after the Pipkin beating and was suspected of leaving the country. He is still at large.

As sordid as his clients' cases were, Goodman denied that his family was affected by his career choice. In a 1978 interview he told a reporter, "I will do anything not to miss a PTA meeting. I won't discuss anything of a business nature at home. In the first place, what my clients tell me is privileged information, and second, I don't think it's healthy to bring my type of practice into a home environment."

After seven years of unsuccessful attempts to have biological children, Oscar and Carolyn Goodman pursued adoption — not once, but four newborns in less than four years. Oscar Jr. arrived in 1969, followed by Ross in 1970, Eric in 1971, and Cara in 1973. With Oscar on the road, Carolyn simultaneously raised three children in diapers. By the time Oscar Jr. was out of diapers, Cara had joined the family.

Oscar Goodman traveled almost constantly for his high-flying organized-crime and bookmaking clients. He might have caught heat from the FBI and prosecutors, but he was treated like a conquering hero by his children when he returned home at the end of the week. Years later, he looks back fondly on those days.

"I had the best of it," he said. "I think I changed one diaper. I took one look, didn't like what I saw. I got home, had my paper, my martini. I had an 'Ozzie and Harriet' home life. I was lucky. And it's all because of Carolyn."

In the middle of the infant and toddler madness, Carolyn finished her master's degree at UNLV.

"He changed one diaper, OB's [Oscar Jr.'s]," Carolyn recalled without a trace of bitterness in her voice. "He got up once, too, in the middle of the night. It's simple, really. We decided that I would stay home and raise the kids and be with them. After seven years, we adopted Oscar Jr., and we felt very blessed. And then, of course, once we found we had room in our hearts for one child, we just wanted more."

Ross and his father share similar birthmarks and Cara and her mother bear a striking resemblance. The Goodmans celebrated their family and Oscar learned a lesson he'd carry with him the rest of his life.

"When I was growing up, I didn't know anyone who was adopted," he said. "Once we adopted, we began to realize how many parents adopt. At times it seemed that everyone we met was adopted. It's not about biology. It's about family."

It's another reason Goodman insisted on flying home every Friday after a trial. His life was calloused, but his heart was with his wife and kids, so much so that some of his fellow attorneys noticed and later remarked that he never fooled around on the road.

"If I have the family I have, it's because of Carolyn," he said. "Carolyn did it by herself. I realize that. Her only salvation was when I would fly back to Las Vegas on Friday night. After I gained a reputation as something more than a shyster mafia lawyer, judges understood that I really needed to fly home on Friday and they'd let me go early to catch the last flight. I'd get home and we'd have a babysitter for Friday night. It was her only relief, and we'd go to the old Bootlegger and have dinner."

"Anyone who says that raising children and running a household and doing the laundry and the shopping is not exhausting work has never done it," Carolyn said. "It's tremendously exhausting. You really have to give up yourself, and you do because you love them, but by the end of each week it also makes you a blithering idiot."

Carolyn arranged a break in her routine by corraling the four children into the car and taking them shopping at the local Ronzone's department store, three toddler boys and Cara in a stroller. It was, she recalled, like herding cats. She'd never let them out of her sight — trying on a new dress was an adventure with four little ones jammed behind the curtain in a fitting room.

When Carolyn managed to get a babysitter, she played competitive club tennis and won her share of tournaments and trophies. One match, however, was interrupted by a breathless call from a babysitter.

"Mrs. Goodman," the frightened woman exclaimed. "I had to call the police. Oscar Jr. is up a tree and can't get down."

For the most part, the children's home life was idyllic. They went to public schools and entertained themselves around the house with a Doberman-mix mutt, a three-legged Pomeranian, and a 60-pound pig given to the Goodmans by R.C. Farms.

The family eventually parted with the porker after it grew to an intimidating size. Years later, Goodman would settle for a backyard pond full of Japanese koi.

A trip to the supermarket was an exercise in policing the boys from the inevitable dismantling of goods located on the bottom shelves, and in the evening the four children all ended up in the same bathtub.

"It was all or nothing," Carolyn recalled. "I couldn't just wash two and let the other two wander around the house."

At the end of the week, Oscar Goodman returned tired, but quickly rejuvenated by the inevitable greeting he received at the front door by the children with their hand-painted signs and toilet-paper streamers. A four-star general never had it so good.

While her husband made headlines, Carolyn Goodman quietly ran the household and was active in developing the fledgling Meadows Playhouse, while also finding time to volunteer at the March of Dimes, American Cancer Society, Jewish Federation, National Jewish Appeal, and Equal Opportunity Board. She was an EOB counselor and its only white employee. She gained the respect of her peers as a proponent of integration in Las Vegas after walking unescorted through the West Side only hours after the civil unrest that took place in the wake of the assassination of Dr. Martin Luther King Jr. She remained devoted to the cause of civil rights in a Southern Nevada that had only begun to awaken to the disparity between African-Americans and the lily-white casino culture.

Shortly after arriving in Las Vegas, Carolyn took a secretarial job at the Riviera. She was employed for a short time as secretary for entertainer Louis Prima, then went to work at Caesars Palace during the years Meyer Lansky, who was suspected of privately influencing the casino through a series of frontmen and investors, was represented by her husband.

Caesars executive Nate Jacobson once quipped to Carolyn Goodman, "Why are you with scrambled eggs when you can have roast beef?" But she stuck with "scrambled eggs" even as he gained a reputation that would make some wives blush, even in what passed in the '70s as society in Las Vegas.

7

A Fool's Gold Rush

The timing was almost perfect. By mid-June 1978, the FBI had developed a massive amount of information in connection with its wide-ranging investigation into Anthony Spilotro and the mob's influence in the Las Vegas casino business. For weeks, wiretap and eyewitness surveillance had logged the activity of Spilotro and his associates, including Herbie Blitzstein. Electronic surveillance specialists had logged nearly 8,000 conversations on 278 reels of tape. What the cagey and increasingly paranoid Spilotro didn't know was that the FBI had also managed to plant an undercover agent in his inner circle in the form of a "reputed diamond fence" named Rick Calise. His real name was Rick Baken and he was the best undercover agent in Las Vegas FBI history. One key to the investigation was ascertaining the suspected criminal activity going on behind the scenes at the Gold Rush jewelry store on East Sahara Avenue.

In mid-June, the FBI had been up on wiretaps for 79 days. On June 19, the FBI executed 83 search warrants simultaneously to make it difficult for the suspects to warn each other. When the feds converged on the front door of the Gold Rush, Spilotro sprinted out the back, running for his house at 4675 Balfour

Drive. He managed to get there just ahead of the feds.

"During the Gold Rush search, the feds were coming to Tony's home," Goodman said. "He ran into his house — and there was plenty in the home the FBI would have been interested in — but Tony held them at bay. He held sixteen FBI agents at bay all by himself, while things were happening in the house to make sure that they came up with zip, which is exactly what they came up with. It was pretty brave on his part.

"He told them they weren't coming in. They said they were, and he told them they weren't. They had guns, he didn't. It's amazing, one little Ant. He kept them out long enough for me to get there. The government was crying about obstruction of justice and everything, and I told him, 'Ah, let them come in.' By that time, there was nothing to worry about."

In the wake of the search, Spilotro made contact with his men on the street and assessed the damage. Then he received a call from the new guy, Calise, who said the FBI had visited him and had shown him a *Time* magazine article indicating Spilotro was the Mafia's Las Vegas enforcer. Calise said he didn't know what to do. Spilotro said he would meet him in a parking lot and from there take him to a man who could help him. The man was Oscar Goodman.

Rick Baken had worked undercover for many years. He'd managed to infiltrate Carlos Marcello's New Orleans crime family and had dined with hoodlums from across the country. He was such a successful undercover agent that he was able to arrest Spilotro soldier Ernie Davino three times under three different identities. But he never dreamed he would one day walk, wearing a bulky NAGRA tape recorder strapped to his lower back, into what federal authorities believed to be the inner sanctum of the mob in Las Vegas. For years the FBI and The Organized Crime Strike Force suspected Goodman of obstructing justice by assigning attorneys friendly to his interests to represent lesser players in cases involving Spilotro and the Outfit. That way, they surmised, Goodman could be tipped off if one of those defendants ever tried to cut a deal that would endanger his own client. It was how Goodman ensured that the mob's tattered code of silence, called *omerta*, would be honored, authorities believed. Snitches were not only repugnant to Goodman's nature, but they were dangerous to his clients.

After all their years of dreaming of nailing Goodman, this was their big chance. All he had to do was instruct Baken to see one of his own associates and the obstruction argument could be made.

Instead, Goodman recommended several competent attorneys not associated in any way with his law firm. One of them was noted criminal defense specialist Barry Tarlow. In fact, Goodman did something no one in government expected. He comported himself in an ethical manner. Baken's recording yielded nothing remotely capable of resulting in a criminal charge against the man they for years had assumed was a trusted counselor to the mob.

A day after the office visit, Goodman received a call from FBI Special Agent in Charge James Powers and Organized Crime Strike Force Attorney Geoffrey Anderson. Powers said, "We want you and Spilotro over here immediately."

"I said, 'Do you have a warrant? Then Spilotro's not coming,'" Goodman recalled. "I went over to the FBI building, walked into Powers' office, and had never seen such a serious look on a G-man's face. They said that the guy I'd been talking to the day before, Rick Calise, was in reality an FBI undercover agent named Rick Baken. And if anything happened to him, they would hold me responsible. I laughed. I said, 'If you think I'm going to provide insurance for that guy, you're out of your mind.' I got up and walked out the door."

Privately, however, Goodman was briefly paralyzed by the revelation. Questions raced through his mind: What if he'd said something that made him sound like a tough guy, or a wiseguy? What if he had dealt Calise's case to a local attorney who specialized in representing some of Spilotro's pals? What if he had made a single off-the-cuff remark about Spilotro's operation?

Once the shock wore off, Goodman grew angry. The stench of the insult filled his office, making him want to vomit. After all his years in the business, this was the level of respect he engendered from the government. He'd known there was no love lost between the Justice Department and himself, but he'd always believed there was a mutual respect, the kind heavyweight fighters have for each other. He never dreamed that his prosecutorial nemeses would try to set him up in his own office.

Instead of retreating, he went on the offensive, blasting the government with a vicious fervor he had never before shown.

Goodman told the press, "It's just a blatant act of government misconduct. I think it's clear from their actions that they'll use any means to justify an end. And that's not the way our laws are designed. The concept of planting an informant in the defense camp is repugnant to the very principles of an individual's expectation of confidentiality of his attorney-client communications. Certainly, a deliberate intrusion is even more constitutionally repugnant than an inadvertent intrusion … and a violation of the Sixth Amendment."

In court motions attempting to void a subpoena of Spilotro, Goodman wrote, "One reason, as illegitimate as it may be, for the government to maintain its desire to subject Mr. Spilotro to the grand-jury process is to generate a public animus against him. … It is clear from the facts that Calise was the pursuer and Spilotro the pursued. Repeatedly, without urging or insistence by Spilotro, and without exigency, the undercover agent attempted to gain access to Spilotro's attorney."

He lunged at anything that moved. When FBI Assistant Director James Decker told reporters that Baken was being hidden to protect his life against retaliation by the mob, Goodman slashed away. Baken, in fact, had been showing up for court proceedings in the days following the search warrants.

Goodman wrote in a letter to the media: "The entire thrust of the government's position was that Mr. Spilotro was a menace and a criminal, which is the theme that the government has been playing and replaying in their investigation of matters in the Las Vegas area and elsewhere, knowing that a press release like this [stating that Baken was in hiding] would engender hatred towards him and his family. The real facts concerning the FBI undercover agent's position are that he is not in hiding, that his whereabouts are not being kept secret, and he continues to function in a routine manner as an FBI agent in the Las Vegas community.

"Mr. Decker's statement to reporters appears to be an attempt by the government to gain sympathy for its position through misuse of the press by relying upon the dissemination of blatant falsehoods.

"Such actions are reflective of a Gestapo mentality and are becoming a matter of course in Las Vegas.

"I was raised in the tradition that when the government said something, you could believe it. I always used to believe it. But now, after these experiences with the FBI, I question every statement. I never know when the government may be lying."

Noting that government agents, in their arrogance, had lost sight of the fact that his clients were at a distinct disadvantage when pursued by the long arm of the law, Goodman struck again and again with motions to have the property of Spilotro and Allen Glick, whose home and office were also searched under the warrants, returned immediately. Although the search-warrant affidavit in the Gold Rush case was being kept under seal, Goodman's own sources made it clear the government had cast too wide a net. With that knowledge, Goodman fought to view the search warrant, then began to build his argument that it was too broad and, therefore, flawed.

Goodman caught an early break when his friend U.S. District Judge Roger Foley ordered that the transcript of the Calise meetings in his office be turned over to Goodman. Foley, as well as Goodman's old friend Harry Claiborne, who'd been appointed to the federal bench, were mighty critics of the Strike Force and the FBI in Southern Nevada. Other than ruling on stay motions, they refused to hear any Strike Force case that came before them. The judges recused themselves from the Argent case. As a result, the case was transferred to Los Angeles. On November 9, 1978, in Los Angeles, after reviewing motions prepared by California attorney Frank Rothman, U.S. District Judge Warren Ferguson speed-read the FBI's 150-page affidavit and ruled that the government's one-size-fits-all search-warrant application in the Gold Rush case was too general as it pertained to Argent's Allen Glick.

"We fought the American Revolution to prevent actions like this," Ferguson said. "… The magistrate committed a serious error when he issued these warrants."

Seized materials began to be returned to Glick. Then it was Spilotro's turn. Within months, a court determined the Gold Rush searches lacked specificity as they pertained to Tough Tony and were thrown out. By then, the FBI knew plenty about

Spilotro and his criminal enterprise, but continued to be con-
founded when it came to making him pay for his activities
outside the law.

? ? ?

In August 1978, Las Vegans Jack Gordon, Sol Sayegh, and
Joe Daly were charged with attempting to bribe Gaming Commission Chairman Harry Reid. Reid was offered $12,000 to
support a proposed regulation allowing Gordon's carnival-
style gaming devices to be distributed to Nevada casinos. Reid
reported the bribe attempt to the FBI and the three men were
arrested.

Gordon was a long-time hustler who had owned conces-
sions at Circus Circus and pieces of local massage parlors.
Sayegh owned the Carpet Barn, Nevada's largest floor-cover-
ing store. Daly was a Gordon flunky. Though Reid was best
friends with Goodman's former law partner Jay Brown, Goodman represented Gordon and Sayegh in the bribe case at a
time the FBI had overheard Kansas City's Nick Civella and
Las Vegas mob conduit Joe Agosto refer to Reid as their ally
and "Mr. Clean Face."

In October, while federal charges against Spilotro in the Gold
Rush case were still pending, the state finally moved to have
Tony Spilotro placed in the Black Book, which consisted of persons excluded from entering a casino. Although the Black Book
was a largely artificial tool used almost exclusively for public-
relations purposes to make Nevada appear tough on organized
crime, it was a signal that Spilotro's days in Las Vegas were
numbered. Without casino access, he would be forced to remain
on the street. Tom Carrigan, chief of investigations for the Control Board, and Jeffrey Clontz, the Deputy Attorney General
assigned to the regulatory body, submitted evidence linking
Spilotro to organized crime, including a Chicago Crime Commission report and newspaper and magazine articles.

"Why now?" Goodman asked. "Nothing has changed.
Tony Spilotro has lived in Nevada for years. What has changed,
however, is that Nevada fears federal intervention into gambling. State officials weren't concerned until the federal government began their chase of Tony Spilotro."

On the afternoon of October 25, 1978, Sol and Marilyn Sayegh's six-year-old son, Cary, was kidnapped from the playground of Temple Beth Sholom's Albert Einstein School downtown. Although a $50,000 reward was immediately offered for the boy's return, he was never seen again.

Was it a random act of violence, or was the elder Sayegh being punished for endangering the mob's Las Vegas operations with the Reid bribe attempt? In light of Carl DeLuna's threat against Allen Glick only months earlier in Goodman's office, could a message from the mob really be ruled out?

Or had Sol Sayegh, fearing retaliation from persons unknown, sent his son to live with family in Israel? Sayegh was also known as a degenerate gambler and for a month rumors circulated that the boy had been taken in retaliation for debts owed.

Within weeks, authorities settled on a suspect, small-time criminal Jerry Burgess, who had made an incriminating call to authorities not long after Cary Sayegh's disappearance. But the case against Burgess was thin.

"I was trying a case in Salt Lake City for 'Fat Sam' Calabrese," Goodman recalled. "The case ended in a mistrial and I was going to fly to New York to surprise Carolyn at her father's induction as president of the New York Medical Association. I flew back without telling her, rented a tux at Macy's, and arrived in time for the reception. Her first words to me were, 'Go home. Sol's son was kidnapped.'

"I managed to put aside my animus for the FBI after Sol Sayegh asked me to work with him to try to solve the kidnapping," Goodman remembered. "I literally became strange bedfellows with Jerry Dougherty and John Bailey of the FBI, along with Dave Dunn of Metro. We bunked down at the Sayegh residence where we all slept in the same room. We tried to get into Burgess' mind. He claimed he was walking down Las Vegas Boulevard in front of the Westward Ho when a payphone rang. He answered the phone and heard an anonymous voice tell him something very important could be found at the bottom of a ravine. That's what he told Sol, whom he'd known for several years. The FBI sent me out with the boy's grandfather to what was at that time the remote desert area of Mojave and Pecos. We climbed down into the ditch and found what Sol's wife later identified as the boy's shoe."

Burgess was tried on the murder charge, but acquitted. He was later convicted of armed robbery and received a long prison sentence. A suspect was never charged in the kidnapping and the boy's body was never recovered.

? ? ?

Earlier that year in August, a strange thing happened in the world of organized crime. As part of the Strike Force's attack on the hidden owners of Las Vegas casinos, a federal grand jury in Detroit returned indictments of Aladdin Hotel entertainment director James Tamer, General Manager James Abraham, Michigan bail bondsman Chuck Goldfarb, and former casino manager Edward Monazym. The 22-count indictment alleged that the four had engaged in racketeering activities on behalf of Detroit Mafia boss Vito "Billy Jack" Giacalone and St. Louis organized-crime interests.

The Detroit indictments weren't surprising, given the government's deep penetration of the Argent casinos and the Tropicana.

What *was* surprising, however, was that Oscar Goodman represented not a single defendant in the case.

? ? ?

It's difficult to fully appreciate how all-pervasive Goodman's law practice really was in those years. *Las Vegas Sun* columnist Paul Price was kidding on the square when he cracked, "Friends are concerned over the whereabouts of attorney Oscar Goodman. He hasn't been on TV or had his picture in the papers for three days." Goodman's face and name made local newsprint day after day for weeks on end. And once the Spilotro affidavits in the Gold Rush fiasco were unsealed, the *Chicago Tribune, Chicago Sun-Times, New York Times, Washington Post, Miami Herald,* and *Wall Street Journal* sent investigative reporters to Las Vegas to get the story on the mobster and his mouthpiece. The Little Guy had become big news across the country.

Goodman found it increasingly difficult to defend his client against the court of public opinion. To newspaper readers and TV news-watchers, Spilotro was "Tony the Ant" and "Tough Tony," the Chicago Outfit's enforcer on the streets of Las Vegas. Even in Las Vegas, where locals have traditionally maintained a romantic view of the members and associates of organized crime who were largely responsible for building the city, Spilotro had become a sinister symbol. Guilty? Of course he was guilty. Now all the G-men had to do was prove it.

Predator though he may have been, Spilotro had plenty of fans on the street. Gambler Vinny Montalto, who would later work as an electronic surveillance expert for Goodman's law firm, was one of them.

Many years after Spilotro had come and gone, Montalto recalled some of Tough Tony's observations.

"Tony had the gift shop at the Circus Circus and he was telling me about a meeting he'd just had with Jimmy "The Weasel" Fratianno, who had come to town to see him," Montalto recalled. "Afterward, Tony said, 'This guy's no good.' I asked him why and he said, 'When I went to buy a pack of cigarettes I pulled out my money and I saw him counting it. Never trust a man who counts your money. When someone counts your money, they're no fucking good.' It was a few weeks after that that everyone learned that Fratianno was a rat. But Tony knew it just by watching him.

"Tony used to say, 'You can only eat one steak at a time.' By that, he meant, don't get too greedy. Tony was very aware of what people around him were thinking. He would say, 'You eat alone, you choke' and 'Fast pay makes fast friends.' And when one of his guys started sounding off he'd say, 'My friend, do whatever you're big enough to do.' Tony didn't say a lot, but when he spoke everyone knew exactly what he meant.

"He also knew that his biggest problem wasn't getting caught for something he did, but getting set up by someone else. He would tell Oscar, 'The only thing I can't defend against is the frame.' And he told everybody else, 'I don't want to cross the street without Oscar Goodman.' He knew what he was talking about."

"Mr. Spilotro has been the victim of scorn and derision in this community and his jewelry-store business has suffered," Goodman argued in the court of public opinion. And, he told

the *Wall Street Journal*: "I'm firmly convinced that the government has as its ultimate goal the elimination of all legal gambling and that Las Vegas is the scapegoat."

Was Oscar Goodman, in his relentless belligerence, standing up for the rights of the accused and attempting to counter
the assault on Nevada's lifestyle? Or was he simply grand-
standing, building his notoriety to scratch a fame itch and
pump up his hourly fees?

Chicago native Billy Vassiliadis, who would become
Nevada's most respected political advisor, moved to Las Vegas in 1974 and was struck early on by Goodman's status standing next to Tony Spilotro.

"The first couple of things that struck me about him were,
one, that if I was in trouble I would want that guy," Vassiliadis
said. "I'm sort of a civil libertarian myself. Here's a guy who's
got an unpopular client and an unpopular cause and he's out
there leading the charge face first. He's not ducking it. And
he's not defensive. He's on the offensive. He's chasing it. I
thought, 'That's a pretty strong guy.'

"The most visible thing I remember about him is a picture
of him in Chicago walking across the street with Spilotro.

"Clearly, after a while I realized he was as much a media
star as a good lawyer and it dawned on me as I got more ma-
ture and understood more about these things that there was
probably a real effect to the good for his clients. The other thing
is, I always wondered why a guy that talented would represent Tony Spilotro." After working in Southern Nevada politics for a few years, Vassiliadis came to realize Goodman more
than most had tapped into an incredibly effective emotion with
the local populace: distrust of the federal government.

"I thought Oscar was on the cusp of that," he said. "I
thought Oscar elevated it to new heights. One of his talents
that people don't give him enough credit for, and that's not as
calculating as people think it is, is an intuitive sense for how to
push the public button. I think he read the tea leaves far earlier than a lot of the media and politicians did. He knew there
were a lot of people here who hated the feds and he struck
that nerve. It was a pretty gutsy move, a pretty ballsy thing
attacking the FBI. He never made Spilotro a sympathetic figure, but his message was pretty damn strong. 'They're intru-

sive. They set people up. It's entrapment. The wiretaps are all over our town. They're in our casinos. They're violating our rights.' You probably had at the time thirty thousand dealers saying, 'Yeah, they're violating our rights.' And then you had all these Sagebrush Rebellion folks pissed off, saying, 'Yeah, they're violating our rights.' I think he tapped into something well before others did.

"What effect it had on cases, I don't know. How much it helped Spilotro, I don't know. But it made Oscar a legend."

8

Jimmy Chagra's Luck

With the possible exception of Tony Spilotro, in the late 1970s Jamiel "Jimmy" Chagra was the worst-kept secret in Las Vegas.

Of all the suspected drug traffickers who made Las Vegas a second home during the era, Chagra was destined to become the most notorious. The middle of three brothers from a simultaneously celebrated and scorned Texas legal family, Jimmy was the non-lawyer in the Chagra clan. Older brother Lee was a nationally recognized defense attorney known for representing drug traffickers and motorcycle-gang leaders. Younger brother Joe was following in Lee's footsteps.

Jimmy was the Chagra who needed to keep a lawyer handy. In a few years, he went from a low-ranking associate of Texas drug kingpin Henry Wallace to the central figure in a multi-million-dollar marijuana and cocaine smuggling ring with connections stretching all the way to Colombia. In Las Vegas, he flashed his cash at every turn. Much of what he earned he lost at the tables.

On frequent trips to Las Vegas, he arrived with millions in cash stuffed into suitcases. One way or another, he shared the wealth. He lived like a sultan in the Frank Sinatra Suite at Caesars Palace. He was such a big player that his former fashion-model wife, Liz, was given a new Lincoln Continental as a gift from the casino. He was also a pampered player at Binion's Horseshoe Club downtown.

Although he listed his occupation as gambler, he was not particularly proficient in the casino. Whatever his skill level at the tables, he was an abject sucker away from them. He became easy pickings for country-club rummy sharks and put more than one golf hustler's child through college after second-best performances on various courses around Las Vegas.

With no credible means of support, Chagra became a yardstick by which all other players were measured as he gambled like there was no tomorrow. After his brother Lee was shot to death in 1979 — some organized-crime sources claimed he was murdered over a botched drug deal involving $450,000 of New York mob exile Joseph Bonanno's money — Jimmy Chagra's intensity at the tables only increased.

"Jimmy was very generous with me," Oscar Goodman recalled. "One time he asked me to meet him down at the Horseshoe, which was his hangout and where he ultimately met Charlie Harrelson, and where Harrelson cooked up his idea, supposedly. Jimmy said to me, 'Come on, let's play craps.' I told him I didn't know how to play and had no intention of learning. I've got enough of a problem losing money on stinking football, basketball, and baseball games, and if I knew anything about hockey I'd lose money on that, too. I don't need to learn to shoot dice. But I go with him anyway, and we're down there at the dice table shooting craps, and he wins a lot of money. He hands me twenty-five grand in cash just for standing there. And I said, 'What's that, a retainer?' He said, 'No, just take it.' I said, 'I don't want to take something for nothing.' He said, 'Don't worry about it, just take it.' That was my first real experience with him.

"The first time I really appreciated how much the Chagras were worth was when I saw Lee at the Kentucky Derby. He was in the Colonel Winn Room, where, if I remember correctly, the minimum bet is either fifty or a hundred dollars. He told the clerk he wanted a certain horse and the clerk asked him for how much. Clerks use a machine to ring up each ticket. Jimmy said, 'Just keep your finger on the button.' And so the clerk did. The machine was rattling like a machine gun. Cha-ching-ching-ching. He made the odds on the horse go from dog to favorite by the time he got through betting.

"Money meant nothing to those fellows, they had so much of it. And I didn't realize the source of it at the time. Jimmy and I started talking down in Kentucky, and he said, 'I may need you. I'm under investigation.' That was at a time he was under investigation for marijuana and cocaine and he hired me shortly after Lee was murdered."

In February 1979, a federal grand jury in Midland, Texas, returned a five-count indictment against Chagra, accusing him of conspiring to import marijuana and cocaine. Bail was set at $1 million, and Chagra was represented by his younger brother Joe and Oscar Goodman. At the time, word circulated in Las Vegas that Goodman had received a $1 million retainer in cash.

꿍 꿍 꿍

Up until his indictment, Las Vegas was good to Jimmy Chagra. It was a place where his money didn't make him stick out much, a place where he could, at least superficially, have an excuse for his lifestyle. Caesars was a casino unaccustomed to turning away a high roller. Las Vegas casinos have been a playground for drug traffickers, arms dealers, and money launderers for decades and Caesars rarely blushed at a cash customer, no matter how mysterious. Off the Strip, Chagra did what every other wiseguy looking for a good gamble has done. He pocketed his bankroll and headed downtown to the Horseshoe, where the only reputation the Binion family was concerned about was their own.

The casino family's patriarch, Lester "Benny" Binion, was a former racket boss in Dallas who had loaded his family and his illicit fortune into a Cadillac at the end of World War II and driven, just ahead of the sheriff, to Las Vegas to start a new life as a legitimate casino operator. A stint in Leavenworth for tax evasion officially ended Benny's career, but he turned over the gambling and occasional money-lending operation to his sons Jack and Lonnie "Ted" Binion. Jack inherited his sense of responsibility and a head for accounting from his mother. Ted loosely patterned his life after his father, who had killed three men, ordered the deaths of several others, and maintained associations with a rogue's gallery of Mafia dons and hoodlums while in the rackets. In Las Vegas, the Horseshoe was known for its Texas chili, $2 steaks, World Series of Poker, and no-limit gambling.

What other casino men called notorious, Benny Binion considered colorful. Although his donations had built a local Catholic church, Benny was most at home sitting at his table in the Horseshoe coffee shop, with friends ranging from local judges and defense attorneys to murderers on parole and visiting cowboys from his 160,000-acre Montana ranch. Jimmy Chagra and what remained of his money were welcome at the Horseshoe. According to Gary Cartwright's brilliant story of the Chagra clan, *Dirty Dealing: Drug Smuggling on the Mexican Border and the Assassination of a Federal Judge*, Jimmy gambled millions in cash at the Horseshoe and often won.

When Jimmy and Liz Chagra and their young daughter relocated to Las Vegas from El Paso, Texas, in 1978, they moved into a house at 3115 Viking Road, unknowingly across the street from Oscar and Carolyn Goodman. Chagra had so much money he attempted to buy the Goodman house as a maid's quarters. Perhaps sensing the government might suspect he was bringing his work home with him, not long after, the Goodmans moved to a house on Bannie Lane in the upscale Scotch 80s enclave not far from downtown. Even then, Goodman could not know the impact Chagra would have on his life.

In representing Chagra, Goodman found himself in a familiar place: single-handedly battling a regiment of government investigators and attorneys bent on destroying his client. Gone for Goodman were the days of *mano a mano* courtroom sparring. Now, every time he entered court, he faced clusters of prosecutors who carried the bludgeon of the federal RICO and Continuing Criminal Enterprise statutes, which withered most defendants and sent them crawling toward a plea bargain.

But Goodman was no dealmaker. He'd become so disliked inside the Justice Department and sneered so brazenly at the system that invariably his communications with opposing counsel were brief and hostile. If a defendant wanted to cut a deal, he could hire any of a growing number of former federal prosecutors who had switched hats in order to make money. With Goodman, a defendant got a true believer, one who would rather die than lose.

Jimmy Chagra needed all of that and more if he were to escape spending the best years of his life in the penitentiary. He was already a prime suspect in the attempted assassination of Assistant U.S. Attorney James Kerr, a San Antonio prosecutor who had often butted heads on drug cases with Lee Chagra. Worse, the drug indictment had been returned in Midland, smack in the middle of the jurisdiction of U.S. District Judge John Wood, Jr. Known as "Maximum John" for his propensity to hand out crushing prison sentences to drug offenders, Wood made no secret of his animosity toward and disgust for Lee Chagra and his associates. By many accounts, Wood had abandoned the pretense of judicial fairness in drug cases. He'd become the quintessential second prosecutor in the courtroom, where he often mocked defendants and took particular glee in meting out severe punishment.

In Wood's court, however, Goodman's manner betrayed none of this knowledge. Goodman and Joe Chagra successfully sought to have his bail reduced from $1 million to $400,000. Jimmy Chagra was temporarily free, pending the outcome of a trial set to begin April 2, 1979.

After obtaining bail for Jimmy, Joe Chagra and Goodman set out against the odds to have Wood recuse himself. The defense attorneys filed 31 motions before the court, each of which was shot down. Wood, who commonly violated the rules of judicial conduct by courting the press, then retaliated by unsealing the five-year-old transcripts of a grand-jury investigation of the Chagras and drug trafficking as a gift to the media and prosecution. The grand-jury material was unrelated to the latest indictment, but served as fuel for the anti-Chagra sentiment in the press. Picking a jury in Texas would not be easy.

The odds grew longer after the government turned drug kingpin Henry Wallace, whom they remade as a lesser player as the case against Chagra came together. Chagra was hit with a Continuing Criminal Enterprise drug-kingpin charge. Overnight Chagra went from the possibility of spending 15 years in prison to life without parole in the court of his family's mortal enemy, John Wood.

¶ ¶ ¶

Back in Las Vegas, the 39-year-old Goodman worked at a breakneck pace. Damning FBI affidavits were being unsealed that tied Spilotro and the Chicago mob to the Argent Corporation and Allen Glick. The affidavits also revealed the FBI's belief that the Tropicana was controlled by Midwestern Mafia families. The national media went wild.

In the wake of his son's kidnapping, Sol Sayegh's trial was severed and postponed indefinitely.

Goodman attempted to move Frank Rosenthal's civil rights lawsuit against state gaming officials to federal court.

On top of all that, Goodman got involved when Culinary Union Local 226 secretary-treasurer Ben Schmoutey was indicted on federal charges linked to the firebombing of several non-union restaurants in the city — restaurants targeted for organization by Schmoutey's Culinary.

Schmoutey came to power in Local 226 as a direct result of the 1977 assassination of secretary-treasurer Al Bramlet. Although Schmoutey was never charged in the murder, his close associates, father and son Tom and Andy Hanley, were convicted of murdering Bramlet and sentenced to life in prison without parole. They also admitted conspiring with Schmoutey to firebomb the restaurants. The feds also knew Schmoutey took orders through Tony Spilotro from the Chicago Outfit.

Meanwhile, Goodman was jumping through full-time hoops in the Chagra case. It was Goodman's first big narcotics trial, but his approach did not vary. He attacked the government at every turn, while working to establish his presence before the judge. It was clear from the outset that Wood wasn't interested in appearing impartial, however. Claiming potential jury bias, Goodman sought to have the case transferred from Midland to Las Vegas — unsuccessfully.

Out on bail, Chagra returned to Las Vegas, but found his notoriety made him too hot even for Caesars Palace. So he took his action exclusively to Binion's. Although a few Las Vegas insiders remember Chagra as a fearless and savvy gambler, most knew him as an arrogant rube whose greatest attribute at the tables was an apparently unlimited source of cash. He was an egotistical card player, as fond of throwing his weight around and attracting a crowd as playing the hand dealt. He was a mark on the golf course. And the sloppy management of his fortune made him irresistible to scofflaws. By all appearances, that's what attracted career criminal Charles Harrelson to him. Harrelson and his running mate, Hampton Robinson, intended on separating Chagra from some of his fortune. As they got to know each other, however, another relationship developed, one that included talk of assassinating federal Judge John Wood.

If Chagra was nervous about his chances of winning an acquittal on drug charges in Wood's court, his actions did not betray the emotion. He maintained a high profile at the World Series of Poker and took time to discuss the odds against him back in El Paso. "With Judge Wood on the case? About fifty-fifty."

"And without Wood?" the reporter asked.

"Much, much better."

Oscar Goodman and Joe Chagra continued submitting motions. The trial date was moved from May 29 to July 24 and Judge Wood surprised the attorneys by agreeing to shift the case from El Paso to Austin. Wood appeared to be far more concerned about the appearance of propriety in the wake of the assassination attempt on federal prosecutor James Kerr, who was shot and nearly killed. Privately, he suspected the Chagras were behind the Kerr murder try, and Goodman attempted to shed light on the judge's bias by noting those sentiments in a motion to compel his recusal. The motion failed.

Although no stranger to reporters and not above leaking information to the press that was damaging to a defendant's case, Wood issued a gag order silencing the attorneys. But he declined to accept the 24-hour security he was offered. Instead, Wood and his wife, Kathryn, quietly moved from their home in El Paso to their Austin condominium at the Chateaux Dijon development in time to enjoy the Memorial Day weekend.

9

Offing Maximum John

On the morning of Tuesday, May 29, 1979, Wood awoke and prepared for an uneventful day of calendar calls. The postponement of the trial date of the Chagra case, which had attracted media attention from throughout Texas, enabled the judge to relax at his Austin getaway, where he brushed up on his tennis game and occasionally went fishing.

Eyewitnesses noticed Wood leave his condominium and walk to his sedan parked on the street in front of the building. He set his briefcase inside the car, then opened the driver's door.

What witnesses remembered hearing next was the blunt *pop-pop* of a car backfiring. From across the street one man saw Wood take a step back, turn at the waist as if someone had tapped him on the shoulder, then tumble in a heap on the asphalt.

Within moments, Kathryn Wood was at her husband's side. Although she attempted to comfort him, he was already dead. A bullet fired from a high-powered rifle had entered his lower back, blown through his spine, and savaged his internal organs. His aorta and liver were pulverized. The coroner characterized the damage as a "snowflake effect."

By the time the ambulance removed Wood's body, the most intensive and costly FBI investigation since the assassination of John F. Kennedy had begun. In the days to come, newspaper headlines trumpeted the details of Wood's demise and politicians filled rotundas with rhetoric about the state of crime in America.

Within a few weeks, the FBI had collected thousands of pieces of information, none of which pointed to Wood's killer or prosecutor James Kerr's shooter.

Federal investigators believed Goodman was well aware of the Wood murder contract. Agents bought without first-hand proof the rumor that Goodman had been present in the coffee shop at Binion's Horseshoe the day Harrelson was hired to take out the federal judge. Goodman flatly denied any association with the crime, dismissing such stories as evidence only of the immense animosity frustrated feds had with him.

The story, however, continues to shadow Goodman's career and was repeated in Jim McManus' book, *Positively Fifth Street: Murderers, Cheetahs, and Binion's World Series of Poker.* "With Chagra on trial in Texas for heroin trafficking, Jack, Ted, and Benny convened in Booth 1 of the Horseshoe coffee shop with Oscar Goodman, the hyper-aggressive young Philadelphia attorney representing the accused. The upshot of that meeting was a $50,000 contract for Charles Harrelson (actor Woody's father) to assassinate U.S. District Court Judge John Wood — or so the lore has it."

(In June 2003, Goodman received an apology from publisher Farrar, Straus and Giroux and a promise that the damning passage would be deleted from future editions of the book. Although the agreement was sealed, it was rumored Goodman and attorney Anthony Glassman received $50,000 to walk away from the threatened litigation. Wrote publisher's counsel Paul J. Sleven, "We would like to assure you that the book was not intended to state as a fact that Mayor Goodman was present at any such meeting or was in any other way involved in the assassination of Judge Wood." The letter became part of a full-page advertisement in *The New York Times* weekend book review.)

The FBI's problem was narrowing the list of potential suspects; defendants who believed they had been mistreated by

Wood were legion. Former federal prosecutor John Pickney had gone so far as to warn Wood that his role as the enemy of the defense was impossible to miss. A fellow federal judge remarked that Wood's style was bound to get him in trouble sooner or later. He had many enemies, most notable of whom were the brothers Chagra.

If the Chagras differed from the rest on the lengthy list of suspects, it was because they made their feelings about the judge known in motion after motion filed in his court. While many concealed their hatred for the man, the Chagras were anything but subtle. They were up front.

Upon learning of Wood's assassination, Chagra became physically ill. He knew it meant he would now be the prime target of the FBI.

Meanwhile, if such a thing were possible, he had more pressing concerns. Wood's replacement, U.S. District Judge William Sessions, presided over the drug-trafficking case and proved every bit as tough a taskmaster as his late predecessor. During the trial, the government took advantage of its deal with Henry Wallace, who by many accounts had been the leader of the smuggling operation, to define Jimmy Chagra as the boss. Goodman's every move was blocked. What's worse, Chagra insisted on testifying on his own behalf. On the stand, Chagra, who was known throughout the region as a drug trafficker, claimed under oath he had never smuggled drugs despite much evidence to the contrary. Near the end of the trial, Goodman returned to his motel room to prepare his closing argument and received a call from his wife informing him that his father had died.

"I was absolutely devastated. I was distraught. I didn't know where I was. The next morning I went to the judge and told him I had to back to Philadelphia because my father had died."

"No, Mr. Goodman," Judge Sessions said. "You're a professional. You can argue the case."

"For the first time in my career, I was disoriented in the courtroom. It had to be the worst argument I'd ever made in my life.

"The jury deliberated two hours and found Jimmy guilty. Maybe because the judge had a guilty conscience and knew that he could have contributed to the conviction because I wasn't in my right mind, he let Chagra out on bail. Chagra ordered a private plane to fly me back to Philadelphia.

"Then he disappeared.

"When Jimmy took off on the federal drug charges, he set himself, Liz, and his son up in a little farm-style place in Johnsontown, Kansas, across from Kansas City," Goodman said. "He and his wife and children lived there under assumed names. No one knew who he was. The FBI had no idea where he was. He could have lived there undetected for a hundred years. All Jimmy ever really wanted was a TV set; he had a little satellite dish so he could watch his sports. I mean, he had it made. He could have stayed there forever. Then he made a horrible mistake. He came back to Las Vegas.

"He couldn't stay away. He came back to have cosmetic surgery done and he was driving down the street when he got caught. When he was arrested, he had several hundred thousand dollars in diaper boxes in the back seat of his car. Dave Hanson, the Metro detective, didn't recognize Chagra. But Chagra recognized Hanson, got out of his car, and said, 'I give up.'

"Judge Sessions gave Jimmy thirty years on the drug convictions. When they brought him back to prison, his luck got a lot worse. Sessions sent Jimmy to Leavenworth, where he was in the wrong place at the wrong time. As lucky as I've been in my life, Jimmy was just as unlucky. When he got to Leavenworth, he walked into a place where the visiting room is bugged. Not because of Jimmy, but because of another of my clients, Nick Civella, who was also in Leavenworth. If you stay around long enough, everything comes together.

"Those recordings at Leavenworth were bad for Nick Civella, but they gave Jimmy even worse problems. It was then they began to pick up Jimmy's comments on the Wood murder. When Liz comes to see him, he talks to her about it. And his brother Joe comes to visit him, and Joe is his lawyer at the time and certainly not a suspect, but then the government hears Joe, who'd had a couple conversations with Charles Harrelson, talking about where the gun stock, supposedly part of the murder weapon, was thrown.

"When they weren't whispering to each other, Jimmy and Liz passed notes. The FBI even put a screen in the toilet trap to catch the paper after Liz tore up the notes and flushed them. They listened to everything they whispered to each other, and the government had snitches on the inside. Whatever electronic devices the government used, they were very effective. The more they whispered, the louder their voices got. It was very sophisticated. They could not keep a secret.

"They got the recordings, but they didn't get, in my opinion, the appropriate court authorization to listen to those recordings, because they were relying on the court authorizations used to listen specifically to the Civella conversations. Strike Force boss Mike DeFeo, who hated Las Vegas more than I could ever explain, was on the other side of the aisle and he argued that the magnitude of the crime was so great and so heinous, the assassination of a federal judge, that he really didn't care whether the law was followed and he was sure the court would sustain whatever the government did. And he was right.

"It was then I really knew I had an uphill battle."

Initially, Goodman didn't know that attorney Joe Chagra, his co-counsel in the first drug case, at the recommendation of his brother Jimmy had taken on Charles Harrelson as a client. It was one of the biggest mistakes Joe Chagra ever made and he eventually paid dearly for failing to be his own man.

A few months into the FBI's investigation, agents caught a break when Harrelson was arrested outside Houston on weapons charges. With his previous felony convictions, which included a contract-murder rap for which he received a 15-year sentence, Harrelson faced a lengthy prison term. But as an experienced con, Harrelson had no intention of wasting away in a sweaty state penitentiary. He dispatched one of his lawyers to U.S. Attorney Jamie Boyd's office to craft a deal: He would plead guilty to assassinating Judge John Wood as long as he could do so within the federal system, avoid the death penalty, and not be compelled to snitch on anyone else. He wanted to serve his time in Leavenworth with the possibility of parole, no matter how distant.

But Boyd wasn't interested. He was busy running down leads for the Chagra investigation supplied by a favorite informant, a fast-talking con named Robert "Comanche" Riojas. Although Harrelson's offer was rejected, he gave the government enough information to let the prosecutors and agents know he was their man in the killing of Woods. It was almost as if he wanted to make sure he received credit for the crime.

? ? ?

After only a few months in prison, Jimmy Chagra was falling apart. He talked tough, but he couldn't adjust to life on the inside. He gambled from behind bars—at one point lamenting on tape that he had lost more than $1 million since hitting Leavenworth—and maintained constant contact with his wife and his brother Joe. They talked on the phone nearly every day and the FBI focused parts of its investigation on those phone conversations. In the process, Jimmy implicated his wife and only surviving brother in the plot to assassinate Wood.

While Jimmy melted on the inside, thanks to a virulent cocaine habit, Joe was ruining himself on the outside.

At one point, Jimmy began plotting a prison break the likes of which Leavenworth had never seen. He soon realized he would need help, so he enlisted the services of a hardened con named Jerry Ray James. James had helped lead a mass butchery during a riot at the New Mexico State Penitentiary. A gang of inmates managed to secure a list of prison informants and the result was a rampage of murder and mutilation in which the penitentiary's machine shop was used to its full potential as a chamber of horrors. Suspected snitches and prison guards were murdered in the most grisly fashion imaginable. Some were decapitated, others castrated, sodomized with axe handles, or blow-torched beyond recognition. And James, whom authorities considered a '70s-era Dillinger, was in the middle of all of it. He was certainly not intimidated by Jimmy Chagra's escape plan. Chagra trusted him almost immediately and didn't think twice when James casually began dropping the name Charles Harrelson. (Harrelson is the father of actor Woody Harrelson and the brother of the polygraph examiner, Leonard Harrelson, in the Lewis Crockett case.)

Harrelson, it appeared, had mentioned to more than one inmate that he'd been responsible for murdering the federal judge and the word got around. Harrelson also claimed that

Dixie Mafia hitman Lawrence "Little Larry" Culbreath had killed Wood. James seemed to have plenty of information, all of which piqued Chagra's interest.

Meanwhile, Harrelson was beginning to feel the heat. After his arrest on gun charges, he was transferred to a Houston jail and sent word to Joe Chagra that he needed legal assistance. Joe responded by meeting with Harrelson, one of a series of mistakes the youngest Chagra brother would make.

Harrelson dumped out intimate details of the murder to Joe, including where he'd hidden the murder weapon. Joe, in turn, wasted no time returning to Leavenworth to relate the information to his older brother. Their conversation was purely incriminating.

"Well, shit, they're already offering him deals, Joe," Jimmy said.

"No, they haven't offered him any deals."

"… Well, he's gonna get life."

"He thinks he might beat the case," Joe said.

"If he beats it, I'm worried."

"… Little Larry's got something to do with it," Joe said. "It was a waste of time going to see Harrelson. I don't like Charlie."

"The guy's gonna talk. He's talking already."

"I don't think so. I think that's his ace in the hole."

"Maybe you better go get that thing, man," Jimmy said.

It was clear from the conversation that the "thing" was the high-powered rifle used to fell Judge Wood.

Then Joe Chagra began to feel some heat of his own. In a later conversation, Joe said, "I don't underestimate anybody. I haven't done anything. What have I done? What am I going to jail for?"

"I don't know, but they're going to try to put that on you. You don't have to do anything to go to jail, you know. There's fucking thirty-thousand people in here that ain't done nothing."

"They've done something. They've all done something to be sitting here."

"You've done something too, Joe."

"What have I done?"

"You know Harrelson knocked off the judge."

"I don't know that."

"You don't know that. Shit."

"I don't know if he did it or not. Maybe he did. Maybe Little Larry did it."

Then Jimmy Chagra said, "Look, the FBI knows I hired him to do this. They know that. Do they, or not?"

"No, they don't know. They don't know. They can't prove it."

"… They don't have to prove it, Joe. Can I tell you something? They'll get liars to get up there and say it."

In other conversations, Chagra elaborated his escape plan, vouched for the criminal capability of Jerry Ray James, was certain escape-conspirator Calvin Wright was cooperating with the FBI, and called for the deaths of Charles Harrelson and former drug-trafficking-partner-turned-federal-informant Henry Wallace. He also managed to hopelessly entangle himself in the escape plan and further implicate his brother and wife in the plot to assassinate Wood.

In a prison conversation in November 1980, Liz Chagra told her husband, "I'll never forgive you if I go to jail, Jimmy. I'll never forgive you!"

"You're not going to jail," Jimmy Chagra told his wife.

It was one more lie in a life riddled with deception, and one more complication at trial for Oscar Goodman.

10

Trial of the Century

For a man who professed such desire to escape the confines of Leavenworth, Jimmy Chagra and his big mouth had brought down the full power of the United States government on him. The pit he had dug for himself, his cronies, and his family appeared to be bottomless. Within two years of the Wood killing, the FBI and Justice Department had collected enough witnesses and amassed enough physical evidence to win the indictment of Jimmy Chagra, Charles Harrelson, Joe Chagra, Liz Chagra, and Jo Ann Harrelson for his murder. Although the feds had developed a wide network of informants on the street and behind prison walls, Jimmy Chagra played Santa Claus with his inability to keep his mouth shut. Cocaine had Joe Chagra chattering like an auctioneer. The pressure turned Liz Chagra's nerves to jelly. Harrelson couldn't stop bragging about his misdeed. And Jo Ann was a victim of ignorance and circumstance.

One by one, they all fell.

As part of his plea agreement, Joe Chagra admitted he took part in the conspiracy to murder the judge, but refused to testify against his brother. He received a 10-year sentence, with parole eligibility in 54 months. Although courtroom observers considered it a great deal, it was a lengthy sentence for a man whose greatest sin was being related to Jimmy Chagra.

Liz Chagra was also ready to deal. As a newly born-again Christian, she gladly renounced her sins. She wrote a thoroughly incriminating letter to Wood's widow, Kathryn, in which she admitted carrying the cash to make the payoff for the murder. In it, she explained how she had been pulled into the crime:

"He [Jimmy] took me inside and asked me to deliver some money (which, by the way, I did deliver money for Jimmy's gambling debts on many, many occasions). Anyway, I protested because we had several guests at our house and I was seven months pregnant and mostly because it was 110 degrees outside. I asked him to send his bodyguard. That is when he took me aside and spoke sternly to me. He said that this was for the payoff for your husband's murder and he could only trust me, his wife. At that point I can honestly say I was shaking and told him I wouldn't do it. But Jimmy persisted and I weakened and ended up involving myself in this crime."

When a deal failed to materialize, she wound up on trial with Charles and Jo Ann Harrelson in San Antonio. Given that the trial was in the John H. Wood Jr. Memorial Courthouse, Liz Chagra didn't stand a chance.

All three were convicted at trial. When the jury foreman announced Liz Chagra's conviction, the jury box erupted in sobs. It was clear the jurors believed that she had committed a crime, but her greatest offense was in remaining married and loyal to Jimmy Chagra. Despite what obviously was a minimal role in the criminal conspiracy, Liz Chagra was hit with a 30-year sentence. She received five-year concurrent sentences for obstruction and income-tax evasion.

Jo Ann Harrelson, who had picked up the money, received a 25-year sentence from Sessions for obstruction and lying before the grand jury.

Charles Harrelson, who was convicted of the killing, received a double life sentence to run consecutively. He also faced sentences totaling 70 years on various state charges and was looking at the death penalty if the state of Texas decided to try him.

? ? ?

Oscar Goodman admits he finds rays of hope under the darkest circumstances. It was that way in the case of the U.S. versus Jamiel "Jimmy" Chagra. Though the earlier convictions devastated Liz and the Harrelsons, they set in motion a chain of events that helped Jimmy Chagra.

First, after much prodding from Goodman, Sessions finally agreed to change the location of his trial from Texas to Jacksonville, Florida. The judge, of course, wasn't trying to do the defense any favors when he granted the change of venue to the John H. Wood Memorial Federal Courthouse.

Prior to the change of venue, Goodman recalled riding in a cab in San Antonio. On the way to the courthouse from the airport, the cabby struck up a conversation.

"He asked me what brought me to town and I told him I was a lawyer," Goodman said. "He immediately asked me if I was working on the Chagra case and as I started to answer, he launched into a diatribe about how he hoped they nailed the bastards who killed the judge, who was a wonderful man and had been dedicated to fighting crime and the drug war in San Antonio. He went on and on and I kept my mouth shut. He said that they should take Chagra and hang him from a flagpole, put honey on his eyes, and ants on the honey. And that would be too good for him Then he turned to me and asked who I worked for.

"I told him I worked for the FBI."

In court, the defense table included only Goodman and Chagra. The government side was a veritable convention of prosecutors, FBI agents, and legal assistants. By physical appearance alone, the courtroom was heavily weighted to one side. The image was not lost on jurors.

The prosecution eventually realized that Jacksonville wasn't San Antonio or Midland, that the Florida jurors felt they owed nothing special to a deceased federal judge from Texas, and that one man's show of prosecutorial unity is another's display of intimidation. But at the outset, it appeared that nothing could erode the prosecution's confidence.

Thus, the Mexican piñata. Rumors circulated around the courthouse that the prosecution had purchased a piñata in anticipation of its victory party in the case against Jimmy Chagra. And, of course, no party is complete without champagne, and the government had bottles ready to ice, as well as little plastic glasses poised for a victory toast. Goodman noted the arrogance, catalogued it, and said nothing. Sometimes arrogance was justified and even a layman could see that Goodman was a decided underdog in what some journalists referred to as the Trial of the Century.

The four counts of Jimmy Chagra's indictment were bombs riddled with trip wires. Chagra was accused of obstructing justice, conspiring to distribute a small mountain of marijuana, conspiracy to commit murder, and murder itself. With plentiful wiretap surveillance, along with the testimony of cooperating witnesses and paid informants, Goodman's task was monumental. And the government knew it. By the attitude of Justice Department veteran prosecutors Ray and Leroy Jahn, a husband-and-wife team poised on the precipice of a career-making victory over the man who ordered the hit on Judge Wood, it was clear to Goodman that this was a case they believed they could not lose.

To defuse the bomb, Goodman knew he would have to concede parts of the indictment or risk losing credibility before the jury. From the evidence presented, it was obvious Jimmy Chagra had conspired to ship vast quantities of marijuana and planned his own escape from Leavenworth penitentiary. To deny the obvious would ruin any chance to beat the charges relating to the murder of John Wood. That made his opening statement crucial. Where the government could crank up the condemnation and conjure saintly images of a fallen federal judge, Goodman had to all but admit that his client was guilty of some of what prosecutors alleged or lose the jury on the first day of trial.

While they might not have been familiar with Maximum John Wood, the jurors also owed nothing to Jimmy Chagra. And as the tape recordings collected while Chagra was in Leavenworth clearly showed, he was no one to pity. How could Goodman encourage the jurors to suspend their natural human tendency to rush to judgment?

Goodman made the first of several wise moves, though at the time, his decisions must have further buoyed the prosecution's confidence. During his opening statement, Goodman attacked the government in what had become his usual style. He took time to criticize the presence of FBI agents sitting with the Jahns. And he went on to paint a picture of the lawlessness in U.S. District Judge Wood's courtroom in 1979, behavior that manifested in a vendetta against attorneys Lee and Joe Chagra and their troublesome brother Jimmy. The battle between the judge and the brothers was widely known in Texas and abundantly documented in court.

Goodman attempted to use his apparent weaknesses as strengths. Chagra was no stranger to the court system. In fact, he had run up against Judge Wood and lost in the Midland, Texas, trial. He was already faced with a long prison sentence and the new federal charges promised to add perhaps five years to his overall sentence.

This led Goodman to ask the jury, "Is someone going to hire someone to kill a federal judge over a five-year differential?"

It wasn't a murder-for-hire plot, Goodman proposed, but extortion after the fact. Harrelson saw Chagra as a mark, as evidenced by his attempt to con him out of several hundred thousand dollars in a rigged poker game in Las Vegas, and the Wood assassination was Harrelson's chance for the score of a lifetime.

Following the defense's tentative opening gambit, Ray Jahn addressed the court. "Jimmy Chagra tried every legal means to remove Judge Wood. Jimmy Chagra decided to have him murdered. It was the only recourse, the only solution for Jimmy Chagra. Fate intervened and Charles Harrelson offered his services. There will be no evidence presented that Jimmy Chagra pulled the trigger."

With that, the government began presenting its voluminous, thorough, and expensive case, with an eclectic array of witnesses ranging from Wood's wife to multiple-offender Jerry Ray James. Government agents had managed to piece together an incriminating note passed from Jimmy Chagra to Liz Chagra, which had been retrieved in pieces from the trap they'd installed in the toilet drain. The prosecutors had even assembled an intricately detailed model of the San Antonio apartment complex where Wood was murdered.

However, Liz Chagra could not be compelled to testify against her husband. And as part of his plea agreement, Joe

Chagra would not be forced to deliver what surely would have been incriminating testimony against his brother.

As he prepared for trial, Goodman received a letter from former client and convicted felon Andy Gramby Hanley, who was part of the father-and-son hit team in Las Vegas. Hanley informed Goodman that Jerry Ray James had already received some of the $250,000 in reward money for his cooperation against Chagra. In fact, Hanley said James had already bought his wife a Mercedes. Oscar Goodman received assistance in the Chagra defense from a most unlikely source—his wife Carolyn.

"It was one of the few times my wife assisted me with a case," Oscar Goodman said. "I had her listen to the tapes. I needed help. It was a very tough case, and I didn't like to talk to lawyers about my case. That's just not my style. I do everything myself. People might not believe that, but it's true. They think that I have a staff of people working for me to handle every detail, but I do all my own research. I do all my own writing. What you read, that's me. Truth is, I'd rather be a research lawyer and a writer than an advocate in court, but you can't make a living doing that.

"Carolyn listened to the tapes. I needed a sounding board. She listened to my theory, what I planned for my closing argument, and she thought everything I said was consistent with the evidence. She said, 'Oh, you've got this case won.' She heard in the tapes that Jimmy Chagra was a braggart, trying to be a big shot in prison, bragging in order to save himself. What bigger thing could a prisoner brag about than killing a federal judge?

"It's about as macho as you can get in the federal prison system. And I wanted to have people within the system say that this was a real way of getting respect and being considered to be a strong guy who wasn't someone who'd be pushed around—who wasn't some rich soft guy. So I found out who six or seven of the toughest prisoners in the United States were and issued subpoenas for all of them. Terre Haute, Lewisburg, Marion. All across the country. I got the toughest prisoners in the system, the killers, the worst, and set it up to bring them all to Jacksonville for the trial.

'Well, the Director of the Bureau of Prisons in Washington

had a fit. He called up Sessions and said, 'Who the fuck is this guy? He's gonna create the biggest escape in the country. They'll get out of that box in Jacksonville in two seconds.'

"So Sessions called me in, and I told him my story, and he said to me, 'Well, I can't stop you from doing it, but you can't have these people coming into the local jail. You'll create a major security problem.' I pressed my theory and said I had to talk to these people. So he had them transferred to the federal prison in Atlanta. This was the time that the Cuban Marielitos were there after landing in Florida.

"I got there on a Sunday before the trial. These were my witnesses and I interviewed the toughest guys in the world. It was almost as if the guards wanted me to get hurt. They let me go into the room by myself and turned me loose. The Marielitos were coming in, speaking Spanish and staring at me. They weren't happy to see a white face dressed in a suit. They were mean angry people and they weren't high on authority figures. So I kept telling them *'abogado, abogado,'* which was the only word I could think of [Spanish for "lawyer"]. I finally finished my interviews with all these felons. And then I decided not to use them. As the trial started, I learned the government was going to use Jerry Ray James as a witness.

"Jerry Ray James is one of the greatest embarrassments in the history of federal prosecution. When they decided, in their zeal to put away Jimmy Chagra, to stoop so low as to use this vicious, evil, conniving human being, this subhuman being, they handed me a mallet to hit them with.

"The more I learned about him, the more I realized James cut one of the great deals in history. It was outrageous, but I saw that the government was stopping at nothing to get its man."

In addition to James' activity in the grisly New Mexico prison riots, by the FBI's own admission James was a career criminal with more than 30 felony arrests. As a condition of his agreement to pardon James as part of the deal with the Justice Department, the governor of New Mexico himself received assurances that James would never set foot in his state again.

The Justice Department was even willing to purchase testimony in order to get Jimmy Chagra. In hustling his way out of a double-life sentence in Leavenworth, James managed to get the government to agree to pay him a $250,000 bonus if Chagra was convicted. At the time of trial, James' wife was seen riding in a Mercedes, which was believed to be purchased with proceeds from his agreement to cooperate.

Worst of all for the prosecution, after two years, the multi-million-dollar investigation failed to produce a murder weapon or an eyewitness to the crime. Several witnesses, under hypnotic suggestion, recalled seeing a man fitting Harrelson's description, but the case relied heavily on tape recordings and jailhouse statements. In a desperate effort to compel the testimony of Liz Chagra, the government went so far as trying to label Jimmy Chagra a bigamist and force her to take the stand without invoking the marital privilege against rendering incriminating testimony against a spouse. In this instance, Judge William Sessions ruled in favor of the defense.

Sessions, a future Director of the FBI, delivered the eulogy at Wood's funeral. Despite his obvious affection for the deceased, Sessions declined to recuse himself. He also beefed up security for trial and even wore a flak jacket. During the proceedings, masked SWAT police guarded the courthouse.

Most of the prosecution's case rested on its presentation of the tape-recorded material and the testimony of a few key witnesses. The tapes were devastating, but there were so many of them, Goodman noticed the jury losing interest after the first few days. As the case wore on, they were being rocked to sleep by an overconfident prosecution.

But Jimmy Chagra was wide awake. He tried not to wince as time after time he overheard himself talking about the murder of the federal judge and the government's pending investigation.

At one point in trial, he pulled out a notebook and wrote to Goodman, "How in the fuck did your wife say you had a chance to win this case after listening to those tapes?"

Goodman wrote back, "Because I'm fucking brilliant, that's why."

The government spent a fortune to construct a model of Wood's apartment complex that was precise to the minutest detail.

Goodman had a visceral reaction to the model. Something wasn't right. Then it hit him.

He asked the judge's clerk, Sarah Burgess, for some Kleenex and a Magic Marker, preferably a green one. He rolled some of the tissue into balls and colored them with the green marker.

The courtroom was silent. Neither the judge nor the jury saw the method in his apparent madness.

Then he placed the tissue balls on the miniature trees, which he'd noticed were barren despite the fact the shooting had occurred on May 29. The exhibit had been constructed from photographs taken in winter, when the trees had lost their leaves.

Goodman graphically showed that the trajectory of the bullet could not have been as the government theorized. The leaves would have been in the way.

Then it was time for Jerry Ray James to take the stand.

The Jahns, despite their vast experience, did not fully recognize that there would be a huge difference in jurors' minds between key witnesses Joe Chagra and Jerry Ray James. Where Chagra had credibility and little to gain by testifying against Harrelson—he did, after all, receive a 10-year sentence for his minor role in the conspiracy—James had every reason to lie. He was not only winning his freedom by cooperating, but he was in line to collect a six-figure paycheck in the process.

James testified that Chagra had boasted of planning to kill Wood. Although his words were damning, his character was made to order for Goodman.

Goodman's argument against the recorded evidence was brilliant in its simplicity. Jimmy Chagra, in his attempt to be accepted among the hardened cons in Leavenworth, had only bragged about having a hand in the Wood murder in order to improve his stock inside the penitentiary. He hadn't actually done anything, only lied to a few fellow cons to remain in their good graces. James admitted on direct examination that Chagra was a big talker; he recounted all the big drug scores Chagra plotted from behind bars. James even recalled Jimmy boasting of offing a man named Mark Finney and burying him in a shallow grave in a stand of pine trees outside Austin.

By the time Goodman had a chance to cross-examine Jerry Ray James, the trial of Jimmy Chagra was nearly a month old. The jurors had heard enough from the prosecution, and the case, save for one outburst from Chagra during James' testimony, had reached a turning point.

Oscar Goodman seized the moment.

His version of the facts of the case was that Jimmy Chagra had been victimized by a homicidal extortionist named Charles Harrelson. Oscar argued that Chagra had never agreed to pay to have Wood killed. Instead, he was forced to hand over nearly $200,000 after the fact in order to prevent Harrelson from implicating him in the crime.

"Mr. Chagra was doing an awful lot of talking to show he was important — that he was heavy into criminal activities, right?" Goodman asked James.

"Yes," came the reply.

Years later Goodman recalled, "Jimmy was surly. He was brusque. He was really trying to be a tough guy. I'd been around plenty of the real thing, and he wasn't it. I knew it was an act he was putting on in order to get along in prison. He was trying to show he was tough. 'I killed this guy, I killed that guy. I did this, I did that.' It was part of his personality, but Jimmy also had a glint in his eye. He did have life in them, and after all of his gruffness, he would start laughing as though the whole thing was a game."

The prosecution rested its case on a Friday, and Goodman spent the weekend mulling his defense strategy. If he attempted to match the government blow for blow, he'd risk losing the jurors on the one hand or rekindling their interest in the prosecution's case on the other. It was clear they'd been less than enthusiastic listening to hour after hour of taped testimony; going over the same ground might only stoke their curiosity. Instead, he decided to minimize the damage and focus on the undeniable flaws in the character of Jerry Ray James, the government's key witness. It was a risk Goodman had to take if he was going to save Chagra's life.

On Monday morning, Goodman called James to the witness stand. Heavily prepped for trial, James anticipated being grilled for days at a time. Instead, Goodman kept his inquiry brief. His defense lasted just 12 minutes.

"Describe how Mr. Chagra told you he killed Mark Finney," Goodman said.

"I think he said he shot him."

"Are you sure of that?"

"I'm sure he told me he offed him," James said.

"You're as sure of that as you are that Mr. Chagra told you he murdered Judge Wood?"

"That's right," James said.

"No more questions," Goodman said. The prosecution appeared momentarily perplexed.

Then Goodman added, "Call Mark Finney."

The supposed dead man strolled into court and raised his right hand. Goodman could barely contain himself.

Once Finney settled in, Goodman asked him, "Mr. Finney, how are you feeling?"

"Pretty good," Finney said.

"Did Jimmy Chagra ever point a gun at you and shoot you?"

"No, sir."

"No more questions," Goodman said. In a moment, he turned for dramatic effect and added, "Your Honor, ladies and gentlemen of the jury, the defense rests."

It was a once-in-a-lifetime moment, the kind of drama that usually took place only in an episode of "Perry Mason." The entire weight of James's testimony crumbled before Ray and LeRoy Jahn's eyes and settled at their feet. If the star witness could not be trusted, then the jury might ask what else was hollow about the government's claims.

During closing arguments, prosecutor John Emerson delivered an impassioned plea for the jury to find Jimmy Chagra guilty. He reminded the jurors of Chagra's own recorded words as he admitted hiring Charles Harrelson to kill Judge Wood. But the prosecutor had to know the case was lost. Chagra would be convicted on the drug charges; that much was so evident Goodman all but stipulated to the crimes. But the murder was different. Because the government had resorted to using the unreliable Jerry Ray James, reasonable doubt had been established.

Goodman focused most of his closing argument on shooting holes through the government's theory of the case. First, he reminded the jurors to keep the events in their proper order.

"I submit that this case did not take place in a vacuum," he said. There was, after all, the assassination attempt of U.S. Attorney James Kerr to consider.

"Somebody took on a certain ruthlessness, a certain callousness, in the Western District of Texas before Jimmy Chagra was even indicted on the drug charge for which he was ultimately convicted ..."

Goodman added that, unlike so many others who might have been motivated to kill Judge Wood, the Chagra brothers were different. While others whispered about Wood's lack of fairness in the courtroom, the Chagras shouted openly. Their attorneys filed motion after motion accusing the judge to his face of being unfair. Then Goodman restated his theory that Jimmy Chagra was guilty of braggadocio, not murder.

"I can't look at you and candidly state to you that Mr. Chagra did not want to escape from Leavenworth, doing thirty years without parole," Goodman said. "The means he chose are incredible. ... I submit that it was a sad, sad situation where a human being was looking to break loose from his cage—not to obstruct justice, but to get out."

But what about the candid conversations between Jimmy and his brother Joe? Again, Goodman implored the jury to put those remarks in perspective—that of a man mired in prison and dreaming of his freedom.

"I submit that Joe Chagra was doing what Jimmy Chagra was doing with Jerry James. He was placating.

"Once again, I can't tell you the words aren't there. But I can tell you that when you listen to the words, you see what Joe Chagra time and time again says, 'I don't know what I'm doing here. I don't know what we're talking about. I don't know what's happening.' Time and time again."

In closing, Goodman delivered what would surely go down as one of the most dramatic, some would say outrageous, lines ever uttered in a federal courtroom.

"Based on the evidence which has been presented to you in this case by the prosecution against Jimmy Chagra, I submit to you that the ultimate tribute that you could pay to the Honorable John H. Wood, Jr., who sat as a United States District Judge, sworn to uphold the laws of the United States, the ultimate tribute you could pay to him would be to return a verdict of not guilty."

Goodman recalled years later, "Basically, if you don't have a jury in your pocket by nineteen minutes, in my opinion, you don't have them at all. You're going to lose them. You're going to bore them. But in that case I did a six-hour summation without stopping. Without stuttering. Without one, 'Uh.' Not one hesitation. And no notes. The transcript reads like a novel. On that day, I *was* brilliant."

The jury began its deliberations on Friday, February 3, 1983. A day later, jurors were still listening to portions of the tape-recorded evidence. By Saturday afternoon, word surfaced that jurors had come to an agreement on two of the four charges. Later, Goodman recalled his reaction when he heard that the jurors had requested a burn bag in order to eliminate any evidence of their deliberations.

"It was then I knew they had listened and that they were with us. Why else would they need to destroy their notes? If they had been siding with the government, there would be no repercussions. And I was right. By Monday afternoon they returned a verdict of not guilty on the conspiracy charges. Jimmy was convicted of obstruction and drug smuggling, but he was acquitted on the murder count. At the time, I called it the most important acquittal in the history of jury trials."

Jimmy Chagra called it nothing short of a miracle. "Thank God for Oscar Goodman!'" he called out to the press.

If Ray and LeRoy Jahn were dejected, they tried not to show it to reporters. Besides, from all appearances, they still had an ace in the hole — the presence on the bench of presiding Judge William Sessions. The jury might have spoken, but the judge had the final say when he sentenced Chagra on March 18.

"I'm glad I won it there," Goodman recalled. "If I had won it in Las Vegas, there would have been a full-scale investigation into case fixing and jury tampering. Truthfully, I don't know how I overcame those tapes. It was one thing to have Jimmy talking with Jerry Ray James about murder. That was a lot of macho talk, the kind of thing that goes on in prison. But the other tapes were different. The conversations between Jimmy and his brother were devastating."

At sentencing, rather than socking Chagra with 25 years, in addition to the 32 years he was already serving on drug and tax convictions, Sessions added only a decade to his existing sentence. Chagra would be eligible for parole in 2007.

In keeping with his reputation as a man incapable of exercising his right to remain silent, upon sentencing, Chagra told Sessions, "You don't care about honesty or truth. One day you and I will stand before a higher judge. If you can live with the sentences you give me, so can I."

And in the end, the judge did something that courtroom observers must have found almost amusing. Sessions fined the defendant $220,000.

It was less than a single evening of gambling in the high-rolling life of the great Jimmy Chagra, and about the price paid for the assassination of Federal Judge John H. Wood.

11

Tony in Trouble

The minute his flight from Florida touched down at McCarran International Airport in Las Vegas, Oscar Goodman headed directly to his office. He was greeted at the door by dozens of lawyers and friends who congratulated him on the incredible acquittal of Jimmy Chagra. His office was filled with balloons, bottles, and streamers.

"At the party there were all sorts of people from around town and they looked at the case the way I looked at it," Goodman said. "It was a big victory against incredible odds. I had never been in a situation where there was so much acclamation. Lawyers from all over the country were sending champagne. And I didn't even get a chance to enjoy it.

"I came in, said hello to everyone, then ran over to the jail, because Tony Spilotro was in custody. It was the only time he was ever in custody while I was his attorney. He wouldn't let anybody else represent him on a bail motion.

"Tony had been indicted for killing two small-time scufflers in Chicago, Billy McCarthy and Jimmy Miraglia. One of the deaths had been particularly grisly, with the victim's head being placed in a vise and squeezed until his eyeball popped out. In Chicago, it was known as the M&M murder case.

"The Chagra case moved me up a few notches. It gave me phenomenal credibility at a time I was known for the most part for representing so-called mobsters. I'd been fighting what I call 'the Vegas image' a long time, but every judge followed the Chagra case because of John Wood. Wherever I went, thereafter, I was treated a lot differently. There was more respect, a little distance, and no more wise remarks about Vegas, about the mob. I was serious as far as judges were concerned. It was significant as far as being a career builder. I always had plenty of clients, but now I had the respect of the judiciary."

Goodman had always commanded the respect of the Las Vegas judiciary, where he was suspected of being a little too close to judges from the county to federal levels. It only added to his legend when, within hours of returning to Southern Nevada, he secured a low bail for Spilotro and got him released. When asked about the release years later, Goodman would only smile and say, "It's pretty extraordinary to get a defendant out on bail where there's an extradition issue and the case would be tried in Chicago."

If law enforcement thought that was odd, their curiosity increased when Goodman and his client waived a jury trial in Chicago in favor of a bench proceeding before Chicago Judge Thomas J. Maloney. It was the kind of rare move that was guaranteed to generate whispers of case fixing.

§ § §

After securing Spilotro's release at home, Goodman took his family to Israel to celebrate the bar mitzvah of youngest son Eric. Upon returning to the United States, he was informed that his talkative client Jimmy Chagra had met with a federal prosecutor and attempted to cut a deal to help his wife. Chagra agreed to admit culpability in the attempted murder of prosecutor James Kerr in exchange for a lighter sentence for Liz. But the deal he cut proved once again that he wasn't much of a gambler: Liz Chagra's 30-year sentence was cut to 20 years. Given the toll lengthy prison terms take on most people, he hadn't helped her much.

"Liz is the one I feel most sorry for," Goodman said. "When I learned she had cancer, I fought like hell to get her out on a compassionate release. But they really wanted to hurt her. Of the forty agents who worked on the Wood assassination case, I think thirty-eight of them wound up divorced over it. It tore apart a lot of people on both sides. As a crime, killing a federal judge is just about the most heinous act in the system.

"Liz was a victim in that case. And even the FBI knew it. One agent, Mick McCormick, joined me in imploring the court to give Liz a break and let her out of prison so she could see her family and die at home. But they refused. And the way they treated her in prison was an abomination. The parole and probation officers were pigs."

Liz Chagra died on September 11, 1997, of cancer, without ever gaining her release.

ƒ ƒ ƒ

Defending Tony Spilotro and the various interests of the Chicago mob and its satellite operations was more than a full-time job. While Goodman prepared for the M&M murder case, he was also plotting strategy in the brewing federal investigation of Allen Glick's Argent casinos. In addition, there was the Schmoutey union bombing case to monitor and three dozen less sensational legal matters hanging in the balance. Goodman entertained reporters' questions daily and it was a rare morning that his name was not in print in at least one of the three Las Vegas daily newspapers.

"Oscar attracts so much attention that some lawyers think he places calls out to reporters before hitting town," Vinny Montalto said. "But he doesn't, of course. It's just him and the clients he represents. He's always in the middle of it and after a while, the press gravitates toward him. And it doesn't hurt that he's a great quote."

Attorney Dominic Gentile observed, "Oscar has a tremendous flair for the dramatic and is an extremely flamboyant lawyer. In some cities, that would have worked against him because, historically, mob guys like to avoid the publicity. And Oscar never saw a microphone he didn't like. He got an opportunity to be very public and outspoken about his feelings about the way the laws were being put into effect at that time and argued that those laws were unconstitutional and trampled upon certain civil liberties of his clients. Remember, the Black Book, which we now take for granted, was only a few years old when he began practicing here.

"What made Oscar seize the moment? I think it was his personality. He was a smart lawyer who was full of energy and loved the limelight, and this gave him an opportunity to exploit it.

"I came from Chicago, and in Chicago the last thing on Earth any mob guy wanted was a lawyer who was going to create attention. I happen to know from first-hand discussions with clients of mine that Chicago mob guys directed a great deal of concern and criticism at Tony for getting so much publicity, and these were people who were much older than Tony. In Chicago, they outranked him. I know that his high profile was a subject of criticism and they blamed his lawyer for it. They never criticized Oscar's ability, but they criticized Oscar's philosophy."

Added another longtime criminal attorney: "Tony stayed out of jail, but he wouldn't have had such a high profile if Oscar didn't use him to get publicity for himself. Of course, he might not have stayed out of jail as long as he did if Goodman hadn't been constantly harassing the G in the newspapers."

Some of his attorney friends were unimpressed by his high profile.

"Oscar is a pretty good attorney, but he's a shameless self-promoter," one long-time colleague says. "He was always quick with a sound bite and he got very lucky coming to Las Vegas when he did. He was the only lawyer in town and he made a killing here, but it wasn't because he was a brilliant person. Face it, the guy's ego is enormous."

On the other hand, this same lawyer couldn't knock Oscar's professional behavior. "Goodman was in Chicago representing Spilotro at a time so many attorneys were taking care of the judges. You almost had to if you were going to be effective for your client. I never remember Oscar having anything to do with that stuff. The guy was ethical. He never played around on the road, never took anything illegal. He likes to drink gin and bet sports. But he didn't play games in the courtroom or anywhere else. There's something to be said for that."

In Chicago, Goodman didn't need shadowy contacts. Tony

Spilotro and the Outfit had more than enough. The FBI and police in Las Vegas and Chicago believed Spilotro used some of those contacts to put in the fix in his double-murder trial. Some of the strange occurrences were not lost on his defense attorney.

"I was on a whole new playing field in the M&M murder case," Goodman said. "Trying a murder case in Las Vegas was a fairly straightforward process. But Chicago was different. During the weeks leading up to trial, I associated with Tony's long-time Chicago lawyer Herb Barsky, who was one of the old-time players in the city. He was a Chicago insider who, legend had it, could get things done throughout the system. Herb has an elegance about him, a certain refinement that belied his reputation as a guy capable of fixing any problem that emerged at Twenty-sixth and California, the address of the courthouse. Herb was not a cigar-chomper. He was very smooth and I watched every move he made.

"Despite what the government was leaking to the press and the fact that Cullotta the rat was making all kinds of allegations, the government had basically nothing fresh linking Tony to a murder committed more than twenty years earlier.

"When we were notified that we had drawn a judge named Thomas J. Maloney, Barsky was happy. He said we had found the right court, which meant nothing to me. Then Barsky strongly suggested we forego a jury trial and allow the judge to hear the case. I was surprised, but I was still trying to read the landscape.

"Tony liked the idea, but in my career I'd tried it only once, and that was in Las Vegas at the insistence of a client who was up on income-tax charges and had drawn Harry Claiborne as a judge in federal court. I knew Harry. The client knew Harry. He swore they were close friends and that the judge would never rule against him because of that friendship. I refused at first, but he insisted. And I'm convinced Claiborne was harder on him than he would have been had my client just taken a damn jury trial. Claiborne convicted him and threw the book at him.

"But Barsky and Tony were persistent, so I eventually agreed to go along with them. My trial preparation didn't change a bit, but it was obvious from the outset that the case was weak. The two-man prosecution team was doing its best, but at one point I noticed something in the pretrial discovery material that deeply concerned me. An automobile was spotted in the area of the murders that Tony might have had access to. It was a new way to link him circumstantially to the scene of the crime where the vise was used, and throughout the trial I expected the prosecutors to bring it up. It was one of those details that could have tipped the scales against us. But they never touched it. Perhaps it didn't dawn on them. I certainly wasn't going to tell them.

"The only thing fresh the prosecution had going for them was the testimony of King Rat Frank Cullotta. This miserable son-of-a-bitch sat up there and lied. He lied and lied. He even lied about the reason he decided to become a rat against the guy who was supposedly his best friend. He told the court that the government produced a tape-recording of Tony sanctioning Cullotta's murder. It was a lie he told his mother and his girlfriends and anyone who would listen, but it was complete bullshit. We subpoenaed the tape and, guess what, there was no tape. No tape!

"Although you'll never get them to admit it, the government never got squat in the way of convictions for turning Frank Cullotta. He admitted murdering four people, and his testimony was useless because he refused to tell the truth. If he told the truth, he would have had to admit that Tony called him a little girl. Nobody in Tony's world trusted Cullotta, because all their lives he'd always been a little girl. It's why even people like Herbie Blitzstein and so many other people in Tony's life all warned him about Cullotta. Tony used Cullotta because Cullotta had the My Place bar and pizza joint. Tony could hang out there. Cullotta married little Nicky Costanza's daughter. Costanza was a real wanna-be, and Cullotta was a wife-beater.

"I blame Cullotta becoming a rat in part on Tony, though. The reason Cullotta broke *omerta*, the code of silence, is in part because Tony didn't take care of Frank when he got into trouble. Cullotta believed he would be taken care of, that his family would receive an envelope when he got in trouble, and that a lawyer would be hired to defend him. But Tony didn't take care of him. Why? Because he didn't believe Frank was with him. Cullotta was a hanger-on. Tony didn't want him around, but he was still part of the group. And Cullotta got his revenge.

"He called people who would take care of him. He called the FBI. And suddenly he went to the other side. The change came overnight. Cullotta became like a little G-man. It's the old story about these guys: 'You have to slap them once to get them to talk, but you have to slap them twice to get them to stop.' Cullotta was a chatterbox.

"My history with Cullotta was brief. He came to the law office before a court appearance without a tie on and I told him, 'You should wear a tie to court.' He said, 'I don't know how to tie one.' I showed him how to tie a tie. In retrospect, I should have tied it tighter.

"I used to keep a fake Rolex watch on a coffee table in my office as sort of a thief meter. If a client couldn't be trusted not to lift the watch, I certainly couldn't trust him in my office. Cullotta noticed the watch and later lied about it in the book *Casino* when he accused me of wearing a fake Rolex. I don't wear a Rolex. I own several, but I don't wear one. But that was Cullotta. He was a liar and a thief through and through. I made sure he was not a factor in the case against Tony."

§ § §

Complicating matters was Cullotta's admitted role as the shooter in the 1979 murder in Las Vegas of Sherwin "Jerry" Lisner, a white-collar criminal and drug dealer who dreamed of bigger scores and moonlighted as a Drug Enforcement Agency informant. Drawn to Spilotro's power, though never considered one of Tough Tony's rough-and-tumble crew, Lisner was an associate at a time in Spilotro's life when he was growing increasingly paranoid. With government agencies probing Spilotro's activities on many levels, Lisner was called to Washington to meet with federal investigators on a matter unrelated to his relationship with Spilotro. Not that Spilotro believed that.

Taking no chances, he dispatched Frank Cullotta, a go-fer and hanger-on from the old days on the streets of Chicago, to take care of the problem. Cullotta, a burglar by trade but also a proficient killer, solicited the assistance of Chicago hitman Wayne Matecki. While Matecki listened for signs of police activity on the scanner in the vehicle parked in front of Lisner's Las Vegas home, Cullotta knocked on the con man's door. He talked his way inside and when Lisner turned his back shot him twice in the head.

Cullotta told *Casino* author Nicholas Pileggi what happened next:

"He turns around and looks at me, 'What are you doing?' he says. He takes off through the kitchen toward the garage.

"I actually looked at the gun, like, 'What the fuck have I got? Blanks in there?' So I run after him and I empty the rest into his head. It's like an explosion going off every time."

Cullotta eventually finished the job after Matecki handed him more rounds. In all, Cullotta shot Lisner 10 times before dragging him into the backyard and dumping him in the family pool.

Watching Cullotta, Goodman immediately knew the informant had been "born again," a phenomenon common to many convicted killers and thugs who, in leaving their mob family, become members of the FBI's family. They act more like avenging angels than men with blood on their hands, more like government agents than many of the actual G-men. Goodman used that knowledge against Cullotta as he built his case.

Meanwhile, Tony Spilotro remained uncommonly cool. He showed no sign of the anxiety attacks and heart trouble that later kept him in bed for days on end while the government worked round the clock to lock him up for good. He was more at home in a courtroom than a lot of attorneys and through experience in the system he knew that, for him, waiting for trial was far harder emotionally than the trial itself. Trials were battles and confrontation was something Spilotro knew plenty about. He reveled in a fight for his life. He ate well, rose early each morning to speak privately with his lawyer, and after a long day in court, made sure Goodman experienced the flavor of Chicago.

"During the trial, Tony took me to a great restaurant where they had Romanian skirt steaks with garlic," Goodman said. "A lot of garlic and the little red pizza peppers. It was the greatest, but when I woke up in the morning, it smelled like I was in a gym with about forty guys. Our rooms just stunk from garlic and we would laugh about it.

"Wherever we stayed, Tony was always in the next room. He wanted to keep me close to him. He had this terrible habit when he got up in the morning. He would make enough noise to wake me up. And he couldn't sleep past about four o'clock, so he would get up and he would order coffee from room service and I would always hear the glass tinkling, and after a while I knew that he was up and it was time for me to get up, too. I would go over to his room and he would insist that I have coffee with him and we would discuss what was going to happen that day. It was like that every morning."

Spilotro enjoyed the benefit of time in the M&M murders, which were nearly a quarter-century old. He was also suspected of enjoying an unholy relationship with the judge, though Goodman claims he saw no evidence of it.

"In Illinois courts, after the prosecution rests its case, it's common for the defense to file a motion to dismiss due to a lack of evidence. In Tony's case, it was obvious the prosecution suffered from a lack of evidence. I made what I thought was an excellent argument and the judge ruled against me. I was devastated. In my mind, I'd clearly shown the flaws in the case. It left me taken aback a bit. I wasn't going to put Tony on the stand. I was really worried.

"I said to Tony, 'We're history.' Tony said, 'Don't worry about it.'

"In retrospect, it should have made me wonder more than it did at the time. I was too worried about presenting a defense. The defense was brief. Obviously, my client hadn't been at the scene of the crime and Frank Cullotta was a proven liar. I had shown that much when I cross-examined him. I had a sleepless night, which is usual for me, prior to making the closing argument in the case. The prosecution got to go last. Finally, the judge came back and ruled the prosecution hadn't proven guilt beyond a reasonable doubt.

"I don't know whether anybody got to Mahoney. I certainly saw no evidence of that. But the most amazing thing was that the prosecution didn't use this piece of devastating evidence. Being able to place a car at the scene of the crime, a car Tony had access to, could have been devastating. I think it would have been enough to convict him. But they didn't touch it. That struck me as odd then."

There wasn't much time to dwell on it. The government had several other cases pending against Tony, including his role in the shooting of Jerry Lisner in Las Vegas.

"I remember being in Art Nasser's law office when we heard that Tony had been indicted for the Lisner murder, a murder Frank Cullotta admitted committing. Tony was accused of ordering Cullotta to shoot Lisner. There was a million-dollar bail for Tony in the case. No one thought we would even get bail. But I reminded the court that he was already making an appearance in the M&M case and the best they could do was wait in line.

"John O'Brien was the magistrate. He was a real straight guy, all-government, but he agreed to the request. I managed to get Tony out on his own recognizance via a long-distance phone call from Chicago to Las Vegas. In Las Vegas, Judge Earle White wanted to arrest him on a Black Book issue, but Tony never missed a court date. He wasn't about to run away. He was a fighter. They had to give him that much."

The M&M case cemented the Spilotro-Goodman friendship as something greater than an attorney-client relationship. Privately, Goodman took note that despite Spilotro's chronic coronary ailment—he would eventually have open-heart surgery—the Little Guy would never consider delaying his court date or moving to postpone a trial. Spilotro was slowly being consumed by the pressure, but he was doing all he could not to show it. It was a brand of stoicism that Goodman, an admirer of strong men, came to respect.

"I probably liked Tony as much or more than anyone I ever represented," Goodman said. "He was very good to me in the sense that he made a concerted effort to shield me from any kind of discussion about criminal activity. It's almost as though he was protective of me. He didn't want me ever to get involved in a situation where I would have a problem as a result of being associated with him. There was a tremendous sensitivity there.

"Spilotro was also very good to me financially. He was very good as far as sending business my way. I had an awful lot of Culinary Union business and an awful lot of fellows from around the country who had problems, who Tony knew, and I would represent them. He afforded me the opportunity of fulfilling my own prophecy of defending the Constitution. If there was ever a target, he was a target, and I really believed that if I could protect him, I was doing everyone a service — by protecting him legitimately based on legal grounds and legal arguments. There was no wiseguy stuff, no rough stuff.

"And I think Tony was genuinely interested in my family. He gave my daughter a little matchstick necklace with a ruby at the end and she really cherished that. We always had a good time.

"We were back in Chicago after the M&M case and Tony and Nancy and Carolyn and I went to see Freddy Bell and the Belltones. At the time, Nancy Spilotro was an animal activist. She wasn't feeling any pain that night and she saw a woman wearing a rabbit-pelted coat. Nancy was never one to shrink or run away from a situation. She was very vocal, especially when she had a little booze in her. And she just started crying, 'That poor little rabbit,' over and over again. And we were laughing."

No tears were shed that night for Billy McCarthy, Jimmy Miraglia, Red Klim, Jerry Dellmann, Marty Buccieri, Tamara Rand, Jerry Lisner, those who came before, and those to come.

12

The Rise and Fall of
Mr. Frank Rosenthal

With its 24-hour action and freestanding legal sports books, sun-baked Las Vegas must have looked like heaven to Frank Rosenthal when he moved there, just ahead of the law, from Chicago by way of Florida in 1967. Las Vegas was the ultimate juice town and Rosenthal had built-in contacts in the sports-betting fraternity. For a man with a keen eye for a bet, a reputation as a fixer and for being one of the best handicappers in the country, and connections with the Chicago Outfit, Las Vegas had the makings of the Promised Land.

But controversy, law-enforcement scrutiny, and the occasional arrest on gambling charges followed Rosenthal wherever he went. Like Jimmy Chagra, he was incapable of doing anything quietly. Personal protestations aside, he'd long since become a name in the shadowy netherworld of sports betting and by the time he arrived in Southern Nevada, he was well-known to police and the FBI. Although Las Vegas was a place where many men with notorious pasts had managed to shed their rap sheets like snake skin and reinvent themselves as legal and respectable businessmen, Lefty Rosenthal would not be one of them.

He'd been in town less than a week before his first encounter with officers of the Metropolitan Police Department's brutish but effective organized-crime squad known as the Task Force. The men who comprised the Task Force were a mixture of linebacker-sized thumpers and skilled undercover operatives who had the place wired. When a wiseguy set foot in the city, they knew about it within 24 hours. Any hoodlum whose profile was likely to cause Las Vegas a public-relations problem was left with a simple decision: Leave Southern Nevada on the next flight out of McCarran Airport or face the consequences. The consequences, local legend held, were of the most serious sort. Every man on the force was fiercely loyal to Sheriff Ralph Lamb, the most powerful politician in Southern Nevada, who ruled Clark County with an iron hand.

But Frank Rosenthal was something of a fighter himself. He'd been arrested many times and was unimpressed with the cops' crude methods. Over the years, he'd managed to make his way through a treacherous world without taking a felony conviction. He pleaded no contest in 1961 to attempting to bribe a college basketball player in North Carolina and had appeared before the McClellan Subcommittee on organized-crime's influence in gambling. Although Rosenthal was believed to have fixed numerous sporting events and operated under the intimidating hand of the mob, he was no felon and, therefore, had it in his head that when he moved to Las Vegas to make a fresh start, he would be treated like a legitimate citizen. He was wrong.

Rosenthal spent his days at the Rose Bowl Sports Book and his nights on the Strip cocktail circuit, hanging his hat at the Tropicana and making a second home at Caesars Palace. It was during one of his late-night forays that he met statuesque blonde and former showgirl-turned-chip hustler Geri McGee, whom he later married. In time, Frank and Geri Rosenthal were sighted mixing with casino bosses and the legal set, what passed for elite society in Las Vegas in the '60s.

When Rosenthal, Elliot Paul Price, and others found themselves in the middle of a federal sports-gambling investigation, Lefty called on Goodman for help. During the course of the case, Goodman missed a deadline for filing a document. It was a mistake made by most young lawyers and many experienced ones, but Goodman faced a dilemma: If he kept quiet, he would almost surely be able to bluff his way past his clients, who were not lawyers and didn't have a full appreciation for the rules of procedure. Or he could tell the truth and face whatever consequences accompanied the admission. He opted for the truth.

"I told Rosenthal about my mistake and he said, 'No problem, as long as you told me. Never lie to me.'"

But didn't Goodman perceive that as a threat?

"It wasn't a physical threat," he said. "It was more of a reminder that he could always go use Percy Foreman, Mike Tigar, or Bennett Williams" — competing defense lawyers who'd take Lefty's money.

Other Las Vegans weren't as kind to Rosenthal, whose reputation for arrogance was surpassed only by his propensity for menacing and degrading underlings. He quickly became known as a big-league ball-buster who demanded absolute loyalty and perfection in the work place.

His notoriety and profile grew considerably in 1974 when he emerged as an executive consultant to Argent's Allen Glick, the upstart "instant" Chairman of the Board of Nevada's biggest gaming company, brought to life like Dr. Frankenstein's monster by millions of dollars in low-interest loans from the Teamsters Central States Pension Fund. Glick was named B'nai Brith's Man of the Year and was the visible and quotable young phenom who projected Argent's image as both the largest and fastest-growing casino company in the city. Standing directly behind (and sometimes in front of) Glick was Rosenthal, who wielded infinite power in the casino and increasingly made management decisions without consulting the chairman. Stardust insiders began to notice that Rosenthal couldn't stand for Glick to receive credit that Lefty believed was his own due. Years before Rosenthal finally was forced out of Las Vegas, his ego was already getting the best of him. Law enforcement would get the rest of him.

"I had no idea what I was involved in," Goodman said. "I had no idea the mob ran those casinos until I listened to the tapes. Up to that point, I always thought Glick was the one in charge. To me Rosenthal was as he portrayed himself, even though when they were together, it was clear that Glick was intimidated by Rosenthal's presence. He definitely paid deference to Rosenthal. Rosenthal had an aura about him.

"In retrospect, it's obvious to me Glick had to have been a part of the whole deal. No question about it. There's no way he could not have known what was going on. He was not a dope. And look at the deal he cut. He walked away from a massive organized-crime skimming operation with millions of dollars and today lives like a country gentleman in San Diego. If I'd known then what I know now, I would have been able to take money with both fists instead of being on a monthly retainer. But my sixth sense of staying clear of trouble kicked in and I didn't get more heavily involved."

Similar to the ownership points Goodman had been suspected of being offered in the old Bingo Palace—a casino operation that state Gaming Control Board investigators linked to mob ownership—the same deal was available to him at the Argent Corporation casinos. It was an offer he could refuse.

Rosenthal fought to obtain a gaming work card in 1974, but licensure as a key employee included an intense background check, with special attention paid to an applicant's friends and associations. That, simply, was Rosenthal's problem: Many men with worse criminal records than his worked in the casino racket, but Lefty's life-long friendships and business associations with men such as Tony Spilotro and Chicago Outfit lieutenant Fifi Buccieri created a seemingly insurmountable obstacle. His claims of legitimacy were falling on deaf ears.

He won a temporary reprieve when the Nevada Supreme Court partially concurred with District Judge and Rosenthal friend Joseph Pavlikowski's ruling that the Nevada Gaming Commission's decision had been hasty and, therefore, unconstitutional. Subsequently, the Nevada Supreme Court ruled that minor sections of the Nevada Gaming Commission regulations were unconstitutional, because they deprived Frank Rosenthal of his work card "without prior notice and an opportunity to be heard."

Then, after the state Legislature, in response to the Supreme Court's decision, passed a law mandating that anyone found unsuitable for a gaming license could not be employed or have a contract with a casino licensee, except as an entertainer, the ever-creative Rosenthal re-emerged at the Stardust as Food and

Beverage Director, then Entertainment Director.

And entertain he did, with a positively surreal weekly Vegas television chat program called "The Frank Rosenthal Show!"

"It was the worst show in the history of shows, but in those days everybody watched it before they went out Saturday night," Goodman recalled. "They wanted to know what Frank was going to say about the Gaming Control Board and they wanted to laugh. It was a completely Vegas program. There were the Lido girls, Barbara Beverly and Kim Cornell, Henry Shed on the piano, Denise Clemente at the microphone. It was an adult 'Arthur Godfrey Show.'"

Or, perhaps, a Vegas version of *Guys & Dolls*. Mob bookmakers Joey Boston and Marty Kane, who at the time worked for Rosenthal in the Stardust when they weren't laying off pieces of the action to illegal bookmakers from coast to coast, made regular appearances on the show. Although Frank Sinatra made an appearance, Rosenthal's guests ran more toward Frankie Valli and O.J. Simpson. Rosenthal delivered over-the-top accolades and below-the-belt criticism. But nothing he said during his slice of Vegas television history could save his future in the gaming industry. He was on his way out.

The press and TV-land fans might have had a chuckle over Rosenthal's performances, but the state's gaming regulatory authorities were not amused. The FBI, Metro, and Gaming Control investigators all believed Rosenthal was the Chicago mob's inside man at Argent Corporation and that Glick was a glorified front man. In June 1978, Rosenthal was called forward yet again for licensure as a key employee.

Goodman sued again, seeking an injunction and a judicial review of the state gaming regulations that enabled the Control Board and Gaming Commission to deprive Rosenthal of his due-process rights. In typical fashion, Goodman shouted that the government was perpetrating an unconstitutional sham and argued that it was wrong to take away Rosenthal's job without a hearing.

Goodman twice took Rosenthal's issues to the Ninth U.S. Circuit Court of Appeals, which on May 6, 1981, dismissed his case against Nevada's gaming regulators. The decision effectively defined the state's right, through the apparatus of the Gaming Control Board and Gaming Commission, to regulate employees in a privileged and licensed industry without the level of due process afforded persons accused of criminal acts. Rosenthal was going down fast.

§ § §

Frank Rosenthal's next super-heated fight with the state came when he was nominated for inclusion on Nevada's List of Excluded Persons, more commonly known as the Black Book. But by then, he had greater worries on his mind, and his increasing inability to control his anger manifested in public outbursts. At one point, he all but accused then-Gaming Commission Chairman Harry Reid of betraying an off-the-record promise to him. Every epithet and threat made sensational news copy, but only continued to sink Rosenthal in political quicksand.

Most observers knew that Lefty was doomed, but he himself appeared not to recognize the fact. He struggled mightily against being inscribed in the Black Book, a fate from which no one had ever escaped. But Rosenthal was not like most other nominees, men who through criminal conviction and media exposure had become so notorious that they didn't bother to forestall the inevitable. This man was determined to maintain his status as a legitimate wiseguy in Las Vegas and Goodman took his battle back to the Ninth U.S. Circuit Court of Appeals for a third time.

One of Rosenthal's most vocal advocates was Dean Shendal, a long-time Las Vegas casino man with a reputation as one of the toughest men ever to walk the streets of Las Vegas. Shendal had been suspected of being a hitman and maintaining ties to top organized-crime figures, including Chicago's Sam Giancana and Anthony Salerno. To this day, he remains a favorite of Oscar Goodman.

"Dean Shendal is a great man and a priceless Las Vegas character with the kind of personal courage you don't find in many men," Goodman said. "This guy, pound for pound, might be the toughest man with two fists that I've ever met. He agreed to testify at one of Rosenthal's hearings. Dean was a gaming licensee and, at that time, owned his own slot machine company. He had his own reputation as a guy with certain connections, but he flew up to Carson on his own dime to testify before the Gaming Control Board. He gave Rosenthal accolades and vouched for his character.

"At one point, one of the Board members made the mistake of asking Dean who was paying him. Well, when someone questioned his personal integrity, he grew livid. He said, 'You sons of bitches! Nobody pays for my testimony. I'm telling the truth.' He turned around, walked out, got on a plane, and flew back to Las Vegas.

"You see, I don't think Dean Shendal would have come forward, and risked what he risked by coming forward, had he really known that the Stardust was mob-controlled. Dean was very savvy. If anyone on the street knew what was going on behind the scenes, it would've been him. And he wouldn't have gone near that hearing out of a concern for losing his own license. Everyone knew about the Stardust and the other casinos after the wiretaps were unsealed. Then the facade fell apart. But up to that point, it was a pretty good facade."

It can be difficult for outsiders, or anyone who relies on such extravagances as a solid legal footing or simple logic, to comprehend the caprice and hypocrisy of the Gaming Control process. The greatest sin in Nevada hasn't so much been mob association or, in the case of top politicians in the state, accepting lavish favors from mob-controlled resorts. Rather, it was betraying the state's mob secrets by attracting undue attention. For a city built from the desert sands upon a foundation of hype and bluster, the best profile for a casino man has always been a low profile.

To better understand Rosenthal's precarious place in Las Vegas history, it's essential to appreciate the events that swirled around him. First, his trusted position with the mob was on shaky ground. Second, his public comments were getting increasingly caustic and irresponsible—no friend of Anthony Accardo or Nick Civella had his own television talk show. And third, the FBI had learned that Spilotro, his life-long friend, was having an affair with Geri Rosenthal, who was flaunting the arrangement.

Worse than that, in Kansas City, the Civella crime family decided Rosenthal was far too friendly with the FBI. After all, for all the legal trouble the bosses were finding themselves in,

Rosenthal had not been touched. That was all the proof men of the caliber of Civella and Frank Balistrieri needed to label Rosenthal a snitch.

At one point, Civella contacted Goodman and asked him, "Is he crazy?"

"No, I don't think he's crazy," Goodman replied.

Later, at Nick Civella's racketeering trial, FBI Special Agent Gary Hart, in a damning indictment of Goodman's alleged role within organized crime, asserted that Civella's use of the term "crazy" was actually a code word. He was in fact asking the attorney whether Rosenthal could no longer be trusted and therefore needed to be eliminated permanently.

"The FBI agent who testified said that if I had agreed with Civella, Rosenthal would have been killed," Goodman said. "I didn't know it at the time, but I apparently saved his life."

But was Rosenthal a snitch?

Rosenthal vehemently denies it and Goodman seems to back him up.

"There are snitches and then there are snitches," Goodman said. "There is such a thing as a dry snitch, a person who talks to the FBI or police, but doesn't necessarily say anything. I think Frank Rosenthal enjoyed playing with people in power. He played with Phil Hanifin, Bob List, and Harry Reid via Jay Brown. I think a lot of people played the game with him. But did he sit down and say, 'Make a deal for me not to be prosecuted'? I don't think so. I think he'd been through too much in his life to become a rat."

? ? ?

Frank Rosenthal's relationship with Tony Spilotro and the rest of the mob went south for good on the evening of October 4, 1982, moments after Rosenthal finished having dinner at Tony Roma's on East Sahara with bookmaking pals Marty Kane, Stanley Green, and Ruby Goldstein. Rosenthal walked across the parking lot, got into his Cadillac Eldorado, turned the ignition, and the world erupted before him. Flames engulfed the car. Then the Cadillac was rocked a second time. Only luck saved Lefty. The bomb had been planted under a steel plate welded to the bottom of the luxury car. The plate deflected the impact of the initial blast and Rosenthal was knocked clear before the second explosion.

"I thought Lefty was dead for sure," Marty Kane said in a rare interview. "He was still steaming when I got to him. His head was smoking and his hair was burned off. He was stunned, but he was also mad as hell. He asked me to get him a doctor, but he was more concerned that his kids knew he was all right than anything. And he never said he thought Tony was behind it."

"From the look of the car, you never would have believed there was any way anyone could have survived," said Metro detective Don Dibble, who arrived on the scene shortly after the explosion.

Attention immediately focused on Spilotro, the perfect suspect, given that he was having an affair with the victim's wife. On the other hand, it was clear that Tony and Lefty were no longer on speaking terms and even the murderous Spilotro would be expected to have had better sense than to invite such unwanted attention by blowing up Frank Rosenthal's Cadillac in the middle of Las Vegas.

"Here is where I was again naive about what was happening with him," Goodman said. "Tony, whom I saw nearly every day in my office, never said one thing about Rosenthal to me that was ever insulting. And vice versa. You would think if they had a blood feud going or there was an affair going on, they would have been sniping at each other. But nothing. They never said a bad word about each other.

"And I had no knowledge of the relationship with the wives. I was over at Rosenthal's home all the time, even during the time he was supposedly having all his trouble with Geri and Tony. He worked out of his home. It was his office. Geri treated him like a king.

"Frank and I weren't talking much at that time, but after the bombing, I went over to his house. He looked like a plucked duck, sitting there with his hair burned off and lots of cuts and stitches. As the years have passed, people have tried to say Tony was responsible for bombing Rosenthal. All I can say is, it was absolutely not his style. He would have been able to arrange a meeting with Rosenthal. Not in the deepest recesses of my mind did I suspect Spilotro had something to do with it."

Although no one was ever arrested for attempting to assassinate Rosenthal, the local-police consensus was that Spilotro was behind the bombing. But, as Goodman insists, the method simply didn't fit Spilotro's modus operandi.

It was, however, the signature of mob families throughout the Midwest. Car bombings were common in Kansas City, Cleveland, and Milwaukee, the murder method of choice of Milwaukee crime boss Frank Balistrieri, who ended up serving a lengthy prison sentence, in part due to Rosenthal's inability to keep the Argent house in order. In fact, Balistrieri was known in organized-crime circles as the "Mad Bomber" and federal wiretap surveillance recorded him blaming Rosenthal for the family's troubles. Mere weeks before the Rosenthal bombing, he told his sons Joseph and John Balistrieri that he would exact a measure of "full satisfaction" from Lefty. And Frank Balistrieri—known as a man with a hatred for underlings who maintained a high profile—always meant business.

Although Nick Civella suffered from terminal lung cancer, his previous question of Goodman—was Rosenthal crazy?—reverberated with a deeper meaning in the wake of the bombing. Of course, Goodman would never admit as much to the FBI or Metro Police, who had tormented him for the better part of two decades. He'd let them find their own suspects.

Mob snitch Frank Cullotta speculated, in Nicholas Pileggi's *Casino: Love and Honor in Las Vegas*, that Geri Rosenthal's drug-dealing biker pals in Southern California were likely responsible for the attempt on Frank Rosenthal's life. With Lefty out of the way, Geri might have made a sizable score from the estate.

Despite all the evidence to the contrary, Metro's Intelligence cops named Spilotro as their chief suspect. Trouble was, their chronology was wrong and they failed to see the bigger picture. Frank had filed for divorce on September 11, 1980, more than two years earlier. The danger of a liaison between Tony and Geri was not that it would set off a battle among local hoodlums, but that it would signal the bosses once and for all that the men they'd sent to handle business in Las Vegas were incapable of doing the job and had to be replaced.

As multiple federal investigations of the hidden ownership and casino skimming at the Argent resorts and the Tropicana began to unfold, the suspicions of the bosses proved more than justified.

Rosenthal had been fortunate to survive the car bombing with cuts, bruises, and burns. Geri Rosenthal wasn't so lucky. On November 6, 1982, only a month after the attempted hit on her ex-husband, Geri Rosenthal was found near dead of a drug overdose at the Beverly Sunset Motel on Sunset Boulevard. She died three days later. Although a coroner ruled her death accidental, she had courted disaster for more than two years by bragging about her illicit affair with Spilotro, as well as about the off-the-record business that took place at the Stardust and other casinos not-so-secretly run by the mob.

Just 10 weeks later, on January 20, 1983, embattled Teamsters Central States Pension Fund fixer Allen Dorfman—another man who liked to brag about his position in organized crime—was shot to death in a parking lot outside a Chicago restaurant. Dorfman had faced a lengthy prison sentence for racketeering, which in turn made him vulnerable to a government offer to testify against his long-time benefactors in exchange for leniency. He never got the chance.

Even Joe Agosto, the Sicilian-born "Cleveland native," failed to make it to trial as a mob turncoat after seeing the writing on the wall from the Rosenthal and Dorfman outcomes. Under the obvious threat of assassination at the hands of the Civella family, Agosto agreed to cooperate with the FBI and enter the Federal Witness Protection Program. But after blowing open the hidden ownership of the Tropicana and Argent hotels and nailing numerous high-profile Las Vegas developers and casino executives for their long-time mob associations and business contacts, Agosto died of a heart attack that August.

Whether the deaths were from homicide, suicide, or natural causes, it wasn't looking good for Argent Corporation insiders.

But what of the mouthpiece who had represented the corporation, Spilotro, Rosenthal, and even Agosto?

It's logical to presume that Goodman's life also hung in the balance as the violent and increasingly paranoid mob bosses attempted to clean up their mess the old-fashioned way, by eliminating potential witnesses.

Goodman denies he was ever threatened or nervous during those desperate days — despite the fact that FBI agents, Organized Crime Strike Force prosecutors, and Metro Police investigators all believed he was a trusted *consigliere* to a network of mob families who were behind the Argent and Tropicana skims. Instead, he insists that Spilotro took care to keep him separated from conversations that might complicate the attorney-client relationship.

Rosenthal didn't want to believe it then, but he had busted out of Las Vegas for good. And what, finally, happened to the bookmaker-entertainment director-TV star who had barely escaped with his life?

Life after Lefty didn't improve fortunes at the Stardust. In early 1983, Gaming Control Board investigators uncovered what they believed was a new casino skimming operation and peeled back another layer of the resort's ownership. Rosenthal moved his two children to upscale Laguna Niguel, California, and watched an unprecedented storm sweep over Las Vegas and the casino industry.

13

A Family in Decline

On March 12, 1983, about the time Rosenthal was moving into his high-security Southern California enclave, Nick Civella, patriarch of the Kansas City outfit, succumbed to lung cancer. Civella's personal health mirrored that of his family, or *brugad*. He was serving a four-year sentence for conspiring to bribe a Fort Worth prison warden to gain a favorable transfer for his nephew, Anthony "Tony Ripe" Civella, in what had become known as the "diamante cinco grosso case" when he became ill. Though Civella was still under indictment in the Tropicana casino skim, the cancer diagnosis rendered that situation moot. The heart, soul, and brains of the Kansas City mob gained a compassionate early release, but he died only two weeks later.

Civella was a charter member of Nevada's Black Book of persons banned from entering casinos, along with notorious gangsters such as Marshall Caifano. Not that it stopped him from showing up. He wielded considerable influence at the Tropicana and the Argent casinos, while simultaneously keeping an iron hand on the Teamsters Central States Pension Fund through his personal puppet, union president Roy Williams. Civella traveled to Las Vegas often. Wearing a wig and beard, he stayed at the Tropicana and Dunes hotels and was treated like royalty right under the noses of state Gaming Control Board agents. In a rare 1970 interview, Civella scoffed at law-enforcement's claim that he was a mob boss.

"I even deny, to my knowledge, that organized crime exists in Kansas City," he told a reporter.

Likewise, Oscar Goodman's response in interviews was to deny by omission the existence of an underworld crisis in Las Vegas or an organized underworld at all. He always described Nick Civella in almost endearing terms. Without ever acknowledging he knew intimate details of the family's criminal activities, Goodman was deeply impressed by Nick's knowledge of the law, philosophy, and literature. But there were times his association with the Civella family became a bit unsettling.

"I remember one time going out to eat in Kansas City with Carl DeLuna, Tony Civella, and his father Carl," Goodman said. "It was a little restaurant in a mall and the waitress seated us. I was in a booth with the window behind me. And Carl says, 'No, you never sit with your back to a window.' And he meant it. All the things that people find so intriguing in the movies, these men took very seriously. In their lives, they had lost friends who had made such a mistake.

"The [Civella] brothers were all different, but they treated me very well. Anyone who knows me knows I'm a sports fan, and from Philadelphia, so when the Phillies played the Kansas City Royals in the World Series, Nick Civella came up with tickets for me. Despite what the government believed about him, Nick did not live extravagantly. Most of my clients, for whatever reason, perhaps tax or other reasons, had very ordinary lifestyles. They didn't drive big cars. They lived in row houses, in neighborhoods where they had their power. Very few were flashy. John Gotti was an exception. The other ones were sort of quiet fellas. The modern-day ones like Nick want people to feel their presence.

"Everyone thinks I'm the richest guy in the world because I represent them. They figure these guys have more money than God. I'm not saying they don't pay, but they certainly don't pay as much as a physician who's in trouble and needs Oscar Goodman. Or a lawyer who's in trouble or a corporation that's in trouble. Their payment takes various forms.

"For instance, here's how I met Tommy Lasorda, the former Dodgers manager and a fine guy. I'm at the World Series in Kansas City. I'm sitting in the first row and he's sitting in the fifteenth. He's the manager of the Los Angeles Dodgers and I have better seats than him. He sees me and I hand him my card. Oscar who? He wants to know. I'm in the first row because, as a perk, Nick Civella got me six tickets, right behind home plate. Not a lot of guys could do that.

"You want to go to a show or a restaurant in any city? You're in New York and you can't get into a particular place for months in advance? You call up one of these fellas. I don't have to give the maitre d' three hundred bucks when I sit down. I don't have to give him anything. I do, because I like to be generous, but everything's always taken care of for you. I don't know how they do it."

¶ ¶ ¶

The Civellas were legends in Kansas City and a popular subject in the press, generating more than 150 news articles between the 1960s and early 1980s. Whether or not the mob existed, there was no denying that the Civellas' formidable influence stretched from Kansas City to the Las Vegas Strip. The government had the tapes to prove it.

Civella's novel plan to beat FBI telephone wiretaps by hiding under the cloak of attorney-client privilege — he and trusted lieutenant Carl DeLuna made a habit of using their lawyers' offices for meetings and important calls — was shattered by an FBI bug planted at the Kansas City law offices of Quinn & Peoples. The wiretap captured 54 phone calls from Civella in a single day as he conducted the family's business. Those taps, along with the bug planted in the home of Civella relative Josephine Marlo, gave the FBI a graduate course in the way the mob did business.

Monikers flew like confetti in the Kansas City investigation. Nick Civella was "Mr. Zio" and "Uncle," his nephew Anthony was "Tony Ripe," brother Carl was "Cork," DeLuna was "Tuffy," Rosenthal "Crazy," Glick "Genius," and another Nevada politician was "Our Bobby." For his part, Goodman was referred to on tape as "Senior."

Teamsters President Roy Williams didn't merit a nickname, but the press labeled him the "kept man" of the Civella family. After agreeing to cooperate with the government, Williams admitted selling out his union brotherhood and his vote as a trustee on the Central States Pension Fund for $1,500 a month from the mob from 1974 to 1981.

The tapes turned Nevada's much-hyped system of casino regulation into little more than a bedroom farce. "These defendants have dealt a severe blow to the credibility of the state and the industry and have made a mockery of the Nevada regulatory procedures," federal prosecutors wrote in their memorandum to U.S. District Judge Joseph Stevens in the Civellas' trial over hidden ownership in Las Vegas casinos. The Civella family "virtually ran a major casino from Kansas City."

The tapes raised the specter of political corruption at the highest levels of Nevada's gaming regulatory system when Agosto was recorded making a reference to a "Mr. Clean Face," speaking of then-Gaming Commission Chairman Harry Reid, who could fix all their troubles. Although Rosenthal accused Reid and even Nevada Governor Robert List of double-dealing, an investigation established no credible evidence that either man had acted inappropriately.

Goodman remained adamant that he'd declined to socialize with the boys from Kansas City, but one source close to Goodman recalled a time Nick Civella joined Goodman for a private dinner. It was a minor exception to his long-held rule. Years later, Goodman remembered Civella's Las Vegas excursion only as a dinner meeting between attorney and client. There were many such meetings in the wake of the November 5, 1981, federal indictment charging Nick Civella and 10 other men with 17 felony counts related to the casino skim at the Tropicana.

Although U.S. District Judge Joseph Stevens was hardly empathetic to the needs of the defense, in December 1982, he did delay the start of the Kansas City case to accommodate Goodman's representation of Jimmy Chagra in the assassination of John Wood. In doing so, he showed an uncommon respect for the lawyer and the system.

Still, the defendants were dead from Judge Stevens' first gavel. Joe Agosto, the little man with the funny hat who had appeared to Goodman and all the world as nothing more than a delivery driver and semi-skilled producer of the *Folies Bergére*, returned to haunt the mob as a key government witness. Agosto's information, combined with the tapes recorded at Josephine Marlo's house, boxed in the mobsters and their minions. The prosecution showed convincingly that from January 1, 1975, to April 1, 1979, the period covered in the indictment, the Tropicana operated under the hidden influence of the Kansas City mob. Agosto was the Civella clan's overseer. Veteran casino man Carl Thomas designed the skim, which was carried out by Tropicana employees Donald Shepard, Billy Caldwell, Jay Gould, and others.

The Tropicana skim was almost quaint by modern Las Vegas standards. For all the trouble the Kansas City mob got into over the Tropicana skim, a white-collar crime, the total distribution was bush league compared to today's gambling economy and the paper-bag system of payouts was downright comical. By October 1978, Shepard, Caldwell, and Gould were siphoning about $40,000 per month in untaxed cash profits and funneling it to Kansas City through a series of couriers: Agosto to Kansas City residents Carl Caruso and Charles Moretina, who handed it personally to the Civellas, who then chopped it up and sent cash packets to Chicago mob titan Joseph Aiuppa and underboss Jackie Cerone.

That $40,000 represented the best of times at the Tropicana. When business was slow, the monthly take was less than half that amount and by the time the cash trickled down, the Mafia kingpins received little more than walking-around money. When the Tropicana fell on hard times, Agosto was compelled to make up the difference by contributing his own savings to the skim.

Meanwhile, one of the most underhanded business moves in the history of the casino racket occurred at the Tropicana when chemical-plant heiress Mitzi Stauffer Briggs was persuaded to invest millions in the resort as a "part owner." Agosto was the key insider who gained Briggs' confidence. She was charmed by his thick accent, romantic attentions, and apparent knowledge of hotel operations and the casino business. She couldn't have placed her trust in a worse person than Agosto, who was funneling as much cash as he could to the

Midwest. Briggs eventually went bankrupt and later was sighted in Las Vegas working at a hotel gift shop.

Then came what would later be remembered as the Las Vegas version of the St. Valentine's Day Massacre. On February 14, 1979, coordinated searches were conducted at several key Kansas City suspects' homes. It was the same day $80,000 in casino skim found its way to Kansas City. The FBI had the money from Las Vegas, proof in itself of hidden ownership. They also uncovered a diary filled with code names and meticulously recorded expenses at Carl DeLuna's home.

DeLuna, an otherwise savvy criminal, had done the unthinkable: He'd reduced to paper the cash flow of the Tropicana skim—right down to the penny. That included his own personal expenses for the smallest items. Knowing that confusion led to mistrust and mistrust led to an early grave, he'd gone out of his way to make sure none of his peers could ever say he was a less than honest mobster.

DeLuna's "honesty" cost him dearly.

At trial, Goodman was assisted by attorney David Chesnoff, whose eyes were opened to the high stakes his senior partner played as a mouthpiece for the mob.

The Civella brothers of Kansas City took a genuine liking to Oscar Goodman. DeLuna, the family's top lieutenant, hung on his every word. They appreciated him so much that when he flew back to Kansas City for the clan's many legal proceedings, the family made sure their favorite attorney was comfortable, safe, and well-fed—but always with his back to the wall.

? ? ?

While Nick Civella languished in prison, Goodman helped fight to sever his trial from the rest of the Tropicana defendants. He effectively persuaded the government to write off its pursuit of the man, who was dying of lung cancer at a time Agosto, too, was almost too sick to appear at trial. It was a race between the Grim Reaper and the government to see which would get the Kansas City mob first.

One by one the rest of the defendants fell. Nick Civella avoided prosecution the hard way, by succumbing to cancer. Charges against two of the 11 defendants were dismissed before trial.

Defendants Donald Shepard, Billy Clinton Caldwell, and Joe Agosto cut deals. Bingo Palace and Slots A Fun owner Carl Thomas, who'd set up the skim at the Tropicana and advised on the skim at the Argent casinos, sent shock waves through the city when he was indicted as a long-time mob front man.

At trial, a physically failing Agosto described his rise to power inside the Tropicana. He told the jury, "The cage is the heart of the hotel. You control the cage, you control the entire money operation of the hotel. I acted like I was owner of the hotel. I was in charge of the day-to-day operation. I took that authority on myself. Mr. Civella congratulated me for having the ability to establish a bridgehead in the Tropicana Hotel. He instructed me then it was about time I started to do something for him and to initiate the skimming. He hadn't received any skim money from me yet. He expected me to proceed. The agreement was that the stealing would not exceed $50,000 a month. I established the limit not to be over $50,000 — they had much bigger aims."

Agosto also testified that he secretly contacted Nick Civella in an attempt to quiet Frank Rosenthal, either by oral directive or the old-fashioned way. Rosenthal's TV show, incessant news conferences, and inflammatory style increased the already-intense heat on Agosto and the Kansas City owners. At one point, Agosto told DeLuna that Rosenthal was an informant who would "bite the hand that feeds him" in order to avoid prosecution.

"The guy is dead," DeLuna told Agosto.

"Evidently, Mr. Civella did not succeed in taming him, but that does not mean he didn't try," Agosto told the court, perhaps alluding to the car bomb that nearly killed Rosenthal.

Goodman managed to fluster Agosto on cross-examination, at one point getting him to admit he had twice lied to Nevada gaming regulators about whether he'd admitted to Briggs, his paramour and Tropicana investor, that he was stealing from her casino, but the damage was done.

The Carls — Thomas, DeLuna, Civella — along with Charles Moretina and Anthony Chiavola, Sr., were convicted by the all-woman jury. DeLuna, the loyal underboss and meticulous notekeeper, was slammed on 13 counts for a total of 30 years. Thomas was sentenced to 15 years in prison, but agreed to cooperate in a limited fashion. He saw his sentence reduced to two years and the charges against him in the pending Argent case were dropped entirely. "He made sure he didn't say anything that would hurt the family," one long-time mob insider said. "He took care of people." The information Thomas provided the government managed not to harm DeLuna or any member of his friends in the Civella family.

? ? ?

Agosto died soon after of a heart attack. (In mob lore, Agosto is believed by some senior organized-crime figures to have faked his death and been sent into hiding by his federal protectors. No evidence of this has ever been made public.)

Although Goodman represented DeLuna in the Tropicana trial, that representation had become an incredible tangle of legal conflicts. Prosecutors commonly filed numerous motions to force his disqualification. But Goodman's presence was essential, not only for the fierce advocacy he provided at trial, but for his institutional knowledge of all the players and their crimes. Outside the courtroom, the FBI continued to privately suspect that he had held more than an attorney's status with the Civellas. Inside, prosecutors focused on Goodman's representation of nearly every major player in the Tropicana and Argent cases. At one time or another he'd been retained by Nick, Carl, and Tony Civella, DeLuna, Thomas, Glick, Agosto, Spilotro, and Rosenthal.

The conflict finally did hamstring Goodman in the Argent casino skim case, indictments for which were unsealed while the Kansas City trial was still going on.

The FBI was already hearing reports that the devastated Civella family was seeking assistance from long-time business associates in the Chicago Outfit. But by then, the Chicago mob had plenty of its own problems to contend with. Tony Spilotro had dug a hole for himself that threatened not only his life, but the lives of those closest to him. One of those close associates was his favorite attorney.

Not that Goodman had much time to worry. His long-time friend and one-time mentor, U.S. District Judge Harry E. Claiborne, had entered the fight of his life and wanted Oscar Goodman at his side.

14

The Trouble with Harry

E ven those who knew and loved him had their doubts as to whether outspoken defense attorney Harry E. Claiborne possessed the temperament to be a U.S. District Judge. Appointed for life, federal judges are known for their august demeanors and imperious ways. Many are black-robed prosecutors and only a handful have gained their appointments after a career spent representing accused killers, gamblers, and income-tax evaders. Claiborne was definitely in the minority.

Although his parents stressed the importance of education, Harry Claiborne came from humble Arkansas roots. A celebrated storyteller, Claiborne was fond of the true tale of how his father had once backed down the Grand Dragon of the Ku Klux Klan of MacCrae County, Arkansas, and had prevented a lynching of a black sharecropper. He was equally proud of how his mother, who taught school for 42 years, had stood up for integration during the 1950s in racially divided Arkansas.

That progressive independent streak was handed down to rail-slim Harry. During World War II as an Air Force military policeman stationed in Santa Monica, California, he balked at rounding up Japanese citizens bound for internment camps. He was subsequently transferred to Las Vegas and the future home of Nellis Air Force Base. Claiborne made Las Vegas his home after the war.

He began practicing law in Las Vegas in 1946, dabbled mostly unsuccessfully in politics, and gained a reputation as a superb defense attorney who filled a courtroom with theatrics and country charm. Claiborne met Oscar Goodman not long after the young Philadelphian and his bride arrived in Las Vegas in 1964. Goodman fondly recalled watching Claiborne work the courtroom as if it were his own personal stage.

Within a few years, the two began working cases together. They represented Frank Rosenthal on work-card issues, former Metro Intelligence detective Joe Blasko — one of Anthony Spilotro's guys inside the police department — in a beating case, and child-molester Lawrence Arvey, who left the country after winning a post-conviction bail release thanks to his two attorneys.

Claiborne began representing Mustang Ranch brothel baron Joe Conforte in the mid-1960s and won an acquittal for him on white-slavery charges in 1968. Claiborne and Goodman later unsuccessfully defended Conforte and his wife Sally on income-tax-evasion charges.

United States Senator Howard Cannon employed Claiborne to help oversee a controversial recount in his 1964 race against Paul Laxalt, which ended with Cannon winning re-election by just 48 votes. In 1978, Cannon chose Claiborne to fill a vacancy on the U.S. District Court bench and used his considerable clout to shepherd his nomination through the Senate.

Blessed with the gift of understatement, Claiborne donned the robe of a federal judge on September 1, 1978, and offered, "I plead guilty to being colorful."

Less than two years later, the FBI was looking into Claiborne for allegedly enlisting private investigator Eddie LaRue to plant a listening device in the home of a former girlfriend. Although the suspicion was never proved, this action by the feds with the approval of new FBI Special Agent in Charge Joseph Yablonsky set the tone for a long series of future battles.

FBI boss Joseph Yablonsky made little secret of his contempt for Las Vegas and its corrupt good ol' boy political network, which included certain federal judicial appointees. He let it be known that the Bureau believed Claiborne's background investigation, conducted on all federal appointees, had been rushed through in the name of political expediency, helped along by high-ranking United States senators. Claiborne's long-time association with Dallas racket boss-turned-Las Vegas casino legend Lester "Benny" Binion, for example, had not been fully explored. To Yablonsky, Claiborne was a high-priced defense attorney who had the moral compass of an alley cat. The FBI man told associates that early on, his office began hearing rumors of Claiborne fixing cases that came before him.

Federal judges are appointed for life, but that doesn't mean the job is free of politics. For more than 30 years, Claiborne had been a fire-and-brimstone defense attorney who lived in the courtroom — not a well-heeled litigator, administrative-law specialist, or former federal prosecutor.

But it was Claiborne's liberal rulings from the bench, calls that made it clear he put the interests of Las Vegas before the law, which made him appear suspicious. In August 1979, Claiborne blocked an attempt to close the Aladdin casino, which had historically been the site of hidden ownership, mob association, and financial folly. He dismissed a firebombing conspiracy case against Culinary Union leader Ben Schmoutey for what he cited as a lack of evidence.

Then Claiborne released sealed FBI affidavits in the Tropicana casino skimming case, a decision that was overturned by the Ninth U.S. Circuit Court of Appeals. He followed that with a decision to throw out minor corruption charges against Teamsters Union official Rudy Tham, one of the men who had been instrumental in the funding of Las Vegas. Claiborne even interceded at the state level to come to the aid of his lawyer friends Peter Flangas and John T. Ross, when they faced a State Bar Association complaint.

Most of Claiborne's controversial cases in one way or another involved the clients of Oscar Goodman.

Claiborne was in trouble outside court as well. His personal finances were a shambles. Accustomed to earning a handsome six figures as a defense lawyer, he was forced to live on the $58,000 annual salary a federal judge received. By 1980, he was busted and contacting old friends for loans. Admitting he was in desperate financial straits, Claiborne also wrote a letter to a former client in an attempt to collect legal fees he'd earned before becoming a judge.

? ? ?

The former client was Joe Conforte, who had problems of his own.

Central Casting could not have come up with a more stereotypical pimp, political fixer, and exploiter of women than Mustang Ranch brothel owner Joe Conforte. He was a squat little man with a pencil-thin mustache, a thick Sicilian accent, and a Napoleon complex. Crime and political corruption was the sewage he wallowed in. Claiborne and Goodman had represented Conforte in his various legal entanglements, including a rapidly expanding Internal Revenue Service investigation that threatened to end his reign as Nevada's leading whoremaster.

In 1960, Conforte was convicted of extortion in Nevada and was sentenced to prison. A short time later, he pled guilty to federal income-tax evasion. At one point, Conforte had filed five years worth of tax returns without filling in such details as his gross income or personal deductions. He was released from McNeil Island federal prison in 1965.

Conforte was acquitted in 1968 on Mann Act charges (transporting women across a state line for prostitution purposes), but by 1970 he was back in court after the Internal Revenue Service filed a civil complaint calling for condemnation of several trailers used at the Mustang Ranch. Although he eventually prevailed in that case, too, Conforte had established himself over the prior decade as a criminal and tax scofflaw who was especially adept at endearing himself to Nevada politicians.

By the mid-'70s, Conforte and his wife, Sally, were again in federal court on tax-evasion charges. Convicted on four of 10 counts, Conforte's career and freedom appeared to be forfeit. Faced with a long prison term, the repayment of more than $15 million in back taxes, and the loss of the Mustang Ranch, Conforte fled to Mexico and then Brazil, where he lived like a prince instead of a pimp on the lam. From the comfort of his Brazilian hideaway, Conforte proceeded to cut one of the sweetest, and most outrageous, deals in the history of the Justice Department. In effect, Conforte was being given a free pass. He would have his tax debt forgiven. He would serve a minimal jail sentence, just 15 months on his income-tax conviction and, concurrently, up to 18 months for attempting to bribe former Lyon County District Attorney John Giomi. In return, Conforte agreed to provide testimony that Las Vegas Judge Harry Claiborne had solicited and received two bribes totaling $85,000.

According to Conforte's scenario, he paid Judge Claiborne $30,000 to quash subpoenas in a pending income-tax case. The balance of the bribe was to advise Conforte when the Ninth Circuit was going to render its opinion on his appeal so that he could flee ahead of the law. The truth was that although Claiborne delayed issuing the subpoenas and failed to recuse himself from his former client's case—a move that in itself raised eyebrows—the subpoenas were eventually issued. The second bribe, Conforte alleged, came after Claiborne promised to overturn the pimp's tax conviction. The truth was that although the 20-year sentence was reduced on appeal to five years, the conviction was not overturned.

But the allegations and the truth were close enough for government work, and on December 8, 1983, U.S. District Judge Harry E. Claiborne was hit with a seven-count indictment for bribery, tax evasion, and lying on a federal judicial disclosure form. The charges stemmed largely from damaging information provided by Joe Conforte and, if convicted on all seven counts, Claiborne faced the possibility of a 39-year prison sentence and $121,000 in fines.

Leading Claiborne's defense was his close friend Oscar Goodman.

❡ ❡ ❡

It was clear from the outset that Claiborne, a Democratic administration appointee, would not receive much more than whispered moral support from Nevada's Congressional delegation. U.S. Senators Paul Laxalt and Chic Hecht, both Republicans, remained entirely in the background and GOP Congresswoman Barbara Vucanovich insisted that the Claiborne affair was best handled in the courts. Only Democratic Congressman Harry Reid, Frank Rosenthal's old nemesis from the Nevada Gaming Commission, attempted to intervene with FBI Director William Webster on Claiborne's behalf. Although Reid had hoped to get an opportunity to rebuke the actions of

Yablonsky and lobby against the sole use of Conforte as a prosecution witness, in the end his meeting with Webster was brief. Claiborne received no 11th-hour help from Washington.

In all, three separate federal grand juries would weigh evidence against Claiborne over a period of more than three years. One grand jury in Portland, Oregon, investigated an alleged bribe Claiborne received there as a visiting judge, but declined to indict.

During the grand jury proceedings, Claiborne refused to take a leave of absence from the bench, a move that only hardened the resolve of the FBI men and federal prosecutors who pursued him. What Claiborne considered to be the actions of an innocent man wrongly accused, they saw as the decisions of an arrogant man who believed he was above the law. Tendering his resignation and returning to private life was out of the question — even if it was a move many federal insiders believed might have saved him from facing felony charges. Claiborne was a wily veteran when it came to reading the legal landscape, but when it came to his own predicament — standing in the gunsights of the FBI and U.S. Attorney's office — he apparently failed to see the trouble he was in.

As the pressure mounted in the months before indictment, Claiborne remained true to form by openly criticizing government prosecutors, Internal Revenue Service agents, and the FBI. He called the Department of Justice's Organized Crime Strike Force prosecutors "rotten bastards" and "crooks" who only went after the "little fish" and were afraid to touch the criminal whales. He referred to Washoe County District Attorney Cal Dunlap as a "legal whore" and a "boy."

Goodman fought to prevent the bribery indictment from proceeding to trial in Reno's U.S. District Court before Judge Walter Hoffman. The trial venue had been moved from Las Vegas to Reno due to a sweeping one-sided campaign of support conducted by the *Las Vegas Sun* and its publisher, longtime Claiborne friend Hank Greenspun. The *Sun's* articles accused FBI SAC Joe Yablonsky and his men of government misconduct and the use of illegal means to indict Claiborne. Goodman was quoted in and appeared to be the source of most of those articles. He seemed to revel in the court of public opinion, as Greenspun and his investigative reporters, fed daily by private investigators working for Claiborne, wrote article after article raising the issue of FBI misconduct. Unsophisticated at dealing with an adversarial press, Yablonsky rose to the bait almost every time, generating still more front-page news stories and biting Greenspun editorials.

In an effort to stop Claiborne's slide toward infamy, Goodman generated dozens of motions and objections. He argued that Claiborne was a victim of selective prosecution. He argued that the confidential grand jury process had been hopelessly compromised. He argued in favor of unsealing the three grand juries that had considered evidence of wrongdoing on Claiborne's part.

? ? ?

Although Claiborne's allies at the *Las Vegas Sun* had printed a small mountain of inflammatory articles, Goodman claimed that the case had been prejudiced by prosecution leaks to the media. He also claimed that he and Claiborne had been the subject of an extensive five-year government wiretap campaign on their offices and demanded to see the transcripts of the illegal listening. No such evidence was provided, nor, the prosecution claimed, did it exist.

He argued most vigorously that government misconduct had run rampant in the FBI's investigation of a sitting judge. As evidence, he submitted the comments of grand jury member Hazel Vaara, who had asked to be excused from the process after complaining that "the government was attempting to 'pressure' the grand jury to return an indictment against Claiborne." That potentially devastating piece of evidence, however, did not stand up to scrutiny. It was based on hearsay, Goodman was forced to admit during a hearing in which Vaara denied she'd ever spoken the words.

The specter of casino man Lonnie "Ted" Binion's role in the 1979 shooting death of gambler Rance Blevins was raised in another motion, which claimed the FBI tried to pressure Horseshoe employee Walter Rozanski into admitting he had taken the murder rap for Benny Binion's drug-addicted son. Rozanski had pleaded guilty to voluntary manslaughter and received probation. (Goodman represented Rozanski and worked out what most courtroom observers considered an impossible deal: probation despite eyewitnesses who told police they saw Rozanski shoot Blevins in the head. After coaching from Goodman, Rozanski said his 9 mm pistol had gone off accidentally.) The motion said that the FBI claimed Benny Binion had funneled $300,000 to District Judge Carl Christensen to ensure probation for Rozanski, for which Claiborne had acted as the middle man. The agents attempted to force Christensen to revoke Rozanski's probation after Rozanski refused to take a polygraph examination. Christensen vehemently denied accepting a bribe, but admitted he'd been visited by FBI man Joe Yablonsky, who requested the Rozanski polygraph. Christensen balked at Yablonsky's plan.

Goodman even filed a motion seeking more time to prepare more motions. At one point he submitted a one-inch-thick stack of newspaper articles, 115 from the *Sun*, as background material for Judge Hoffman's perusal.

Finally, Goodman filed one motion too many. When he demanded to know upon what legal authority the judge was assigned the case, any fantasies the defense might win over Hoffman were dashed for good.

One by one, Judge Hoffman rejected every motion set before him; in the process, he discounted the defense's contention that Claiborne was a victim of an overzealous FBI. He also cast aside Claiborne's largely unsubstantiated claim that his law office had been illegally bugged and the phones at his Plaza de la Cruz home had been tapped in violation of federal law. Claiborne, who as a defense attorney was regionally famous for his ability to dazzle judges and juries, was becoming increasingly desperate.

The fact was, Claiborne had represented Conforte on white-slavery charges and had socialized with him, a criminal client, violating a basic rule of professionalism. Not only that, but as a judge, when he was informed of the government's criminal case against Conforte, he failed to immediately recuse himself. In addition, he occupied the bench during proceedings involving his friend and own attorney, Oscar Goodman.

Claiborne's personal relationship with Conforte returned to haunt him in court documents alleging that the judge had been provided with prostitutes for six years and that the brothel baron had used Claiborne, when he was still an attorney, as a conduit to local politicians. Conforte was notorious in Nevada political circles for using his working girls to ply favors, or extort them outright, from elected officials who frequented his Mustang Ranch.

Claiborne was bound to face criminal charges and, no matter the outcome, possible impeachment. When every one of Goodman's motions failed, he attempted to circumvent the judge by raising a key constitutional issue at the Ninth U.S. Circuit Court of Appeals: whether Claiborne could be tried on a felony charge prior to an impeachment proceeding. Although indicted U.S. District Judge Alcee Hastings had failed in a similar request, eventually proceeding to trial and winning acquittal, Goodman stressed the difference between the two cases—what he saw as the vindictive actions of the FBI and U.S. Attorney's office in Southern Nevada.

Goodman wrote, "Judge Claiborne is the first U.S. Judge in our nation's history to assert that the Constitution, at a minimum, requires that this court conduct an evidentiary hearing to determine, prior to trial, whether the government's investigation or exercise of prosecutorial discretion was tainted by a motive to retaliate against him for the manner in which he exercised the judicial function in cases to which the government was a party."

Again Goodman focused on Yablonsky's office and the federal prosecutors who had made no secret of their contempt for Claiborne. They believed the judge had fixed cases and taken bribes.

"Claiborne has demonstrated a sensitivity to the rights of the individuals who appear before him that has compelled him upon occasion to reject the products of zealous government investigations and positions vigorously asserted by its attorneys. Both on and off the bench, he has vigorously criticized what he saw as a misuse of prosecutorial resources when they came to his attention as a judge."

In the end, the Ninth Circuit rejected Goodman's plea. Claiborne was headed for trial—his old client and friend, Joe Conforte, ready to take the stand against him.

？ ？ ？

With the trial on track in Reno, Goodman and Hank Greenspun had lost their home-court advantage. In Las Vegas, Goodman's name struck fear in the courts and the *Sun* publisher was a legend. In Reno, under the iron hand of Judge Hoffman, the newspaper's endless droning about a grand government conspiracy — much of its arguments based on the most frivolous foundation — gave Greenspun the appearance of an increasingly desperate vaudevillian searching for a friendly audience. It made Goodman appear the second banana. And none of it figured to help Claiborne's chances in the long run.

Undaunted, Goodman countered by questioning the process by which the government had indicted Claiborne in the first place. Goodman learned, in the case of Miami lawyer and gambler Paul Ashe, that Las Vegas FBI boss Joe Yablonsky had attempted to set up Claiborne. Ashe and Yablonsky had met during the FBI man's time working undercover in South Florida. Later, when Yablonsky found out that Ashe was being coin-cidentally defended by Oscar Goodman at trial in Harry Claiborne's court against charges of defrauding Las Vegas casinos of $54,000, he was ecstatic. If ever a perfect opportunity to nail two men Yablonsky believed to be thoroughly corrupt had knocked on his door, this was it. So Yablonsky personally met with Ashe to offer him favorable treatment if he agreed to tempt the judge with a $50,000 bribe. Ashe never made the offer to Claiborne and was eventually handed a three-year sentence.

The move was pure Yablonsky, who was known in the FBI as the "King of Sting." Problem was, the king had broken the rules when he approached an indicted person who'd already retained counsel. Assistant U.S. Attorney Randy Rukstele, who prosecuted Ashe, said in an affidavit, "I advised Mr. Yablonsky that his having contacts with Mr. Ashe in the absence of Mr. Goodman was a potentially dangerous situation and that all future contacts regarding Mr. Ashe would have to be between me and Mr. Goodman. Mr. Yablonsky agreed with me and indicated he would not have any more contacts with Mr. Ashe."

Coupled with Yablonsky's failed attempt to persuade District Judge Carl Christensen to order a polygraph examination for Walter Rozanski, the Ashe incident clearly illustrated to

Goodman the lengths to which the FBI chief was willing to go to build on Conforte's wobbly bribery claims.

Yablonsky continued to be the subject of an almost daily assault of negative news articles in the *Las Vegas Sun*. The FBI boss was blistered in front-page "Where I Stand" editorials and battered by stories of suspected abuse of office under banner headlines. Greenspun had run guns to a fledgling Israel and bravely battled Senator Joseph McCarthy, but this time he had lost his sights in an all-out effort to protect his friends. Although Yablonsky brought some of the abuse on himself with his inability to read the local political landscape and an arrogance not uncommon to FBI men who looked down on Las Vegas, the *Sun's* crusade coincided with Yablonsky's unprecedented anti-corruption efforts.

? ? ?

To illustrate both the arcane legal technicalities in the system and the fine line that the friendship between a defense attorney and a U.S. judge draws, it's instructive to examine the Ashe case a little more closely.

When Ashe was solicited by Yablonsky to sting Claiborne, the offer was designed to trip up not only Claiborne, but also Goodman. Goodman's conflict in the case was clear: He served as Ashe's attorney as well as Claiborne's, not to mention appearing on behalf of Ashe in Judge Claiborne's court. Goodman swiftly withdrew as Ashe's lawyer, but his new attorney, Jeffrey J. Fitos, went on the attack: "Throughout that time period, Judge Claiborne and Oscar Goodman were engaged in an attorney-client relationship. As a result of this relationship, Judge Claiborne became privy to extrajudicial information that the defendant had been approached by the FBI to act as an agent of the government in the investigation of Judge Claiborne's activities on the bench."

Fitos also accused Goodman of short-circuiting a potential deal between Ashe and the FBI.

"Mr. Goodman told Ashe not to accept the offer, thereby acting specifically on the point of conflict. Defendant would clearly have benefited, not marginally, but greatly, from an offer of leniency or clemency.

"Accepting defendant's allegations as true, once Judge Claiborne heard of the FBI offer, it was impossible for him to remain on defendant's case as an impartial judge.

"Judge Claiborne knew Mr. Goodman represented the defendant in his courtroom and should not have sought Mr. Goodman's counsel. ... Mr. Goodman desired that the case go to trial rather than to serve the best interests of his client. Mr. Goodman's failure to seek and negotiate plea offers demonstrates the adverse effect his interest in his own aggrandizement had on his representation of defendant."

The problem with Fitos' argument was one of chronology. Although Goodman and Claiborne enjoyed a long-standing personal friendship and that fact alone raised the issue of conflict, Goodman did not begin representing the judge until August 1982 — several weeks *after* Ashe was convicted of defrauding Las Vegas casinos of $54,000.

ʔ ʔ ʔ

With all of his motions quashed by Judge Hoffman, Goodman worked feverishly to build a defense against charges stemming from Claiborne's badly botched 1978, 1979, and 1980 tax returns and misrepresenting his income on a federal financial-disclosure statement in 1978 prior to taking the bench. Goodman also had to fight charges that Claiborne had taken $30,000 from Conforte during a stay in Reno on December 14 or 15, 1978.

Working from the government's set of facts, Goodman found an air-tight alibi for Claiborne during that 48-hour period. He had spent much of that time at the Horseshoe Club with his long-time friend, Benny Binion. But instead of the alibi vindicating Claiborne, it served to create the suspicion that Goodman was weaving witnesses and affidavits out of whole cloth. More affidavits and motions were prepared, but on March 12, Judge Hoffman allowed the prosecution to expand their chronology of the alleged bribe to begin as early as December 11, 1978.

"We are surprised and we are bothered and we are deeply disturbed by the latest move by the government!" Goodman roared. "I can't remember being as angry and outraged."

Hoffman goaded Goodman, "You get outraged easily." But he added, "I recognize your valiant effort."

Trying to turn the tables, Goodman next argued that chief prosecutor Steven Shaw of the Justice Department's Public Integrity Section was playing a "guessing" game with the case and was "tailoring the facts to the testimony."

"If we're playing by the rules," Goodman continued, "the government should be held to their theory of the case. This is not a crap game, even though we're in Nevada. We're not shooting for somebody's life here."

It didn't help that one of the defense-team members, attorney John Squire Drendel, was portrayed in the press as something of a co-conspirator after it was learned he had met with prosecution witness and Conforte lawyer Stan Brown. During the FBI and Justice Department probe, Drendel approached Brown, who later recounted their conversation to the court:

"What do you hear about Harry?" Drendel asked.

"I heard the heat's on," Brown replied.

"Can you corroborate the thirty and fifty?" Drendel asked, supposedly referring to alleged bribes.

"Yes and no," Brown replied.

Drendel was booted from the case.

Then, just a few days before trial, Goodman received another setback from the Ninth U.S. Circuit Court of Appeals, which rejected outright his argument that Claiborne, as a sitting federal judge, had to be impeached by Congress prior to undergoing any criminal proceedings. The court wrote: "It can scarcely be doubted that the citizenry would justifiably lose respect for and confidence in a system of government under which judges were apparently held to be above the process of the criminal law."

There was one ace left in the deck. Privately, Goodman recognized a familiar strategy on the government's part. Prosecutors were placing too much weight on the testimony of a severely conflicted witness. One who, if cross-examined properly, would become the defense-team's best friend. That witness, of course, was the brothel baron, Joe Conforte. Although his government advocates fought to keep his lengthy criminal record out of the press, Conforte's career was far too notorious to sweep under the rug.

❡ ❡ ❡

True to form, the government's star witness was an oily pimp who had cut the deal of a lifetime. The prosecution was stuck with a devil of its own making and Goodman took full advantage of the image.

"I run a whorehouse," Conforte told the jury at the outset of his testimony.

It was downhill from there. Conforte punctuated his statements with vulgarities, was caught in inconsistencies, then under pressure lost his train of thought and developed memory loss.

The jury couldn't help but wonder: How could anyone take the word of Joe Conforte?

In the end, few did. The first trial lasted 19 days and ended when Judge Hoffman declared a mistrial after the jury failed to convict on a single felony count. With Conforte as its star witness, the government had gone 0-for-7.

Conforte bellowed in the press about challenging Claiborne to a polygraph test, but the damage was done. Not only was Conforte's brief career as the government's star witness finished, but the bribery case that had been the crux of the FBI's intense investigation lay in ruin.

By late June, word leaked that the Justice Department harbored serious doubts about relying so heavily on Conforte. Prosecutor Steve Shaw's next move was the most important he would make: Instead of retrying the case adorned with the reeking albatross, Conforte, around its neck, prosecutors simply dropped the bribery charges against Claiborne and went forward on the tax charges. Never mind that the tax issue was originally raised, in large part, to bolster Conforte's bribery allegations. Conforte, his sweet deal secured, vanished from the case and resumed his vacation in Rio de Janeiro.

The obstruction-of-justice charge, which stemmed from the supposed Drendel-Brown conversation, was also dismissed. The government's battle against Harry Claiborne was reduced to a dry but devastating tax case. Accountants and tax preparers were not nearly as colorful as Joe Conforte, but they would prove more effective in court.

Without Conforte, Goodman had no devil to cast in his

courtroom drama. The defense's government-vendetta theory was moot in the face of three obviously ill-prepared tax returns. Harry Claiborne was in big trouble.

As the second trial drew closer, Goodman decided to make a risky move: He filed a motion demanding Hoffman recuse himself from the case for bias.

The accusation was clear. Hoffman, recognized as one of America's most capable federal judges, considered absurd the defense contention that Claiborne was the victim of an FBI vendetta. He called the newspaper articles pointing to possible ethical wrongdoing on the part of Yablonsky and his men "trash" in open court and was unlikely to change his tune in the second trial. Hoffman had also denied every single defense motion, allowed the defense a mere four months for case preparation from the day of indictment to the first trial, and ridiculed both defendant and defense attorney in court.

Walter Hoffman, however, wasn't going anywhere. Goodman's tactic did put him on the spot: Had Goodman sealed his client's fate with the judge by accusing him of bias? Or had he ensured Hoffman would take extra care to be fair?

Opening arguments in the second trial of U.S. District Judge Harry Claiborne began on August 2, 1984, with Oscar Goodman downplaying the government's tax case. Goodman told the court that Claiborne was guilty only of investing too much trust in his tax preparer, Jerry Watson, and accountant, Jay Wright. Claiborne, jurors would learn for the first time, had pre-signed his tax forms and turned over his IRS obligations to his experts.

These "experts," the evidence showed, however, were not deserving of the title. Watson, who processed the 1980 tax form, was not a certified public accountant. And Wright, Goodman alleged, had failed to properly calculate the judge's 1979 income taxes.

"It's not enough if you find that Judge Claiborne was careless or Judge Claiborne was negligent, [but] whether or not he acted willfully, with some kind of bad purpose," Goodman implored. "Perhaps shame on Mr. Wright. Perhaps shame on Judge Claiborne. But Judge Claiborne had every reason in the world to trust him."

The third count, failure to report a $75,000 loan on his 1978 federal financial-disclosure form, amounted to what Goodman shrugged off as a "misunderstanding." Claiborne claimed he had received a generous $100,000 gift from former Dunes Hotel and Casino operator Sid Wyman, but kept the money in a shoebox secured inside a Binion's Horseshoe casino safe deposit box belonging to Ted Binion. By the time of trial, Wyman was deceased. No one asked Ted Binion whether the money was actually his and not Claiborne's. Although witnesses in the first trial testified that they'd been present in the Dunes suite the night Wyman gave Claiborne the $100,000 in $100 bills, the explanation was unlikely to play well before a panel of jurors mostly unaccustomed to such an event occurring to a man who would later become a federal judge.

Wright was a devastating witness. Weak as some of his testimony might have been, he clearly recalled writing a note to himself regarding the $75,000 in question: "Borrowed to pay taxes in 1977." The only one who could have told him that, he said, was Harry Claiborne.

"Claiborne didn't say who he borrowed it from," Wright testified.

During a break in the proceedings, Ted Binion left the courtroom gallery and approached Goodman and Claiborne with an idea: Couldn't the judge just take the stand and admit that he had a drinking problem and, in the process of having his income drop from $375,000 a year to his $58,000 judge's salary, unintentionally botched his tax returns? A proud Claiborne refused to entertain such drama.

As any taxpayer knows, every defense argument suffered from a basic flaw that would not be lost on the jury: Ultimately, a citizen is responsible for his own tax forms. Goodman's protestations notwithstanding, Claiborne's tax forms bespoke a level of irresponsibility that was criminal on its face. A cook or cabdriver would be expected to read his own completed tax form before signing it; an experienced lawyer and sitting federal judge had no less responsibility.

Ultimately, the tax documents themselves proved deadly. They were so sloppily prepared that a schoolboy would have noticed their obvious flaws. The prosecution presented its case for two and a half days, then rested.

Co-counsel J. Richard Johnston and Goodman immediately moved to dismiss the three charges against Claiborne, claiming the government had failed to prove willful intent on the part of the defendant.

Predictably, Hoffman wasn't buying it. The jury would decide whether Claiborne had willfully misreported his income taxes.

There was little to argue on the facts, which prompted Oscar Goodman to continue to attack Judge Hoffman. Hoffman, in turn, was still seething from the defense lawyer's previous motion calling for recusal.

In one incident, during a break, Goodman approached Claiborne's secretary, Judy Ahlstrom, in the hallway outside court. Ahlstrom had just finished being cross-examined by the prosecution. Minutes later, a marshal handed Goodman a note from Judge Hoffman admonishing him not to talk to witnesses, something the prosecution had commonly done.

"It seems it only works against us, Judge," Goodman sneered, "because when their witnesses leave here, it's all right for them to talk to each other. We take this as a personal aspersion toward the defense, because this is the first time this rule has been invoked."

"This lady was a key witness on a particular point!" Hoffman blasted. "Mr. Goodman, I don't want to cite you for contempt — have a seat, sir!"

Hoffman wasn't finished. Pounding his fist he said, "I say you haven't got a right to get up in this court and say I am biased and prejudiced. ... You can make it in the Court of Appeals, but not here. You keep your mouth shut from here on out, is that clear?"

At that moment, Claiborne grabbed Goodman by the coat and whispered, "If you don't shut up, he'll throw you in jail and then I'll be lawyerless."

Then Goodman deadpanned to the bench, "I understand what the court is saying."

Goodman had gone beyond the brink of contempt, trying everything short of putting Judge Hoffman in a headlock to get him to declare a mistrial. For without one, Claiborne was sure to be sunk by the weaknesses in his character.

Then Harry Claiborne took the stand. He told the court of his Arkansas background and of a life filled with his triumph over adversity. He described himself as an Arkansas country boy who graduated from an obscure law school in 1941, then recalled his service as a military policeman at the future Nellis Air Force Base during World War II and the beginning of his Las Vegas law career in January 1946.

Claiborne testified under careful questioning by defense co-counsel J. Richard Johnston that the blunders made on his income tax returns were not errors of malicious intent, but the unintended mistakes of an honest man.

That included his hard-to-believe story of keeping nearly $100,000 in cash in Ted Binion's safe deposit box for a rainy day.

"Did you ever tell [Wright] that it was a loan?" Johnston asked, referring to the mysterious appearance of $75,000 to pay his outstanding IRS debts.

"No sir," Claiborne said.

"Was it a loan?" the attorney asked.

"No sir," Claiborne replied.

"I have trouble keeping my mouth shut," Claiborne explained to the jury. "I sometimes say things that I think and that don't sit well with some people."

Then it came time for him to be cross-examined. Prosecutor William Hendricks immediately went for the throat. Claiborne admitted he had erred when he allowed his income as an attorney for 1978 to be reported as $22,332, when upon careful consideration the accurate figure was $41,000. Although the judge had amended his 1979 return to reflect the difference, in Hendricks' mind the damage had been done.

"How could you forget half your legal-fee income in just two weeks?" the prosecutor asked. "You want the jury to believe that you filed these 1040 forms without ever looking at them?"

"Yes," Claiborne replied. "I most assuredly do."

Hendricks insisted that Claiborne, desperate for money, had underreported his income by over $100,000, then attempted to hide that fact.

As the jury prepared to deliberate, Goodman made one more motion to dismiss the case against Claiborne due to a lack of corroborative evidence, which boiled down to accountant Wright's testimony and a single note he produced that stated the $75,000 used to repay his tax debt was a loan.

At last, Hoffman appeared to soften, if ever so slightly, toward Goodman.

"I would have to deny your motion, [but] I agree with you," Hoffman told Goodman.

It was a matter for the jury to decide.

? ? ?

In his closing argument, Goodman toned down his bulldog personality and presented the soothing demeanor of a consummately reasonable attorney. He admitted that the defense believed Claiborne had made mistakes, but that those errors did not constitute criminality. Careless, negligent, grossly negligent, yes. But not criminal.

But Hendricks had the upper hand and logic on his side. Late in the trial, Hendricks conceded that there wasn't enough evidence to prove the financial-disclosure charge. The jury would consider only the two tax-evasion charges.

"He's knowledgeable enough to be a federal judge," the prosecutor told the jury. "I think it's clear Judge Claiborne … knows tax law."

The jury deliberated a short time before returning on August 10 with its verdict: guilty on two counts of tax evasion and innocent of lying on a judicial-ethics report. In early October 1984, Judge Hoffman sentenced Claiborne to two years in prison.

"I've always considered that the measure of a man is how he handles adversity, and I'll handle this the same way I've handled everything else in my life—head on," Claiborne said outside the courthouse, the jury's verdict still ringing in his ears. "And I'll pursue the appeal and continue the fight until my name is cleared."

? ? ?

By the time of Claiborne's conviction, Joe Yablonsky was long gone from Las Vegas, but not without leaving a parting shot. "For the good of society, I would rather have ten Confortes walking the streets than one corrupt federal judge. There's no doubt in my mind that he received those bribes."

Tired of hearing Yablonsky attaching crimes not committed to his client, Goodman lashed out.

"Sometimes I wonder if he has any brain at all," Goodman said. "Yablonsky is so poisoned against Nevada, he can't look at the verdict with any sense of reality. Judge Claiborne was exonerated of the corruption charges. Yablonsky should learn to read."

"Yablonsky was a moralist who first concluded Harry Claiborne was guilty and then went out in search of the facts necessary to convict him," Goodman said. "His heavy reliance on the word of Joe Conforte illustrates that. I think Claiborne was being investigated from the moment his name was put into nomination. But as far as a criminal investigation, it was only after they went down to Brazil and spoke to Conforte and got him to come back that the case against Claiborne was made.

"If there's one thing I'm not, it's a moralist. I mean, when people come into my office and sit down, I don't really care if they did what they're charged with. I'm there to make sure that their rights are protected. Big difference. I don't start saying to people, the fellow charged with child molestation, for instance, 'My God, how could you have done something like that?' If he did it, the prosecution has to prove he did it and they have to prove it the right way. I honest-to-God believe, for the system to work, that it's worth letting the twelve guilty go free than convict the one innocent man. Yablonsky could never see it that way. He'd rather have the twelve innocent and the guilty one convicted.

"I believe the jury would have accepted the defense case if Claiborne hadn't been a judge. They hold judges and lawyers to a higher standard than the average person. The jury cannot accept the fact that the judge should be held to the same standards as other citizens — that's the way the system is supposed to be. ... I'm sure the judge will never stop fighting this to his dying day."

Goodman immediately moved to appeal the conviction to the Ninth Circuit. At the same time, he privately prepared for the inevitable final battle against all odds: the Congressional impeachment of U.S. District Judge Harry Claiborne.

That daunting task should have been enough to keep any mouthpiece busy, but about that time Tony Spilotro's world was finally crashing in on him.

15

Fighting Wars
on Two Fronts

L as Vegas had long touted itself as the Entertainment Capital of the World, but by early 1986, the biggest name in the city wasn't spread across a Strip marquee. It was splashed across the front page of both local newspapers. The name buzzed nightly on the airwaves emanating from the local-television news broadcasts. It was whispered throughout the casino industry from the pit to the penthouse. It was not Tony Bennett, Tony Curtis, or Tony Orlando. It was Tony Spilotro.

Spilotro had become a celebrity and by doing so had fallen prey to the same double malady that had led to the deaths of Benny Siegel, John Rosselli, and Allen Dorfman and to the downfall of Frank Rosenthal: a high profile and an excess of ego. Spilotro's celebrity status, combined with all the other problems the mob was experiencing by the mid-1980s, diminished the value of his life considerably.

Spilotro was the top priority of Metro police, the FBI, and the Justice Department Organized Crime Strike Force. Metro Intelligence boss Preston Hubbs had once said, "Let there be no doubt that we consider Tony Spilotro to be the lowest form of human life. This hoodlum, who thrives off the weakness and misery of our citizenry, offers nothing but a disgrace to this community." Hubbs estimated Spilotro's various criminal crews and business associates at more than 150.

Spilotro was a suspect in as many as 25 murders and literally thousands of other felonies ranging from extortion to armed robbery, but thanks in large part to the efforts of Oscar Goodman, had not had even a minor conviction in more than a decade. But time was running out for Tony.

He had come to represent all that was notorious about Las Vegas and had become an immensely popular subject of the media.

The last thing his superiors in Chicago wanted was for a soldier to have his name in the paper daily, because their names invariably were linked to his.

In Chicago, Ron Koziol of the *Tribune* and Art Petacque of the *Sun-Times* blistered the man they labeled "Tony the Ant" in articles that wound up each morning on the doorsteps of Spilotro's bosses. On the street, Spilotro was known as a wily operator and unrepentant killer. In the press, he had become a caricature. And in real life, he was so overwhelmed with anxiety that he kept the covers pulled over his head and was unable to get out of bed on many mornings.

Review-Journal columnist and KLAS-TV newsman Ned Day led the assault in Las Vegas. Taking advantage of his exclusive FBI and Metro police sources, Day generated column after column that both broke news and poked fun at the diminutive mobster and his crew of thugs, burglars, extortionists, and killers. Day's work was so biting that at one point he was offered a job at a major Chicago newspaper.

"Tough Tony Behind Bars: A Columnist's Disaster," read one headline. This March 19, 1986, column, written in Day's trademark tongue-in-cheek style, appeared in the form of a plea to Goodman to save Spilotro, lest the columnist's career be ruined. It read in part:

"So, lawyer Goodman, I made your important client my project. I learned everything I could about him. I wrote a lot about him. I wrote bad things.

"In retrospect, I may have gone too far—like the time I dubbed him the 'Fireplug Who Walks Like a Man.'

"But you have to understand. I was ambitious, you know.

And being a bust-out in previous careers, I had nothing to lose. So I picked on him and a lot of folks thought that was just great.

"... The point is that thanks to Mr. Spilotro's presence in Las Vegas, my career as a newsman has been okay.

"What happens if he goes to the pokey?

"No more short jokes. No more gags about Hoffa Burgers at his restaurant. No more self-righteous anti-mob crusading. I'm telling you, sir, it would be an unmitigated disaster.

"... I'm pleading with you. Please do everything you can for Mr. Spilotro. My career may be riding on it."

¿ ¿ ¿

Spilotro blew up. Goodman subpoenaed Day as a defense witness in the upcoming racketeering and murder case, possibly in retaliation for all the slights on his client, and the columnist once again had a gem of a story when Tough Tony issued him a none-too-subtle threat in the hallway outside court.

In print a few days later he wrote, "'I heard you want to be famous. ... I'll make you famous,' Spilotro said, adopting a cold, steady glare that made me think being 'famous' was not a good thing. 'I know how to make you more famous than you ever thought about. You know I know how.'"

Day, the consummate newspaper smart aleck, was never called to testify.

"I think Tony was a creation of law enforcement and the media," Goodman said years later. "Ned Day used to call him names. He was the Poobah, the Fireplug, whatever. If you get called the Poobah enough, you begin to act like the Poobah.

"There is an attitude on the part of the public, created by media coverage and attention, to want to see some bad come to the individual because he is charged with an offense. Under the law, that attitude is impermissible, and yet it proliferates news coverage in which some reporters and columnists become like Junior G-men. To some extent, Ned Day was that way when it came to writing about Tony Spilotro. Ned was well-known for being, shall we say, laissez-faire and liberal when it came to writing about drug use and the local sex industry, but he affected the character of a criminal avenger when it came to Spilotro. By caricaturizing Tony and making him the object of scorn and ridicule, he not only made my job much more difficult, he also put Tony's life in jeopardy. Which appeared to be what Ned had in mind."

In the Ned Day column under the headline: "How Can Spilotro, Incredibly, Still Walk the Streets?" Day took issue with Spilotro's status as a free man after winning the M&M murder case, having damning wiretap evidence thrown out on technicalities and winning numerous procedural points that effectively delayed his trials.

"Justice delayed is justice denied. Most often the maxim applies to individuals charged with crimes. But what about the rest of us?

"Take, for example, the case of Tony Spilotro, the stubby kahuna of the Las Vegas streets. He still struts around town, despite a decade of government charges that he commands a cutthroat gang of burglars, arsonists, extortionists, leg breakers, and other career terrorists.

"If things go according to form, it'll be 1990 or beyond when his second case goes to trial.

"But what about the rights of society, the rights of law-abiding citizens who want justice? How many burglaries, thefts and extortion schemes can be carried out by a group of career criminals in the next eight years? How many victims will there be?"

Phil LaVelle covered the federal courthouse for the *Review-Journal* and had several encounters with Spilotro. He also gained insight into Goodman's personality.

"In those days, Oscar was in full stride," LaVelle recalled. "He'd leave court and say, 'There's no such thing as organized crime. It's a figment of the government's imagination. Shame on the Justice Department.' He was just 110% in that frame of mind. I couldn't budge him on a damn thing. He was very aggressive, always keyed up, and never looked like he had an off day."

؟ ؟ ؟

Stymied in his quest for a positive forum in Las Vegas, Goodman took his assault on the government to a new level. He went on the attack on national television during a CBS "60

Minutes" segment titled "The Mercenary and the Mouthpiece." The piece focused on the high-wire careers of "Mercenary" Joel Hirshhorn of Miami, noted defender of drug-cartel bosses, and the "Mouthpiece" Oscar Goodman, whose schtick was well-known to Las Vegans, but clearly wowed interviewer Mike Wallace.

"It is not relevant where [criminal defense attorneys] get their money, as far as I'm concerned," Goodman offered, adding that he found the murderous Spilotro to be a "kind, decent, and attentive" client. He described mob killer-turned-government informant Aladena "Jimmy the Weasel" Fratianno as "a piece of garbage." He bragged that he'd "rather go to the can" than betray an attorney-client confidence. On a roll, Goodman added that if he were ever convicted of racketeering or tax evasion, he would "get out of the business and maybe become some kind of revolutionary."

For years afterward, a photo of Wallace and Goodman hung from the wall of the attorney's office inside the House the Mob Built. It was signed, "To Oscar Goodman with much respect, Mike Wallace."

But as Spilotro approached trial in the Hole-in-the-Wall Gang racketeering case, all the press in the world wasn't helping to offset the pile of evidence against the burglars who worked for Spilotro. Frank Cullotta's defection to the government's side only increased the odds against Tony staying out of prison.

Goodman privately argued with the defense attorneys of the other defendants in the case against filing a motion for a change of venue to remove the case to a jurisdiction where his client's name was less notorious. In court, Goodman had learned, notoriety is a form of celebrity and celebrity is capable of grabbing the jury's attention. In Las Vegas, no lawyer had gained a larger reputation than he. Goodman even considered commissioning a public-opinion poll to prove his point, but it wasn't necessary. As the leader of the defense team, he called the shots in what promised to be the final showdown between Spilotro and the government.

The evidence was piled high against the defendants—a motley assemblage of thugs, burglars, suspected hitmen, and former police detective Joe Blasko. Beyond their criminal activity, they all had one thing in common: an allegiance to Tony Spilotro.

But it wasn't his loyal street crew that Spilotro needed to worry about. It was the rats, as Goodman called them, who once again threatened Tough Tony's freedom and his attorney's winning record in court. Although the government hoped to finally get something credible from Cullotta, the admitted killer and Spilotro sycophant, Organized Crime Strike Force prosecutor Lawrence Leavitt caught a break when FBI agents managed to turn mob associate Sal Romano against his former running mates.

In addition to his other legal troubles, Spilotro was also being investigated for an attempt to bribe a caterer into poisoning members of the grand jury. Although the investigation went nowhere, it added to Spilotro's dangerous reputation.

There was little question that the Hole-in-the-Wall Gang was going down for a burglary at Bertha's gift and jewelry shop. After all, the defendants had been apprehended in the middle of the job. But Spilotro was not at the scene, so it would be up to Cullotta and Romano to convince the jury he was the mastermind behind that heist, as well as the rest of the criminal activity.

After more than a week in court, a mistrial was called when two jurors were overheard discussing something about money during a break outside the courtroom. It was never established whether any member of the jury had actually been offered a bribe, but the result gave Spilotro and his men a short reprieve. U.S. District Judge Lloyd George set a new trial date.

The irrepressible Ned Day had a well-timed wisecrack in a column tallying the "winners and losers" in the costly mistrial.

"Winner: Attorney Oscar Goodman, who not only got his client, Tough Tony Spilotro, off the hook, but who also gets to collect a whole new fee when the case goes to trial again in June. No double-jeopardy on lawyers' fees."

"Loser: Oscar Goodman's other clients, whose affairs will have to continue taking a back seat while he concentrates his efforts on his premier client."

That line was not lost on Harry Claiborne. Years later, his friends would say Claiborne had begun to question whether Goodman had given him the best possible defense during the second tax trial in Reno. In an interview with Claiborne in 2002, the former judge said he had no problem with Goodman's representation.

Meanwhile, Tony had won another round on a technicality, but the odds were still way against him. He faced trials for the Jerry Lisner murder and the Hole-in-the-Wall burglaries and had yet to go to trial for his role in the Argent Corporation casino skim case, the debacle for which his mob bosses held him partially responsible.

In Rosenthal's case, Goodman admits having received that phone call from Nick Civella, who asked the loaded question, "Is he crazy?" From the force of the explosion that nearly killed Rosenthal, it's safe to say Civella believed he knew the answer.

But did Goodman ever receive a similar contact from Spilotro's associates in Chicago?

He insists he did not, and that after winning a mistrial on the grounds of possible juror misconduct, Spilotro was poised to return to battle for the three sweeping cases that remained against him. Goodman lacked the personal attorney-client relationship with, for instance, Chicago's Joey Aiuppa and Tony Accardo, that he had with Civella. While wiretap surveillance and court records had established Goodman's close association with off-the-record casino owner and Teamsters Pension Fund insider Nick Civella, the same could not be said for the Windy City group.

But if Tony Accardo had called, Goodman might have been tempted to say Spilotro was crazy. Spilotro's nerves were shot — and not only from his troubles with the law. He'd also made himself a target for elimination by yet another criminal family in fighting for his life. Unlike his associates in the Hole-in-the-Wall case, men who were basically common laborers in the mob's hierarchy, Spilotro had been trusted with some of the Outfit's most intimate secrets. He not only knew how the skim was generated and to whom it went, but he was also aware of the identities of dozens of Las Vegans who remained secretly connected to the Outfit. And not even Oscar Goodman on his home court could ensure Spilotro would beat three more major felony cases.

The Hole-in-the-Wall Gang retrial was scheduled to begin June 16.

❡ ❡ ❡

Goodman has long been an excellent spotter of legal talent. Bringing Steve Stein into the firm is one example. Stein, who had done service with the Knapp Commission on corruption and organized crime, was running the Justice Department's Organized Crime Strike Force office in Philadelphia in 1973 when he encountered Goodman while prosecuting a bookmaking case. He joined Goodman's law practice a year later.

Stein had seen first-hand the government's transgressions in its fight against the criminal element. He'd watched the statistic padding and the outright cheating that went on in the name of what was right. He was ready for a change and was impressed with Goodman's ethics and character.

"Oscar waited until the case was over to approach me, which showed me a lot of moral code," Stein recalled. "He said, 'Are you planning on making government a career?' I said, 'Hell no.'" He joined Goodman, Jerry Snyder, and Leonard Gang in Las Vegas a few months later.

Stein not only knew the law, but he and Goodman shared similar philosophies.

"I saw things working in government that blew my mind," Stein recalled. "I saw things going on within the government and by the government that made me think that maybe they were the bad guys and the guys I was prosecuting weren't as bad.

"I learned a lot from Oscar. Oscar puts on a good show of ego, but he has one of the most down-to-earth, common-sense, brilliant legal minds I have ever met in my life. And, man, can he try a case. I learned more from watching him than I have in many law classes. He's really not as egotistical as people say he is when you get to know him. Of course, he doesn't let himself be a friend to most people. He's got one true friend in his life and that's Carolyn.

"But I learned not long after joining his office that you never call Oscar after 5:30. You never know what he'll say because he will have been drinking, and when he drinks he's liable to say anything — and not remember it the next day."

Stein was given the unenviable task of maintaining lines

of communication between furious federal prosecutors and the law office while Goodman pounded the FBI and Strike Force in the press. If a deal had to be cut, Stein did the dirty work offstage.

"I'm good at that," Stein said years later. "Back then, I had the respect of most of the prosecutors."

A former federal prosecutor said, "Oscar says he never represented people who cooperated with authorities, but that's only technically true. Oscar had Steve Stein if someone wanted to cut a deal with the government."

And if Stein ever felt betrayed by Goodman's treatment, as one critic contended, he showed no sign of a diminished affection for the man.

Then there was David Chesnoff, the young attorney who'd broken in locally with Dominic Gentile and joined Goodman as Judge Harry Claiborne's fight was heating up. Chesnoff emulated Goodman's command of the courtroom and swagger around the firm's legion of mafia clients. In time Chesnoff would become a nationally recognized drug attorney who was despised by federal prosecutors and DEA agents. Chesnoff would recall years later being awed by Goodman's work ethic, by his ability to hit happy hour like a wild man and still get all his work done, by how personally he took the case against Claiborne.

Marty Keach was a Deputy District Attorney in Clark County when he encountered Goodman's guile and juice during a case involving a man accused of lewdness and sexual assault. By the time Goodman finished finessing the case, which Keach recalled was a lock against the defendant, District Judge Earle White gave the accused probation with the condition that he undergo therapy.

Instead, the defendant moved to California, where he rapidly eluded court supervision. Keach was furious and managed to have the man recalled for violating the terms of his release. Again Goodman took the stage, worked his magic, and the man Keach indelicately calls "a sick perverted fuck" received no more than a wrist slap and an admonishment from the judge.

"The long and short of it was, Oscar had something that I didn't fully understand at the time. I didn't know how much stroke Oscar had. He convinced Earle to keep the guy on probation, and I got a good lesson in how the system worked. It was a power play."

Not long afterward, Keach went to work for Oscar Goodman.

"Steve Stein and Bill Terry had been asking me for a year to come to work for Oscar. When I went to work for him, I immediately understood where he was coming from," Keach recalled. "He said, 'We don't got friends. We're lawyers. We represent clients. We make money.' That was always his attitude."

ᶟ ᶟ ᶟ

In the heat of representing Spilotro on multiple fronts and Claiborne during his appeal to the Ninth Circuit, as well as the responsibility of traveling to Washington for the subsequent disgraced judge's impeachment hearings, Goodman signed on to represent embattled San Diego Mayor Roger Hedgecock against allegations of perjury and conspiracy over campaign-finance improprieties involving more than $360,000 in contributions funneled from the J. David Dominelli Company. Goodman replaced Michael Pancer, who had managed to win a mistrial after the jury in Hedgecock's first trial was deadlocked 11-1 to convict.

"William Todd, the presiding judge, had aspirations to the California Court of Appeal," Goodman recalled. "On the Sunday before the trial began, I was quoted in the San Diego paper saying that Todd was arrogant in his demeanor and conduct and biased against my client for political gain. The morning of the trial, Todd went absolutely bonkers. Every day during the ensuing weeks of trial, he constantly made reference to arrogance."

Hedgecock's jury was sequestered, but it didn't prevent a juror from hooking up with a bailiff, who was found to have improperly influenced deliberations.

"The case was hotly contested. And in the end, the jury was out day after day before returning a verdict of guilty. I got a phone call from a San Diego attorney immediately after the verdict and learned that during deliberations, the bailiff had defined for the jurors the reasonable-doubt standard. The only person who can do that is the judge and that helped the jury find Hedgecock guilty.

"Before returning the verdict, some jurors also sneaked out and had sex with each other and the bailiffs, drank vodka and orange juice provided by a bailiff, then returned their verdict. The judge tried to protect the bailiff, Al Buroughs, by telling me to drop dead and that his man would never have done any of this. Even after we'd obtained affidavits from jurors, Todd still turned us down for a new trial. When we took the case to the Court of Appeal, it was reversed. By then Hedgecock had won, but the damage was done. He had been removed from office as a result of his conviction."

Hedgecock, now a popular conservative radio talk-show host in the greater San Diego metropolitan market, saw his conviction overturned with Goodman as counsel by eventually paying a $5,000 fine and serving a short term of probation.

For Goodman, such outcomes, when the alternative is a lengthy prison sentence, are substantial victories.

$$? \; ? \; ?$$

In the middle of the Spilotro fight, developments were coming quickly in Harry Claiborne's appeal. The embattled judge faced two alternatives. He could resign, in which case his struggle would be over. He'd serve his two-year prison term and, once completed, he could go on with his life. Or he could continue to appeal to have his convictions overturned on a number of legal grounds. If he refused to resign, he would surely be impeached. Given the felony convictions alone, that much appeared certain. Into that bitter headwind he marched with Oscar Goodman at his side.

In San Francisco to represent Claiborne before the Ninth U.S. Circuit Court of Appeals, Goodman was joined by former District Judge Thomas O'Donnell, the man who had overturned the Crockett murder case, as well as Claiborne's law clerk Brad Jerbic, the future Las Vegas City Attorney. The defense team dined at Claiborne's favorite restaurant and the next morning were to meet for breakfast. Claiborne arrived, but O'Donnell was nowhere to be seen. "He's not feeling well," Claiborne told Goodman.

Goodman wasn't told until after he addressed the Ninth Circuit that his dear friend O'Donnell had suffered a massive heart attack that morning. Claiborne, on the most important day of his life, had chosen to be at his friend O'Donnell's bedside.

Goodman had plenty of fight left, but his options dwindled after a three-judge panel from the Ninth Circuit Court upheld Claiborne's convictions.

In his opinion, Judge Wilbur Pell revealed his cynicism about the Claiborne case: "We assume that he gained some familiarity with concepts as basic to the tax law as the distinction between ordinary income and capital gain during his law school studies, his 30-odd years of practicing law, and his three years on the bench before filing his 1980 return."

Goodman was reduced to venting his outrage before an unimpressed court. He wrote in part, "The final reality in this case is that a man, innocent of any criminal wrongdoing, has been hounded, prosecuted, and convicted, and that conviction affirmed by the panel, because the man was a judge unpopular with federal agents and prosecutors. ... The panel has simply adopted the contentions of the prosecutors in an effort to find some motive or theory and some evidence to support the convictions. Long ago, Abraham Lincoln commented that the evidence against one of his clients was so thin it looked like the shadow of a sparrow that had starved to death. So it is in this case."

The Ninth Circuit refused to rehear the case before the entire court and Goodman vowed to take Claiborne's case to the United States Supreme Court.

A year to the day after his conviction in Reno, a source close to a House of Representatives subcommittee told the *Reno Gazette-Journal* that it was likely Claiborne would resign before he was impeached. If the source assumed Claiborne would eventually see the inevitability of his predicament and step down from the bench, he or she didn't know the judge. Claiborne was determined to stand before a Congressional firing squad. There was no reasonable likelihood that the United States Senate would overrule a jury's decision. Although historically a tax-evasion conviction had not been deemed "high crimes and misdemeanors," no legal precedent prevented Congress from crushing Claiborne at its whim.

"Unless he is impeached or he resigns, he remains a judge," a Justice Department spokesman said. "The Constitution spells it out that simply."

Unbowed, Claiborne refused to resign, but in so doing courted the ultimate disgrace.

≈ ≈ ≈

Oscar Goodman's schedule left little time for his wife and family, but Carolyn Goodman betrayed no resentment publicly. She had four teenagers to look after and the private Meadows School to groom. She'd served on the founding board of the Hebrew Academy in Las Vegas, had worked on a 10-year development plan for the rapidly expanding Clark County School District, and had chaired the Governor's Council on Alcohol and Drug Abuse in the mid-1970s before embarking on the Meadows, a school she was largely responsible for building from the ground up. She served on every committee at the school, from budget and buildings and grounds to advertising and education. In addition to the traditional classwork, students at the progressive private school were taught basic Spanish and trained on computers.

Rising daily at 4 a.m., Oscar and Carolyn shared the same work ethic and enjoyed the early hours together before the demands of his clients or her schoolchildren began anew.

"I really love my life," Carolyn said at the time. "I feel like a very lucky woman. Oscar travels a lot for his work, but I think that's good for our marriage. It makes us appreciate each other more. He's a very dynamic man, very strong, with a great sense of humor.

"I keep very busy with my kids. Before my two older boys started to drive, I put 30,000 miles a year on my car just driving in town. And I feel my work at the school is very, very important. I think each individual has a responsibility to the world around them. I'd like to see more parents get involved."

"I missed my father, but I remember my mother saying, 'He's out there so you can have the best things in life, the best education,'" Cara Goodman recalled. "Looking back, I think it was very hard for her to maintain her attitude. She took care of all of us while he was gone.

"I've always believed that he would have given up everything for his family," Cara said. "He obviously loved what he was doing, but he was there when we needed him. I think everything that makes him a good lawyer makes him a great father."

At one birthday, Cara remembered making a wish. She told her father, "I wish you didn't have to leave."

Of the stress and hurt feelings of raising the family alone, Cara said referring to her mother Carolyn, "There had to have been difficult times, but she never let us see that."

Privately, despite their schedule and the growing pains of their children, the Goodmans were a generally healthy family. Publicly, Oscar Goodman was in the press daily as the unrepentant protector of vicious killers and corrupt judges.

? ? ?

Tony Spilotro walked into the kind of trap he was known for setting. Word of his mistrial reverberated from Las Vegas to Chicago and he'd gained a reputation in the press for beating the government one way or another. He also had a reputation for shotgunning witnesses against him and it was no secret there was a large reward on the street for anyone who could locate federal informants Frank Cullotta and Sal Romano.

Stories were published, quoting anonymous law-enforcement sources speculating that the Teflon-like Spilotro might be in line for a promotion from his bosses in Chicago. The information almost casually made its way from mob informants to law enforcement, who in turn fed the media. One Las Vegas journalist wrote an article on Spilotro's possible bright future in the Outfit's hierarchy under the headline, "Spilotro Stock Goes Up." Unfortunately for Tony, however, with a new regime in Chicago, just the opposite was true.

Although Spilotro cursed the media, he rarely missed a newspaper story. And he was beginning to believe his own clips. He might have thought the world of Las Vegas revolved around him, but in fact he was out of the loop. With wiretaps rampant and physical surveillance on him running 24 hours a day, he could not realistically hope to communicate long distance with his bosses.

So it must not have seemed suspicious when his brother Michael received a brief message from a connected friend in Chicago setting up a meeting with Sam Carlisi a week before the second Hole-in-the-Wall Gang trial.

But Chicago had changed in the years since Tony had traveled west. Convictions in the Kansas City and Argent casino cases had sent Joey Aiuppa, Jackie Cerone, Joey "The Clown" Lombardo, and Angelo La Pietra to the penitentiary. Tony Accardo was playing out his string in semi-retirement in Palm Springs. Aiuppa's former driver and confidant, Sam Carlisi, had risen to the Chicago Outfit's final table, along with underboss Joe Ferriola. Although stricken with cancer that eventually killed him in 1991, Ferriola had enough strength in 1986 to assume the mantle of the family.

His first order of business was ridding the Outfit of its man in Las Vegas, so in early June, after a sufficient cover story had been floated, a call was made through younger brother Michael Spilotro, a restaurant owner and part-time actor, requesting Tony Spilotro's presence in Chicago.

Although FBI and police sources later reported that both Spilotro brothers were nervous as they traveled back to Chicago, they were apparently not so alarmed that they lifted a finger to prevent what would happen next. After the Spilotros arrived in Chicago, they were picked up by trusted Outfit insiders, who chauffeured them to a meeting with the bosses at an undisclosed location. The car drove south on US 41. They appeared to be heading to Joey Aiuppa's private hunting lodge near the town of St. Anne, Indiana.

¿ ¿ ¿

In Chicago, Anne Spilotro waited a day before calling Chicago police. She knew something was wrong. Then 48 hours had passed since Tony and Michael had failed to check in with their wives. When Tony Spilotro didn't appear for trial on June 16, 1986, U.S. District Judge Lloyd George postponed the proceedings until June 30. Something was definitely amiss. Las Vegas buzzed with the news of the Spilotro brothers' disappearance.

Mob experts such as former FBI man Bill Roemer openly

speculated that Spilotro had gone into hiding to avoid his next date with a judge, but Oscar Goodman feared the worst. It wasn't like Tony Spilotro to run from trouble, and contrary to the belief of some of his Las Vegas press agents, he was really only a soldier in a mob with no more chance of becoming boss of Chicago than he had of becoming the mayor of Las Vegas.

Had they taken time to think it through, the law-enforcement "experts" would have known something was genuinely amiss by the fact Michael Spilotro was also missing. Although he'd been indicted in an earlier racketeering case in Las Vegas, those charges had been dismissed for a lack of evidence. He was indicted in April 1986 for attempting to extort a "street tax" from a group of Chicago pimps. In reality, even if convicted, Michael Spilotro didn't face a long prison sentence. He spent plenty of time in Las Vegas, but kept a comfortable home in the suburb of Oak Park. Michael worshiped his big brother, but he wouldn't have gone on the run with him. And nothing would have kept Michael from calling his wife—unless he was unable. That's why she called the police just a day after he and his older brother didn't return home from their meeting.

On June 17, authorities found the 1986 Lincoln Mark VI the Spilotros had been driving parked at a Howard Johnson's restaurant near O'Hare International Airport. In Las Vegas, U.S. Magistrate Phillip Pro signed a contempt citation against Tony Spilotro for his failure to appear in court, but by then it had become clear the brothers had taken a ride with someone.

"Tony Spilotro never ducked a court date in his life," Goodman recalled. "It wasn't his style. A lot of so-called experts were saying he went on the lam to avoid his upcoming trials, but the truth is he wasn't afraid of the courtroom. He loved to do battle, to go to war with the government. I knew something had to be wrong, because Tony gave no indication that he might not be around for the retrial. I think he looked forward to staring down those rotten rats Frank Cullotta and Sal Romano. He lived for that kind of confrontation."

Goodman insists that he felt no fear for himself or his family and his actions during that dangerous time bear that out. Only a day after Spilotro was reported missing, Goodman traveled to Washington to join federal judge Harry Claiborne.

Before he left for McCarran International Airport and the flight back to Washington, Goodman received a phone call at his home. A voice on the other end of the line told him Tony Spilotro was gone. Many years later, Goodman still declined to identify the voice on the phone.

Tony Spilotro was missing, but Goodman's mind was elsewhere.

♪ ♪ ♪

Upon conviction, Harry Claiborne was sent to a federal prison in Montgomery, Alabama. He was transported from Alabama to Washington to meet with Goodman to prepare for his Congressional showdown. Two days after Tony Spilotro turned up missing, Nevada's senior U.S. Senator, Paul Laxalt, issued what amounted to a warning to Claiborne: Think twice before walking onto the Senate floor and trying your luck in an impeachment proceeding. By then, even Laxalt had called for Claiborne to give up his salary, which by then was $78,200. Although he stopped short of asking the judge to resign, there was no indication in the Senate or House that Claiborne had any chance of prevailing.

"Under no circumstances will he resign," Goodman told reporters, who realized the judge was walking into a slaughterhouse.

Members of Congress from both parties had begun calling for Claiborne's scalp. South Carolina Senator Strom Thurmond shouted for a constitutional amendment that would automatically remove from office any federal official found guilty of a felony. "When convicted federal officials refuse to resign from office, it's a slap in the face of the American people for them to remain on the federal payroll." Thurmond's proposal went nowhere, but it did represent the prevailing sentiment.

Goodman addressed the House Judiciary subcommittee, which was charged with drawing up the articles of impeachment, for three hours. The group wasn't the least bit interested in the defense's vendetta theory. After the morning session, a disheartened Claiborne declined to testify in his own defense and asked to be returned to his cell at Maxwell Air Force Base. He knew he had no allies on the subcommittee and was certain to lose when his case came up for a vote on June 24, 1986. "I haven't heard of anyone who is going to stick up for the judge," an inside source told a reporter.

Claiborne could still resign and spare himself ultimate national humiliation, but time was running out.

෴ ෴ ෴

On June 23, 1986, Michael Kinz went to apply weed killer to the sprouting cornfield he leased on land next to the Willow Slough Preserve in Newton County, Indiana. As he surveyed the soil, he noticed a patch of land that had recently been broken. But it hadn't been tilled. It had been turned over. Having knowledge of the methods of deer poachers who sometimes buried the unused remains of their kill, Kinz called the Indiana Game and Wildlife Agency, which dispatched a field biologist.

After digging a short time, the men uncovered not a deer carcass, but the corpses of two men who had been so badly beaten their faces were unrecognizable. A call went out to the Newton County Sheriff's Office, then to the FBI, and within hours agents were contacting dentist Pat Spilotro with a request: the dental records of brothers Anthony and Michael.

On the day the House Judiciary subcommittee voted to endorse the impeachment of Harry Claiborne, newspapers in Chicago and Las Vegas led with the news that the Spilotros had been found beaten to death and buried in a cornfield located near Morocco, Indiana.

The autopsies were performed in Indianapolis at the Indiana University Medical Center. Dr. John Pless, director of forensic pathology at Indiana University Medical School, determined the cause of death. The Spilotros had not been shot in the back of the head in keeping with a long Outfit tradition, but had been beaten with blunt force, the kind caused by hands and feet. They'd been buried while still breathing. Kent County, Indiana, Coroner Dr. David Dennis determined the brothers died of asphyxiation related to the severe trauma they had received. But, the coroner noted, the Spilotros suffered no broken bones.

In Chicago, Michael Spilotro's attorney Allan Ackerman called the deaths a "shock" and "a pathetic, horrible situation." Horrible and pathetic, perhaps, but hardly surprising given the business the brothers were in and the change of the guard in the Outfit.

Although reporters noted that the Spilotros were found just five miles from a farm owned by Joey Aiuppa, authorities refused to speculate whether the imprisoned mob boss had any connection to the murders.

The Hole-in-the-Wall Gang racketeering trial was delayed a week, and columnist Ned Day had lost his favorite topic for all time. "Forget Metro or the Federal Strike Force," he wrote. "On the tough turf that he ruled, Tony Spilotro's word was the only law that counted. That's why it seems so odd that his mangled corpse now should appear so trivial; just another manifestation of old clichés, just another mobster dumped dead in an Indiana cornfield, or a trash compactor, or a car trunk — you've heard the story before.

"What does it all mean?

"Maybe that's the answer: It means nothing."

But Spilotro's death held powerful meaning for his friend and attorney Oscar Goodman. For the first time in more than a decade, Goodman was not attempting to shout down government prosecutors on behalf of his client.

The quiet, to Oscar, was almost unnerving.

Though Spilotro and Goodman had been joined at the hip for a decade, the attorney received not a single phone call from any law-enforcement agency asking his opinion of who might have been behind Spilotro's murder. Not that he would have received such a call warmly.

"As time went on, I was particularly angry because I was convinced that the FBI never wanted to solve his murder," Goodman said. "Nobody in the world had a legitimate relationship with Tony that was more intense than myself, other than perhaps his wife. And you would think that the least the FBI would do would be to come to me and ask me whether I had a thought as to what happened. They never did. And when I called them on it, they said, 'Well, if we'd gone to you, you wouldn't have told us anything." But what they meant was, 'Fuck you and who cares?'

"These were people who followed Tony day and night year after year, but a few days before he's scheduled to go to trial he returns to Chicago, where all his people are supposed to live, and they choose that time to pull their surveillance," Goodman said. "That's bullshit and they know it. They had to have heard something and they let it happen.

"They didn't even make an effort to find out who did it. Not that I had any idea; I still don't. All I know is that whoever did it had to be very tough, because Tony was a tough, tough guy. I didn't know Michael that well. I knew he was the owner of Hoagie's Restaurant in Chicago and had a very nice wife named Annie. But Tony was tough."

In the weeks that followed the Spilotro murders, investigators began to piece together likely suspects. Veteran FBI Agent Jack Bonino interviewed Betty Tocco, the estranged wife of mob hitman Albert Caesar Tocco, and came away convinced that he'd had a hand in the murders. Knowledgeable sources believe Tocco, Nicky Guzzino, Dominick "Toots" Palermo, and at least one other hoodlum participated in the burial of the two brothers. The man behind the murders, informed mob sources later revealed, was Chicago's new boss, Joe Ferriola.

? ? ?

The House Judiciary subcommittee on courts met the day after the Spilotro brothers' bodies were discovered in Indiana to determine the structure of the impeachment of Harry Claiborne. Within hours, it resolved by a vote of 15 to 0 to forward to the House Judiciary Committee four articles of impeachment related to the "high crimes and misdemeanors" associated with his tax-evasion conviction. Many of the Judiciary Committee members had barely studied the issue and were unlikely to stray from the decision of the subcommittee on courts, whose members had at least cracked the file. It was a political conundrum: The closer Claiborne got to a full hearing on the floor of the United States Senate, the worse his chances became of receiving an attentive audience.

Later that week, Claiborne and Goodman watched the 35-member House Judiciary Committee unanimously vote to impeach. And still Claiborne refused to resign. He never wavered from his cry of innocence.

"I think it will be an uphill fight," Congressman Robert Kastenmeier of Wisconsin said in the understatement of the day. "As these matters go, the conviction and the jury findings make it conclusive for other persons judging the matter. ... Even assuming, for the purposes of argument, the conviction is overturned, the facts relating to Judge Claiborne's behavior cannot be reversed. The conduct remains the same."

Congressman James Sensenbrenner of Wisconsin agreed. He told a reporter, "It's going to be very difficult for a House member who has studied the case for a month or two coming up against Mr. Goodman, who has represented Judge Claiborne for five years. The message I get is that Goodman is very good at getting hung juries. ... My concern is that he is eligible for parole at any time under the terms of his sentence. The Parole Board is meeting July 16. We could have the outrageous situation where the man is sitting on the bench in the day and is in the halfway house at night."

Congressman Harry Reid considered himself an ally of both Claiborne and Goodman, but for weeks he attempted to persuade the judge to resign. Publicly he wouldn't rule out the possibility that Claiborne and Goodman might win the day — "He and Oscar Goodman are going to have to be at the top of their game," he declared, putting a voice to the handwriting on the wall. Privately, he was convinced the judge had no chance.

Although he knew he hadn't been heard sympathetically by the committee, Oscar Goodman refrained from lashing out. "When you explore the issues, you want a total exploration, but I have no quarrel with the way the subcommittee treated me," Goodman said.

Goodman was new to Washington, but it didn't take a Beltway insider to read the playing field. Whenever he broached the subject of resignation, Claiborne would have none of it. For all his troubles, the Arkansas sharecropper's son believed that the system eventually would enable him to prove his case of government misconduct.

But Claiborne had perhaps been reading too many issues of the *Las Vegas Sun*, where the sensational stories of government misconduct were published. All the talk of an FBI vendetta was not supported by facts capable of withstanding careful examination and the dress rehearsal before the House Judiciary Committee made that clear.

Why did Claiborne refuse to resign? Those who knew him believe that, after his tax-evasion conviction, he became obsessed with salvaging his reputation. He had to go down fighting.

"I always believed that in the end, the system would work," Claiborne said in a later interview.

More than a decade after his eventual impeachment, Claiborne was asked whether he believed he received the best representation possible from Goodman. Stories had circulated in Las Vegas for years that Claiborne was dissatisfied with Goodman and was upset by his attorney's nightly drinking. Given an opportunity to rethink his ordeal, Claiborne said he believed Goodman gave his best effort against a stacked deck.

In his arguments in front of the committee, Goodman charged that Claiborne had made powerful enemies as a defense attorney and judge because of his fierce independence and refusal to be intimidated by Strike Force prosecutors and FBI agents. But although committee members might have considered it outrageous for the government to excuse brothel owner Joe Conforte's $19 million tax liability, it wasn't proof of wrongdoing against the judge. Goodman was practicing alchemy before supreme skeptics, who also didn't buy the theory that the FBI's pursuit of private investigator Eddie LaRue, on charges he'd planted a bug on behalf of Claiborne at the home of a girlfriend, had been more vendetta. LaRue had been acquitted, but there had been enough evidence to indict him. And neither was the demotion of DA's office polygrapher Chuck Lee, who had administered a favorable lie detector test to Claiborne in the case, proof that the government was out to get the judge.

Goodman's charge that the FBI had pulled a black-bag burglary of the judge's home in order to photograph his personal financial records was met with derision. Where were the facts to support the allegation?

"You're speaking of people who are going to get somebody's head, political hit squads," Congressman Romano Mazzoli of New York said. But where were his facts? Where was the smoking gun? "At least make reference to factual data, or do we have a tale spun today which might have editorial comment, might have personal communications woven into it? What appears in your brief could very well be your own comment, not so much data."

Furthermore, House counsel Richard Cates made it clear he saw no evidence that the $106,000 tax liability that had led to the two tax convictions in 1983 could be construed to be solely the responsibility of tax preparers. In other words, the argument that didn't work at trial wasn't working before the House Judiciary Committee, either.

Having come to the end of his version of the facts, Goodman was finally reduced to using the newspaper articles. "I understand. I have heard people take that position. I have read letters to the editor. But at the same time, if you're new to the Las Vegas community, where the judge was sitting and where the standard of respect is probably better judged, the whole community, at least ostensibly, is rallying behind him. There are posters. There are billboards. There are buttons."

But Las Vegas, he discovered that day, was a long way from Washington. And the judge's tax figures were a long way from accurate. And Goodman stood legally naked before the committee.

In an attempt to make sense of the fumbled numbers, the House impeachment committee hired tax expert William L. Wilson, who represented a large Midwest accounting firm. Wilson's observation was devastating. For 1980 alone, Wilson used incompetent tax planner Jerry Watson's figures and calculated that Claiborne had underreported his taxable income by $176,943. Claiborne had a net tax payment of $1,103 when he actually owed the government $97,864.

The House Judiciary Committee voted unanimously to forward the articles of impeachment to the entire House for a vote. On June 26, the House of Representatives voted 406-0 to impeach Harry Claiborne. Congressman Peter Rodino and his fellow House managers entered their scorn for the judge into the record:

"Judge Claiborne has brought disrepute upon the federal judiciary. In two years he failed to report over $190,000 in taxable income. Judge Claiborne cashed large fee checks at local casinos, and used the tax refund he received to invest either in quarter horses in Mexico or real estate in Las Vegas. The evidence consistently and persuasively demonstrates that his actions were deliberate, purposeful, and willful. When confronted with his crimes, Judge Claiborne lied under oath. He has refused to resign his office. He has continued to collect his salary while in prison. He has drawn scorn upon himself and the federal judiciary that he represents."

Even in the face of three unanimous votes against him and the strong rebukes from the congressmen, Claiborne refused to quit.

His case was scheduled to make one last stop in the United States Senate, where he hoped to win a hearing before its 100 members, and where it would take a two-thirds majority vote to remove him from office.

? ? ?

By the end of the summer of 1986, Spilotro's name had faded from the Las Vegas and Chicago media. Goodman won a hollow victory before the Ninth U.S. Circuit Court of Appeals on September 26, when it affirmed U.S. District Judge Foley's decision to suppress the evidence obtained during the Gold Rush jewelry-store search warrant; Foley had deemed the language contained in the search warrant unconstitutionally vague. Assistant U.S. Attorney Eric Johnson insisted on taking the matter to the Ninth Circuit, where he challenged Goodman to one of many paper wars the two would wage over the years. The court reviewed the FBI's 157-page search-warrant affidavit, describing it as "a tedious chronology of surveillance and telephone taps, showing a general pattern of criminal wrongdoing without providing strong evidence of isolated criminal transactions; it does, however, provide probable cause to believe that Spilotro supervised a loanshark and bookmaking operation." More than a year's effort by the FBI under Special Agent In Charge Joseph Yablonsky, the period of time in which Agent Rick Baken managed to infiltrate Spilotro's inner circle of thieves and killers, was wasted and thrown out due to a lack of attention to detail.

The Circuit Court plumbed the critical depth of the affidavit in relation to its gross weight and in the end agreed with beleaguered Judge Foley, whose integrity had been so wickedly questioned privately by federal prosecutors and investigators, that the affidavit lacked sufficient specificity.

Goodman and his most notorious client had prevailed one last time, though Spilotro's last battle was won posthumously.

"I never had a bad day with Tony," Goodman recalled years later. "And it's the most amazing thing, but I can't think of any lawyer in the country, with the exception of John Gotti's attorney Bruce Cutler, who would have experienced what I experienced. Until Tony got killed, I didn't realize how much time out of my life he took. It was like I had nothing to do. It was like my whole life was taken up taking care of Tony Spilotro and everything else was ancillary and had to be fit into little niches, but didn't take on monumental proportions.

"I saw that not only was Las Vegas changing, but my practice was changing as well. After Tony died, it was like I sat at my desk and I was hollow."

Except for one thing. After finally stepping through the ropes and climbing out of the ring he'd shared with Spilotro all those years, he now had to go into the 15th round of the fight to save the career of Judge Harry Claiborne.

16

Impeachment Blues

Oscar Goodman flew to Washington, D.C., in late August 1986 to prepare for the Senate impeachment trial of Harry Claiborne. He immediately made himself at home. By definition, that meant securing a comfortable bed and sufficient office space, and making the acquaintance of a discreet bookmaker and a superb martini. He had little difficulty locating any of the four. While he'd been preparing for a trial before the Senate, Washington had been preparing for the impeachment as well. The impending proceedings were nightly topics of discussion on TV news programs and the morning newspapers featured the Claiborne affair prominently.

Oscar Goodman was getting his fifteen minutes of fame, Washington-style.

"The Secretary of the Senate was there. I forget his name offhand, but he was a gracious fellow who was more than happy to handle my football action. I'm not sure if he laid it off or not, but it was great. He was either booking it or he was passing it to a bookmaker, and we settled up every Tuesday. That was a relief, because I hadn't missed a chance to bet on a ballgame since I was a kid.

"We worked hard during the day, but we drank even harder

at night. I found paradise at a splendid restaurant called the Monocle, which was a favorite with members of Congress. People quickly knew where to find me — in the bar talking to Robert Reed, the bartender. Robert was a fine gentleman who poured the best martini in Washington. We used to drink there every night.

"Before long, Robert named a drink after the way I used to prefer my martinis. It was a drop of Scotch, which was swished around the cold glass, then thrown out. He filled the glass with very cold Beefeater gin, then took a glass of ice on the side and placed the olive atop the ice. I mean it was a real alcoholic drink. And they called it a 'Goodman.'

"Everybody knew where Goodman was, because he was drinking Goodmans."

Not that he was taking the process lightly. By day, Goodman and the rest of the defense team faced the grim reality that Claiborne would not, as they'd hoped, receive a wide-open hearing before the entire Senate. To date, there had been no indication that the Senate was going to be any more sympathetic to Claiborne's argument than the House.

Television cameras and Kleig lights were set up in the Senate Caucus Room in preparation for the Claiborne impeachment hearing. In the years before C-SPAN and other television coverage of Congress became commonplace, the presence of cameras and equipment gave the room an especially dramatic appearance. Oscar Goodman and Harry Claiborne might have been focused on trying to impress a group of professional politicians, but the judge was being tried before a nation of Americans who had experienced the Watergate scandal a dozen years earlier. Interested citizens had learned about the impeachment process from events leading up to President Richard Nixon's resignation.

Claiborne spent his nights in the brig at the U.S. Marine base in Quantico, Virginia. By day, he was shackled, handcuffed, and chained to a guard during the trip to the Capitol. Only a plea to the Senate enabled the 69-year-old Claiborne to have the shackles removed once he reached his destination. But security was so tight around the judge that two armed U.S. marshals flanked him at all times and did not permit visitors not associated with his defense team to communicate with him, as though he might have somehow been able to corrupt the halls of Congress.

"At one point I went to Warren Rudman, the senator from New Hampshire, who was my adversary back when I represented Ben Schmoutey before a Senate committee," Goodman remembered. "Rudman was clearly not a friend, but I read in his face that he also believed the shackling of Claiborne was punitive treatment. It was for show and not necessary, and fortunately, he agreed. I persuaded him to allow Claiborne to remain in a 'safe house,' where he had a little TV to watch football games on. When I visited him, the marshalls let me go out and bring back food for him. True to his nature, when I asked him what in the world I could get for him, he said, 'Chili dogs.' So that's what I got him."

Goodman was more concerned with the way Claiborne's case was being treated inside the Senate. The signs went from bad to worse in September, when the Senate rejected Goodman's motion to have the impeachment heard before the full 100 members. Instead, the senators opted for a 12-member panel to hear the facts presented. The panel included a young Senator from Tennessee named Al Gore, Jr.

And there was a problem with the timing of the trial itself. It was scheduled for the final weeks of the session, when the sausage-making legislative process is at its most intense and members of the Senate are most distracted. "That deadline for adjournment would definitely work against the judge," defense-team member and former Senator Howard Cannon observed. "We feel this is a matter of such importance it should not be pushed aside because people want to get out and go home."

"With all the rush," added Senator Paul Laxalt, "it's going to take an extremely conscientious senator to wade through that report."

The impeachment trial came in two phases: the presentation of testimony and the oral argument. But the Senate panel complicated matters for Goodman by limiting the scope of his government-conspiracy defense. Goodman was able to parade witness after witness to testify to the incompetence of the tax preparation and the judge's good name, but he was not allowed to call witnesses who claimed the FBI had sanctioned the burglary of Claiborne's home. Nor was he allowed to discuss the $19 million deal the FBI cut with Joe Conforte to testify against Claiborne.

Goodman presented a line of character witnesses, all of whom held forth about the judge's unimpeachable integrity and impeccable character. *Las Vegas Sun* publisher Hank Greenspun, whose newspaper had long since discarded any pretense of fairness or objectivity in the Claiborne affair, attested at length to the judge's innumerable good qualities and the Justice Department and FBI's many misdeeds in railroading an innocent man.

"No one could have withstood what the government has done to this man," Greenspun said. "I'll say this. I've known Judge Claiborne for twenty years. ... Never have I had more reason to express openly my respect, my admiration, and my gratitude for this man for having survived—to sit before this honorable tribunal, as a last resort, to seek vindication.

"Not only will it be a vindication for this man. It will be a vindication for the checks and balances of this government, the judiciary ... which sadly, sadly, is being destroyed."

Greenspun also focused his ire on his favorite target, former FBI SAC Joe Yablonsky, who he claimed had "poisoned the entire environment about this man so that no one can form an objective judgment about him."

Greenspun, of course, hadn't exactly contributed to the objective study of the case by portraying Claiborne as a simple citizen-victim of an ogre-like FBI. It might have played in Las Vegas, but such sensationalism generated laughter in more sophisticated circles.

If Greenspun and his reporters were in no small part responsible for fanning the flames of federal outrage against Claiborne, the fiercely independent publisher was not going to admit it. The *Sun* printed special editions featuring Claiborne's side of the story and Greenspun handed out copies of the papers. At one point, Greenspun argued with a bailiff and won permission to sit directly behind the defense table. He remained near Claiborne's side throughout the proceeding.

Although Greenspun and Goodman held forth at length about their theory of a Yablonsky vendetta, House Judiciary Chairman Peter Rodino in his opening statement before the Senate impeachment panel said, "You should keep in mind at all times during this trial the kind of man with whom we are dealing. This is not an uneducated man incapable of understanding his obligation to report income and pay taxes. He is a highly educated attorney and learned judge who has participated in criminal tax cases both as a lawyer and a judge. He knew full well his obligation to pay his taxes, understood the meaning of signing his tax form under penalty of perjury, and was well aware of the seriousness of and the penalties for tax evasion."

But what if Claiborne, overwhelmed by making the transition from private practice attorney to federal judge, had signed a blank form and relied on the competence of his tax preparer?

It was a question that intrigued Senator Jeff Bingaman of New Mexico, but impressed few others. Signing a blank tax form seemed the height of irresponsibility to some on the panel. The other senators focused on facts that, outside Las Vegas, seemed to defy reason: the hoarding of the cash gift from Sid Wyman and the fact that Claiborne cashed a substantial IRS refund check at the Golden Nugget.

Goodman fought to win two main points. He submitted further motions to fully explore his vendetta defense and to try Claiborne's case before all 100 senators.

Claiborne's future hung on Goodman's ability to persuade the 12-member panel to open the door to the government's conspiracy against the judge. Without it, he was dead meat. On September 19, Committee Chairman Charles Mathias ordered three federal agents to testify as to whether they had intimidated tax preparer Jerry Watson. The agents denied intimidating him. And Watson's former assistant, Charlotte Travaglia, testified that the man responsible for Claiborne's tax return was unintelligent enough to make errors of such magnitude that the House Judicial Committee's tax expert had uncovered. Arkansas Senator David Pryor, one of Claiborne's few allies on the panel, argued in favor of expanding the scope of the trial.

It appeared to be the break Goodman had hoped for.

"In my opinion, if the senators continue to show the interest that they've been showing and we can continue with the momentum that I think we've developed, I think we can get a full hearing in front of the Senate. I definitely view it as a positive sign. If they were going to turn me down, they would have turned me down today."

As suddenly as the opportunity appeared, however, it vanished.

"We'd better be very, very careful about what we do here," New Hampshire Senator Warren Rudman warned. This senator sensed the importance of the moment. If the committee opened the door for Goodman to present his government-misconduct case, the focus would shift from the tax issue.

"This conspiracy doesn't seem to me to go to the [tax fraud] articles that are before us," Arizona Senator Dennis DeConcini observed.

Finally, Chairman Mathias issued a four-page ruling prohibiting Goodman from presenting so-called vendetta witnesses as part of his defense strategy. It was all over but the final vote.

"You have to remember, the Claiborne case came at a time when the FBI was basically sacred still," attorney David Chesnoff said. "Ironically, our support came from the few senators who were anti-federal people. The people who really hurt us were the liberals. We couldn't break through the liberals. They wouldn't step forward. People like Paul Sarbanes, Joe Biden, and Al Gore, they killed us. Gore even accused Oscar and me of violating the Senate rules by politicking. What a joke. They were politicking on their side and we were supposed to sit silent and take it.

"Oscar was incredibly eloquent. He didn't pull any punches. He laid it all out. It was one of the few times in my life I've actually seen him cry.

"They treated Claiborne worse than Pablo Escobar. What Claiborne didn't recognize was he had the power of the Justice Department going against him. It was too much. Oscar dedicated every minute to Claiborne. I just don't understand where it could have been won."

Goodman was selling hard, but the senators weren't suckers. The same minimalization strategy that had saved the prosecution in the second criminal trial was being followed in the impeachment. And there was nothing Goodman or anyone could do about it.

This was not a murder or racketeering trial in which the rules in court were clearly defined. There were no angles to work, no technicalities that might impress a judge or jury into letting the defendant off. In an impeachment proceeding, the criminal "burden of proof beyond a reasonable doubt" did not apply. The Senate could rule as it wished; it could allow as much or as little testimony as it desired. In effect, the Senate acted as the judge and jury, except that in Claiborne's case, not all the judge-jurors were going to hear the evidence presented in person. Instead, they would read the report of Chairman Mathias, then decide.

Goodman and Howard Cannon, citing the statements of members of Congress during the impeachment proceedings of President Richard Nixon, argued forcefully for the Senate to embrace the reasonable-doubt standard. It was their one hope of opening the door to try their version of the case as a vast government conspiracy to railroad an honest but outspoken judge. During the pre-impeachment hearings in 1974, Sam Ervin, Jr., had offered, "In a case of this kind, if we are called upon to try an impeachment, I would not hope for conviction on any charge unless I was satisfied beyond a reasonable doubt of the truth of the charges." And Strom Thurmond had added, "The penalty of impeachment is severe. It is not a criminal penalty, but I know of no penalty that would be more severe than to remove a president from office. And, therefore, I believe the evidence should be beyond a reasonable doubt." And John C. Stennis had said, "Where any party is charged with an impeachable offense, and is tried by the Senate, be it a so-called minor official on up to the highest office under our Constitution, then I think the proof required ought to be beyond a reasonable doubt."

In presenting his argument, Goodman held a mirror up to the senators, reminding them that it had not been so long ago that their colleagues, some of whom were still serving, had asked that important question. Of course, Nixon had resigned before the Senate came to a vote, thus avoiding the disgrace that accompanied removal from office. Claiborne, possessing none of Nixon's political savvy, would still have none of that. He remained steadfast in his conviction that he was an innocent man, wrongly accused and the victim of wicked circumstance and conspiracy.

During the phase of the process set aside to argue the reasonable-doubt standard, Harry Claiborne argued that he had been a fair and fine judge, one who was independent. And that had been part of his problem. Then he argued that he had done only what the average citizen does when he hires a tax preparer and accountant—he trusts the experts, casually looks over the documentation, and cuts a check to the Internal Revenue Service. In the slow rhythmic style that had become his trademark in the courtroom, Claiborne calmly told the senators that he had been called a liar three times in his life—once by a Justice Department prosecutor in Reno and twice that day by House Judiciary Committee Chairman Peter Rodino and Representative Hamilton Fish, Jr., of New York.

"I want to be honest with every member of this body. I would much rather, right today, be almost any place than here. But I knew when I was convicted that this was the place that I had to come. And I have felt that I was not dealt fairly with on the trial level, in that on the trial level, they refused to hear my pleas, if you please, of government misconduct against me. And the appellate court turned a deaf ear also.

"And I knew that I had to go somewhere. I knew there would be somewhere that somebody would listen. And I told my lawyers and I told everyone that was concerned with my personal life that somewhere along the line, some judge is going to say, 'Wait a minute. Wait a minute. What in the world went on? What happened?' And when the time comes that the judge will say that, I would receive some relief.

"I am not fighting here for a judgeship. That may forever be gone. I am not fighting for my freedom, because I have given up a large part of that, and I know I will give up some more before I am released.

"There is more involved than Judge Harry Claiborne of the District Court of Nevada. And what is involved is a spirit of fair play. What is involved is honesty and decency and what is involved is the independence of the American judiciary."

Goodman was forced to summon all his life experience and legal training, all his gifts of salesmanship and courthouse legerdemain. He also called upon a lengthy list of character witnesses, which ran the gamut of Las Vegas society.

In the end, Claiborne found eloquent and generous allies in Senators Jeff Bingaman of New Mexico and David Pryor of Arkansas. Of the 12 committeemen, only those two spoke out on his behalf.

Pryor made it clear in his statement that he believed

Claiborne had been driven from office by the FBI.

Pryor addressed the assembled members of the U.S. Senate as they convened to decide the guilt or innocence of a federal judge from Nevada. "Today I rise to speak out against the raw and awesome power of the federal agencies of the U.S. government and about an abuse of that power that I truly believe led to the ultimate conviction in the lower court of Judge Harry Claiborne. Mr. President, I rise today to speak for the opportunity, if not the basic right, of every American taxpayer to have the right to face an auditor of the Internal Revenue Service Civil Division to explain their tax return before criminal prosecution starts. Judge Claiborne did not have that opportunity. He was denied it.

"Mr. President, I rise today to speak against what has become the accepted practice of arbitrarily and capriciously targeting individual citizens of our country, of intimidating witnesses in their trials, of forgiving past crimes to testify against particular people, of ensnaring individuals into crime or becoming government bounty hunters."

Before relinquishing the floor, Pryor also lashed out against the FBI and raised key defense questions of vendetta and also conspiracy on the part of Yablonsky.

In his official statement, Jeff Bingaman outlined Claiborne's defense and agreed that the tax-evasion convictions had arisen from "tragic mistakes" and not willful deceit. Bingaman believed that the entire Senate, without considering the full scope of evidence available, could not make a fully informed decision and had done Claiborne an injustice. "In conclusion, Mr. President, we have not given the respondent an adequate hearing to support a conviction on Articles One, Two, and Four. A vote of guilty on each of those articles requires an independent determination as to Judge Claiborne's state of mind and in order to make that determination, we need to hear testimony, not have a select few hear testimony, but actually have the Senate hear testimony."

But even Bingaman admitted there was enough evidence, given the fact Claiborne had been convicted by a jury in the federal tax trial, to remove the judge from office on Article III.

Oscar Goodman, who had clerked for Arlen Specter nearly a quarter century earlier, listened as the esteemed senator from

Pennsylvania summed up the grim reality. Claiborne's conviction alone had sunk him, rendering the Senate's decision a foregone conclusion.

"As Judge Claiborne's case has emphasized, federal judges are unique in that once convicted, even by the trial court system of illegal conduct, the people may not simply vote them out of office if they so choose, assuming that the party refuses to resign. Instead, a judge reluctant to relinquish his office must be subject to the impeachment procedures established by the Constitution.

"The full gamut of those procedures has now been exhausted. Judge Claiborne has had his day in court, before the House, and before the Senate. It is time for him now to become an ordinary U.S. citizen, convicted of a felony offense, who must serve his remaining time in prison, without the reward of believing that he can then return to his bench and resume life as before. Judge Claiborne must pay for the offenses he committed, and can no longer assume the distinguished mantle of a federal judge."

The statement of Senator Al Gore of Tennessee was typical of Claiborne's critics on the committee. "The conclusion is inescapable that Claiborne filed false income-tax returns and that he did so willfully rather than negligently. While I do not believe that the Senate must apply a reasonable-doubt standard in impeachment proceedings, I nevertheless believe that Claiborne has advanced no reason to doubt the conclusions that I have reached about his conduct.

"Although a convicted felon, Claiborne arrived before the Senate as a member of the federal judiciary. He has been afforded the procedural protections which the Constitution reserves for that important position. Given the circumstances, it is incumbent upon the Senate to fulfill its constitutional responsibility and strip this man of his title. An individual who has knowingly filed false tax returns has no business receiving a salary derived from the tax dollars of honest citizens. More importantly, an individual guilty of such reprehensible conduct ought not be permitted to exercise the awesome powers which the Constitution entrusts to the federal judiciary."

? ? ?

At the end of the day, U.S. marshals returned Claiborne in chains to the brig at Quantico. From there, he was transported back to Montgomery, Alabama, where he served the remainder of his sentence.

Upon release in 1989, he returned to Southern Nevada. After sufficient time to recuperate, he began a campaign to have his right to practice law in state courts returned. In 1990, the State Bar of Nevada reinstated attorney Harry E. Claiborne's license to practice law.

Claiborne and Goodman communicated less and less in the months and years following the impeachment. Claiborne made it clear to friends that he believed he'd lost in part because of Goodman's inferior effort. Claiborne, some of his intimates thought, believed one of his greatest mistakes had been to have Oscar Goodman as his attorney. In an interview, Claiborne was far more circumspect, observing in retrospect that no lawyer could have saved him from what he considered a glorified fix.

A former federal prosecutor and tax specialist, who agreed to be interviewed on the condition of anonymity, said he had no doubt about Goodman's effort, but questioned whether it wouldn't have been wiser in the second federal trial for Claiborne to bring in an expert in IRS criminal procedure. It was there, before that jury in Reno, that Claiborne's fate was forged. The impeachment was all but decided by the 12 jurors hearing the tax case against Claiborne, for common sense would dictate that any federal judge who is convicted of a felony has no chance of being allowed to remain on the bench.

Lost on some, however, was the prosecution's strategy. In the wake of the mistrial in the first case, only a few days passed before federal prosecutors re-emerged with the plan to eliminate Joe Conforte from the mix and prosecute Claiborne on the tax charges alone. And it certainly didn't help Claiborne's chances that Goodman and his IRS specialist, J. Richard Johnston, were unable to buy time from Judge Hoffman, who immediately ordered a new trial, minimizing the defense's ability to prepare for the imminent proceedings. If Claiborne was dissatisfied with the mistrial result, he never mentioned it publicly — and there wasn't much time to look for a replacement for Oscar Goodman.

Law partner David Chesnoff said, "I was with Oscar every

day during the Claiborne trial. I watched how hard he worked to try to save the judge. People can say whatever they want now, but Oscar would have done anything to save Claiborne. And Oscar cried when he lost. It was the first time I'd seem him cry. He was heart-broken that he couldn't save Harry Claiborne."

? ? ?

"After the vote, I returned to Las Vegas deeply saddened for Claiborne, but in the short time I'd been there, I'd fallen in love with Washington. It helped, I knew, that I was on television nightly with the top story. The impeachment filled the *Washington Post* and talk of the judge's fight buzzed throughout the city and Congress. Making the speech on the Senate floor, going through the vote, getting the autographed pictures of all these people back there, and all those people telling me what a good lawyer I was, it went to my head like gin.

"Then I returned to Nevada, and said to my wife, 'Sweetheart, it's the greatest city in the world. You've got to come back with me. And I took my wife back there. The Secretary of the Senate, who had been kind enough to book my football bets, made arrangements for tickets for a special, special tour. We had a guard there who took us everywhere. We were treated like kings.

"Then I said to my wife, 'I'm gonna take you to my favorite restaurant, the Monocle.' This was the place where I was a celebrity, where they renamed a gin martini just the way I like it—'The Goodman.' This was the place where I felt like I had arrived.

"And we walked in there. This was two weeks after the impeachment. I came through the door with Carolyn and smiled knowingly, ready for a warm greeting from my good friends at the Monocle. And a man inside the door said, 'Oscar who?' Two weeks had passed and they had no idea who I was. Couldn't care less. I couldn't get a table.

"The drink was gone. I was gone. I went home. It just taught me what Washington's all about—and what politics is about. I learned a valuable lesson that day. Carolyn reminded me of the lesson more than once."

17

The Philadelphia Story

It was with a sense of nervous anticipation, a splash of nostalgia, and not a little irony that Oscar Goodman returned to Philadelphia to represent the Scarfo crime family in a series of criminal cases that had become like so many acts in an epic and bloody drama that intrigued and entertained the citizenry. Not only was Goodman eager to take the stage and strut some stuff in his hometown, but his memories of the day he and Carolyn left Philadelphia for the wilds of Las Vegas, copies of *The Green Felt Jungle* in hand, surely brought a smile. For all the family's warnings about the mob in Las Vegas, one of the biggest mob wars in the nation's history had taken place a short cab ride from where little Oscar had come of age.

City of Brotherly Love, indeed. Police suspected Nicodemo "Little Nicky" Scarfo, his handsome nephew, Philip "Crazy Phil" Leonetti, and their gang of murdering more than two dozen people, corrupting politicians, trafficking in drugs, and committing innumerable acts of extortion and mayhem. Even their top attorney, fellow Philadelphian Bobby Simone, had come under attack and eventually served a prison sentence for tax evasion.

For a generation, Philadelphia's underworld had been managed by Angelo Bruno, a man so low key that he was known as the Docile Don. By 1980, the dawn of the decade that celebrated greed throughout the business world, the traditional rules Bruno had followed were tossed aside like a corpse to the roadside. Then again, "Greed is Good" had always been the mob's motto.

Rising from his status as a small-time psychopath who'd been exiled to Atlantic City in the years before legalized gambling, Little Nicky had done his best rendition of Little Caesar. Climbing to the rank of capo in 1977, Scarfo's stock grew along with the fortunes of the Boardwalk.

By March 1980, Atlantic City was a plum, coveted not only by Bruno, but by the Genovese crime family and other organizations. Bruno's old-school ways and reluctance to expand his turf irritated even his closest associates, and on March 21, 1981, one of the Docile Don's dissatisfied employees, Anthony Caponigro, attempted a hostile takeover by murdering Bruno with a shotgun. His unsanctioned hit was immediately avenged. With Caponigro out of the way, Philip "Chicken Man" Testa became the new boss of Philadelphia.

Philip Testa's reign lasted a mere year before a nail-packed bomb exploded beneath the front porch of his South Philadelphia home, turning the Chicken Man to chicken salad and paving the way for Scarfo's ascension. Police believed Scarfo, with Leonetti at his side, was responsible for more than 20 murders, many identifiable by bullets behind the ears and a trademark "cowboy-style" rope-tying. Scarfo became known as "the man who loves murder" after one former associate told a court that, following the murder of Vincent Falcone, Little Nicky had exclaimed, "I love this. I love this. The big shot is dead. He's a dirty motherfucker. If it wasn't so messy, I'd cut his fucking tongue out."

§ § §

Oscar Goodman returned to Philadelphia in 1986, at age 47, with a tangle of mixed emotions. He thought immediately of his late father, the former prosecutor who had carved out a successful career in private practice in the city, only to fall short

PREVIOUS PAGE: *Oscar Goodman and his most notorious client, Tony "the Ant" Spilotro.*

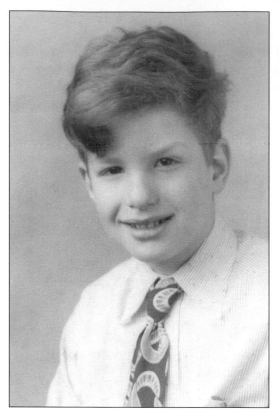

The good boy and protective brother: Oscar Goodman as a kid in West Philadelphia.

Laura and Allan Goodman provided their son Oscar with a stable and creative homelife.

By the 1980s Oscar and Carolyn had emerged as a power couple in Las Vegas.

Portrait of an American family dining in a Vegas showroom: (from left) Oscar Jr., a proud father, Ross, Eric, a blonde Carolyn, and Cara.

Goodman and Jay Sarno celebrate the casino man's victory over IRS bribery charges.

Goodman's friend, Florida lawyer Alvin Malnik, was believed, but never proved, to be Meyer Lansky's protégé.

Lewis "Brown" Crockett was an early Goodman client. In later years he returned to prison and once unsuccessfully tried to set up his former attorney.

Syndicate bookmaker Marty Kane, right, was in a mood to feast at the Bacchanal restaurant at Caesars after Goodman got a gambling charge reduced to a citation. In later years, Kane would take credit for starting Goodman's career.

In his day, Brooklyn-born Bob Martin was known as America's best sports handicapper. A key player in the nation's illegal sports gambling syndicate, Martin was also among Goodman's favorite clients.

Kansas City mob underboss Carl Civella was so stand-up that he refused to flee after he was convicted and headed for a lengthy stay in the penitentiary.

The Little Man, Meyer Lansky. Goodman maintains he never met the mob's reputed financial wizard, though he once represented him.

Jimmy Chagra talks to the press after Goodman walked him on federal charges in the killing of Judge John H. Wood.

Kansas City mob boss Nick Civella was among Goodman's favorite clients and used to sneak into Las Vegas in a disguise to gamble at the Dunes.

At the 25th anniversary roast (of Goodman's law practice) at the Desert Inn with Anthony Civella. "Tony Ripe" was one of many notorious men who mixed with Las Vegas casino executives and judges that night.

Nicky Scarfo, the maniacal boss of the Philadelphia mob family once ruled by "Docile Don" Angelo Bruno, benefited from Goodman's representation of underboss Philip Leonetti, but in the end went the way of most hoodlums.

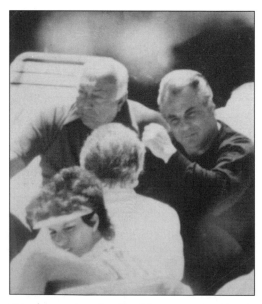

Gambino crime family elder statesman Natale Richichi (top left) was a confidant of mob boss John Gotti (top right).

Tony Spilotro remained out of jail with Oscar Goodman as his lawyer, but he couldn't beat the rap from the Chicago Outfit.

Las Vegas FBI Special Agent In Charge Joseph Yablonsky called Goodman a mob sycophant who went too far in helping to protect suspected killers like Spilotro.

Tony (second from left) and Michael (far right) Spilotro were not only brothers, they also shared criminal intimacies and were rarely without the need of bulldog attorneys, such as Goodman and Jerry Werksman (far left).

Although the stress of Tony Spilotro's business haunted their lives together, Nancy Spilotro remained a fiercely loyal old-school wife of the feared Mafia enforcer.

Chicago native Herbie Blitzstein (right) was Spilotro's most loyal soldier, accompanying him on a variety of daily assignments in Las Vegas. The fact that Blitzstein wasn't killed with Spilotro surprised some authorities. Blitzstein met his own violent end in 1997.

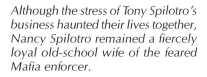

Argent Days: Goodman confers with Allen Glick (left) and Frank Rosenthal (center).

Oscar Goodman with the Rosenthal clan. For a while, Lefty, his wife Geri, and their children looked like a typical American family.

When his Cadillac exploded on October 4, 1982, Frank Rosenthal's days of pretending he was a legitimate guy were over.

The friends of Argent Corp.: (from left) Allen Glick, Goodman, Frank Rosenthal, Joey Cusumano, and Paul Lowden (with their wives). Of the group, only Lowden remains in the casino business.

Harry Claiborne tries on his new robe at U.S. District Court in August 1978. Senior judges Roger Foley (left) and Bruce Thompson (right) show him how it's done.

Brothel-master Joe Conforte ran back to Brazil after burning former client and friend, U.S. District Judge Harry Claiborne. Goodman had represented Conforte and wife Sally, but grew to despise the Mustang Ranch owner.

Goodman played himself in the 1995 movie Casino. He's seen here with Robert DeNiro, whose "Ace Rothstein" character was based on the real-life Lefty Rosenthal.

The referee and the fighter: District Attorney-turned-boxing referee Mills Lane had been Goodman's opponent inside the courtroom, but they remained friends outside it.

Goodman represented embattled San Diego Mayor Roger Hedgecock and won his case on appeal. Hedgecock is now a popular radio talk-show host in California.

At times, Oscar (pictured above with law partner David Chesnoff) and Carolyn Goodman lived in separate worlds: While his clients were among the most notorious men in America, hers were innocent children whom she tutored at the Meadows School.

LEFT: *The candidate. Goodman took his campaign to the people with a tireless grass-roots effort that included many hours working the phones.*

BELOW: *Victory for the outsider. Goodman flanked (from left) by political consultants Mark Fierro and Tom Letizia, and controversial assistant Bill Cassidy.*

At his swearing in, Goodman was uncharacteristically under-stated as he attempted to draw a line between his new career and his controversial previous one.

The mayor cheers for his friends Congresswoman Shelley Berkley and then-U.S. Senator Richard Bryan.

A pair of mayors: Goodman shares a laugh with his predecessor Jan Laverty Jones, who in her eight years in office dramatically raised the profile of the position.

At his State of the City address, Goodman stressed the need for downtown redevelopment.

The self-proclaimed "Happiest Mayor in America" has vowed to reinvigorate care-worn downtown Las Vegas.

of his goal of becoming a judge. And he thought of his mother Laura, the artistic blithe spirit who still lived in a high-rise apartment there. She was sure to be subjected to the inevitable association the public always made between a mob attorney and his hoodlum clients.

"I thought to myself, 'If my father could see me now,'" Goodman said. "These were big cases in Philadelphia. It's a huge media market and the reporters are professional and extremely competitive. They were everywhere, constantly asking questions. In a sense, I was like a movie star back there, but I was smart enough to know that it wasn't me, it was my client. It's like when I represented Tony and people sometimes accused me of courting the media. That wasn't the case at all. What I did was represent the man. Although the headlines read, 'Spilotro Does This,' 'Spilotro Does That,' Spilotro wasn't doing anything. His attorney was. But I got blamed for placing him in the public eye."

There would be no such accusations in Philadelphia, where the press followed like hounds the trail of blood left by Scarfo and his crew.

¶ ¶ ¶

Leland "Lee" Beloff fancied himself a man of his people. Raised in South Philadelphia, the son of a judge, young Beloff was a successful boxer whose rugged good looks and acquaintance with comedian Ernie Kovacs earned him a shot at an acting career. After a handful of movie and television roles, he returned to Philadelphia to begin a career for which he appeared ideally suited: politics. At 23, he was the youngest person ever elected to the Pennsylvania House of Representatives, and even a party switch from Republican to Democrat didn't slow him. Although he'd been suspected of election fraud, nothing stuck to Beloff in the early years. After more than a decade in the state legislature, he moved to the Philadelphia City Council, where his South Philly contacts made him an easy favorite.

One of those contacts was Little Nicky Scarfo.

By the mid-1980s, Beloff and his assistant, Bobby Rego, were ringing bells with local and federal law enforcement for their suspected criminal activities. It came as little surprise when Beloff, Rego, mob hitman Nicholas "Nicky Crow" Caramandi, and Scarfo were indicted on federal charges of conspiracy to extort $1 million from Willard Rouse, III, in exchange for City Council action on two bills that were essential to obtaining $10 million in federal funding for the developer's Penn's Landing project. They were also accused of extorting $100,000 from developer Dr. John Bennett in exchange for help with a union problem and of forcing developer Harry Devoe to provide Beloff's girlfriend with a free apartment in exchange for the councilman's support of a bill to close a residential street in the Old City. The case would be tried in U.S. District Judge John P. Fullam's court. Scarfo attorney Bobby Simone was named an unindicted co-conspirator and Little Nicky was severed from the case and eventually convicted of extortion.

Caramandi and drug-dealing associate John Pastorella agreed to cooperate with the government in exchange for leniency, which placed Beloff under immense pressure. His run of luck appeared over. Through Simone, a desperate Beloff reached out for Oscar Goodman, who brought partner David Chesnoff with him to Philadelphia. The story of Goodman's return to Philadelphia filled headlines. "Beloff Hires Las Vegas Attorney" and "Lawyer Comes Home in Defense of Beloff," the *Inquirer* declared.

As usual, the $87 Horatio Alger story found its way into the lead with ample references to Spilotro, Chagra, Harry Claiborne, and Goodman's trademark custom-made cowboy boots. One writer, Emilie Lounsberry, quoted an anonymous Las Vegas lawyer describing Goodman: "He can be flamboyant when he wants to be, but lower-key than his reputation would lead you to believe. There are times when he can be somewhat flamboyant, but not in the theatrical, Hollywood sense."

"I knew that had I stayed back here, I would have been on someone else's shirttails," Goodman said. "From the moment I got [to Las Vegas], the town was great to me. Everything I touched turned to gold."

Goodman's Midas touch was hard-pressed with Beloff, however. His fervent protestations aside, Beloff was up against a series of damaging witnesses who were willing to link him to the extortion schemes. The tension was getting to the embattled councilman.

At dinner with Goodman, Beloff was drinking and eventually became convinced a group of men in business suits at another booth were FBI agents. Brandishing a fork, he rushed their table and screamed at them. "I know you're with the FBI!"

"Not FBI," one nervous customer replied. "IBM."

A restaurant manager and Goodman helped break up the altercation to avoid having to call police.

At least some of Beloff's paranoia was justified. After all, the government was alleging that at a bar called Marabella's, Beloff had sent a silent signal by rubbing his shoulder twice to indicate the $1 million extortion was on. Beloff could barely move without feeling like he might be acting suspiciously.

Goodman's strategy was the usual: to zero in on the government's use of Caramandi and Tommy Del Giorno, two admitted killers and leg breakers whose rap sheets bespoke long criminal careers. Goodman eventually discovered that the two killers had been given more than the usual meals and protection while under the government's supervision. Del Giorno had once been treated by his law enforcement chaperones to a prostitute after a particularly good day of grand jury testimony.

Discrediting two such witnesses was easy for Goodman and he planned to have a field day.

Prosecutors tried to remind the public, through the media, that whatever their flaws, Caramandi and Del Giorno were once trusted associates of Scarfo and that cooperating Mafia witnesses by their nature were bound to have problematic backgrounds, but such qualifying was drowned out by Goodman's constant pounding at the pair of reformed assassins.

The trial began on March 23, 1987, before Judge Fullam. The prosecution pieced together a case that linked Beloff to extortion and political corruption through his intermediary, Bobby Rego. If Rego's attorney, Joshua Briskin, believed Goodman would lay off his client, he was mistaken. Wherever possible, Goodman carefully used Rego's position in the government's theory of the case to Beloff's benefit.

After the damaging testimony of developers DeVoe and Rouse, Beloff took the stand to profess his innocence. Although he admitted being acquainted with Caramandi and Scarfo, he denied knowing of their reputations as killers and mob figures. Not all of Beloff's side of the story seemed credible, but his presence on the witness stand, with Rego to follow, was a challenge to the jury to measure the relative truth of all those present. And that included Caramandi, Del Giorno, and John Pastorella, who had become an FBI informant.

Goodman battered Caramandi and Del Giorno in his cross-examination, but he went over the top during his closing argument, ramming everything that moved. First, he read the lengthy list of crimes of which Caramandi and Del Giorno had been accused. Then he belittled the prosecution's theory that Beloff had held up the City Council bills for anything but ordinary political reasons. He bashed the prosecution's overwhelming use of surveillance video and audio records.

"Look at this courtroom!" he declared. "It looks like 'Star Wars' in here."

Then he implored the jury to consider what they were being asked to believe: that Beloff, a reasonably respected councilman, had somehow needed to use Caramandi to deliver a message to Rouse.

"Is he gonna use some goon?" Goodman asked, adding in a B-movie accent, "'Hey, Mistuh Rouse. I want a hundred thousand from you. I want a million from you. If you don't gimme the money ...' Come on!"

The jury was in stitches. Prosecutor Ronald Cole wasn't smiling. Then Goodman sealed his closing argument with a variation on a theme he'd been propounding for many years.

"Think about what separates us in our country from the Communists and Fascists, i.e., proof of guilt beyond a reasonable doubt. That is our system, so in the most important day in Lee Beloff's life, I ask you to return a verdict of not guilty on all counts."

The jury deliberated for less than eight hours before reporting to Judge Fullam that it was deadlocked on the extortion and conspiracy counts. Beloff and Rego were acquitted on three lesser counts, but instead of admonishing the jury to go back and try again, Fullam surprised many by declaring a mistrial.

Publicly, Oscar Goodman was elated.

"It feels like a victory," he told reporters. "Anyplace else in the country, I think my client would have a complete acquittal. I think in Philadelphia, there's a presumption that a politician has to be treated harsher than an average citizen. If it were an average citizen on trial, we'd be having a party to end all parties."

Some jurors discounted the testimony of Caramandi and Del Giorno. Others didn't believe the infamous silent hand signal. In the end, one juror, an elderly Italian-American woman from South Philadelphia, held out for acquittal on a majority of the charges.

Beloff used the moment to boast that his political career was far from finished, but it wasn't to be; voters buried him in the next election. By then, he was preoccupied with a second trial. This one was sure to benefit from a more skilled jury selection and a more clearly defined use of Caramandi and Del Giorno. Prosecutors would also take advantage of Scarfo's conviction on all charges in his half of the Beloff extortion case.

That left it up to Goodman to outdo himself in the outrage department.

The second trial began June 23, 1987, and Goodman immediately set to work attempting to dismantle the government's case. He started with the Marabella hand signal.

"It would be impossible for Leland Beloff to see that far across the bar without his glasses on," Goodman offered in his opening statement.

But though he saved the best for Caramandi and Del Giorno, by then they'd been schooled by prosecutors in the art of testifying under pressure. Unlike the first trial, in which Caramandi dressed and acted like a cheap gangster, the second time around he was far more conservatively attired.

Beloff and Rego again took the stand in their own defense, but the case clearly wasn't going as well.

Goodman scrambled in his closing argument. "Lee Beloff is wealthy. He's powerful. He's a politician. He has a girlfriend and he's a friend of Nicky Scarfo, the reputed head of the mob. He's the ideal target upon which careers may be built."

The jury wasn't impressed. It returned guilty verdicts on 11 counts against Beloff and Rego. They were sentenced a week later. Beloff got 10 years in prison, while Rego received eight.

Judge Fullam said Beloff "engaged in corruption of the worst kind. Not only did he sell his office, but he enlisted the aid of organized crime and, in effect, made the City Council one branch of the local Mafia."

Goodman even enlisted high-profile assistance from attorney and Harvard law professor Alan Dershowitz. But it was no use. Judge Fullam had made it clear from the start that he wasn't about to look with favor on corrupt politicians. No one listened when Goodman declared, "He stands before you and feels that he disgraced his family and his name and is now humbled. He has not displayed arrogance. He still hopes for a future as a human being to return to his family and children. He loves his children."

Problem was, Beloff's entire existence was built on arrogance and the only one who declined to acknowledge the fact was his defense attorney. There was nothing to do but move on.

Luckily, there was still plenty of business left in Philadelphia for Oscar Goodman.

That June, 28 people were hit with a federal indictment in a case in which the government alleged the Scarfo family was engaged in a vast conspiracy to dominate the methamphetamine market in Philadelphia through the control of a key ingredient, phenyl-2-propanone or P2P, known on the street as "oil." The biggest names in the indictment were Scarfo, underboss Phil Leonetti, Charles "Charlie White" Iannece, Francis "Faffy" Iannarella, and Salvatore "Chuckie" Merlino. The top players were also charged with maintaining a continuing criminal enterprise; if found guilty of it, the charge carried life sentences.

Scarfo's connections allegedly brought P2P from Europe for $135 a gallon, which was capable of making $240,000 worth of methamphetamine, according to *Mafia Wipeout: How the Feds Put Away An Entire Mob Family*, by Donald Cox. This time Scarfo and Leonetti were tried side by side, with Simone representing the boss and Goodman standing for the underboss. Their strategies clearly reflected a coordinated effort behind the scenes. Other defendants might fall, but they were out to protect the family leaders at all costs.

The trial began December 4, with Simone and Goodman firing away at the notion that real mobsters would stoop so low as to deal drugs and, again, at the incredible absurdity of the government relying on the testimony of Caramandi and Del Giorno.

In their fourth trial in less than a year, however, Caramandi and Del Giorno by then had become experienced witnesses. Each anticipated biting lines of questioning and were not disappointed. They barely flinched at Goodman's portrayal of them as animals and psychopaths who'd "engaged in every crime known to man and breached every commandment known to God." Although there was plenty of evidence that someone had conspired to move methamphetamine through Philadelphia and control those who sold it, little direct evidence—beyond the usual notoriety that accompanied their names—linked Scarfo and Leonetti to the conspiracy. They were high enough up the ladder to be separated from the action by way of several layers of underlings. Simone hammered away at the relative credibility of Caramandi and Del Giorno and at one point even appeared to concede the fact that Scarfo was the head of a Mafia family, in an effort to remind jurors that real "men of honor" didn't deal drugs.

Goodman said, "The buck stops here with you. That's what makes this country different! I don't concede that Phil Leonetti is a member of any secret organization—except out of the mouths of the sewer."

When the jury returned an acquittal, the prosecution and courtroom, dotted with FBI agents, were stunned. Scarfo, Leonetti, and their allies cheered their victory and a shouting match ensued with epithets passing between the mobsters and the G-men. Simone and Goodman reveled in the pandemonium as U.S. District Judge Thomas N. O'Neill Jr. shouted "Silence!" in the courtroom.

Goodman and Simone had made sure jurors remembered Caramandi and Del Giorno for the criminals that they were. So the swift not-guilty verdict gave even the snitches' staunchest government supporters second thoughts about their usefulness in future trials.

For his part, Goodman was now being referred to as "swashbuckling" by some trial watchers. As always, the wanna-be tough guy in the custom cowboy boots couldn't prevent his rhetoric from crossing the line from legal to street jargon.

"The jury did the right thing," he proclaimed. "Caramandi and Del Giorno were the backbone of their case and now it's like a shattered spine. ... I'm happy that this case marks the beginning of the end for these two bums. Let the government put them out on the street and see how they make out. The government has nothing else but the mouths of these two liars."

Veteran courtroom observer and author Donald Cox noted several defects in the government's case, ranging from its inconsistent use of available evidence to the judge's lack of courtroom control. Still, though Scarfo and his intimates were acquitted, most of the remainder of the 28 defendants were convicted and sentenced to long prison terms.

There would be other battles to come, but for the moment Goodman was on top of the world as he drank in the adulation. At one point, several trial followers shouted that he and Simone were the best attorneys in the world.

"You're darn right we are!" Oscar Goodman shouted back.

18

Chicken Wing and the Rats

Those unfamiliar with the ways of the Mafia might believe that Sal "Chicken Wing" Testa would have taken it as a sign the day his father, the "Chicken Man," was blown up by a nail bomb at his South Philly home. Others might have taken the hint and gotten out of the gangster business altogether, getting into insurance sales or shoe repair in a place far from the City of Brotherly Love.

Alas, Chicken Wing was a slow learner. In one respect, it was hard to fault him. After all, with Scarfo as boss, the twenty-something Testa made plenty of money, much of it from trafficking methamphetamine. He owned luxury cars and even captained his own yacht. He was loyal to Little Nicky, had gained a tough-guy reputation after surviving an assassination attempt by the rival Harry Riccobene mob, and appeared headed for the big time as heir apparent to bosshood. Apropos to the Mafia tradition, in early 1984, he proposed marriage to Maria Merlino, daughter of Scarfo capo Sal Merlino.

But Sal Testa's fortune changed overnight after he jilted Maria and embarrassed her papa. Suddenly, Testa was out of Scarfo's inner circle. While others huddled up with the boss, Testa remained in the dark.

Darkness became Testa's permanent condition on September 12, 1984, at a place called Tavella's Sweet Shop. On Scarfo's orders, Nicky Caramandi, Tommy Del Giorno, Charlie Iannece, Joey Pungitore, and Wayne Grande ended Chicken Wing's short career with bullets to the back of the head. Testa's corpse was discovered two days later wrapped in a blue J.C. Penney blanket dumped on the side of Slickersville Road.

Although by 1984 most organized-crime-related deaths in the Philadelphia area were blamed on Scarfo and Leonetti, collecting enough evidence to go before a jury was another matter. That's what made Caramandi and Del Giorno, despite their myriad shortcomings as witnesses, so essential to the government's cases.

John Pastorella, the small-time drug-dealing hoodlum, was in business with Sal Testa, partnered up with Caramandi, and eventually came to wear a wire for the FBI. In time, Pastorella recorded Caramandi discussing a variety of criminal acts, including the elimination of Sal Testa. Presented with self-incriminating statements, Caramandi turned snitch and was joined by Del Giorno.

It was as close to Scarfo and Leonetti as the government was ever likely to get. Scarfo was already serving time on the Rouse extortion and Leonetti's bail on previous felony charges had been revoked. But in keeping with their status as nearly untouchable, both remained strangely confident.

"They're never going to testify against us," Leonetti said. "They don't have the balls. They'll melt."

Goodman stifled a laugh. He'd heard such talk for years. What his mob clients didn't realize was the fact that criminals who flipped and became government witnesses often went through what has been likened to the "born-again" experience in the evangelical Christian faith. They give themselves over to the government, most often the FBI, and become empowered as prosecution witnesses. Such was the case with "Nicky the Crow" Caramandi and Tommy Del Giorno. They'd been reprogrammed. Not only did they no longer consider themselves Mafia thugs, they were now double agents who were bent on stamping out evil for the government.

What did Goodman think of Scarfo?

"Nicky may have been a lot of things, but he was also a

family man," Goodman recalled. "Nicky had two sons, Nicky Junior and Mark. Little Nicky was a nice kid who I considered a hanger-on. He loved hanging around his father's people. He was on the edge of everything and he idolized his Uncle Philip. The other son was quieter. Nicky was sensitive about Mark. Because of the publicity he was getting, the kid was teased constantly at school. Eventually, the kid hanged himself. Although he survived, he remained in a vegetative state and Nicky blamed the government and the media.

"Nicky was just the opposite of Angelo Bruno, who was a quiet guy known as the Docile Don. Nicky preened for the media. He loved to give them the finger. He gave everyone the finger. He always liked to tell reporters and prosecutors to go fuck themselves. He would whisper it in court.

"He certainly wasn't shy. His crew reflected his personality. They were a group of guys who liked to party, liked to be seen at restaurants. And they were violent, at least according to the court transcripts. Philip is supposed to have shot a man in the head for saying he wasn't the best concrete guy in Atlantic City. They killed another man for daring to break an engagement with a captain's daughter. If someone was at a party and didn't say hello to Nicky, he was in danger of losing his life.

"But around his attorneys, Nicky was always upbeat, always positive that he was going to beat the charges he faced."

What prosecutors and investigators lacked in quality of evidence, they more than made up for in quantity of indictments. Scarfo was hit rapid-fire with a series of them. On April 9, 1987, Scarfo and Nick Virgilio were indicted in the murder of corrupt Municipal Judge Eddie Helfant. Then Scarfo and his gang were indicted by the Commonwealth of Pennsylvania in the Testa murder. On May 14, a federal indictment also named Scarfo, Leonetti, and six others in the murder of Sal Testa, with a trial set for early the following year. By January 1988, a federal grand jury had charged Scarfo, Leonetti, and 17 others with racketeering, nine murders, four attempted murders, and a series of lesser felonies in an 88-page indictment.

Obviously, the government was trying to bury the Scarfo mob under a mountain of charges. Some Philadelphia courtroom observers believe federal and state prosecutors and law enforcement would have been far more effective if they'd shared information instead of fighting over which headline-grabbing case would go to trial first. Just as egos had sunk mobsters and their mouthpieces, prosecutors were also susceptible to getting caught up in the media hype and hysteria of the moment.

Into that maelstrom stepped Oscar Goodman, who seemed to thrive in such an atmosphere. Along with Simone, Goodman led a 10-member defense team into what many observers believed was an unwinnable fight. They went up against Philadelphia Assistant District Attorney Barbara Christie, who was escorted into court by jack-booted state troopers and sat alone at the prosecutor's table in an attempt to send a psychological message to jurors. Christie did not lack for confidence. If anything, Goodman believes she overplayed her advantage. She also allowed whispered remarks from the defense table to get under her skin.

"Barbara Christie was like a cocky bantam rooster strutting around the courtroom," Goodman recalled. "She was flanked by state troopers, who wore the jodhpurs and jack boots. They looked like Nazis except for the fact that their uniforms were blue instead of brown. And Nicky and Philip couldn't resist trying to rattle her. They would whisper 'motherfucker' to her, or as Philip always said it, 'motherless motherfucker,' and it would drive her crazy. It happened every time she passed the defense table. She complained to the judge, Albert Sabo, but he couldn't hear anything and would just wave her away. One time, though, one of the defense attorneys, Steve La Cheen, went too far. He said, 'Why don't you go back to the kitchen?'

"The moment he said it, I knew we were in trouble. The expressions of several female jurors just fell. They had obviously heard his remark. I thought we were dead, but then she saved us by responding, 'I don't even cook.' The female jurors, who obviously did cook, were more mad at her than the defendants."

The case centered, once again, on the relative credibility of Caramandi and Del Giorno. Having sparred with them three times before, Goodman was intimately familiar with their modus operandi. By then Caramandi and Del Giorno followed

a predictable pattern, which in Goodman's observation included darkly comical renditions when it came to interpreting
a meeting on the Boardwalk between them and Scarfo. Because
there was video, but no audio, of the meeting, they felt comfortable interpreting the content of the conversation to fit their
testimony. Whether it was drugs, political corruption, or murder, they managed to recall different intimate details of the
Boardwalk meeting each time they took the witness stand.

"I think they were lying and I believe they knew they were
lying," Goodman recalls. "They used the meeting to mean
whatever they wanted it to mean, but that's the kind of rats
they were. The truth meant nothing to them."

With a sequestered jury, the murder trial began April 5, 1988.
Prosecutor Christie focused on Testa's rise and fall from Scarfo's
fickle and deadly graces. While Simone reminded jurors that
none of the talk about organized crime and the Mafia was relevant to the charges the defendants faced, Goodman returned
to Nicky Crow and Tommy Del. He set the stage for his devastating future cross-examination, in which he would dine
Hannibal Lechter-style on their litany of admitted criminal acts.

From the outset, it was clear the defense did not have a
friend in Judge Sabo, who seemed partial to the prosecution
and strangely preoccupied. Defense counsel Joe Santaguida
was cited for contempt after he lost his temper and admon-
ished Judge Sabo to "pay attention." As the defense saw it,
Sabo allowed Christie wide latitude, while cutting short opposing lawyers' examination of witnesses. At one point, the
attorneys had an in-chamber meeting with the judge, where
Goodman's partner David Chesnoff watched Sabo playing
solitaire with cards on his desk.

"I couldn't believe my eyes," Chesnoff later recalled. "He
was playing solitaire. Hey, it was only a death-penalty case."

During trial, prosecutors let on that they believed Scarfo
intended to have defendant Bobby Rego killed. Proving that
mob lawyering isn't all stone-cold seriousness, Chesnoff managed to make light of the purported murder plot.

"During a break I took a piece of paper and drew a sign
pointing to Rego—just in case anybody was going to take a
shot, I wanted to make sure there was no confusion," he said.
"Everyone fell to pieces, including Rego.

"Oscar's cross examination of Caramandi and Del Giorno helped save the case and came at a time we'd lost momentum."

After Simone and La Cheen took after Caramandi, it was Goodman's turn. Using a large chart listing Caramandi's crimes, he started with the gangster's childhood and worked his way toward the present. Beyond the three murders he'd admitted participating in, the chart displayed more than 300 burglaries and scores of other crimes ranging from auto theft to welfare fraud.

At one point, Caramandi admitted, "For two years, I just looked around and hunted to kill people."

Although Goodman had scored points with the jury, he'd also left open the possibility of damaging questions being asked about the Rouse extortion case in which Scarfo had been convicted. Christie seized the moment.

Wrote Donald Cox in *Mafia Wipeout*: "One of the defense lawyers quipped to the media that Goodman should now be called 'Open the door Oscar,' since he had been the one who made it possible to widen the case from just the murder of Sal Testa to other crimes committed by the mob. Many other defense lawyers feared that his ploy marked a turning point against their chance of getting their clients off the hook, since the prosecution could now bring in evidence extending beyond the Testa murder."

"You shouldn't have opened the door," Judge Sabo said. "You should have left it alone."

Christie had won a round, but could not overcome the constant stream of objections and outright harassment by the defense that Judge Sabo appeared unable to quiet. At times, it must have been hard to separate the mobsters from their mouthpieces.

Finally, the trial reached a chaotic pitch. Christie and the defense team constantly objected to each other's questions in a scene straight out of a Marx Brothers movie. Sabo called for a four-day recess: Del Giorno, it seemed, was somehow unavailable to testify. This infuriated Goodman, who for his part had been away from his family with few breaks for the better part of a year. It turned out Del Giorno's son had been arrested.

The delays got to Goodman. Maintaining the proper

rhythm and imagery was essential to his defense technique and the interruptions were killing him. During a recess, in one of the few times in his legal career, he failed to contain his anger.

"Do you know who is holding up this trial? The princess, that's who!" he shouted in Christie's presence. "If this happened in Nevada, she would be disciplined. If her delays had occurred in Nevada, she would be canned by now and the judge would have dismissed the case. ... This is all Judge Sabo's fault."

When he finally took the witness stand, Del Giorno admitted committing crimes ranging from robbery to murder. He also said he'd enjoyed a hooker while under the supervision of a team of New Jersey state troopers, one of whom the killer accused of stealing his money.

In his May 4 closing argument, Goodman implored jurors not to hang his client on the word of two admitted killers whose testimony had been purchased by the government. It was a song he'd sung for years, but he was particularly on key that day.

Rolling like a television preacher, Goodman thundered, "I want you, the jury, to come back and shout to the rafters those words so eloquently spoken by Phil Leonetti, 'Not Guilty! Not Guilty! Absolutely Not Guilty!'"

Courtroom observers said Goodman "starred for the defense" after opening the door to the potentially damaging Rouse extortion admissions. Before the last defense attorney said his peace, Christie took ill and Sabo allowed a lengthy recess. In Goodman's mind, this clearly was yet another attempt to upset the successful rhythm of the team's wave of closing arguments. Later that day, she returned and spent 78 minutes on her closing argument, then Sabo submitted the case to the jury.

After six weeks of testimony and only six hours of deliberations, the jury returned with a paralyzing verdict: not guilty on all charges. Jurors had clearly listened to Goodman and the others on the defense team when they spoke about Caramandi and Del Giorno. Jurors believed the defendants to be guilty, but were not presented with convincing evidence. They had simply not believed the snitches enough to vote for conviction.

Goodman had promised that if the defense prevailed, he

and Chesnoff would skinny dip in the fountain of the Four Seasons Hotel. Although turned back by security guards, Goodman and Simone hosted a gang of nearly 100 people who celebrated the victory of Scarfo and Leonetti in the Testa murder case.

The defendants were the only ones missing from the party, which was awash in expensive Tattinger champagne and $50-a-shot Louis XIII cognac. The affair was catered by the boys from South Philly: hoagies on the house.

Reporters mingled in the crowd and skirted around the edges of the orgy of booze and brash talk.

"I went up to Oscar Goodman, who represented Crazy Phil Leonetti," a *Philadelphia Inquirer* columnist wrote. "As an ice-breaker, I asked Goodman if he was still planning to get naked.

"He said no, and asked me to sit. I did so, hoping to be put at ease by the man known for brilliant defense of heavies. In a kind voice, he said: 'You remind me of a journalist in Las Vegas who did similar work. He passed away. These guys don't like you.'

"I guess I can understand that.

"'They dislike you very much. ... I respect you, but if you're going to write negative stories, you should write the other side as well.'

"That's why I'm here."

"'This is a great day. The message is that you can't build a prosecution on the paid-for testimony of two sleazeballs like (ex-mobsters) Tommy Del Giorno and Nicky Caramandi.'"

Although the columnist fared less well with other members of the mob party, he kept his wits, sense of humor, and life.

The dizzy reverie was to be short-lived. Even the cockeyed optimists in the crowd had to admit Scarfo's gang faced daunting odds in the future trials that stacked up against them.

"Thank God for the American jury system!" a Scarfo relative shouted. "It's great to be an American."

Nicky Scarfo, Jr., added, "What can I say? I'm extremely happy. It couldn't happen to a better bunch of people."

℘ ℘ ℘

"We're bigger than U.S. Steel," Goodman joked *Godfather*-style to reporters during the Four Seasons affair, where $800 bottles of cognac and $100 bottles of champagne flowed like water from the hotel's fountain. But as with all things in life, the party eventually ended and the bill arrived: $16,000.

Those who view the mob as some all-powerful entity should take note of what happened next. When the $16,000 check came, Nicky Scarfo, Jr., son of one of America's most notorious Mafia bosses, couldn't pay it. So Goodman pulled out a credit card and picked up the tab. The Scarfo family, after all, was good for it, right?

Sort of. The family's ready cash was in short supply, so Scarfo offered a 1973 Rolls-Royce, with an estimated value of $20,000, as a means of erasing the debt. Goodman took possession of the vehicle in October 1988. Although he hadn't seen the luxury car, it was, after all, a Rolls-Royce and Scarfo assured him it was in very good condition.

Scarfo had purchased the Rolls in January 1986 from Cream Puff Motors of Palm Beach, Florida, for $25,000, mostly in cash. The vehicle was registered in the name of an associate, Anthony Gregorio, at a time Scarfo and his family were trying to sew up the P2P supply for the lucrative methamphetamine market. Scarfo used the vehicle during meetings with prospective providers of the drug precursor chemical.

Although Goodman had yet to drive the car, he spent $4,000 to have law-enforcement surveillance microphones removed from its interior — surely out of concern that the listening devices would interfere with the radio reception. After a bit of detail work, the classic would be his. He even planned to take out the vanity plate "MOB FEE" for his upscale motorcar.

Goodman's fantasy ended in September 1989, when the FBI seized the Rolls by claiming it was used to facilitate drug trafficking. They added that any lawyer with a vast knowledge of Scarfo's criminal empire ought to have known that. With his law partner David Chesnoff and appeal specialist Peter Goldenberger at his side, Goodman vowed to fight the seizure in the name of justice, the principle of the matter, and perhaps out of anger at potentially being stiffed for that Four Seasons party.

At that time in Philadelphia, sympathetic ears were in short supply where mob lawyers were concerned. Goodman wasn't exactly some down-on-his luck cause célèbre. Some, in fact, considered him the poster boy for all that was wrong with the criminal-justice system. He was, after all, the man who kept standing up and frustrating the government in its attempt to clean up organized crime. There would be no public outrage over a rich lawyer losing a mobster's Rolls-Royce.

"But what about the legal principle?" Goodman asked. "Would even the harshest critic argue that an innocent owner should be penalized for the alleged sins of a previous owner? Of course not. And the law provides for that. But I was expected to know that Scarfo had used the Rolls to further a drug conspiracy that I knew he was not convicted of. I'd have to fight and spend tens of thousands of dollars to get it back, far more than the car was worth. I didn't need the car. To my mind, the seizure was offensive, as are all seizures in my opinion, but this one was even more egregious."

Goodman and Chesnoff argued that, to their knowledge, La Cosa Nostra members abhorred drug trafficking. They argued that even the government's own snitch, Tommy Del Giorno, admitted that Scarfo frowned on drug selling, even though the mob boss practiced a substantial amount of "willful blindness" in that regard, making hundreds of thousands of dollars over the years from everything from P2P sales to shaking down narcotics dealers. Despite clear evidence that Goodman logically could not have assumed the car was used for illegal purposes, the courts, like the citizens, didn't care. District Judge Anita Brody found that he had failed to prove he was not "willfully blind" to the true use of the vehicle and had taken no steps to ensure the propriety of the petrol-burner.

While the Rolls rotted in an FBI outdoor-storage facility, Goodman and Chesnoff fought on. They argued their case in December 1993, four years after the seizure, before the Third U.S. Circuit Court of Appeals, which rendered its decision around Thanksgiving 1994, and finally settled the matter in February 1995. By then, the vehicle had sat through five and a half winters and was 23 years old. A classic it wasn't, but the high court vacated the earlier decision and remanded the case. Goodman, at last, had won possession of his Rolls-Royce.

Chesnoff said, "Seizing attorney's fees was the most recent vehicle used by the government to prevent people from having representation. Now we can fight for our clients, instead of ourselves."

Journalists in Philadelphia and Las Vegas, many of whom had been quick to vilify Goodman's clients, came to his defense on the controversial seizure issue. In Las Vegas, former Nevada Governor and *Las Vegas Sun* columnist Mike O'Callaghan said it best when he wrote, "Las Vegas attorney Oscar Goodman struck another blow for Americans who have come to question the government's abuse of its forfeiture law." Clearly, beyond Goodman's personality was a principle worth standing up for. Trouble for him was, it was sometimes hard to see past his shtick to the heart of the matter.

It would cost Goodman thousands to rebuild the Rolls, but fortunately Chesnoff had a client in Los Angeles who specialized in custom auto-body work. The car was shipped to California, where work on it commenced immediately. Visions of parading his victory around Las Vegas danced in Goodman's head.

But before he could get behind the wheel of his Rolls-Royce, federal agents raided the auto-body shop and arrested its occupants on suspicion of drug trafficking, seizing the car again.

"I've still never driven that damn car," Goodman said.

？ ？ ？

Scarfo and Leonetti had little time to celebrate their victory in the Testa murder case. The United States Justice Department Organized Crime Strike Force had prepared a crushing racketeering indictment alleging the Philadelphia crime family was an enterprise awash in murder. When it finally landed, the indictment accused the Scarfo-Leonetti mob of involvement in 39 acts of murder, attempted murder, murder conspiracy, extortion, illegal gambling, and narcotics distribution. In all, Scarfo, Leonetti, and 15 of their associates were charged. If convicted, it would obliterate their family. United States attorneys Louis Pichini and Albert Wicks, with a string of assistants, walked point for the government. Each of the 17 defendants was represented by counsel.

Once again, the Strike Force was relying on quantity and

the tainted testimony of Caramandi and Del Giorno. This time, they added a mountain of sensational photographs depicting gruesome murders allegedly carried out on orders from Little Nicky and Crazy Phil.

"They were out to impress the jury with the abundance of the evidence, but the problem was little more than the word of Caramandi and Del Giorno linked Scarfo and Leonetti to all those dead bodies," Goodman recalled. "In cruder terms, they were throwing a bunch of shit against the wall and praying something would stick. We had beaten them, and they were attempting to squash our clients under the weight of marginal evidence. But it was still all about the Crow and Del Giorno, and they were still a couple of lying rats."

Goodman had long since proved the most eloquent member of the defense team. He led off the long string of opening statements.

"When [Caramandi and Del Giorno] want liquor, the evidence is going to show that they get liquor," he told the jury. "When they want to get paid for their testimony, the evidence is going to show they get paid for their testimony. … And the evidence is going to show that they're not in some kind of a prison, but they're down by the beach having a better life than you folks are going to have for the next three months. … Now I submit to you that at the conclusion of all the testimony, you're going to be convinced that this type of pact with those type of people invites perversion of the truth. By your verdict of not guilty, you will not permit this courtroom to be a breeding bed of perjury for the spawning of lies."

Though the opening statement by Strike Force Prosecutor Louis Pichini was powerful, the government's case drew laughter when its first witness, Kathleen Residence, took the stand wearing a blonde wig and dark glasses, looking like a cross between an aging Hollywood starlet and a federally protected witness. Residence claimed to have damning evidence linking Scarfo mob member Nicholas Virgilio to the 1978 murder of corrupt Judge Eddie Helfant. Trouble was, when it came time to pick Virgilio out of the many defendants at the defense table, she pointed to Scarfo instead. "If she took off her glasses, she might be able to see," Goodman cracked to the delight of everyone in the courtroom—except, of course, the prosecutors.

Then came Joseph Salerno, Jr., a plumber who had previously admitted participating with Scarfo and Leonetti in the December 1979 murder of Vince Falcone. Salerno's earlier testimony had failed to result in a conviction, but this time his words were weighted by the presence of his father, Joseph Salerno, Sr., who later took the stand to tell about surviving a mob assassination attempt that occurred shortly after his son became a cooperating government witness.

And on it went. Crime after crime. Body after body. Corroborating testimony was slim in some places, nonexistent in others, but there were enough tape recordings to establish a pattern of racketeering activity steeped in blood. The defense was in trouble. While Caramandi and Del Giorno remained suspect, the incriminating law-enforcement recordings of 11 co-defendants raised their credibility. Scarfo and Leonetti were finally sinking under the crushing weight of the federal government's case.

Goodman remained eloquent and wickedly critical of the key witnesses in his closing argument.

"Deals have been made with devils. If you return a verdict like the prosecutors asked for, then you encourage the use of bought-and-paid-for perjured testimony. ...

"The government threw enough mud against the wall and they hoped some would stick against Phil Leonetti, but in his particular situation, it doesn't pass muster — not with the kind of testimony you heard from Caramandi and Del Giorno. ..."

Goodman was right, but nothing he could say would make the jurors forget the grisly photos, the incriminating taped statements of the other defendants, the testimony of Joe Salerno, Jr. and his father, or the prosecution's use of inflammatory rhetoric, such as calling the defendants "Mafia killers" and describing one as a "baby-faced killer," among other names meant to paint a biased image.

After being sequestered for nearly two months during the trial, the jury deliberated 26 hours before returning a sweeping guilty verdict. Neither Scarfo nor Leonetti flinched in the 40 minutes it took the foreman to sort through all the charges.

It had taken 33 days of testimony, more than 100 witnesses, and perhaps millions of dollars in investigative and legal costs, but the government had finally defeated the Philadelphia mob.

Although he was disappointed, Oscar Goodman wasn't completely surprised by the jury's decision. What shocked Goodman at the time of sentencing—when he was fighting for every inch of ground on a hostile battlefield, attempting to save Leonetti from spending the rest of his life in prison—was that his client had been dishonest about his dealings with the government.

"Of all my so-called mob clients, Phil Leonetti was one of the most impressive," Goodman recalled. "He was young and handsome, as handsome as a movie star, but he seemed to possess an old-school set of values, the sort of values I have seen in few of my clients. And he was tough. If what was alleged about him was true, he was a very capable fellow with a gun. And he appeared destined to run that family after his Uncle Nicky was gone. Leonetti had his eye on Atlantic City, where he had more than a few contacts in the casino business. He was bright enough to remain in the seat of power for many years, and I was confident that I would be able to have at least some of the charges against him thrown out, or greatly reduced, so that he might have had to serve no more than a few years. But he was faced with a forty-five-year sentence. His uncle got a fifty-five-year sentence to go with the other sentences he was serving.

"And while I was busy busting my tail for Leonetti, he was meeting behind the scenes with government prosecutors, who must have been laughing their heads off at me. Ignorant Oscar. All I was doing was trying to save his miserable life and he was ratting out his friends and family."

FBI agents and Strike Force prosecutors initially believed Leonetti could help make major cases against New York crime-family bosses, especially Gambino leader John Gotti, in whose company Leonetti had been seen in New York on several occasions. Leonetti might have been able to bolster the credibility of Salvatore "Sammy the Bull" Gravano, Gotti's underboss-turned-government informant. (In the end, Leonetti was brought to New York to testify at Gotti's 1992 trial, but wasn't used. "We won't be needing Leonetti," federal prosecutor Andrew Maloney told his partner John Gleeson. "Sammy will handle whatever they throw at him." And Gravano did. Leonetti had won a free pass for at least nine murders with little appreciable gain for law enforcement.)

Matters became dangerously twisted when Goodman learned that prosecutors weren't just looking for another nail in Gotti's coffin, but also for evidence of impropriety on the part of prominent mob attorneys, himself included. Leonetti told an FBI agent that Goodman had accepted a large sum of unreported cash as his fee. Problem was, Leonetti got the numbers mixed up.

"Leonetti tried to convince them that I had received a large amount of cash as a fee and that I hadn't declared the money. Checkmate, they must have figured. Game over. But I'm not stupid. Even though I believed Leonetti would have been the last person in that family to turn rat, it didn't change the fact that I wouldn't break the law. But it did remind me that I was almost as big a target as the notorious men I represented and that it never paid to socialize with them."

Now that the head of the crime family that had long dominated Philadelphia had been cut off, the situation turned dicey for the lesser players. Less than a year after Scarfo's racketeering conviction, Nicky Scarfo, Jr., narrowly survived an assassination attempt at Dante and Luigi's Restaurant at 10th and Catharine streets in South Philly. The younger Scarfo was interrupted during dinner by a masked man wielding an automatic machine pistol. He was hit nine times, but lived. "I saw the gunman coming toward me, but I didn't see the gun because he had it behind his back," he told his attorney Bobby Simone, who continued to be suspected of acting as a *consigliere* to the devastated crime family.

While Scarfo Jr.'s wounds would heal, Simone's troubles were more lasting. "The glue that held the family together," as Goodman described Simone, was eventually convicted of tax charges related to the family's criminal activities.

"I learned my lesson years ago," Goodman said. "Never get so close to your clients that the government confuses your role. Unfortunately, it was a lesson Bobby Simone didn't learn until it was too late. Bobby was an excellent attorney and a real leader. He kept the defense together. Bobby Simone, more than any other attorney, had the capability to lead the defense team. It's probably one of the things that led to his trouble with the law. He came to be so identified with his clients that the government believed he was with his clients. I don't think he was. But that's always the rub with so-called mob attorneys, especially if they're successful. If they're not careful, the government lumps them in and, like Bobby, considers them part of a racketeering conspiracy. The government basically had nothing on Bobby. Del Giorno is probably the man most responsible for putting Bobby behind bars. Bobby was convicted and sent to prison.

"He did some of his time at the federal camp at Nellis Air Force Base, which if you have to sit in jail is one of the better places to do it. But Bobby didn't do his time well. A Marty Kane or Bob Martin would have used the time to get in shape, lose some weight, eat right. Marty Kane would have walked ten miles a day. But Bobby constantly groused and complained about the food and conditions. Nothing was good. Everything was bad. I visited him a couple times and felt sorry for him. But it was an instance where the counselor should have taken advice from his clients about doing his time. Bobby did his time very, very poorly.

"There's a difference between confusing your role as attorney with your clients' lives and being willing to go to jail for your client because it's the right and necessary thing to do."

It was a lesson defined by Goodman's representation of Gambino crime-family capo Natale Richichi.

19

The Underworld
Turned Upside Down

Critics in the media and law enforcement were generally either entertained or annoyed by Oscar Goodman's
endless "government-intrusion" shtick, but by the late
1980s he'd begun to look like a prophet in legal circles. For all
his hyperbole and courtroom theatrics, the government abuses
Goodman had shouted about for so long were becoming painfully clear even to his many detractors, despite the blood-soaked
evidence that had been piled up against his notorious clients.

Traditional organized crime, meanwhile, was taking a beating. Sweeping prosecutions in the "Commission" and "Win-
dows" cases in New York had devastated the upper ranks of
the five families. Old-school bosses, such as the Genovese
brugad's Anthony Salerno and the Lucchese family's Anthony
"Tony Ducks" Corrallo, were among those hit with 100-year
sentences, and the men replacing them weren't cut from the same
tough cloth. Rampant drug trafficking, and the withering prison
sentences resulting from such activity, had led to unprecedented
defections throughout La Cosa Nostra. There were times it must
have seemed to Goodman that the mob lawyers were the only
ones keeping their mouths shut anymore.

In New England, the Patriarca family was crumbling under the weight of a sweeping federal racketeering indictment that threatened to put away the upper echelon of traditional organized crime in Providence and Boston, including boss Raymond "Junior" Patriarca, Vinny Ferrara, J.R. Russo, Dennis LePore, and a majority of the infamous Angiulo brothers. Within weeks of finally clearing his calendar of issues related to the Scarfo family, including the hand-biting Leonetti whose accusations that his lawyer had accepted hundreds of thousands of dollars in unreported cash turned out to be lies, Goodman was contacted at his Las Vegas office by Dominic Spinale, a local mob figure and casino Black Book member who was related by blood, if not by blood oath, to the Angiulos.

Spinale told Goodman that Vinny Ferrara and J.R. Russo were looking for legal counsel in a case that could put them away for several lifetimes. Goodman agreed to represent Ferrara and provide legal help as needed to Russo, the dapper street boss who was determined to represent himself despite the well-known admonishment that a man who does so has a fool for a client.

The two mobsters didn't know it at the time, but their criminal world had turned upside down. The FBI had somehow managed to plant a microphone inside the home at 34 Guild Street in the Boston suburb of Medford, which as fate would have it on October 29, 1989, was the site of a Mafia induction ceremony. The recording captured for the first time La Cosa Nostra's ritual for turning out "made" guys, right down to the pricking of the trigger finger and the burning of the image of a saint.

"We're all here to bring in some new members into our family, and more than that, to start making a new beginning," Raymond "Junior" Patriarca proclaimed in the presence of Ferrara, Russo, and 14 others. One of those proposed new members was Carmen Tortora.

"Do you want it badly and desperately? Your mother's dying in bed and you have to leave her because we called you. It's an emergency. You have to leave. Would you do that, Carmen?" Patriarca asked.

He answered in the affirmative.

Later, as the men left the house, Ferrara was recorded saying, "Only the ghost knows what really took place over here today, by God."

But he was dead wrong, of course. Patriarca's self-proclaimed time of rebuilding was fated to be blown apart by the Medford recording. The capturing of the ceremony was mortifying, to be sure, but what lay ahead would prove what longtime observers had known for many years: that the FBI was better at shaving the rules than the mob.

How had the FBI gotten so lucky as to plant a bug, of all places, in that nondescript house?

Who had the agents managed to turn into an informant?

One thing was certain: Oscar Goodman could no longer claim there was no such thing as organized crime. The induction ceremony appeared to transcend even his well-honed ability to deny the undeniable — proving that the mob, for all its shortcomings and movie imagery, really did exist as a secret criminal organization. To be sure, had it not existed, Hollywood would have invented it, but the Guild Street ceremony was clear and convincing proof that Joe Valachi, Jimmy the Weasel, and all the other American Mafia turncoats had been telling the truth when they described the ritual swearing in of new made members.

"I received several phone calls from what few federal prosecutors I spoke with, all of whom were only too willing to rub it in," Goodman said. "But what did anyone expect, that I would ever admit my clients were part of a complex criminal organization? That would be like throwing in the towel before the first bell rings. It's never a fair fight. The weight of the government is always greater than any client, and persons accused of crime who have gained notoriety in the media and with the FBI have an even harder time receiving justice within the system. Labeling each man a mobster in court in front of a jury creates the worst kind of bias. It's impossible to overcome. It's why judges don't allow it. So those prosecutors can gloat all they want. I would continue to fight to make sure my clients had the most level playing field possible."

℘ ℘ ℘

In Boston, for nearly 20 years the playing field had been uncannily tilted against the Patriarca family. Investigative journalists and local wiseguys noted the remarkably unblemished legal record of James "Whitey" Bulger, the gangster who ruled the rackets of South Boston with an iron fist. While the Patriarcas and their associates fell like dominoes, Bulger so enjoyed the greatest Irish luck that he was considered one of the craftiest criminals in the city's history. With brother William Bulger rising to the Democratic leadership in the Massachusetts House of Representatives, Whitey was the family's black sheep.

Long after his running mates fell to violence or criminal conviction, the notorious Bulger brother managed to remain on the street. He appeared to have developed a sixth sense when it came to eluding the authorities.

As Goodman came to find out, Whitey's knack for evading the cops wasn't supernatural, but based on a decades-long part-time job as an informant for the FBI. Bulger's handler was a fellow Southie native named John Connolly. Connolly was a street-wise agent and a reliable media source. Local newspaper reporters with the *Globe* and *Herald* could not have known he'd spent much of his career grooming and protecting the Boston office's greatest resource, a man who also happened to head a criminal enterprise that committed numerous murders and countless lesser felonies.

But in the beginning, all Goodman knew was that his client, Vinny Ferrara, was bucking nearly insurmountable odds. In addition to the federal racketeering case, he faced murder charges in multiple jurisdictions and had become a popular topic of scorn with U.S. Attorney Jeremiah T. O'Sullivan, the man responsible for nicknaming Ferrara "The Animal." Around the neighborhood, Ferrara had been known by the less sensational moniker, "Vinny Nip."

"Jeremiah O'Sullivan, the prosecutor in Boston, was speaking before a group of feds and called Ferrara 'The Animal,'" Goodman recalled. "And as always, he said Ferrara was responsible for killing twenty-six people. It's always the same number with these guys. They're always killing twenty-six people. I'd heard about his reputation, and Ferrara was sitting across from me in my office with J.R. Russo, and I have to be honest, I didn't see it. Vinny's sitting across from me and he's telling me he's a Boston College grad with a degree in accounting. He was very articulate in his own way and surely didn't seem to me to be a guy who would kill twenty-six people.

"Then I looked to my left. There was J.R. If there was ever the patrician Italian, he looked it. All of the statues of Cato and the Centurions were cast in his face. He wore these wonderful silk shirts with very big collars, rounded at the end without a tie, and silk suits that fit him perfectly. He was regal.

"These did not look like the kind of guys who were being portrayed by the government as killers. I couldn't wait to represent them, because they were so very bright in the mode of Nick Civella. They were refined. They were a different kind of mobster. One of the guys around them was a man named Dennis LePore. They called him 'Champagne Dennis,' and he was one of many very colorful characters associated with the case."

The case, however, was made virtually impossible to win due to the presence of the FBI's incriminating recordings captured at 34 Guild Street. Goodman immersed himself in those tapes and concluded that they were all but certain to sink what slim chance Ferrara and Russo held. As always, however, there was room for a little gallows humor.

"Jurors who listen to the tape of the induction ceremony will respect the fact that you're loyal to each other, that you're willing to stick up for one another no matter the circumstance," Goodman told them. "But that part about leaving your mother even if she's on her death bed, well, what can I say? The jurors aren't going to like that."

Facing hundreds of years in prison and a daunting mountain of evidence against them, the two were quiet for a moment. Then a sly smile crossed Russo's face.

"Next time we'll leave that out," he said.

On the wrong end of a mountain of damaging evidence, the defense team began stirring up a veritable dust storm of pretrial paperwork. If the prosecution wanted to bury them and obscure the questionable sources of their damning tapes and manuscripts, then the defense would respond in the only way it could — with six months worth of motions before U.S. District Judge Mark Wolf, a former federal prosecutor who nevertheless had become known as a tough but fair trier of fact. In the coming months and years, Wolf would prove to many why he was once on the short list for an appointment to the United States Supreme Court.

For Goodman, the only real hope was in persuading the judge to grant a motion to suppress the induction ceremony and other key court-authorized recordings against his client. He also knew that defendants of such notoriety weren't likely to endear themselves to a panel of their peers unless they were first made to seem almost as human as the average citizen. There was plenty of ground to cover, given that Patriarca was a name synonymous with crime and Ferrara and Russo had been almost as well-known as heavy hitters on the streets of Boston as Williams and Yastrzemski had been at Fenway Park.

Gradually, Wolf appeared to grow intrigued, or at least entertained, by the mobsters' version of events and began to question many of the FBI's investigative techniques, including the use of unnamed informants in its attempt to win court approval for key recordings.

The pretrial motion-to-suppress proceedings didn't lack for Runyonesque color.

"The first thing was their clothing," Goodman recalled. "J.R. Russo went nowhere without looking like a million bucks. He simply wasn't going to participate in the process without his silk shirts with the long collars and his suits that were the best. Ferrara followed him, and with them went the rest of them. If they were going to face the music, they were going in style. They had to have a hearing as to whether they could wear their street clothing instead of their prison garb. This was all prior to jury selection, during the motion to suppress. We were months from actually trying the facts in the case. In other words, few people were going to see what they wore. But every morning we had to have the clothing thing. They had to have their clothes ironed and cleaned. When they went into court they looked like they did when they first came into my office: impeccably dressed in a manner that reflected, shall we say, their station in society."

In other words, they dressed like wiseguys.

"Then there was the food problem. Dennis LePore wanted live food. Frankly, at the start, I had no idea what he meant. He made this impassioned plea to the judge for live food and the judge listened to him day after day, and he finally asked him, 'What is live food?' Live food is like oranges and apples, as distinct from canned, frozen, or processed food. It was very important to him. Eventually, the judge not only allowed Dennis to have his live food, but allowed the defendants to receive meals in their cells that would have made a gourmet envious. They missed their freedom, but they missed no meals.

"Then there was the health call. Everyone had their own ailments. It got to the point where the judge was bringing in Harvard medical professors from Beth Israel [Hospital] to treat these guys. It was the most bizarre experience I've ever had.

"They were caught, but they wanted to have their dignity."

J.R. Russo was struggling to maintain his case after rejecting Goodman's advice and deciding to act as his own counsel. Goodman recalls doing his best to shadow Russo in an effort to prevent him from inadvertently incriminating himself. At one point, Russo nearly cut a deal that, unbeknownst to him, failed to adjudicate all the charges against him, leaving him open to sentencing in a murder case that held the promise of the death penalty. Russo had plenty of experience with the court system, but he wasn't a criminal-defense attorney. However, in terms of the courts, he was like the baseball fan who comes to every game and by the end of the season decides he, too, can play big-league ball.

"J.R. was representing himself and was always very polite to the judge," Goodman said. "But for the fact that I intervened, he would have represented himself into the electric chair. I pulled him out of the electric chair and he was forever grateful.

"The suppression hearing was a great deal of work, but there were times when it was marvelously entertaining for me. We would be there every day early. We had only about an hour a day of court. The rest was filled up with the clothing and food and health stuff. For example, it turns out they were experiencing very dangerous conditions as far as driving to the federal courthouse. There was no downtown jail where they housed federal prisoners and they were all in outlying areas, some as far away as Connecticut. They had to be brought into downtown Boston in these vans. It was dangerous being handcuffed in the vans and not being able to extricate themselves if there was an accident. We had a hearing where the judge actually went down, got in the van, and had handcuffs put on himself so he could work out the problem."

While the defense fiddled, the prosecution fumed. Beneath the surface, Goodman and his fellow counsel were piecing together what they believed was an enormous ethical flaw on the FBI's part: a lack of candid disclosure to the judge in presenting its wiretap affidavit. During the suppression hearing, Goodman began to probe and spar with prosecutors, using his experience to detect the slightest sign that they were misleading the court.

"We spent six months trying to hammer out the motion to suppress, and it was one hundred percent obvious to me that the government was lying through its teeth," Goodman said. "The roving-wiretap issue was a total fraud. They knew exactly where this ceremony was going to take place and they could have gotten a conventional wiretap. The guy, Francesca, signs out of the prison saying he was going home on furlough for family business, which is very funny. The FBI followed him into the home in Medford. They put the bug in the home. All they had to do was get a regular wiretap, but they went in under this silly pretense. I think the judge saw it too, but he just couldn't prove it. It got to the point where the judge was getting fed up with them.

"I never went home. We worked day after day in court and night after night on our strategy. The judge was very demanding. Every night I had to write a brief. Every morning I had to get up and submit it. It sounds like we wasted a lot of time, but Wolf was getting to know these guys. He was getting acquainted with my client and he was getting to see through the FBI and its methods, which, in the long run, was very important not only for Vinny and J.R., but for future cases in Boston.

"In his final opinion, he said these people have families and they are men of their word. They may be outlaws, but they have their own code of honor and at least they uphold it and that's admirable. He said they care about their children and their wives and the schools they go to and the fact that they're educated and that they get religious training. So he was finding all the good things, which helped at the time of sentencing.

"When the government heard that, they went out of their fucking minds. They went nuts that somebody could say something good about *omerta* and their lifestyle. The truth is I would have liked to try all my cases in front of [Judge Wolf] because there was never a doubt in my mind that he was listening and was attempting to be fair, which is so rare on the bench. After six months, I finally went home for Martin Luther King weekend. Then I got a call from him at home.

"The judge said, 'Mr. Goodman, I'd like you to come back here. Nobody can resolve this case other than yourself and I think this is probably a good time to do it. I want you to come back here and sit down with the government on Monday and get this case resolved.' So I went back and we worked it out.

"I was the first one to call them liars. I was the first one to put the prosecutor on the stand. I was the first one to show that what they were doing was wrong. People will look at the twenty-two years that Vinny got and say it's outrageous, but he was facing three death-penalty cases. I resolved the case in my client's favor. Vinny was dead on certain of the cases and he was facing death-penalty cases in Connecticut. My deal included Connecticut, the U.S. Attorneys, everything. Everybody signed on to the deal. Twenty-two years is a long time. I'm the first one to tell you that. But it's a lot shorter than the death penalty."

♪ ♪ ♪

The case against Patriarca, Russo, and Ferrara did more than just humanize the defendants in the eyes of the judge. It also broke trail for future inroads into what would emerge as the greatest scandal in the history of the Boston office of the FBI.

Goodman is particularly proud of the role he played in getting to the heart of the FBI's secret relationship with Whitey Bulger and his underboss and chief Mafia messenger, Stevie "the Rifleman" Flemmi. The revelations later gave Ferrara, through the efforts of Boston counsel Anthony Cardinale and Goodman's law partner David Chesnoff, a chance to gain an early release for crimes that the vast weight of the evidence would indicate he committed with malice.

"In a way, the original deal showed that the government had something to hide," Goodman said. "It served no purpose for them to cut anyone a deal. They were all goners. They had Vinny dead to rights and didn't pull the trigger. There was a reason for it. I had caught them lying and they knew it, and I think the judge knew it, too."

While Ferraro and the rest were sentenced in 1992, it wasn't until several years later that the truth was at last fully revealed. By the mid-1990s, however, the defense team's probing turned up enough evidence to devastate the U.S. Attorney's Office and the FBI. The game was up and in 1995, Bulger was finally indicted on racketeering-related charges stemming from his longstanding role as the king of South Boston. Even then, Bulger slipped into hiding after apparently being tipped off that he'd been exposed as a "top-echelon informant" for the Bureau.

His job had been dangerous but simple: Give reliable information on the Mafia to Connolly, who in turn used the background to help the FBI make cases against the Angiulo family. But on the street, the world is anything but simple.

Other FBI snitches with homicidal pedigrees also emerged, including Bulger's long-time associate Stevie Flemmi. Angelo "Sonny" Mercurio, for example, admitted he'd been an FBI informant at a time he'd been ordered by Bulger to carry out a hit, which was unsuccessful, on rival crime boss Frank Salemme. By turning a blind eye, it was almost as if the Boston Bureau was sanctioning homicide. The defense had a field day.

With men such as Flemmi, Mercurio, and mob-associate Johnny Martorano ratting out both the underworld and their former federal handlers, it was only a matter of time before Agent John Connolly, all the while professing his innocence, was eventually also indicted. In the ultimate irony, Bulger and Flemmi were listed as co-defendants with their former handler.

"I can see the value of using you people," Bulger had told Connolly after deciding to become an informant more than 20 years earlier. "It's good to have friends in law enforcement."

Those words would return to haunt both men. So would the words of Judge Mark Wolf on September 15, 1999, as he issued his devastating 661-page ruling: "In 1861, Lord Acton wrote that 'every thing secret denigrates, even the administration of justice.' This case demonstrates that he was right."

Wolf granted the suppression of evidence based on false

and misleading affidavits filed by the FBI, which had failed to disclose its network of relationships with Bulger's crew. The federal government was forced to acknowledge that by protecting Bulger for a quarter-century, it had coddled a drug-dealing killer, allowing him to operate his deadly rackets in exchange for information that led to the convictions *of his rivals* from the Mafia.

Wolf scrupulously catalogued incidents of suspected FBI corruption within the Boston office and the withholding of evidence from the judge and, in doing so, opened the door for the eventual overturning of previous felony cases, including the one against Ferrara. In July 2000, Goodman's partner David Chesnoff filed a motion for a new trial based on the revelations outlined in Wolf's ruling. Of course, Ferrara's appeal was complicated by the fact that, if his case were overturned, his deal with the government would be voided, and he'd again face the likelihood of a death sentence.

At one point, speaking of Mercurio, but revealing his disgust for the whole Judas network, Wolf said, "You're a criminal. It's not too much for me to expect that even as a cooperating witness, you're not going to be a fully honorable man."

Three thousand miles away, the judge's words were music to Oscar Goodman's ears.

"Finally, after more than thirty-five years in the legal profession, a judge finally admitted the obvious — that men who were dishonorable in life don't don a white robe and halo once they get in bed with the FBI," he said. "It was a long time coming."

The Bulger scandal prompted the Justice Department to rewrite its lengthy guidelines concerning confidential informants. In the wake of the revelations, FBI officials argued that, although the Bulger mess was embarrassing, the corruption was limited to Boston.

As always, they would get an argument from Oscar Goodman.

❦ ❦ ❦

It was hardly the first time Goodman had encountered federal agents willing to mislead the court on the witness stand in an effort to save their case and protect their confidential sources. During Goodman's representation of the nation's vast network of illegal bookmakers, he had come face to face with agents who were willing to dissemble the facts and dared him to challenge them. In the 1970 26-city bookmaking case, he'd helped spot a forged signature on a wiretap affidavit, which got dozens of felony charges dismissed against organized crime's largest betting ring.

Another case involved suspected illegal bookies Harmon Northrup Swanson, Larry Werry, and James Wiley. When a wiretap affidavit was written, it told of two confidential informants who attested to illegal activity taking place on phones operated by the suspects. But there was only one informant. The information the one informant provided had been divided into two in order to beef up the agent's claim of wrongdoing.

Before a Special Attorney for the Department of Justice and an FBI agent verified that there had been only one informant, Organized Crime Strike Force Attorney James Ritchie told the court otherwise. Reno FBI man John Norris testified that, to the best of his recollection, "It was the suggestion of Mr. James E. Ritchie, the attorney in charge of the investigation, that the information coming from the one informant be separated and reported as emanating from two different sources as a ploy to protect the identity of the confidential informant." Special Agent John Barron testified that he knew of only one informant, but after learning of Ritchie's "positive recollection," he had refreshed his memory and was certain—all physical evidence to the contrary—that there had been two. U.S. District Judge Bruce Thompson granted Goodman's motion to suppress all evidence produced by the wiretap.

"In that case, Bill Cosby was captured on the wiretap calling the race book at a Lake Tahoe casino. He had been betting it locally when he performed in that area and had continued to bet it when he left the state. It was like a hand-in-glove-type testimony.

"The agent was testifying about two informants and you could see that when you looked at the testimony of Informant A and Informant B—it was too perfect. As soon as I saw it, I knew he was lying. So I challenged him. 'This, in fact, has to be one informant,' I said. He said, 'Absolutely not.' I pressed him and I pressed him and I pressed him, and he finally said, 'Yes, it was one informant, but the Strike Force attorney told me to do it.' And who was the Strike Force attorney? Jim Ritchie. I made Ritchie come in when he was head of the Strike Force. Boy, was he nervous. He'd been made head of the Detroit office. Even though the facts said there was one informant, he claimed to remember there being two. Thompson threw the case out."

♪ ♪ ♪

Goodman sometimes managed to prevail even when he caught an FBI agent telling the truth.

FBI Agent Thomas Noble thought he'd found organized crime's Mother Lode. In early 1984 acting on a tip, Noble began investigating what he believed was a massive illegal bookmaking operation with organized-crime ties stretching across the country and including Anthony Spilotro. He obtained a court-authorized wiretap signed by U.S. District Judge Lloyd George and listened to hundreds of telephone calls involving a network of immensely successful Las Vegas sports bettors, who appeared to be led by a non-practicing orthopedic surgeon named Ivan Mindlin, a suspected illegal bookmaker named William "Billy" Walters, and his top assistant Glen Walker. On the street, the Mindlin-Walters team was known as the "Computer Group," in reference to its use of computers to handicap games and speed-dialers to place bets with illegal bookies throughout the United States. At the height of its activity, the Computer Group was placing up to $600,000 in bets per day.

"Walters operates a large bookmaking operation which he uses to place bets with legal and illegal bookmakers for the 'Computer' group," Noble wrote in an affidavit. "Walters will contact various bookmakers and place bets on desired games and point spreads or Walker will contact bookmakers and 'beards' and instruct them on how to place certain bets for the 'Computer' group.

"Besides this operation, Walters controls a bookmaking operation under the guise of the C & B Collection Agency."

As he listened, Agent Noble grew increasingly excited. At

last the Bureau had tapped into what he believed was a vast underground river of illegal bookmaking activity, a main artery in the national gambling syndicate. Small-time mob figures Dominic Spinale and Eddie DeLeo, both of whom reported to Spilotro, appeared to play a role in the network. He immediately began gathering evidence to take to the Justice Department's Organized Crime Strike Force, whose prosecutors would in turn present it to a federal grand jury.

Although Noble didn't realize it at the time, there was a fundamental flaw in his theory. To be sure, several of the suspects had backgrounds in illegal bookmaking and, indeed, at least one was taking side action while working for the Computer Group. But the majority of the defendants were cogs in a well-oiled wheel that was *placing* bets — not *taking* them. Illegal bookmakers were often targeted by local and federal prosecutors, but not the players. The difference, it appeared, was lost on Agent Noble, whose dream of solving the mystery of a massive multi-state bookmaking empire was dashed by the reality that the Computer Group was simply a collection of bettors who played the daily odds on ballgames the way day traders take on the stock market.

The Computer Group, however, was not an average gaggle of gamblers. Far from it. One informant told Noble that the group had beaten the bookmakers for $25 million betting on professional and college football and college basketball. It was so successful, in fact, that it was compelled to use numerous "beards," individuals who disguised their alliance with the Computer Group in order to place their bets (and have them accepted).

The first search warrant was served in 1985, but by the time the FBI and Justice Department sorted out the evidence, nearly five years had passed. What began as a bookmaking case wound up being an illegal gambling investigation. Then the government dropped the hammer: 19 defendants were hit with 120 gambling-related felony charges. Walters and Mindlin faced more than 400 years in prison. Even Walters' wife Susan was charged with 13 felonies for her role as her husband's accountant.

"Is it in the national interest for our government to spend millions of dollars of manpower to go after nineteen people who are betting on ballgames?" Walters asked *Washington Post* reporter Bill Brubaker.

Ironically, the Computer Group was being prosecuted for beating America's illegal bookmakers out of millions of dollars. If anything, its success put the illegal bookies in peril. The Computer Group even bet thousands with illegal bookmaker Mat Marcus while he was fronting for an Internal Revenue Service sting operation, which eventually was disbanded after losing $600,000.

Billy and Susan Walters retained Oscar Goodman. Anticipating the indictment, Goodman volunteered to quietly surrender his clients. They were, after all, at worst two successful gamblers who kept homes in Ft. Lauderdale and Las Vegas. Not exactly Bonnie and Clyde.

Instead, the FBI sent agents with guns drawn to the Ft. Lauderdale house, where Susan Walters' mother was staying, frightening the elderly woman. In Las Vegas, agents arrested the Walters at their home, handcuffed them, and hauled them away. Goodman later wrote in his "notice of outrage," "Prosecutors have dispatched their constables to literally shackle and lead legitimate citizens from their beds to drag them to courthouses through the land." He also noted that a copy of the *Review-Journal* lying that morning in the Walters' driveway featured a front-page story on the "secret" indictment.

Goodman's strategy of outrage resounded in Las Vegas, where gambling had been legal since 1931, casino owners were considered solid citizens, and a large segment of the population bet sports, played cards, or pulled slot handles. Fielding a sympathetic jury wouldn't be difficult.

Fielding a favorable ruling from a judge, however, was another matter. The case drew U.S. District Judge Lloyd George, a prosecution-oriented tough-sentencing jurist with whom Goodman had consistently been at odds. The group retained other top local and national attorneys, including Richard Wright, a prosecutor turned defense attorney who had fought Goodman and Harry Claiborne in the case in which Sarno and Mallin were accused of bribing an IRS agent, as well as Morris Goldings, Ken Hense, and Laura Fitzsimmons, the defense-team's only woman.

Las Vegas Organized Crime Strike Force attorneys Jane

Hawkins Shoemaker and Kurt Schulke faced the unenviable task of prosecuting a gambling case in the gambling capital of the world.

Although direct evidence linking the Computer Group to organized crime was tenuous, Noble noted in his affidavit that in the early 1980s, mob associate Dominic Spinale had received wagering information from Glen Walker and passed it on to Tony Spilotro. Mindlin also made use of Spinale, the agent observed. But what did it mean?

Potentially more damaging to the Las Vegas hierarchy was the connection between the Computer Group and prominent locals, including developer Irwin Molasky, who, although not indicted, was forced to retain counsel, obtain immunity, and answer questions about his links to the betting cartel.

As the trial drew near, Walters became increasingly concerned for his wife. The angle-shooting Kentucky native who had plied his trade as a car salesman and illegal bookmaker before joining forces with Mindlin in Las Vegas, made a decision to speak to FBI agent Noble in an attempt, as he would later describe it, to educate him about gambling and demystify the Computer Group. The two agreed to meet under the condition that Goodman, whose reputation for refusing to represent defendants who cooperated with the government was well-known, not be notified. A meeting was then arranged with Judge George and on April 1, Walters appeared in court without counsel present.

Walters supplied a long list of names of gamblers, filling an affidavit which he would later call absurd in an attempt to appear to be giving Noble useful information. In reality, Walters was passing on street gossip and the sort of information many of the city's cab drivers already knew about organized crime. Walters did, however, burn Mindlin by implicating him in a $20 million money-laundering scheme involving the Barbary Coast Casino on the Strip. "Mindlin received money from the Barbary Coast in the form of checks made out to 'dummy' corporations," Noble wrote in his report. "These checks were then laundered through Bahamian banks."

No criminal charges were ever filed based on the information provided by Walters. Walters, in fact, denied being an informant. His alacrity in dealing with the feds, however, branded him a snitch on the street. Inwardly, Goodman seethed over the prospect of representing someone who went to the FBI behind his back. In his upside-down world where the good guys wore the black hats, a client who cooperated with federal investigators flew in the face of his convictions and was bad for his image. Outwardly, on the other hand, he sought to seize the moment and do what he did best — put the government on the defensive. He filed a massive motion before the court, alleging outrageous government conduct on the part of the FBI and Strike Force for allowing the secret meeting to take place. Goodman spared no one, not even Judge Lloyd George.

It was a rare opportunity to turn up the heat on the judge, a devout Mormon who took great pride in his image and reputation in the community. George was infuriated over Goodman's accusations.

By late July, Goodman's motion had had its desired effect. George abruptly announced that he was recusing himself from the case. Goodman then took the opportunity to tell Walters to find himself a new mouthpiece. A judge from outside the district was selected to hear the case. To the defense, almost anyone was a better choice than George, the staunch conservative who seemed to see Walters and the group as Al Capone and his Outfit. Judge Clarence Newcomer of Pennsylvania presided and his balance was immediately apparent. The case ran its course, but without someone to vilify the gamblers from the bench, the jury relied on the overwhelming evidence that the Computer Group was a betting operation — not layoff bookmakers for organized crime — and where would Las Vegas be without gambling? The jury voted not guilty on 64 counts and hung on 54 others, which the government dismissed "in the interest of justice."

Although trial observers credit Wright, Goldings, Hense, and the others, Goodman is just as certain the Computer Group would have been doomed without his inflammatory motion alleging outrageous government conduct.

"To call him a rat, I'm not sure it's accurate," Goodman recalled years later. "Walters called me and told me that the judge had called him into his chambers without me. I was at a Passover seder. When I finally got all the material and the facts became known, I found out it wasn't the first time Walters talked to an FBI agent. He had talked to an FBI agent who told him, 'Don't tell Oscar.' When he was back in Louisville, he'd also talked to an agent. [The FBI parted with its usual protocol and revealed details of Walters' approach to the government. He had contacted Louisville, Kentucky, FBI Agent Jim Morello, who in turn had made the connection with Noble. A clandestine meeting took place in New Orleans, where information was brokered with a goal of dismissing charges against Susan Walters.] I understood his motivation, but it upset me greatly and I told him to get another lawyer."

Walters received stellar representation from attorney Richard Wright. Although no one close to the Computer case admits it was Goodman's intention to entangle prosecution-friendly Judge George, the inflammatory motion had that effect.

"Billy Walters would be in prison today had I not taken the judge with me," Goodman said. "Judge George felt that Walters was a bad guy. He felt that he was the new Spilotro. He would never have recused himself. It was a strategy to get the judge to disqualify himself, but I never dreamed they would bring in a judge from Lancaster, Pennsylvania, who had a pretty good way about him and didn't come in with any preconceptions."

After the trial, Goodman lost more than just a generous client in Walters. He also lost other top gambling clients, including Jack Binion and the lucrative Binion's Horseshoe account. While Goodman was calling Walters a snitch, Walters, in turn, told associates that Goodman had been ill-prepared to take on the massive case. It was one of the few times in Goodman's career that a client questioned his work ethic.

A decade later, with the passage of time and through his newly acquired political lenses as mayor of Las Vegas, Goodman recalled, "We shook hands. Billy always treated me right and we've put whatever differences we had behind us. He was probably the most generous client I ever had. He was always grateful. He always gave bonuses. He was a charming guy, a real good businessman. Billy was one of the smartest clients as far as having a good mind that I've ever represented.

"I blame the fact that he spoke to the FBI on the indictment of his wife. I think it got to him that they would go after her and in that regard, I can't blame him. I really think he wanted to talk to the FBI and convince them that he was actually merely a big bettor and wasn't a bookmaker, which was right. But the FBI was too stupid to understand it. In those days, Noble had the Yablonsky mentality, where he felt all gamblers were second-class citizens and should have inferiority complexes because of who they were.

"They should have never met alone with Walters knowing that I was his lawyer. It was totally unethical, but it's not surprising, because they don't have any ethics. They know they're not supposed to interfere with the attorney-client privilege once a defendant has an attorney. If, in fact, Walters said, 'I want to make a deal; I'll give you Oscar,' then they don't have to call Oscar. But if they want to talk about the case, they never should have talked to him.

"It was me against the judge. It just so happens Walters was the beneficiary. Judge George and I didn't talk to each other for four or five years afterwards. He hated me and I wasn't particularly fond of him. Then I was up in Reno on a case. Lloyd George took me aside and said he knew we'd had a strained relationship and he was sorry that it had taken place. I was amazed he apologized to me. I went home and thought about it all night. The next morning I called him and asked if I could come up and see him. I met with him and apologized for being an asshole. Since that time, we've formed a respectful relationship. I even think of us as good friends. Even to the point that when the new federal courthouse was being dedicated in his honor, he asked me, as mayor of Las Vegas, to be a guest speaker. That's coming a long way."

ʔ ʔ ʔ

The game was changing before Goodman's eyes. Although the FBI had bungled the Computer Group case, its relentless pursuit of the mob was having the desired effect. Traditional organized crime was being run into the ground. With few exceptions, the traditional mob's big moves in the rackets had degraded into half-hearted muscle jobs and made-for-indictment FBI undercover traps that were irresistible to life-long criminal minds. The story of Colombo crime-family capo Charlie "the Moose" Panarella is one such example.

Philosophically speaking, Panarella was a man after Goodman's own heart. Born in 1922, Panarella's life had been a study in Cosa Nostra politics and laws. He was also a construction worker and union organizer whose authority around the job site in New York was well-known and feared. He'd risen through the ranks quickly by once taking a baseball bat to a man who had made the mistake of showing disrespect to family boss Joseph Colombo. Panarella's reputation for violence included a legend in which he castrated a tardy loanshark before killing him.

Goodman represented Panarella in the early 1990s on money-laundering charges stemming from an attempt to purchase a New York horse farm. Although he was convicted of taking part in a plan to launder up to $1 million through the Maxim Hotel and Casino, it was also true that the case had largely been a sting manufactured by the FBI and carried out by its immensely effective undercover man, Charles Maurer.

It was clear to Goodman that federal authorities were playing a game by using Panarella's rank and reputation to create a case sure to grab a few positive headlines.

"It wasn't bad enough that there was plenty of crime on the streets," Goodman said. "People were dying. There was plenty of actual drug dealing going on, plenty of bank robbery, murder, and mayhem. And don't forget the billions changing hands illegally on Wall Street with insider trading and phony-stock scams. But those crimes aren't guaranteed to grab a headline. Charlie 'the Moose' Panarella is good for a headline, so they had to structure a case in order to entrap him as some sort of mobster.

"He was basically an old man who'd had some problems in the past, but was living quietly and really minding his own business at the time of the case," Goodman recalled. "They were leading the horse to water they provided, and when he drank they arrested him. People may not want to acknowledge it, but there's a tremendous bias against some ethnic groups in this country. Charlie's was a nothing case that was blown out of proportion because of his reputation and his Italian surname."

Notwithstanding Goodman's protests, Panarella, Dominic

Imperio, John Terranova, and Nelson Pereira were approached by an FBI agent posing as a representative of a drug cartel who offered to purchase John Terranova's horse farm in Old Westbury, New York, for $500,000 in illegally obtained cash. After an initial contact, Terranova paid an $18,000 brokerage fee for what he believed was a legitimate sale of his farm. The government was also accused of holding onto the $18,000 of Terranova's money after his arrest. Panarella said he wanted nothing to do with the transaction, but was only helping a couple of friends. Each man was charged with a single count of conspiring to structure a financial transaction designed to evade Internal Revenue Service reporting requirements.

In reality, there was no drug money. In fact, the drug dealer in the case, Anthony Perri, worked as a confidential informant for the FBI and was himself under suspicion of narcotics trafficking at the time he agreed to cooperate in what Goodman, predictably, called a manufactured crime. Perri, an admitted crack-cocaine addict, later claimed the government reneged on its agreement to reward him with up to $100,000 for helping them make the case against Panarella and his associates.

Panarella, then 71 years old, was placed under house arrest after a judge set bail at a half-million dollars for the non-violent charge. He was placed in home confinement for 550 days before trial and eventually pleaded guilty to a single count of conspiracy. He was sentenced to 18 months in prison in connection with the 1992 incident and served 15 months. His name was added to Nevada's casino Black Book in 1997.

Ironically, Goodman knew plenty about government informant Anthony Perri, whom he'd represented on a previous felony case.

Providing defense counsel for the mob had come to this: attempting to prevent 70-something clients, who were arguably under arrest more as a source of generating big headlines than as menaces to society, from rotting in the penitentiary for crimes concocted by the good guys.

Goodman was growing restless. It was clear, even to a man who swilled nostalgia the way he threw back Beefeater martinis, that the best of those Runyonesque days were gone for good. The G might have occasionally trampled the rights of the accused and in so doing pummeled everyone's rights, but its efforts had been brutally effective against organized crime. If only privately, Goodman had to give his enemies that much.

The truth was, Goodman was getting tired of the sameness of so many of his cases. He began to think about running for political office and was developing a special fondness for the idea—as outlandish and controversial as it seemed at the time—of becoming the mayor of Las Vegas.

But before he climbed the steps to a place at City Hall, Oscar Goodman would first have to keep himself out of jail.

20

Last of the Stand-up Guys

G oodman's heart jack-hammered and his stomach roiled. He could taste the bile in his throat. Standing in the court-room of U.S. District Judge Phillip Pro, he felt the eyes of his family and the legal community upon him. Would he stand up for his ancient hopelessly entangled client, Gambino crime-family capo Natale Richichi? Or would all the tough patter he'd uttered over the years turn into so much hot air?

For more than a year, Goodman had represented Richichi, but now it was the attorney who was in need of representation. This time, more than a client's freedom was on the line. Goodman's own freedom, as well as his legal career, were at stake as he fought the court's order to disclose the basic details of his financial compensation by Richichi, who'd been caught in an FBI investigation and faced a lengthy prison sentence for crimes ranging from money laundering to attempted bribery of a union official.

Richichi had been a confidant of Gambino boss John Gotti and had run the family's pornography and gambling rackets for many years, generating great riches. Now weakened by emphysema, Richichi had begun using oxygen to assist his breathing. But even though his days on the street were done, his condition had done nothing to lessen his position within his crime family. Nor had it sated his criminal desires.

The FBI finally had Richichi nailed, but the federal law-enforcement machine appeared to be on the verge of a far more satisfying catch: the ultimate mouthpiece with the whiplash sneer and the custom-made cowboy boots.

Was Goodman somehow being punished for his withering shot at Judge Lloyd George? Or had he finally crossed the line that separates client advocacy from criminal contempt? He was about to find out.

⸮ ⸮ ⸮

On April 19, 1994, Goodman walked into Pro's courtroom accompanied by law partner David Chesnoff for a hearing on the attorney's flat refusal to turn over basic details of the source of Richichi's fee arrangement as required by IRS form 8300. Goodman had left the sheet blank. Failure to comply meant up to $100,000 in fines and a criminal sanction.

Goodman held out.

He was determined not to cave in—perhaps out of stubbornness and principle, but possibly out of an abundance of caution. Richichi was, after all, under indictment as a powerful Mafia boss who hadn't held a legitimate job in decades. Assistant United States Attorney Jane Hawkins Shoemaker and Department of Justice attorney John C. McMillan, Jr., asked the obvious question: "Where would such a man get the money to pay a lawyer, if not from the commission of crimes?"

"None of your damn business," was Goodman's reply.

"Essentially, the government's position is simply that neither the Sixth Amendment nor the Eighth Amendment is applicable to Mr. Goodman's claims of privilege in this context," McMillan told Judge Pro. "As I pointed out in the government's written memorandum, your honor ... the Ninth Circuit has already held that merely requiring a defendant's lawyer to testify does not constitute a material interference with his function as an advocate or operate to deprive the accused of a fair trial.

"It's our position, particularly after reviewing Mr. Goodman's response brief, that there simply is ... going to be no problem on the Sixth Amendment basis with Mr. Goodman's giving over the fee information requested."

McMillan was right. Several courts, including the Ninth U.S. Circuit Court of Appeals, had ruled that providing basic fee information for tax purposes doesn't violate the attorney-client privilege, the Sixth Amendment right to a fair trial, or the Eighth Amendment prohibition against excessive fines.

Sensing the worst, Goodman still refused to concede.

"I didn't know Mr. Richichi before he was arrested on an indictment and went up to see him in the Marshal's cell," Goodman told the court. "But what they want from me is fee information, which I submit is different than the fee information that the cases speak about, which are usually involved in an investigation concerning drug trafficking where there's an interest on the part of the government to see whether or not an individual is receiving monies from, let's say, a kingpin, in order to silence the mules. ... This is a situation where if I am forced to divulge this information, I will actually be ... providing a last link for the government's case to show that my client had access or control over certain monies that ended up being given to me as an attorney's fee. And I don't see how, under that circumstance, the government can so cavalierly state, as has been stated to Your Honor today, that I would be able to retain my position as Mr. Richichi's attorney, that I wouldn't have to be a witness in the case."

It was easy to see how Pro and the prosecutors could believe Goodman was playing games with the court. Goodman had unsuccessfully fought such orders in the past. He knew the rules. He even acknowledged that similar arguments had failed in other courts and resulted in hefty fines for the attorneys involved.

So they were not amused when he said, "I cannot tell the court that I personally receipted any monies; my office did. The receipt was for the monies actually received, those monies were deposited in the bank. Taxes are paid on those monies, so as far as the government is concerned, from our perspective, we're being law-abiding citizens as far as our tax obligation. As far as the information they want, that's where the quarrel exists."

Called before a federal grand jury, Goodman asserted his

attorney-client privilege in violation of a court order and stood silent. His act of defiance was a textbook example of contempt of court.

When he came back before Pro on May 13, 1994, he explained to the judge that he had meant no disrespect, but made it clear he wasn't about to comply with the court's request. Although the threat of going to jail had become very real, as Goodman argued it, the threat to a suspect's right to a fair trial was in even more jeopardy.

'I'm going to make a concerted effort to get the Ninth Circuit to change its position ... and to expand the attorney-client relationship and the Sixth Amendment protections to a person who's being investigated by multiple grand juries," Goodman told the court.

His allies in the defense bar believed he was playing a longshot at best. His enemies at the U.S. Attorney's Office believed he was pandering to the media and the defense bar. Pro respectfully took Goodman's plans for appeal under submission. But Goodman had left the judge no choice and everyone knew it.

"Well, I suppose the record is clear, Mr. Goodman. You did appear before the grand jury and refuse to produce the records, and that remains your position at this point then, is that correct?" Pro asked.

"That's correct, Your Honor," he replied, feeling his blood pressure surge.

"All right. The court then ... does find Mr. Goodman in contempt for ... failing to comply with the grand-jury subpoena *duces tecum* and the order of this court of April 26, 1994 ... that he therefore be taken into custody pending compliance with the subpoena. ... The order of incarceration will be stayed pending appeal."

With wife Carolyn in the gallery taking it all in, Goodman felt sick to his stomach. He was blind with emotion. He had second-best cards and he knew it, but he still wouldn't give in. Was it ego? Was it a need to be perceived not as a money-hungry defense lawyer, but as a protector of trial rights for all defendants? Or had he simply overplayed his bluff hand and after all these years — much to the elation of the Justice Department, the U.S. Attorney's Office, and the FBI — been trapped into eating his own rhetoric?

Goodman had battled the government throughout his career to prevent ever having to fully disclose fee records. In 1979, while representing the Argent and Tropicana casinos, he fought unsuccessfully — after avoiding repeated requests by his prosecution nemesis, Las Vegas Strike Force attorney Geoffrey Anderson — in a case heard by then-U.S. District Judge Harry Claiborne. His struggle had come full circle.

By late June 1994, Pro had run out of patience and Goodman had run out of time. A gathering of lawyers and Goodman allies, carrying signs that read "Free Oscar," "Save Confidentiality," and "Protect the Sixth Amendment," lined the sidewalks outside the Foley Federal Building. As television cameras soaked up the moment, they shouted, "Hey, hey, ho, ho, let the 'O' go!" Criminal defense attorney Tom Pitaro said, "Oscar is the symbol today, but it's the clients, the American people, that will be the real victims. Two hundred and seven years after the enactment of the Constitution, we shouldn't be fighting for it here on the streets of Las Vegas."

Strike Force Attorney Jane Shoemaker echoed the government's collective sentiment that Goodman was again turning the process into a public-relations stunt, but it had become equally clear that the threat of jail hadn't cowed Oscar Goodman.

Nor had it made him any less cocky.

"If they think money means more to me than jail time, they're nuts," Goodman told reporters from the courthouse steps. "The greater good here is to protect the citizens of the United States of America and unless attorneys do that, the Constitution won't be worth two cents. The government has realized I will stay in jail for principle. They cannot break me."

But even as he spoke those words, he knew he was acting. The government could break him — and would try by bleeding him dry. He might laugh at the $25,000 fine and $2,500-per-day assessment the court had ordered, but he also knew the contempt citation had no sunset provision. It could go on indefinitely.

To counteract the pressure cooker of the courtroom, Carolyn took Oscar for a quiet weekend at Dana Point on the California coast. He ambled into a hotel bar and ran into several federal prosecutors. Frank Marine, a Washington prosecutor, recognized Goodman and related a story to him. Like many others in the federal arena, they'd heard of Goodman's brush with a contempt citation and his abject recalcitrance when it came to cooperating with what they believed was a simple court order. Goodman immediately bought a round of drinks.

"I had to play the role with them," Goodman recalled years later. "I wanted to show them I could take whatever the judge dished out standing on my head."

But it was more serious than that.

"Hey, Oscar, you've got problems," Marine said.

"I have deep pockets," Goodman bragged.

"It's not money," said the fed. "They're going to indict you for criminal contempt out of Washington. It's serious."

It was all Goodman could do to smile, but he finished his martini and several more that evening. An indictment transcended Pro's admonishment and fine, which in all likelihood would have expired in a few months with a new empaneling of the grand jury. An indictment changed everything. The facts were clear. He was certain to be convicted. With a conviction, his career would be over. The Justice Department's undeclared war on America's criminal defense attorneys continued unabated. He was trapped.

After returning to Las Vegas, he conferred with Richichi, informing him of the government's plan. Richichi let him off the hook.

"You're no good to me in jail," Richichi said. "Give them what they want."

Still, Goodman was defiant to the end, submitting forms that contained little more than his name and Social Security number.

"They weren't complete by any means," he later recalled. "There was no way they could help the government's case against my client. But this time Shoemaker didn't say a word. It was obvious what they wanted: a victory over Oscar Goodman."

Ironically, the Strike Force didn't need any extra paperwork to prove its case against Richichi. The 75-year-old Gambino capo, a long-time confidant of John Gotti, had run the crime family's pornography holdings in Florida, New York, Nevada, and elsewhere for nearly a decade since the demise of predecessors Robert "DeBe" DeBernardo and Ettore Zappi. In Florida, he faced extortion and racketeering charges in connection with the control of several topless cabarets. In Las Vegas, he was charged with conspiring to bribe an International Stagehands Union official in association with a cut-rate leg show at the Dunes Hotel. In reality, the union official was FBI undercover agent Charles Maurer, but the substantial evidence against Richichi made a conviction all but certain.

Known to associates as "Big Chris," Richichi was a throwback to the days when the mob respected its code of silence. When people on the street spoke of Big Chris Richichi, the words "stand-up" and "old school," and "a man's man" were often mentioned. But at a time he ought to have been thinking of retirement, this mobster was about to be overwhelmed by modern law enforcement. He wisely cut a deal in the Las Vegas case — which included his wife Joan and son Sal, who later saw all charges against them dismissed. He then went back to Florida for one last fight, with Oscar Goodman at his side.

"Here's a guy who probably had more ladies on his knee than Bill Clinton," Goodman said. "He loved his wife and daughter and his Solly, as he called his son Sal, more than life itself. He really, honestly, legitimately loved his family, but he also had a whole different life. He had his Gotti life. He never said anything bad about Gotti. He was there with him, very close to him, and it turned out he was the most trustworthy man in his life. Natale Richichi was the real McCoy.

"My favorite Richichi story goes back to when we were down in Palm Beach at the Chesterfield Hotel preparing for his federal case in Florida, and Richie "the Fixer" Perry came up from where he was staying in Miami to see my opening argument. He spent the night and the next morning we three went down and had breakfast. The bill came to about twenty-three bucks and Richichi gave the waitress a hundred dollars. She came back with the change, and Perry said, 'Oh, the Count never wants change.' Because he looked like a count. Well, word spread quickly and when we came back from court, everyone referred to him as the Count. They thought he was royalty. They had no idea he was there for a criminal case. To them he was the Count. He had that kind of air about him. It was great.

"He was into pornography and was considered a very tough guy. It was his background, certainly. Richichi read *Sleepers*, the wonderful book by Lorenzo Carcaterra, which is a true story of the brutal treatment of juvenile offenders in the Wilkinson Home for Boys in New York, and said it was a hundred percent accurate. He'd been there. He'd lived through the abuse. Some of the kids, and they were kids, were criminals by the time they entered that place, and others were made into hardened criminals by their experience. He'd had friends he grew up with go to the electric chair.

"It's something we never talked about, but everyone knew the odds. They were extremely long, but Richichi was a fighter. The government had plenty of evidence, including a string of rats, Michael Peter being the biggest, and a few people in Richichi's life who were suspected rats. Kenny Guarino, for instance, received friendly treatment from the government, which was something I could never quite understand after he and Richichi each pleaded guilty to conspiracy to defraud the government. Richichi was old and sick and got six years. Guarino received five to eleven months at a halfway house."

But it was Michael Peter who figured to give Richichi the most trouble. A one-time Cornell University student, he was as arrogant as he was successful and took advantage of Gambino family contacts—including an association with Florida-based capo Jimmy Williams—to grow his business empire. Before he fell, Peter owned or managed more than 50 topless cabarets in the United States and Europe, including six in South Florida. His businesses employed 5,000 people and grossed $100 million a year by combining upscale stripping with a sound business plan. His Pure Platinum and Dollhouse III each generated $100,000 a week in cash from horny locals and tourists.

Peter was charged with allowing the Gambino family to keep a hidden interest in three of his clubs and making regular payments to Richichi. He faced up to 40 years in prison and fines and forfeiture of $17 million in assets. Although the government's case was considered weak, he cut a deal, pleaded guilty to a single count of mail fraud, and received a wrist slap.

At trial, Richichi was found guilty and sentenced to 72 months in federal prison, the equivalent of a life sentence as Goodman saw it.

Even though he couldn't save Natale Richichi and Charlie Panarella, Goodman came away with the kind of warm memories that other men might reserve for their favorite uncles. The fact that Richichi was a top confidant to the most wanted man in America and Panarella once stuffed a man's own testicles down his throat did not dim Goodman's affection toward them. If anything, they seemed to add an air of intrigue that had otherwise been missing from Goodman's life since the death of his friend and top client, Tony Spilotro. His public protests to the contrary, these were not just clients. These were friends he respected.

As a memento of Goodman's stand-up performance in federal court, Richichi and Panarella gave him a gift that perhaps only men of their trade would truly appreciate: a set of large steel ball-bearings mounted on a plaque.

Given their reputations, it was high praise, indeed.

21

Bright Lights, Billable Hours

Although in many ways his law practice had never been more successful, by the mid-1990s something was missing from Oscar Goodman's professional life. His routine was much the same as it had been the previous three decades. He still rose before 5 a.m. and put in a full day, bet on anything that moved, and drank a pitcher of martinis before dinner at Piero's with Carolyn. But as much as he might have denied it at the time — if anything, his list of clients had become more colorful — some of the electricity had gone for good.

Life just wasn't the same without La Cosa Nostra.

Goodman made do with a rogue's gallery of characters torn straight from the pages of the *National Enquirer* and combined it with his trademark gift of self-promotion to keep his practice stimulating and his mug in the spotlight. He would say it was good for business, but it also fed his ego the way Beefeater gin tickled his liver.

There was Jack Gordon, whom Goodman had represented 15 years earlier in the case involving the attempted bribery of then-Nevada Gaming Commissioner Harry Reid. Gordon, a long-time promoter with a pencil-thin mustache and the reputation for slippery business ventures, had been found guilty of conspiring to bribe a public official and served three years in prison. He returned to making a buck with flash-in-the-pan pop stars, one-hit wonders, and tabloid freaks. For a time, he managed and was married to tabloid celebrity LaToya Jackson, who became better known more for her famous brother Michael, her tell-all memoir, and her volatile relationship with Gordon than for her ability to carry a tune. Gordon was in many ways the consummate Las Vegas sleaze, who'd come up as a carney and remained, at heart, a dubious deal-chaser.

Jackson filed for divorce in 1996, claiming she was the victim of beatings and mental cruelty by Gordon. The tabloids had a field day with their personal circus — Goodman avoided looking like the ringmaster by sending the Gordon-Jackson file to attorney Neil Beller.

After parting ways with LaToya in a deal Goodman helped broker, Gordon returned to tabloid print when he became the manager of the brief and forgettable career of John Wayne Bobbitt, the ex-Marine who rose to international notoriety after his wife, Lorena, severed his penis with a carving knife. Subsequently, Bobbitt put in short stints as a porn actor and a Nevada brothel employee. Around that same time, Gordon signed Bobbitt's girlfriend, Playboy Playmate Kristina Elliott, to a promotional contract that called for Gordon to receive up to a third of her earnings as a nude model. At one point, Gordon was found in contempt of court and served 10 days in jail after it was revealed he'd threatened Elliott after she pressed charges against Bobbitt for battery. "If John goes to jail, people will find your body in the bottom of Lake Mead," Elliott claimed Gordon told her. By then, however, Goodman had farmed Gordon out to law partner David Chesnoff.

Country singer Tracy Lawrence was known for his hits "Sticks and Stones" and "Any Fool Can See," but when he was arrested for whacking around his wife, former Dallas Cowboys cheerleader Stephanie Lawrence, he was wise enough to call Oscar Goodman. As always, Goodman's zealous defense of his client was in the public eye.

"He's as not guilty as I am," he told reporters. "If he hit his wife, then I hit my wife. And I never hit my wife, and you can ask her. If I can't win this case, I'll pay you my fee. I'm gonna beat them up."

Never mind that an officer's report revealed the victim's head was lumpy with welts. Goodman responded by suggesting that the complaint was little more than fabrications motivated by an estranged wife's greed. Lawrence pled guilty to a misdemeanor battery charge and paid a $500 fine, but probably got the inspiration for a few "hit" songs out of the experience. The couple later reconciled and, in true country-western fashion, broke up once more.

For a time, Goodman represented the owners of an upstart North Las Vegas hazardous-waste disposal company called U.S. EnviroMedical Corporation, which was accused by local authorities of burying tons of contaminated hospital waste beneath its own headquarters. Despite Goodman's protests that his clients had been maligned by a competing disposal firm, U.S. Med eventually ceased operations.

In the late summer of 1994, Goodman received a call from O.J. Simpson's manager in connection with the football star's arrest on murder charges. Simpon's man was attempting to assemble a team of top-flight lawyers to represent him. But Goodman had his own problems. Not only was he representing Richichi on felony charges in Boston, but he still faced the threat of jail for contempt. Goodman was offered $25,000 just to fly to Los Angeles for a meeting, but declined the offer. Just as he'd turned down an offer to join the defense team of former Panamanian President Manuel Noriega a few years earlier, Goodman wasn't interested in playing a supporting actor's role in the courtroom. Nor was he interested in cases that would take him away from home for months at a time. In quiet moments, he began to anticipate a time when two of his own college-age boys, Ross and Eric, might one day join his law firm.

But for a man in his mid-50s who appeared to increasingly desire to shed his reputation as a mob lawyer, Goodman's client list seldom strayed far from the shadowy world of the street. After so many years, it was where he found himself most comfortable. Problem was, the men with whom he seemed to share such affection had all but vanished from the scene.

One man who returned to the scene was Carl "Tuffy" DeLuna, the Kansas City mob underboss who was convicted in the Argent and Tropicana casino skims and gained his freedom in 1995 at age 68 after 16 years in the penitentiary. Organized-crime experts agreed that DeLuna was capable of revealing information about the mob's secret ownership of several Las Vegas casinos in the 1980s that could ruin the careers of several Las Vegas casino bosses.

Surely Goodman knew what DeLuna could do. But he also knew DeLuna's pedigree: strictly old school.

"He is the prototypical 'not that kind of guy,'" Goodman said. "He's the original zipper mouth. He wouldn't do anything ever to hurt anybody. No way."

Which only further convinced those who believed in DeLuna's encyclopedic knowledge of the history of the Las Vegas skim that Tuffy was in line to receive a windfall in exchange for his long years on the shelf. It gave new meaning to the adage "silence is golden."

? ? ?

Although DeLuna was his major Kansas City mob client to make the news, it was Goodman who rose to controversy after it was reported that he, law partner David Chesnoff, Missouri attorney and former federal prosecutor Byron Fox, and the political consulting firm Public Issue Management Inc. stood to divide $6 million if they succeeded in helping Las Vegan Bruce Becker gain a license to operate a Jefferson City riverboat casino. It was the first time since Goodman's days representing Argent Corp. that he'd come so close to owning a piece of a casino.

Fox, a prominent mover in Kansas City political circles and a close friend of Goodman and Chesnoff, had also represented members of organized crime. The presence of Goodman, Chesnoff, and Fox added the spice of the mob to newspaper accounts. The alleged failure to disclose resulted in misdemeanor criminal charges being filed against Becker, allegations that were later dismissed—but only after his license application was rejected by Missouri gaming authorities.

Privately, Goodman suspected one of Becker's competitors, perhaps Nevada casino licensee Paul Lowden, of working to scuttle the deal. Ironically, there was a time Lowden, former owner of the Hacienda and Sahara resorts, had been on friendly terms with Goodman, Argent front man Allen Glick, and future casino Black Book members Frank Rosenthal and Joey Cusumano. Goodman had gone to Lowden and offered him a shot at participating in the casino. Lowden apparently thought that Goodman was threatening him to go into the deal.

❡ ❡ ❡

Goodman's persona as a mob lawyer not only defined him, but also had an effect on other criminal defense attorneys.

Dominic Gentile said, "Oscar's big high-profile clients from the old days were gone. I think Oscar basically ran out of those kind of clients — not because they wouldn't hire Oscar, but because they weren't around anymore. The FBI and other agencies drove the money out of Italian organized crime and after the Scarfo trial there was really nobody left. Oscar had become so identified with being a mob lawyer that Rick Wright and I basically benefitted from all of the publicity that Oscar had received over the years. Clients came to me and told me flat out that they'd contemplated hiring Oscar, but they were afraid because he was so identified with being a mob lawyer."

"There's a big difference between being an advocate and being a mouthpiece," one former federal prosecutor said. "Saying there is no mob, that the FBI is a bunch of Nazis, that Spilotro was a good guy, that prosecutors were mentally deranged, that's disgusting. He knew who Spilotro was and that he was a cold-blooded murdering sonofabitch. If you lie down with dogs, you're going to get up with some fleas."

But Dick Crane, another veteran Strike Force prosecutor, disagreed.

"Oscar had a job to do and he did it well," Crane said. "He battled. He was supposed to battle. That was his job. It was his job not to get along with us, and he certainly didn't. He was a fighter, but I don't think he went too far.

"Oscar's very clever and a very able advocate, a smart guy. His job is to make government do its job and prove its case, but his job is not to say there's no such thing as the mob or to call FBI agents, many of whom have dedicated their lives to protecting us against thugs and rogues, the bad guys.

"In all the time I dealt with him, he never had a reputation of fucking around on his wife. I never heard anything but that he was a good family man. There's something to be said for a guy who raised four kids and every one a success. I think that's very telling about the man."

Goodman had become such a media celebrity that it was sometimes difficult to separate his egotistical public persona from the man. No matter how he was in his private life, in public he was larger than life.

"Oscar has always been out for Oscar, but we're all ego-maniacs," a former federal prosecutor said. "The best of us are ego-driven. This is not a game. This is life and death and there's no second place many times. You either win or you lose, but there's still an application of ethics to our profession. That's the difference, and I don't think Oscar got that."

"You've got to understand something about being a trial lawyer," said one with thirty years experience. "It's not about just knowing the law. A lot of guys know the law and can't win a trial. The difference between being a good trial lawyer and being an excellent one is not only being smart, but you have to have a lot of self-confidence. When you stand up in front of that jury, you have to convey that you know what's going on and that what you say is gold and they can trust you. They must believe you're the man and you're going to be honest with them and that you're the one looking our for someone's rights.

"It takes a big ego and a lot of self-confidence to stand up in front of twelve people and convince them that you're right and the government is wrong. One thing about Oscar, he doesn't have a weak personality. He believes when he stands up there he can't be beat. That's what's required to win. If you're the least bit timid, if you show the least bit of weakness, you're done—particularly in criminal cases, where the jury doesn't believe your client is innocent until proven guilty and the entire power of the government is against you."

A veteran lawyer and longtime Goodman watcher observed, "Oscar has always had a big ego in court, but you don't necessarily have to be that way in everyday life. Sometimes he gets carried away."

"We're in there for the game, for the sport of it," Goodman law partner Marty Keach said. "We like to fight and we like to win. We don't like to fight the weak. We like to fight the strong, and the strongest of the strong. Oscar is always the lead, except for the ones he tried with me. He let me carry the weight and I loved him for that.

"It's no different that a heavyweight fight. Anybody can beat the stiffs. Give me the best. That's what I want to go up against. Being a trial lawyer is not for the weak, and Oscar isn't weak."

≀ ≀ ≀

The strange but lucrative cases continued to pour into Goodman's office. The offers that called for cross-country travel were declined or turned over to partners. Goodman was attempting to stay closer to home, but he agreed to defend Carson City oral surgeon Dr. Gregory Minton, who was accused of sexually molesting several female patients while they were under anesthesia. Despite substantially damaging testimony against the dentist, Goodman managed to persuade a jury that the memories of no fewer than seven patients were all somehow faulty. He focused on flaws in the government's theory on the molestations and exploited the prosecution's failure to do its job thoroughly by checking out details of the dentist's office.

Each witness had someone in the waiting room who was told that the doctor had molested them. The doctor's employees said they were told to turn down the lights, turn up the radio, and leave the patient in the dental chair.

"The judge, Archie Blake of Yerington, couldn't wait to sentence Minton to a million years," Goodman said. "Every motion I made was denied. I went home one weekend during the trial and attended a party Carolyn was giving for the Meadows School at our home. Former Los Angeles Dodgers manager Tommy Lasorda was the guest of honor and I had him autograph two baseballs — one for the judge and one for the prosecutor. When the trial resumed, I gave each a baseball. For some reason, I never lost another motion."

Edward Becker, an investigator, author, and himself a nationally recognized expert on organized crime, represented the conservative Accuracy In Media at the Minton trial. Although the group had no official role in the trial, Becker's presence served to temper what he considered the heavily lopsided coverage in the local press. He noticed a dramatic shift in the tone and tenor of reporters' coverage after Goodman took on the case.

"On a daily basis, it was being very widely covered by the *Reno Gazette-Journal* and the local *Appeal,* the Carson City paper," Becker recalled. "I was the one who brought Oscar into it. I made Minton fire his attorney, who wasn't getting the job done. I said to Minton he'd get out of this by hiring Oscar. Oscar asked for a big fee right from the start. The guy took a loan on his house and was very good at paying Oscar. We had a lot of reporters, who of course wanted to see Oscar.

"I think Oscar scared the prosecution. You've got a hard-living District Attorney, and he has a woman who is his aide and does most of his work. Now in comes Oscar and we've got this guy out of the water. Oscar was his typical self. He'd get up and shout at the judge and the attorney. He was very intimidating. That's Oscar, I guess.

"Until the Minton trial, I knew Oscar only through the mob stuff. During the trial, I got a feeling of what he was really all about when I saw him work. We'd go to Adele's restaurant in Carson City and he'd buy me dinner, but he was all business. Afterward, he would go to the damn library at night after court and work until ten or eleven o'clock. It wasn't like he was a dilettante or a showboat. He was a real hard-working attorney. He's a pain in the ass, but somehow down deep I feel he's honorable.

"He's a gambler. We'd fly back on the plane. He'd order martinis for both of us. He kept busy making out his basketball picks."

For one of the few times in his career, Goodman enlisted the services of a medical expert in a criminal case. Dr. Ron Siegel was a UCLA professor and author of several books. He was considered an expert on the effect certain anesthetic drugs had on female dental patients. He testified that a number of patients, including some of his own, had hallucinated that they'd given oral sex to the dentist. The strategic testimony appeared to impress several jurors.

About the time the jury began deliberations, Goodman encouraged Becker to leak the results of a privately administered polygraph that showed Minton had been truthful when he'd denied molesting his patients.

"When the jury came in not guilty, Oscar invited the jury to his house for Thanksgiving," Becker remembered. "There were tears in Oscar's eyes when he won that case. It was amazing."

❡ ❡ ❡

It's understating matters considerably to say that winning an acquittal for a dentist accused of perverse acts was unlikely to hold Goodman's interests. He managed his cases, bet his ballgames, and relished his free time spent with Carolyn at their high-rise condominium on Coronado Island. Oscar and Carolyn tried to spend at least a few days during each summer's month-long thoroughbred racing meet at magnificent Del Mar Racetrack. But the born actor was bored away from the stage. He looked forward to the September 1998 premiere of *Mob Law*, a British documentary about his life and legal career.

Paul Wilmshurst's Oscar Goodman odyssey began when the writer and film director picked up a London newspaper and read a story about the notorious mob mouthpiece. Wilmshurst decided then that Goodman's life was the stuff of American legend and as a bonus, potentially provided a vehicle with which to study the history of Las Vegas. The idea for the documentary *Mob Law: The True Story of Oscar Goodman* was born.

"He's a big character in the history of the town — and in his own right," Wilmshurst remarked. "And he's worked with a lot of interesting people."

Once again, Goodman would be identified with his clients, but this time the link produced a documentary of his life, not merely the scorn of a prosecutor or a few newspaper headlines.

The film's line producer, Gary Johnstone, observed, "Hopefully, the image we're going to give is closer to the real Las Vegas. One of the most exciting things is just the light — the battle between the light God supplies and the light neon supplies. We want to record that battle."

But it became just as clear that the filmmakers also wanted to record the battle between good and evil — with Goodman as a likable devil. Wilmshurst, through the Big Table Film Company, began shooting the documentary in October 1997. The film was shot in both black-and-white and color with a style reminiscent of Joel and Ethan Coen and used a haunting music score written by Daniel Pemberton. Actor Anthony LaPaglia narrated.

Goodman's clients had been repugnant and his own actions showed he knew far more of their world than he cared to admit, but there was something about the mob lawyer the camera found intriguing. By all appearances, Goodman granted Wilmshurst and his crew total access, going so far as to include home-movie footage of his own bar mitzvah, as well as the inside of his home in Las Vegas' upscale Scotch 80s neighborhood.

"They're pulling no punches," Goodman told *Review-Journal* film critic and reporter Carol Cling, adding his trademark darkly comic twist. "I don't have any censorship powers — if I don't like the final product, all I can do is have them killed. No lawsuits — that's the final solution."

It was the characters, Goodman not least, who carried *Mob Law*.

Wilmshurst was able to interview on camera men such as Colombo crime-family capo Charlie Panarella, who would have never dreamed of showing his face or speaking on the record to an outsider. But he would do almost anything for his friend Oscar. There were also local mob associates Joey Cusumano and Dominic Spinale, suspected hitman Dean Shendal, and a host of others.

Adding to the documentary's credibility was the participation of former FBI undercover agent Rick Baken, who had infiltrated Anthony Spilotro's crime crew and once wore a wire into Goodman's own law office in an attempt to catch the attorney obstructing justice. And there was former Las Vegas office Special Agent in Charge Joe Yablonsky, whose righteous indignation made him appear like *Les Miserables'* Javert to Goodman's Jean Valjean.

While Goodman portrayed himself as a man in love with the Constitution and protecting the rights of the accused at any cost, Baken and Yablonsky were used as foils in the film. Yablonsky was unable to contain his contempt for Goodman, speculating that he had been part of a fixed murder case on Tony Spilotro's behalf and had gained an unhealthy and perhaps unholy strength from associating with mobsters.

Although top-heavy with biographical material—the camera crew even visited Goodman's old Philadelphia row house after receiving a police escort into a neighborhood gone from middle-class Jewish to working-class black—the action led up to an odd but entertaining climax. Goodman in his black Mercedes was pitted against Baken in his white sports car at sunset on the edge of the Las Vegas Valley. Although the symbolism was forced, the overstatement appeared to fit the character of the man and the town. Goodman and Baken traded angry remarks as the sun set on their era, but in the end Goodman managed to steal the scene by bidding his former adversary farewell with a surprisingly cheerful, "Drive safely."

It was just the sort of eerie surrealism that had been so much a part of Oscar Goodman's normal private life and bizarre public legal career.

The 92-minute *Mob Law* premiered to a full house at a movie theater inside the Orleans Hotel and Casino as the top attraction of the fledgling Las Vegas International Film Festival. It was not reported that Goodman and his law partners Marty Keach and David Chesnoff guaranteed a capacity crowd by buying up blocks of tickets. Several Southern Nevada judges and other public officials were in attendance, along with a number of lesser underworld figures and those Goodman clients not excluded from the casino due to their listing in the state's Black Book.

The documentary was popular in Great Britain, where it first showed on Channel 4. It received a series of mostly favorable reviews in a number of national newspapers and magazines and served to illustrate, equally, Goodman's controversial status as a top mob lawyer and his apparently unlimited capacity for ego gratification. He reveled in the adoration, basking in the opening-night spotlight.

Then he watched as the story of his life went straight to video cassette and relative obscurity as a Fox Lorber and WinStar Home Entertainment release. The video carton depicted Goodman in what he sometimes called his mob lawyer suit, with half his face obscured by a shadow in a clear statement of the documentary's ambiguous message. *Mob Law* didn't find the audience of Scorsese's *Casino*, but it was also nothing Oscar Goodman felt compelled to apologize for as it went public.

Goodman's restless intellect and ego began to manifest in regular appearances in the role of Every Defense Attorney opposite former Clark County District Attorney prosecutor Tom Leen in a weekly short-format television debate on KVBC-TV, the Las Vegas NBC affiliate. Both men were well-suited for their parts as bookends on opposite sides of the legal system. Goodman and Leen took turns, oftentimes degrading their differences into name-calling diatribes reminiscent of a couple of "Saturday Night Live" characters, but the audience was enthusiastic. Within the two-minute format, Leen questioned Goodman's morality and Goodman roared about the Constitution.

More than comic legal relief, the program allowed Goodman a forum to espouse a number of his personal beliefs and pet theories about society, which he postulated would run more smoothly — and far less hypocritically — if petty drug use and prostitution were decriminalized. Goodman ad-libbed while Leen appeared rehearsed and ready for the courtroom. A showman at heart, Goodman was in his element. Even his most routine volleys were as jagged as carnival glass.

And he often went too far, so far over the top that his point was obscured by his outrageous arguments. At home, Carolyn Goodman cringed at her husband's antics. In his relentless zeal to win every imaginable battle, Goodman also uttered a number of wickedly boorish comments from his character as the Uber Mouthpiece. At one point he dragged out his pet plastic rat and banged its head repeatedly, saying that was what should happen to government informants. Another low point came when Goodman told Leen that women sometimes lied about rape. Although he wasn't wrong from a statistical standpoint, the inference viewers were left to draw was that he meant a great percentage of them lied, so most rape was not a serious offense. Such outrageous acts of overstatement occasionally made Carolyn Goodman flinch, but Leen's most pointed rhetoric did nothing to pierce Oscar Goodman's *Hindenburg*-sized hyperbole.

Goodman later insisted it had only been a silly television show. Surely, no one would remember his most ill-advised comments. Fewer still, he was certain, would care that he'd advocated legalizing hookers and pot. Not unless he did something really outrageous, like run for public office.

§ § §

Not all Goodman's mob clients had retired.

On the street, Richard Perry was known as one of the sharpest minds in the sports-betting business, but he specialized in the fix. From horseracing to basketball, he scatter-shot angles at a variety of sporting events and picked up the moniker "the Fixer," along with convictions for corrupting harness races at Yonkers Raceway in 1974 and for conspiring to rig basketball games at Boston College in 1984. Perry was also a fixture at New York's Rucker Basketball Tournament, where many of the nation's top prospects gain their first wide exposure. Perry, author David Porter observed, "always seemed to have an angle on whatever big games were going on around the country."

In Las Vegas, Goodman and his partner David Chesnoff were called to assist Perry who was in yet more trouble, this time after photographs surfaced in the *Review-Journal* of the Fixer in a hot tub with members of the University of Nevada-Las Vegas' championship basketball team. The scandal helped lead to the ouster of UNLV Coach Jerry Tarkanian and ushered Perry's name into the state's Black Book in 1992. After busting out of Las Vegas, Perry moved to South Florida, where he sometimes kept company with Gambino capo and Goodman client Natale Richichi. In conversation, Goodman waxed nostalgic about his visits with Perry and Richichi.

It became clear that Goodman was fond of their street stories and the Fixer's head for numbers. Their felony status was of no concern to a man who'd spent most of his adult life in the presence of notorious men.

§ § §

When asked to define organized crime, one-time Gaming Control Board Chairman Shannon Bybee once said, "Anybody that Oscar Goodman represents." While the remark generated laughter, Bybee reflected a prevailing view of Goodman—a view the mob lawyer only occasionally bothered to correct. Privately, however, he sneered at the lack of respect he was afforded by men he believed were inferior attorneys who'd risen to power through a long tradition of Nevada juice, instead of doing combat in the courtroom. Over time, even some retired Justice Department attorneys, such as former Organized Crime Strike Force leader Richard Crane, gave their devil his due.

"Oscar was a fierce adversary in the courtroom," Crane said years after their last battle. He would later endorse Goodman's mayoral candidacy. "He was well-prepared and very aggressive in the courtroom, but he never crossed the line."

What about the sentiments, sometimes attributed to Strike Force legend Michael "Iron Mike" DeFeo, that Goodman, Claiborne, Judge Foley, and others were members of a corrupt cabal that served to protect organized-crime interests in Las Vegas for a generation?

Crane, now a private-practice attorney who serves as chief counsel for Coast Resorts casino company, shrugs at the conspiracy theory.

"They had everything but proof," Crane said.

Says one former prosecutor, "It's no secret that Oscar was a big reason Tony Spilotro stayed out of prison, but as much as people hate to admit it, that was his job. I think he was probably too close to the mob socially, and whatever he says nowadays, he really liked some of those guys who were nothing more than pieces of shit. But there's a difference between the mob and a mob lawyer. The difference is, Oscar was never indicted, never convicted, never sent to prison, and never clipped."

Others in the system remained forever suspicious of Goodman's character.

"There are two different types of attorneys when it comes to the mob," former Las Vegas FBI Special Agent in Charge Joe Yablonsky said. "There are attorneys who represent the mob. And there are mob attorneys. And Mr. Goodman was proud to be called a mob attorney. [His relationship with Spilotro] went far beyond the norm of attorneys and clients.

"When I look at him, I think of him as the kid on the block who had the shiny bicycle that nobody wanted to play with.

He was kind of looking for some sort of acclamation. Las Vegas was a perfect place for a Philadelphian to come to achieve what he's achieved.

"One of my theories about criminal defense attorneys, many of them, part of their practice is to turn lies into truth and truth into lies. After a while, they become confused about what the truth is and what the lie is."

The mention of Yablonsky's name rekindled Goodman's fiery rhetoric:

"Joe doesn't get it and never will. He'll never understand that just because the FBI says something doesn't make it true. The instances of lies and cover-ups inside the FBI are legion, yet all Joe can do is focus on me. He's obsessed. I'm in his head. I've driven him crazy, and I couldn't be more pleased.

"Yablonsky said I like men because I couldn't have children or some shit. The fact is, I like to be around strong men. I'd like to think I have something in common with them. Yablonsky was crazy, in my opinion, and that made him dangerous. It wasn't his criminal investigations that were a problem. It was his tactics that were underhanded. It was his view of Las Vegas and everyone in it as bad that made him dangerous."

As the 1990s played out, Goodman became even more convinced that the ever-creeping hand of the government had reached so far into the justice system that it not only was willing to present its own set of killers as credible witnesses, but was also willing to lie to judges, mislead grand juries, even attempt to put defense attorneys in jail, to reach its goal. Wherever the weight of the process was greatest, and the FBI, DEA, IRS, and Justice Department had the most on the line, the Constitution wasn't worth the paper it was printed on.

In his view, it wasn't that his clients hadn't committed many of the acts alleged. It was that the fair-trial process was being bastardized. After all the mobsters and their mouthpieces were gone, it was the process that mattered. And it was being subverted on a disturbingly regular basis in high-profile cases in which the government had the greatest investment of time, money, and ego.

The government hated to be upstaged or proved wrong and Goodman was not a congenial combatant. He gloated in victory, snarled in defeat, and never gave an inch. Prosecutors had been his clients' mortal enemies and that made them his enemies, too. Even after 35 years, he remained a one-man revolutionary whose deep distrust of government bordered on anarchy. Long-time observers of Goodman saw a man who would rather have thrown a bomb in the courtroom in order to make a statement than cut a deal for his client. Oscar Goodman would never go quietly into that good night.

22

Devils and Angels

When word circulated on the afternoon of September 17, 1998, that Lonnie "Ted" Binion had been found dead at his house on Palomino Lane, a short distance from Goodman's Bannie Lane home, those who knew the troubled Las Vegas casino man assumed what Metro police at the scene initially believed: The hard-partying 55-year-old had finally succumbed to the drugs that had consumed so much of his life.

Ted Binion had done his best to emulate the style of his father, Horseshoe Club patriarch Benny Binion, but had fallen prey to the hedonistic lifestyle that the monied elite so easily find in Las Vegas. Ted's longing for Las Vegas' mobbed-up good old days and his penchant for keeping young girlfriends and smoking black-tar heroin cost him millions of dollars and much of his adulthood. Although he possessed a $1 million home in Las Vegas, a sprawling ranch property in the rural Southern Nevada community of Pahrump, an expansive family ranch in Montana, and an estimated net worth of $70 million, Binion was in the middle of breaking up with his hard-bodied live-in girlfriend, Sandy Murphy, when she called 911 and told the operator she'd been unable to revive him.

Minutes after the police arrived at Binion's home, Oscar Goodman received a knock at his door from Nick Behnen, the husband of Binion's Horseshoe operator, and Ted's sister, Becky Binion Behnen. Nick and Ted had long been at odds, ever since the Gaming Commission had removed the black-sheep Binion from the Horseshoe due to his drug addiction and mob association. Ted believed Nick and his kid sister were feeding Gaming Control Board investigators damaging information in an effort to force him out of the casino.

Goodman had been Ted Binion's attorney and friend, and at one time borrowed $250,000 from the casino man to pay a debt incurred by the collapse of a tax shelter. He'd repaid the loan and like many Las Vegans had maintained a friendship with the roguish but affable Binion.

Goodman later recalled that Behnen appeared to have tears in his eyes.

"You've got to get over to Ted's house," Behnen said. "He's committed suicide."

"Suicide?" Goodman thought. That didn't sound like the Ted he'd known.

Goodman got in his car and drove a half-mile to the Palomino Lane house, where police swarmed and friends of the deceased, including contractor Rick Tabish and attorney Richard Wright, were standing around. Metro officers at the scene said it appeared Binion had accidentally overdosed, as evidenced by a prescription bottle for the sedative Xanax found near the body. To all the world it appeared Ted Binion had died the way he'd lived: as an addict. An autopsy later revealed Binion had large, if marginally lethal, amounts of heroin and Xanax in his system, with what Chief Medical Examiner Dr. Lary Simms described as an unusual amount of heroin in his stomach, as if he'd swallowed the stuff instead of smoking it, in a manner commonly known as "chasing the dragon."

"He was one of the best guys I've ever met," Goodman told reporters who knew Binion as a tough-talking violence-prone ne'er-do-well. Once again Goodman revealed his taste in humanity.

But a strange thing happened on the way to burying Ted Binion. His estranged sister Becky, initially, and eventually the rest of his family, began to suspect foul play. Footwork by private investigator Tom Dillard established a clandestine relationship between Murphy and Binion's new friend, Montanan Rick Tabish, who was arrested with three other men two days after the apparent drug overdose in the act of digging up an estimated $7 million in silver bars and coins from an underground vault at Binion's Pahrump ranch.

Just days after Binion's death, Murphy delivered silver coins to Goodman's law office, then changed her mind and removed them. She told confidants that she didn't trust Goodman, a friend of 30 years of the deceased and his clan. Goodman was off her case a short while later, but continued to be rumored to participate as a trial consultant by proxy through private investigator William Cassidy.

Despite those facts and his friendship with the deceased, Goodman initially agreed to defend Sandy Murphy. He and his partner David Chesnoff stood by Murphy as she fought to receive a portion of Binion's estate, approximately $3 million including the Palomino Lane house, that he'd set aside for her in his will only months before his death.

In probate court on Murphy's behalf, however, Goodman and Chesnoff found themselves up against long-time friends Richard Wright, Harry Claiborne, and Bruce Judd, all of whom believed that Binion had been the victim of a homicide, not an accidental drug overdose. Goodman considered such talk absurd in the face of Binion's longstanding heroin habit.

Although District Judge Michael Cherry eventually ruled that Murphy was entitled to her portion of Binion's estate, by then the police investigation, combined with the work of Dillard, had begun to uncover circumstantial evidence that Binion might have been the victim of murder.

A few weeks later, Goodman quit the case as he pursued a run for mayor of Las Vegas. Murphy stated publicly that she'd felt abandoned by trusted counsel. And after her arrest with Tabish on murder charges, questions arose as to whether Goodman had benefited from hundreds of thousands of dollars worth of silver Murphy was suspected of pilfering from the Palomino Lane house after Binion's death. Goodman denied receiving any silver and said that, in fact, he'd returned much of Murphy's retainer.

But rumors persisted throughout the Binion murder case that Goodman was confidentially consulting for the defense through his assistant, Bill Cassidy. Irish businessman and Murphy benefactor William Fuller, a red-haired octogenarian whose sudden mysterious presence only added to the intrigue of the case, was suspected of hiring Goodman. More false speculation, Goodman argued.

On September 15, 2000, a jury convicted Murphy and Tabish of causing the suffocation death of Ted Binion. The defendants were sentenced to life in prison with the possibility of parole. On July 14, 2003, The Nevada Supreme Court overturned the convictions and ordered new trials.

? ? ?

As an attorney, Gerard Bongiovanni's legal career had been distinguished only by his role in the controversial protracted litigation following the 1980 fire at the MGM Grand (now Bally's) in which 82 people died. So it was understandable that many downtown courthouse observers were surprised when Bongiovanni won a seat on the District Court bench in 1990. Perhaps they were further surprised when they began to hear within weeks of his election to the bench that he was taking money to fix cases. Perhaps not. Bongiovanni chose for his assistant a de-robed Justice of the Peace named Delwin Potter, an attorney whose own career had been defined by a prolific role as a stipend-hungry "Marrying Sam," the term for JPs who focus on the lucrative Las Vegas wedding business.

At the same time the rumors were swirling around Bongiovanni's courtroom, producers Jeff Kutash and Martin Romley had had a falling out with the owner of the Riviera Hotel-Casino, Meshulam Riklis, over their popular *Splash* production show. With its breakneck pacing, scantily clad showgirls, million-gallon aquarium replete with "mermaids," and "Dome of Death" motorcycle trick riders, *Splash* was everything middle-class tourists loved, and newspaper critics hated, about Las Vegas. The disagreement between the producers and the owner resulted in a lawsuit, which wound up in Bongiovanni's court.

Kutash was no stranger to the shadows of the entertainment business, having had a relationship with Colombo crime-family capo Michael Franzese.

In 1996, Kutash, Bongiovanni, and the judge's friend and bowling partner Paul Dottore were indicted on racketeering, wire-fraud, and conspiracy charges related to the show producer's alleged attempt to pay the judge $5,000 to fix the case against Riklis.

Until then, Dottore was known on the street as little more than a small-time scam artist with a big mouth, a wanna-be who talked like a connected guy. At least in the case of his relationship with Bongiovanni, he wasn't lying, or so it seemed. Dottore, it would turn out, had other connections, too.

Kutash hired Oscar Goodman. Bongiovanni retained pugnacious local criminal-defense lawyer Tom Pitaro. For Goodman, the legal scenario was a variation on a theme. In order to make its case against the judge, the government first needed to prevail over Kutash, who appeared to be the more vulnerable defendant. With Dottore cooperating with police, the trials of Kutash and Bongiovanni were severed. Kutash went first in what some courthouse observers believed to be a practice run prior to the showdown with the judge.

Former Riviera showroom manager Starlee Leavitt testified that she'd approached Dottore, with Kutash's approval, with a plan to fix the Riklis case. "I thought Mr. Kutash was trying very hard to make a partnership work, and I knew that Mr. Riklis was being difficult and—these are my words—maybe a little underhanded in dealing with him," Leavitt told the court on August 28, 1997.

Leavitt, who received immunity in exchange for her testimony, tearfully told the jury Kutash had told her, "I'll take it under advisement," when she informed him that Bongiovanni had agreed to accept $5,000 to rule in his favor.

Dottore had gone so far as to hand Bongiovanni marked bills, which police later removed from the judge's back pocket. Goodman wasted little time plowing into Dottore's checkered past and easily characterized him as a Judas who had sold out his best friend Bongiovanni for money, as well as to save his own skin with the feds, who'd also nailed him in a bank fraud in which one victim was more than 80 years old. With a face straight from a penitentiary yearbook, Dottore was a loathsome witness and an almost gleeful Goodman made him squirm.

"Oscar told me he always knew when he had a witness at his mercy," Vinny Montalto said. "When the witness goes for a drink of water, he's got them. I've watched him in court dozens of times and every time one of the witnesses goes for the water, he's done."

Goodman's strategy received a big boost from Terry Salem, a con man and mob associate turned government informant, who'd played a key role in the bank fraud but managed to cut the sweetest deal of any of the suspects. Salem worked exclusively for the FBI for 16 months in 1994 and 1995, earning $3,000 a month and a free pass to pursue his white-collar criminal enterprises. Like Dottore, Salem pleaded guilty to reduced charges in exchange for his testimony that Kutash had paid the Bongiovanni bribe. So advantageous was Salem's agreement with the government, he wasn't even forced to return or pay taxes on the money he stole in the bank-fraud case.

Goodman managed to severely damage the marginal credibility of Dottore and Salem, but he felt that Starlee Leavitt had been more effective with jurors. Her role made sense and provided a link between the defendant and the judge. Near the end of the prosecution's case, a decision was made: Put Kutash on the stand. The jury needed to hear him say he never paid a bribe. After all, he had far more credibility in the community than the informants. Unfortunately, he also had a few problems. There were the troubling phone records, which appeared to establish a pattern of contact that fit the government's theory of a conspiracy. There was a bank withdrawal, which occurred at about the time the bribe was alleged to have been paid. And there was the envelope Leavitt said Kutash had given her, which she believed was filled with $5,000 in cash.

Then it was FBI case agent Jerry Hanford's turn to take the heat. Hanford, a respected veteran, had followed the stench of corruption wafting from Bongiovanni's courtroom since shortly after the judge took the bench in early 1991. He'd pieced together what appeared to be a solid chain of evidence that placed cash bribes right in the judge's pocket. But Goodman managed to turn the tables on the respected FBI agent and supervisor, as he'd done so many times before, by raising the image of a law-enforcement investigation that was too willing to believe the words of criminals desperate to cut a deal to save their skins.

For those who had followed Goodman's career, it was déjà vu. The stage and bit players may have changed, but the message he was speaking was the same. And the jurors were listening.

Goodman and Kutash also received two big breaks. At the time of the alleged incident, the FBI was wiretapping Dottore's phone line and heard him discuss with Leavitt the issues related to the Kutash civil case against Meshulam Riklis. But on October 15, the day the bribe was to have been delivered, the government wasn't listening, so prosecutors had no voice recording, only a phone record of a call being made between Leavitt and Dottore. The following day, Bongiovanni granted Kutash's request for a temporary restraining order in his civil case. But prosecutors had made a mistake common to many complex criminal cases. In an effort to be precise, they had boxed themselves in to facts so specific they allowed for no inconsistencies. For example, as evidence of wrongdoing, the government cited a $5,000 corporate check cashed by Kutash's partner Martin Romley on October 16, 1995 — a day *after* the supposed cash exchange was made. In his closing argument, Goodman went to great lengths to exploit the flaw in the government's case.

Only later was it determined that the date used by the government had been the day the check was processed by the bank, not the day it was cashed. That date? October 13, 1995.

Exploiting the pungence of the government witnesses, the inconsistency in the supposed bribe check, and the rare appearance of a client on the witness stand, Goodman managed to persuade the jury to vote to acquit Kutash on all charges. The jury deliberated less than eight hours before rendering its verdict. Although at least one juror was apologetic for voting to acquit Kutash, the show producer celebrated and announced that he was planning to produce a Joe Palooka show for Las Vegas with the help of Oscar Goodman, who was a life-long fan of Broadway.

"This is a very rare occasion in this building," Goodman said, exiting the federal courthouse. "They tried to put an innocent man in prison for their self-aggrandizement, and thank God the jury wouldn't let them do it."

The effect of the Kutash acquittal reverberated throughout the local justice system and set the stage for Tom Pitaro's dramatic victory on Bongiovanni's behalf. In his case, Pitaro used much the same strategy Goodman had employed — batter the government witnesses and humanize the defendant. Bongiovanni also took the stand in his own defense and jurors came away impressed, despite the dramatic evidence pointing toward guilt. Bongiovanni was found not guilty on October 30, 1998.

"I try my case based on trying the government," Goodman said later. "If they can show that they got my man without breaking the law, then they're entitled to him. And in every case they broke the law. I don't think I've had one case where the government didn't break the law. You shouldn't have to try a perfect case to get a conviction, but you should have to play according to the rules. They were always breaking the rules. Maybe they didn't do that with guys other than Italians. I don't know. But in just about every case I ever had, they broke the rules.

"Look at Kutash, a perfect example. I just destroyed them with the way I tried the case. This poor FBI agent, Jerry Hanford. I got him on the stand and destroyed him. By the time I got through with him, it didn't matter whether Kutash did it or didn't do it. It didn't matter because Hanford gave the kitchen sink to the rat Terry Salem. He let Salem keep everything, things he clearly wasn't entitled to, cash that he not only hadn't earned, but that the evidence showed he'd stolen from an old man. The jury just wasn't going to tolerate it. Maybe part of it is that I get outraged at it and the jurors see that, and the jurors don't tolerate that. Maybe my outrage is louder."

⸮ ⸮ ⸮

But would even Oscar Goodman's gift of outrage overcome the public's perception of haunted heavyweight boxer Mike Tyson?

It was hard to believe it could.

Tyson was a street thug from the Brownsville section of Brooklyn. As a reform-school teenager, he became the pet project of trainer Cus D'Amato, who along with managers Jimmy Jacobs and Bill Cayton remade Tyson in pugilistic "Pygmalion" fashion. They taught him fundamentals, instilled a modicum of discipline, nurtured his love of the fight game, kept him out of jail, and turned him into a seemingly unbeatable warrior who became the youngest heavyweight champion in modern boxing history. When one by one those positive influences either died or became estranged from Tyson, he returned to his street ways. He also linked arms with fight promoter and occasional-Goodman client Don King. Along the way, Tyson was convicted of rape and became entangled in a series of embarrassing altercations on the street and with the law.

But nothing in Mike Tyson's checkered résumé compared to his actions on the night of June 28, 1997, at the MGM Grand Garden in Las Vegas in a heavyweight title fight against reigning champion Evander Holyfield. In front of thousands of screaming fans and millions of television viewers, Tyson was in trouble in the third round. Holyfield appeared to butt Tyson, who responded by twice biting the champion's ears, ripping half of one of them off. Referee Mills Lane, the former Northern Nevada District Attorney, District Court judge, and longtime Goodman adversary, disqualified Tyson. A riot ensued that rocked the boxing racket.

"At that fractured moment, I truly believe Mike Tyson went nuts," Lane later wrote in his autobiography, *Let's Get It On*. "And by doing so, he disgraced all of us boxers, professionals and amateurs alike."

The world of boxing echoed the referee's sentiment and the world at large appeared to have had enough of Tyson's animal act. The prevailing pressure in the media was sweeping and singular: Ban Tyson for life from ever setting foot in a ring in Nevada, the big-money fight capital of the world. If that happened, his career would effectively be over.

Don King, Mike Tyson's promoter and manager, made a desperate call to Oscar Goodman. The wheels began to turn. King also hired Sig Rogich, a Nevada political consulting giant and advisor to presidents Ronald Reagan and George Bush, who began to pursue a course toward calming the media. An apology was written for Tyson to parrot to the press, but it did little to stanch the international flow of negative publicity. Pundits and professional fight-game observers began calling for a lifetime ban for Tyson, who'd already strained even the boxing racket's broad ethical boundaries with his rape conviction and persistent police problems.

Goodman stepped in with law partner Marty Keach and attempted to turn the tide before the Nevada Athletic Commission, a panel of laypersons appointed by the governor. Mills Lane and several of the commissioners, including Chairman Dr. Elias Ghanem, were men Goodman had known for many years.

For his part, Ghanem was one of the most enigmatic characters in Las Vegas. A practicing physician whose clients had once included a heavily medicated Elvis Presley, Ghanem had amassed a fortune and formidable political influence since immigrating to Las Vegas from Palestine. As a campaign fundraiser, his circle of political associations stretched from City Hall to the White House. Goodman had represented Ghanem at a time when the FBI and IRS were investigating a number of suspicious activities that resulted in damaging publicity, but no charges filed.

"During the IRS investigation, it was one of the few times in history where we actually convinced the prosecution not to file charges against him based on what our defense would be," Goodman explained. "Elias had quite a bit of money that he hadn't declared to the IRS. His father was from Palestine and when he came over, he gave Elias an awful lot of money, and we argued that it was that money, rather than money he didn't declare from his income, that the IRS had discovered. And they bought it.

"So I had a very good relationship with Elias, ostensibly. But he was part of the power elite in Las Vegas and I was not. As a result of that, he was a friend of Frank Schreck and all the casino owners, with whom I had no relationship—or an anti-relationship. I'd helped Elias at a critical time in his career, but I'm not sure how much that counted with him.

"With all the hundreds of thousands that he raised for people in various political campaigns, when I was running for mayor, I think Elias gave me a grand and raised no money. It was all right, but I guess it surprised me a little.

"But far beyond that, I admired Elias for his courage and grace facing a devastating disease, cancer. He was one of the most gallant men I've ever met in the sense that he lived with this horrible disease and the pain. He had cancer in every part of his body. I give him so much credit. I have nothing but admiration and respect for him as far as his bravery. But, you know, that fight game stinks." (Ghanem died of cancer in 2001.)

Although Goodman won't admit that anything unethical or untoward occurred on Tyson's behalf, it was clear to observers that Tyson was receiving the best treatment possible from his allies on the Nevada Athletic Commission. The reason was simple: At that time, his career was still an economic engine that generated millions for Las Vegas.

Goodman had represented King for many years on the delicate matter of contract negotiations with heavyweight fighters, including former champion Larry Holmes. When King and Holmes parted ways, it was Goodman who met with both men at 3 a.m. in the coffee shop at the Riviera Hotel and drew up their agreement on the back of a napkin. In years to come, Holmes often told reporters that he'd been cheated out of a fortune by Don King, but the Easton, Pennsylvania, fighter declined to take his former promoter to court.

With his violent crime-riddled background and rags-to-riches life story, King was the sort of man Goodman had long been enamored of. But Goodman's romance with his clients' public personae was tested by King, a former Cleveland numbers banker who had served time for manslaughter and had been involved in at least one other violent death.

In 1966, King was arrested after bystanders witnessed him stomp to death a small-time drug dealer named Sam Garrett, who made the mistake of owing King $600. Despite outweighing Garrett by 100 pounds, King held a gun on the man while kicking his brains out. "Don, I'll pay you back the money," Garrett had gasped before lapsing into unconsciousness. That incident helped give King the reputation as a mob-associated bad guy who was willing to do anything to get ahead on the street.

"He already was a force of nature," Jack Newfield wrote in *Only in America: The Life and Crimes of Don King*. "He possessed the alchemy of a brilliant strategic mind, working-class ambition and anger — and no conscience."

Mills Lane wrote in *Let's Get It On*, "Don King reminds me a lot of Rasputin, the Siberian monk who attached himself like a leech to the Russian czar Nicholas II and his wife. As the story goes, despite numerous attempts on Rasputin's life, including feeding him enough poison to kill any ten men, the court sorcerer just couldn't be knocked down for the count.

"And so it is with King, who has had the hounds of hell on his heels for more than a decade. ... Regardless of the odds stacked up against him, King somehow managed to dodge the silver bullet."

Mike Tyson's first manager, Bill Cayton, once observed, "Don King can cast a spell over people that makes Svengali look like a rank amateur."

That spellbinding ability appears to have worked on Goodman, too.

King brushed aside scandal and talk of mob associations for years. He'd been accused of tax evasion and money laundering, corrupting fights and robbing fighters, even manipulating ABC's "Wide World of Sports" boxing championships. Nevertheless, while King's accusers came and went, King continued to prosper. In the process, he established a power base that included a variety of Strip casino resorts that hosted prize fights — with some help along the way from Oscar Goodman.

Goodman began preparing to argue for leniency for Tyson, who was certain to be suspended by the Nevada Athletic Commission, but without help might be swept away forever.

"I'd been a boxing fan most of my life and I'd represented Sonny Liston in a dispute early in my career," Goodman said. "When Larry Holmes was having problems with Don King, I represented Larry. When Holmes was later called before a commission investigating corruption in boxing, I was with him then, too. I'd been acquainted with Don for a number of years and I know this will strike some people as odd, but I never had a problem with Don. He has a reputation in the media that had no basis in reality in my experience. He was nothing but honorable and generous with me."

Generous though he may have been, King's star-crossed reputation continued taking a beating on many fronts. As if in cosmic preparation for defending Tyson's combination of pugilism and cannibalism, Goodman was also asked by King to represent Oliver McCall in front of the Athletic Commission, after the flash-in-the-pan heavyweight champion suffered what appeared to be a nervous breakdown and began crying prior to the fifth round of his February 7, 1997, fight against Lennox Lewis. McCall was also suspended and Goodman pleaded for his client to receive counseling and a second chance. "Oliver was suffering from an illness at the time and shouldn't be treated any different than a boxer who has the flu," Goodman told reporters. "Oliver will be back in the ring and make himself proud. He is very anxious to fight again. Whatever psychological problems he had have been resolved."

Within a few months, the suspension against McCall was lifted.

Goodman could ensure the fighter had an opportunity to return to the ring one day, but the ghosts that haunted McCall's troubled psyche were nothing a lawyer could exorcise. McCall's comeback was unsuccessful, but he often called Goodman to chat about the ups and downs of his life outside the ring.

How important was Goodman's presence at Mike Tyson's hearing?

It's difficult to say, due to the abundance of backroom politics present in any King debacle and the boxing racket in general.

But as *Review-Journal* reporter Warren Bates noted, Goodman's reputation focused a story, which had generated tabloid headlines from coast to coast, on its legal aspects. As veteran attorney Mace Yampolsky pointed out, "There's definitely a quote-unquote Oscar Factor." That wasn't lost on reporter Bates, who penned a sidebar headlined, "Tyson Hires Heavyweight Lawyers." As usual, Goodman was called a "mouthpiece for the mob." Clients Meyer Lansky, Anthony Spilotro, and "John Gotti confidant Natale Richichi" were given all but law-partner status. Bates, an experienced reporter, peppered Goodman's résumé with cases involving former San Diego Mayor Roger Hedgecock and former U.S. District Judge Harry Claiborne as well. Even at home, Goodman was a lawyer who was almost as big a story as his client.

"It was my office that had laid the legal foundation for what happened with Tyson," Goodman recalled. "We'd represented Murad Muhammad when he faced revocation and we got the commission to rule in an either-or manner. Either a fine or revocation. We saw it coming with Tyson and were able to use Murad

Muhammad on Tyson's behalf because Muhammad was a court win, a legitimate court win, in front of District Judge Donald Mosley. The key was to keep Tyson's career alive. Everyone acknowledged that he had to be punished. We wanted to avoid the equivalent of the death penalty. The decision was made even before I was hired. But it was important for me to make a statement. The effect was to save Tyson's career. As far as the world is concerned, I did. But there was a tremendous amount of backroom play. Understand that Tyson was a commodity of Nevada, an earner. If there was a way to keep him alive, that was the objective. And we figured out a way to keep him alive."

Tyson was fined $3 million and his license was revoked with the provision that he could reapply after one year.

"It had to be a year," Goodman said. "To take more than a year he'd rust. A year was the right decision. I got exactly what I wanted. That was a hundred-percent win as far as I was concerned."

Las Vegas criminal defense attorney Dan Albregts told a reporter after the commission hearing, "I thought he did a great job. It was a typical Oscar job. Not only was he representing his client, he was trying to create a record in case they banned him for life and they'd perhaps have to go to a higher body for an injunction. It just comes from human nature that people are going to be interested in what he has to say."

Noteworthy in all the Athletic Commission hearings in which Goodman participated is the almost total lack of adversarial questions regarding the attorney's position on behalf of his notoriously troubled clients. Where others might have laughed Tyson and McCall out of their hearings, the Nevada commissioners made their positions clear, while remaining courteous to Goodman. It was clear to observers that there really was an "Oscar Goodman factor."

Only three months after Tyson's July 9, 1997, revocation, the nation's sports press began talking about a comeback for the ear-shredding former heavyweight champion. In the months to come, Tyson was involved in a bar brawl with heavyweight thug Mitch Green, broke a rib in a motorcycle accident, filed a $100 million lawsuit against King, sued his managers Rory Holloway and John Horne, was sued by two women who claimed to be victims of physical abuse, was compelled to pay former trainer Kevin Rooney $4.4 million, got into an altercation with another driver after a fender-bender in Gaithersburg, Maryland, was sued for criminal assault, and was the subject of a psychiatric report that called him depressed and lacking in self-esteem.

Despite all that, on October 19, 1998, the Nevada Athletic Commission voted four to one to lift Tyson's suspension only fifteen months after nearly severing Evander Holyfield's ear.

ჵ ჵ ჵ

In December 1998, Goodman stood before the state Pardons Board to plead the case of convicted killer Peggy Wham, who was dying of cancer. Wham had been convicted of setting up the 1983 murder of her husband, Keyboard Lounge owner Harry Wham. She received life in prison without the possibility of parole. After 15 years in the penitentiary, the ravages of stomach and pancreatic cancer had shrunk her body to less than 80 pounds.

"When I first went to see her at the Southern Nevada Women's Correctional Center five months ago, she was robust," Goodman addressed the Pardons Board, headed by then-Governor Bob Miller. "Now I dread every time I go there because of the deterioration I see before my eyes. See for yourself. Radiation and chemotherapy are too much for her to take. She has lost sight in her right eye. She has a very short life span, not much time left. … You do have a venue of compassion."

In a rare move, the Pardons Board voted unanimously to immediately release Peggy Wham, who cried as she hugged her attorney.

Oscar Goodman had prevailed against the system, this time not through roaring bombast, but by gently persuading the Pardons Board and setting the stage for it to show mercy to a dying woman—albeit a dying woman who, in her prime, had hired a stone-hearted hitman to murder her husband.

ჵ ჵ ჵ

An angel among the wiseguys, the photograph of Tommy Allison stuck out in Oscar Goodman's law-office gallery. The mob attorney's inner sanctum was lined with photos and court-room-artist sketches of some of America's most notorious men. There was "Little Nicky" Scarfo and "Crazy Phil" Leonetti, "Tough Tony" Spilotro and Vinny "the Animal" Ferrara. All those tough guys and a hundred more.

And then there was Tommy Allison, a severely handi-capped boy who stared at the camera from his hospital bed. The image never ceased to stop visitors cold and reminded even the most cynical among Goodman's clients of the bless-ings in their miserable lives.

Born in 1981, Allison was one of the million-to-one kids who contracted encephalitis at age two after receiving a measles-mumps-rubella vaccination. Tommy was blind and deaf, but Goodman knew he was full of life. The boy's mother, JoAnn Allison, attended to her child's never-ending needs 24 hours a day. The mother's search for an attorney eventually led her to Goodman's outer office.

"I'll never forget when the receptionist called me and said, 'There's a woman with a child out here who has to see you.' I had no interest. I said, 'Is it a criminal case? No? Then send them someplace else. I do criminal work.'"

But the receptionist persisted and Goodman got up from his desk and walked to the outer office. There he saw a wheel-chair-bound child rendered completely incapacitated by a re-action to a common vaccination.

"When I got there I saw JoAnn and Tommy, and right off the bat I knew I had to do something to help them."

Goodman knew he was in for a devil of a time getting a pharmaceutical company and insurance provider to pay for the damage done. Courts had consistently rejected most pre-vious claims of medical malfeasance in vaccination cases, judges logically ruling that the greater good of the vaccine outweighed the admittedly rare risk of a severe reaction.

Keach hammered through the case against long odds after a local ambulance chaser fiddled with it for three years. Mat-ters went from bad to worse when it appeared the case might not be allowed to reach the trial stage. Keach kept shooting angles, first receiving a favorable recommendation from pedi-atric immunologist Kevin Garrity, then against long odds man-aging to persuade Charles Poser, chief of pediatric neurology at Harvard, to act as an expert witness. After a review of MRIs, Poser was 100% sure that the vaccine had caused the child's devastating maladies.

Drug manufacturer Merck moved for summary judgment by applying the same legal theory that protects government contractors from liability with a form of institutional immunity. District Judge Del Guy agreed.

Keach and Goodman appealed and after five years were granted a hearing before the Nevada Supreme Court. It would be the last oral argument heard in the old courthouse and it would be a doozy.

Goodman moved into first position because of his long standing before the court. He went against the equally experienced Rex Jemison and the result was a 3-to-2 decision in favor of the boy, making landmark product-liability law in Nevada and a first in the rest of the country.

That meant the case would return to the district court level for trial. With such a victim, there was no telling how high the jury award might go. In the end, Merck attorneys decided not to take a chance and moved to settle and seal the case for a substantial sum.

"I would not have won in front of the Supreme Court," Keach said. "They wouldn't give it to me. But Oscar is different. He's like one of those veteran pitchers who makes the great pitches and gets the close calls."

JoAnn Allison didn't know it the day she met Goodman, but having him take Tommy's case at that point in his legal career was this mother and son's dream come true. Goodman's name alone gave the case, despite its shortcomings, a chance to proceed through a local system where similar litigation had failed. Once Goodman convinced the Supreme Court to allow the case to proceed, a trial date was set. It was only then that attorneys for the insurance provider began to get anxious. On the day before trial, a confidential settlement was reached that kept Tommy and JoAnn Allison comfortable for many years to come.

The case revealed a side of Goodman few in the legal community had ever seen. The hardball-playing mob attorney had a heart like everyone else.

Tommy Allison was a teenager when he died October 19,

1999. Goodman eulogized, "JoAnn was a saint and Tommy is an angel."

Goodman's eyes always cloud over when he talks about the Allisons.

"In my career I represented a lot of people. Spilotro, Rosenthal, and many others, but Tommy was as significant as they were, if not more so. He was a very special moment in my life.

"That's why I always kept his picture in the middle of my rogue's gallery."

An angel among the wiseguys.

? ? ?

Some called it typecasting. Others called Oscar Goodman appearing as himself in Martin Scorsese's mob epic *Casino* the role of a lifetime in a legal career filled with role-playing.

The movie, which starred Robert DeNiro playing Frank Rosenthal and Joe Pesci as the Tony Spilotro character, sparked local debate on the so-called "good old days" when it was generally agreed that the mob in various manifestations had run Las Vegas. Goodman defended the image of the older city, which existed less than a generation earlier, before Las Vegas was dominated by publicly traded corporations that promoted gambling as entertainment and a trip to Sin City as fun for the whole family. "I think Las Vegas was a much more vibrant dynamic place in those days. It was full of glamor and glitter. Now it's a family-oriented destination, a lot different than the old days."

Although plenty of locals agreed with him, his romance with the past did nothing to change Goodman's image as a Mafia mouthpiece. On the contrary, it made him easier to criticize.

"I think that type of nostalgia is very misplaced," former federal prosecutor Stan Hunterton told a reporter. "In reality, these were gangsters, cruel arrogant people. If you step back and look at the end of that era, Rosenthal had his car blown up and was lucky to be alive. Allen Dorfman was killed. Tony Spilotro was killed. It's like a phenomenon of snakes eating each other. When you have a bunch of snakes in a meadow and you start a fire around the periphery, the snakes will eat each other."

Goodman had spent much of his legal career calling Hunterton and his prosecutorial peers just such names.

"During the filming of *Casino*, I got the chance to meet the stars and Martin Scorsese and found them to be very interesting people," Goodman said. "Carolyn and I invited DeNiro, Pesci, Nick Pileggi, and Sharon Stone over for my wife's brisket dinner. Word got out that they were coming over, and I suddenly started hearing from Steve Wynn, who at that time lived with his wife Elaine near our home on Bannie Lane. Steve is very big on celebrities and knows plenty of them. Steve was very insistent that he and his wife also be invited to the dinner party, and so we were glad to have him. The dinner was marvelous, Sharon and Elaine Wynn even helped Carolyn clean up and the only downside was Pesci's stinking cigar."

Goodman, meanwhile, fielded daily interviews from curious reporters seeking one-liners about the good old bad old days. He rarely failed to oblige. As filming drew to a close and word circulated that the movie would be more than a little unkind to the memory of his client and friend Spilotro, Goodman began hearing from Tough Tony's nuclear family. They were deeply hurt by his participation in such a film. He'd allowed his runaway ego to ruin long friendships with the Spilotro family, relationships that would never be fully repaired.

Later he admitted, "I made a mistake. I didn't read the script first to see how Tony would be depicted. I enjoyed being a part of the movie and I found the stars and Scorsese to be interesting people, but I wish I'd never done it. I thought it would be a more balanced portrait of everyone, but I should have known better.

"The scene with the vise, I represented him on that case. Tony was found not guilty. The picture portrayed the allegation, but it didn't follow through with the end result.

"The premiere in Los Angeles was very glamorous, and of course we wouldn't have missed it, but as soon as I got there I saw Frank Cullotta, the rat who had been an advisor on the film, peering from behind a pillar at me. He didn't have the guts to look me in the eye. In retrospect, my participation in *Casino* was a mistake. Although it was fun and good for my ego, I hurt members of the Spilotro family, which wasn't my intention. I got carried away with the thought of being in a movie and didn't understand exactly what the movie was about. In the movie, Tony is portrayed as a really bad guy who never helped anyone and did drugs. Tony was never convicted of a crime while I was his attorney, helped a lot of people get jobs in the casino business, was always a gentleman around my family, and never, ever, to my knowledge, touched drugs."

Had he learned his lesson? It seemed unlikely. As mayor a few years later, Goodman lobbied to win a bit part in the hit HBO television series "The Sopranos," at one point having his controversial confidant and liaison Bill Cassidy ask the mob show's star, James Gandolfini (when filming *The Mexican* at the Plaza), to have Goodman play a corrupt Atlantic City mayor (a role Goodman would have been familiar with after representing the Scarfo family, which had corrupted Atlantic City mayor Michael Mathews.)

More than anything, the *Casino* experience was a sign that Goodman and his city had changed. He was still a top mob attorney. Trouble was, his backyard was no longer full of mobsters. Unless he wanted to travel, and the Claiborne, Chagra, and Philadelphia ordeals had cured him of that bug, there weren't many high-end organized-crime cases out there. And the street-corner thugs and half-assed wiseguys who still found their way into newsprint couldn't afford his fee.

By late 1998, Oscar Goodman's private political cravings began anew. Would the man who had convinced the world that he was proud of being a mob lawyer, even though there was no such thing as the mob, actually pull the trigger and announce that he intended to run for office?

Conventional wisdom dictated that he'd never succeed. His name was well-known, but so was Capone's. From a traditional political standpoint, Goodman's notorious clients gave him more baggage than the Caesars Palace bell desk. He couldn't do it. He could dream, but could not actually seek election for the office that he craved: mayor of Las Vegas.

Or could he?

23

The Candidate

Although no one who understood the Machiavellian history of organized crime would easily believe it, the seeds of Oscar Goodman's 1999 mayoral candidacy were not sewn in the backroom of some smoke-filled mob social club, but in the hallowed halls of Haverford College when he made an unsuccessful run for student-government president. Goodman's overwhelming need to perform before an audience began surfacing early in his life, in activities ranging from school plays to second-string football, then manifested later in his entourage of hangers-on as an undergrad and even in keeping some law partners at his side, in part, to provide a laugh track for his sarcastic wit. Those who've watched him perform before juries will agree that Oscar the lawyer is at his best when thinking on his feet with his client's freedom on the line. Watch him tear into a hostile witness on cross-examination and you can almost feel the heat of the footlights as he commands the stage.

Over the years, he'd toyed with the notion of running for public office. There was talk of a judgeship appointment during the mid-1970s when Mike O'Callaghan was governor, thoughts of a run for lieutenant governor, even an earlier aborted mayoral run. But local political wisdom dictated that the public would never really trust the candidacy of a nationally recognized Mafia mouthpiece. Goodman had been photographed more times with Spilotro than Tony had with his own kids.

"Plenty of name recognition, but plenty of negatives," Las Vegas political consultant Don Williams told him. "Too much baggage."

Baggage? Goodman had enough political baggage to keep a battalion of bellhops hustling for a year. There was the ghost of Tony. There were the names of hundreds of wiseguys Goodman had stood up for over the previous 30 years. This was the man who'd declared to reporters that he would rather have his daughter date Spilotro than an FBI agent, that as far as he knew his clients were upstanding citizens, that the Mafia didn't exist, that drug trafficker Jimmy Chagra wasn't responsible for the murder of a federal judge, that the murderous Phil Leonetti was the victim of a law-enforcement vendetta, that marijuana and prostitution should be decriminalized, and so on. This was the man who played himself in *Casino*. It was easy to presume that this was a man with a vulnerable background.

But Goodman also had a formidable intellect and genuine charisma, the kind cookie-cutter candidates couldn't obtain from even the priciest political imagemaker. He was also a favorite of local reporters, a veritable quote machine who'd chronicled his career in many hundreds of newspaper stories and TV segments.

Oscar Goodman had negatives, but he appeared to have few secrets. His flaws and friends were well-documented and many locals considered him a fascinating character. Even Nevada's premier political consultant, Billy Vassiliadis of R&R Partners, would admit as much. "He's an interesting guy," Vassiliadis commented with considerable understatement. "With his trial experience, he's a great speaker. He's media savvy and he's colorful. I think he can capture some people's imagination. Remember, 'Jesse the Body/Mind' Ventura is governor of Minnesota."

Not that Vassiliadis was endorsing Goodman's candidacy. Few members of Nevada's political machine were willing to come within a mile of the man. It's not that they thought he lacked the ability to do the job. A circus chimp could handle the traditional ribbon-cutting and City Council-leading duties of a part-time job that paid $45,000 a year. It was Spilotro's ghost that gave them pause.

"I think Carolyn Goodman would make a great mayor, but not Oscar," political consultant and former presidential advisor Sig Rogich said.

Other local powerbrokers echoed Rogich's sentiments. Goodman was colorful, but he didn't fit the mold of the new sanitized corporate structure.

Traditionally, the Las Vegas mayor's position was held by men with personalities so bland and colorless they barely photographed. Oran Gragson had been a furniture dealer who once sold mattresses to a local brothel. He was square, reliable, and spoke with a dramatic speech impediment. Bill Briare was the only hail-fellow-well-met to hold the office in a quarter century. He gave way to local businessman Ron Lurie, whose administration was marked by monotone speeches and an ethically questionable land deal.

Then came Jan Laverty Jones, a Stanford graduate and Las Vegas car dealer whose family had owned a supermarket chain. Her eight years were marked by a series of downtown redevelopment proposals, at least one of which took advantage of controversial eminent-domain laws to acquire prime property to convert small Fremont Street businesses into a parking garage. Jones was fond of wearing mini-skirts and brought an unprecedented effervescence to the office. She was bubbly — and keenly politically motivated. As a sitting mayor, Jones twice ran unsuccessfully for governor.

When her second run for governor fell short, Jones decided not to run for a third term and threw her support behind 10-year City Councilman Arnie Adamsen months before official filing for the office began.

As ever, Goodman first discussed the possibility of his run with Carolyn, who'd seen him chafe at the confines of his law practice.

"Oscar had been disenchanted with the criminal practice for probably twelve to fifteen years," Carolyn recalled. "He kept asking me, 'What do you think?' and I said, 'Why don't you teach at a law school? Why don't you write a book? Why don't you paint? Why don't you do a lecture series? Why don't you run for office?' And the answers were always 'No,' but running for office tweaked him a little bit.

"I'm going to say probably eight years ago we talked about it a little more seriously and I said, 'I think you could win.' He said, 'Yeah, but I've got all this baggage and everybody says I can't.' He said, 'I'm going to call Don Williams.' Don came over to the house. He said, 'I'm going to have a poll taken. I'll go out to UNLV and have their pollster do a poll.' I said, 'Oscar, this is ridiculous. Obviously a poll is going to be negative. You should just put your hat in the ring and run.' They took the poll and it was negative, and that really soured him for a little bit. But not long after we were back discussing it again. 'What should I do?'

"Finally, he kept bringing it up and not even thinking of what it was he wanted to run for. I don't even think that had crystallized for him. I've always been most enthusiastic, because I know how brilliant he is, and how funny he is, and how charismatic he is."

He also met with his children, all of whom by then had graduated college and were beginning their professional careers. They were concerned their father would be vilified by the press and those who would connect him with his unsavory clients.

"No one wanted him to do it," Cara Goodman said. "He'd been interested in running for office for a long time. I can always remember him toying with the idea. Everything had just died down. I thought, 'Why stir this up again?' The press was going to attack him. He could retire and be a professor, or go play baseball. We told him, 'Don't do this.'

"But when he decided that it was something he needed to do, we immediately supported him. We just didn't want him to get hurt."

Goodman had heard talk of his connections to organized crime for decades. The issue was more a threat to his family than to himself. After all, when you've spent your life in the company of notorious men, what's a few mean-spirited words in the press?

So the Goodman family met again to discuss the substantial downside to Oscar's run for mayor. This time, instead of fretting over possible fallout and embarrassment, Ross, Cara,

Eric, and Oscar, Jr., were unanimous: Their father should go for it.

In the interim, Goodman had piggybacked on a Mason-Dixon public-opinion poll that measured positive and negative name recognition for prospective mayoral candidates, including former City Councilman Steve Miller, former County Commissioner Jay Bingham, City Councilman Arnie Adamsen, developer Mark Fine, and lawyer Oscar Goodman. The numbers were impressive. The poll showed that, in terms of name recognition alone, Fine had no chance: Though he was socially connected, he wasn't well-known. In a short 90-day campaign it would be nearly impossible to raise his name recognition enough to be competitive. Miller was well-known as a firebrand one-term councilman who, since being voted out of office, had spent several years avenging his loss by writing broadside editorials for weekly newspapers. Bingham, a homebuilder who'd become a multimillionaire while in office, had been pro-development as a commissioner, had high name recognition, and was well-respected within Southern Nevada's politically active Mormon community.

Finally, Adamsen was considered the favorite to replace Jones. He fit the mold established by Gragson and Lurie. He'd been an active Democrat and a blackjack dealer and title-company officer before being elected to the City Council. He was the sort of politically tepid public official developers and casino owners felt comfortable supporting during campaigns — and intimidating thereafter.

Then there was Oscar Goodman, whose high name recognition rivaled the political gadfly Miller's. Goodman's negatives were also high, but the poll showed that many of those who knew his name approved of him. The numbers were far from perfect, but they indicated that he had a fair chance against Bingham and a good chance against Adamsen or Fine.

If his own family endorsed his candidacy and the polling numbers didn't set off any fire alarms, what was he waiting for?

Ironically, Goodman, who seemed acquainted across America with everyone in organized crime at least on a professional level, knew few members of Southern Nevada's political-consultant Mafia. Besides, with the exception of Don Williams, a gun-slinging individualist, the establishment's political fixers were already lining up on the side of the safe candidates, Bingham and Adamsen. Goodman needed someone to turn to and Tom Letizia fit the bill. Though he wasn't really in the campaign-running racket — he sold advertisements and did voice-overs for commercials for a living — he was competent and loyal. Goodman contacted him to hash out the possibilities.

He also contacted associates in the legal community and veterans in the media.

"I spoke with Oscar five days before he declared his intentions publicly," criminal defense attorney Dominic Gentile recalled. "I could see he was serious. He called and asked me, 'What do you think? Can you come over here and see me?' That was on a Thursday or Friday and Jay Bingham was still in the race. I sat back and I thought to myself, 'This is a perfect scenario for Oscar. He's a leader by nature. He was kind of played out at the law office, and he'd have to be reinvented, and that was going to take a while. I said, 'You know, you really should go for it.' I told him that I thought it was absolutely the right move."

When he heard the news that Goodman was running for mayor, reporter Phil LaVelle could only smile. "He's a showman," LaVelle said. "He's got a certain entertainment quality to him. It just struck me as perfect for Oscar."

By the first of March, barely two months before the primary, Adamsen and Bingham were considered by the political press to be solid front-runners. Fine, who had spoken with Goodman about their possible candidacies and agreed that he would not run if Oscar decided to enter the race, filed without notifying his long-time friend and real-estate investment partner. The slight served as a wake-up call to Goodman and was his first lesson in political friendships.

With the close of filing for the office set for the end of the business day on March 4, 1999, Goodman was running out of wiggle room. After soliciting further opinions of family and friends and even querying a few reporters, he returned to his strength, Carolyn.

"He really didn't make up his mind to run until the last minute," she recalled. "When I left him in the morning I said,

'What are you going to do?' And he said, 'I don't know. I'll let you know by quarter of three. You have to come.' And sure enough, at two-thirty he said, 'I'm running. Get on down here.'"

Letizia scrambled to put together a press conference at Goodman's Fourth Street law office, known to some reporters as the House the Mob Built. Reporters who'd watched him in the courtroom and holding forth before banks of television cameras had never seen him so nervous. His hands visibly shook and at times his voice trembled. He was dressed impeccably, a little too swell for a local politician, in a dark blue Brioni suit and his trademark custom cowboy boots. Two dozen well-wishers were joined by almost as many television and print reporters. With Carolyn and Ross Goodman standing by, along with Rabbi Philip Goodman and peripatetic law partner David Chesnoff, Goodman announced a candidacy that had been rumored for weeks. He seemed to be the last person to know he was running for office.

On unfamiliar ground, he wasn't quite sure how to comport himself. His talk sounded more like a classic Goodman closing argument growl than the launch of a campaign to represent a city as its mayor. He sounded more angry than excited.

Goodman seemed surprised when reporters started asking questions about himself rather than one of his notorious clients. It was a defensive feeling he'd often fight in the coming weeks. The first of what would be hundreds of questions about his representation of mobsters were fired at him and he managed to field them without pointing fingers or accusing anyone of being a government rat.

"If Mr. Spilotro did anything wrong, shame on the prosecutors for not being able to convict him," Goodman said, applying his personalized sense of logic. "I'm proud of the work I've done my whole life. I've represented people by upholding the Constitution.

"The juices are flowing. I've never done anything in my life other than to win it. I'm dead serious and there's no joking around here. ... The thing I have is my intellect. If you want someone who is smart and who will keep the city in the forefront and moving forward, I'm your man. I want to be Las Vegas' ambassador to the rest of the world. ... Life is a series of challenges. I love the practice of law and I'm recognized by my peers as among the best. Now I want to take my experience and energy and utilize it to better the City of Las Vegas. … I want to become a spokesperson throughout the world so that everybody will know we live in the jewel of the desert."

Then he said something that was guaranteed to send shivers down the spines of his opponents.

"I'm gonna spend whatever it takes and I have plenty of people ready to help me—two hundred thousand, five hundred thousand, two million—whatever it takes."

As Vinny Montalto recalled, "After Tony died, Oscar lost a lot of interest in what he was doing. He still worked hard, but most of the people he'd represented were in jail or dead. He moved a lot of cases to David Chesnoff and Marty Keach, who made a lot of money thanks to Oscar. That's why I think he got so interested in the idea of running for office. From one day to the next he was and then he wasn't running. He collected a few promises from people with money around town and then made his decision. It was the first time in a long time I'd seen that spark in his eyes."

In truth, Goodman had locked up few commitments beyond those in his personal circle of allies in the legal community. But he possessed two things his opponents could not match: a personal wealth estimated at more than $10 million and a wicked—possibly unhealthy—competitive streak. If he was jumping into the race, he was doing so to win.

One challenge Goodman overcame when he decided to run for office was a mild case of germ phobia. In recent years, he avoided shaking hands with some people, but once he decided to file for the mayor's job, the feelings of unease disappeared.

Informed of Goodman's entry into the race, a somewhat smug frontrunner Arnie Adamsen said, "You've got to be kidding me. This is great. I love it. The more the merrier."

Jay Bingham also attempted to take the news lightly, almost as if Goodman's candidacy was not something to be given serious thought: "The race will be interesting and lots of fun."

But the words rang hollow. Within days, Bingham announced that he was pulling out of the race due to a previously undiagnosed heart condition. His withdrawal fueled speculation that he was uninterested in challenging Goodman in a negative campaign that might have splashed mud on his own candidacy.

After surviving the first press conference of his new life as a political candidate, Goodman did what he does best: He smiled for the cameras and led a parade of supporters up Fourth Street to make it official at the Clark County Election Department. His wiseguy friends, clients, and well-wishers were mostly absent from his announcement. It was a phenomenon that would repeat itself often in the coming months: For all his public appearances, speeches, and rallies, none of his former clients approached him to inadvertently create a devastating photo opportunity for an opponent. The street guys wished him well, but stayed away.

"It's something I'm actually proud of," Goodman said. "There were no meetings. I never sent Joey Cusumano or Big Chris Richichi or Charlie Panarella a message. They knew how important this was for me and they stayed away out of respect. And I wasn't about to shun them, either. These are people I know and like. They're my clients, but they're also people I enjoy talking to. I've never shied away from friends, but they knew that being seen with me would be misinterpreted by the press and seized upon by my political opponents. So they stayed away. That's the kind of guys they are."

Vinny Ferrara and Jimmy Chagra also stayed away, but that was not necessarily by choice. They weren't scheduled to be released from federal prison until well into the 21st century.

ʔ ʔ ʔ

The mayor's race in Las Vegas is officially a nonpartisan affair, which was probably good for Goodman considering the fact he'd changed his party years earlier from Republican to Democrat, but had never been active in a campaign. Mayoral candidates run in a May primary format. Unless one candidate garners more than 50% of the votes, the top two finishers move on to a June run-off election.

While the press was getting used to the idea of his candidacy, Goodman was busy spending 14-hour days campaigning. If politics was a popularity contest, then Goodman's boyish longing to be liked by everyone would serve him well. He worked from a lengthy daily schedule full of the usual speeches before senior-citizen groups and women's organizations, then improvised with unannounced appearances outside the front door of the Costco and Wal-Mart stores. What he knew about political strategy could fit on a matchbook, but he made a promise to himself that no one in the race would work harder. More than anything else, in the coming weeks Goodman would out-work his opponents, sprinting from one political function to the next, then collapsing at the end of the day with a pitcher of Beefeater.

Campaign adviser Jim Ferrence was won over by Goodman's energy and ability to grasp issues and political nuances quickly. Mark Fierro's visual conceptions helped to produce smooth effective spots and Letizia ran the office and handled the fund-raising sprint, but it was Ferrence who balanced the other two, managed the sign placement, coordinated the grassroots cam-paigning and get-out-the-vote effort, and attempted to craft a winning strategy for Goodman. Ferrence, the campaign's man-ager, rapidly learned that his candidate defied the usual po-litical convention.

"I think his lack of political sophistication ended up help-ing him," Ferrence said. "My political instincts were always contrary to his, and he always turned out to be right. My in-stincts told me he should distance himself from all the mob stuff and from the start he wrapped his arms around it and hid nothing. And he was right to do that. He has a better un-derstanding of people than I do."

Oscar Goodman's strength was meeting people and win-ning them over — not fretting over the details of the City Char-ter.

"One thing we had to change immediately was his televi-sion persona," Ferrence said. "His first TV spots were of him in the boardroom challenging his opponents and saying 'let the debate begin.' When I first met him, I had no idea he and Carolyn had adopted kids. In fact, I'd never even heard of Carolyn Good-man. We had to personalize him. If I give myself any credit, it's for recognizing that fact. The truth is, Oscar and Carolyn have a touching personal story and that needed to get out.

"That led to Mark Fierro and Carolyn sitting down and going through the family scrapbook. That's when Carolyn said that, although her husband was busy, he never missed a soccer game and was always there for his kids. That's a striking departure from the image the public had of Oscar Goodman as the tough mob lawyer."

It was noteworthy that none of Goodman's three closest advisers came from the heart of the community's long-established political machine. Fierro was a creative mind, a firebrand, and a slick former TV news reporter. Letizia sold ads for a living. Of the three, only Ferrence was considered a young prospect with a big future in the game.

"We were all, in a sense, on the outside looking in and that includes Goodman," Ferrence said. "I was in a position where it wasn't going to be bad working for Oscar, win or lose. And then I saw what we faced from the establishment. Two days after I met him, the 'Anybody but Oscar' editorial ran in the *Review-Journal*. Within that week, people from the Chamber of Commerce were going through the halls of the Legislature saying Oscar was going to be a disaster for the community and early on I think that's the way they really felt. They didn't sense the tide turning until it was much too late.

"The sort of sanctimony they displayed was really too much. The idea that Oscar Goodman's election was going to change everything or in some way harm Las Vegas was silly. And I have to admit it was enjoyable to see some of those people eat crow."

When a person decides to run for office, it's often easy to see which ones listen closely to the advice of their consultants and handlers: Their normal way of dressing changes overnight. They start looking like their constituent groups. As Las Vegas mayor, Jan Jones dressed in short skirts and high heels. When she became gubernatorial-candidate Jan Jones, she started wearing studious wire-rim glasses, navy blazers, and khaki pants. Overnight she went from hussy to preppie.

On the campaign trail, Governor Bob Miller once visited an edgy leather gay bar in Northern Nevada. Instead of the sort of conservative suit he wore with other constituent groups, Miller donned a leather jacket in an apparent attempt to blend in with the crowd. He wanted a look of the man of the people and wound up with the look of the Village People.

Goodman's small cadre of insiders immediately tried to

change the way he dressed, which was sort of a cowboy-boot-wearing Philadelphia lawyer. Goodman was proud of his dozens of boots and suits and, if pressed, could talk clothes like a Fifth Avenue tailor. He needed to loosen up, they said. Wear some jeans to Costco. Get comfortable.

He flatly refused. He'd worn suits every day for decades, unless watching a ballgame around the house, sitting in a box seat at Del Mar, or relaxing on the beach at Coronado. So suits and boots it was, often in withering late-spring weather. At city-park barbecues, at St. Patrick's Day parades, in front of Costco greeting customers like one of the employees—he looked like a $400-an-hour attorney.

? ? ?

Goodman's political honeymoon didn't last long.

On March 9, the *Las Vegas Review-Journal*, Nevada's largest newspaper, blistered Goodman with an editorial headlined, "Anybody but Oscar." With only the hand-wringing warnings of the development community and Chamber of Commerce and a file full of clippings of the Mob Mouthpiece to go on, the scorching editorial did what many effective newspaper opinions do, namely, turned its subject into a caricature in order to prove a point.

Goodman was credited for his legal skills and University of Pennsylvania education, but was lambasted as precisely the wrong man for the job, boasting that he was a "barrister-to-butchers" who "carries so much baggage he could be Sky Cap of the Century at McCarran International Airport.

"... Mr. Goodman once proclaimed the mob doesn't exist. ... As a philosopher once put it: You can deny the existence of electricity, but grab a high-voltage wire and it will kill you just the same.

"... Can you imagine this man contemplating Metro's budget or being generous with the organized crime unit? And as the most visible personification of the 'new' Las Vegas, he'd be a PR catastrophe."

Infuriated by the head-on attack, Goodman responded with a March 21 essay titled, "Newspaper Was Badly Mistaken: I Am Not My Clients."

"The Constitution guarantees our rights, but those constitutional rights are written on a piece of paper. They do not mean a single thing unless there is someone to enforce them for regular people. That is where I come in.

"… Why would the leaders of a respected newspaper go out of their way to besmirch my unblemished record of service to the community and the Constitution of the United States?

"I suspect you made this significant error because my candidacy represents change, and change is something the *Review-Journal* has always been slow to accept."

He then went on to remind the skeptics that he'd once been named one of the country's Top 10 criminal defense lawyers by the *National Law Journal*. "I cannot think of a better person to represent the City of Las Vegas and the citizens as professionally and ethically as I have represented my clients.

"I am in this race because I have ideas for our great city. I believe elected officials must do a much better job of managing and planning growth and our traffic problems if Las Vegas is going to be a great place to live in the 21st century. I believe that in the next 10 years, downtown Las Vegas will either become a rejuvenated center where people will congregate, or it will become a very dangerous place for Southern Nevadans. I have a plan to reinvigorate the downtown business corridor. That is why I entered this race, not to get into superficial banter or personal attacks."

Not that he was incapable of superficiality and his own brutal verbal assaults. In fact, Goodman fed off the newspaper editorial the rest of his campaign and beyond, reminding himself of its approximately 200 words over and over again. Not good enough? Barrister to butchers? He'd see who had the last laugh.

Said one long-time political observer, "Obviously, that editorial got under Oscar's skin. It became his rallying cry."

If the largest newspaper in the state was declaring that he wasn't good enough, he'd show them who was boss. First, Goodman would have to overcome his lack of command of the issues and propensity for double-talk. But even the *Review-Journal* acknowledged that he was intelligent and articulate and there was no mention of whether Adamsen and Bingham were educated men who could be called articulate anywhere outside the city limits.

Political commentator Jon Ralston observed, "Whether Goodman's entrance merely adds liveliness along the inevitable road to ex-county Commissioner Jay Bingham's coronation remains to be seen. But if Goodman spends a small fortune, he might be not just a spoiler, he might well be Bingham's general election opponent."

Ralston, a bellwether of the state's political machine, noted the mob-lawyer baggage and saw Goodman more as a spoiler than a serious contender: "If the [primary] turnout equals what it was the last time there was an open seat—which was nearly 51% in 1991—all bets are off and a general election almost a certainty. But if the turnout is half what it was in 1991, it will take only 22,000 votes to win the race in the primary, and my money is on Bingham.

"If Goodman can't help boost turnout to those levels of eight years ago, then his chances of victory will be buried deeper than Tony the Ant rested in that Indiana cornfield."

Tom Letizia queried the state's top political insiders and found all of them working for the opposition—even former White House advisor Sig Rogich.

"I couldn't call Kent Oram, because in the beginning he was working with Bingham," Letizia recalled. "I called Sig and Sig said, 'We'll destroy you if you decide you're going to run.' He was already with Bingham. I respected Sig's advice, but I felt differently. Truth was, I was so excited because I always believed in Oscar. I'd always known how strong and popular he was as a criminal lawyer. I just knew how people loved Oscar Goodman. But Jay Bingham was our major hurdle."

With the press focused on the safer and less flamboyant candidates, Goodman would be lucky if he wasn't arrested for endangering the town. But strange things were occurring throughout American politics, as evidenced by the resounding election of former professional wrestler Jesse Ventura to the office of governor of Minnesota. It was possible, even likely, that Las Vegas voters weren't as afraid of Goodman's candidacy as the press and casino-developer community.

Las Vegas oddsmaker Jackie Dell made Goodman a 17-to-1 underdog.

Goodman obviously wasn't intimidated by the long odds or the fact that such mainstream institutions as the Greater Las Vegas Chamber of Commerce had already cast their lot with Adamsen. He attempted to win over the chamber during a meeting.

"He used his wit to disarm his opponents," Fierro said. "The only tough meeting we ever took was with the chamber. When he spoke the room went absolutely quiet. You could have heard a pin drop, and at one point he looked at everyone at every table and said, 'Oh, now I'm not so nervous. I know every single one of you. I've done work for some of your families.' It was very effective and personal. As he was leaving, he greeted Claudine Williams, the casino industry legend, and shook her hand, getting tangled in the enormous diamond ring she wears. He said, 'I'm sorry. I was trying to slip it off your finger.' Everyone busted up. At that moment, you knew nobody was going to raise a finger to help Arnie. They saw Oscar's magic and how he worked people."

What few observers could measure with certainty was the relative unimportance with which the public perceived the position of mayor of Las Vegas. Political hacks and flacks talked long into the night about the chances of Bingham, Adamsen, Fine, and even Goodman, but the public could have cared less. After all, it had elected a kind-hearted furniture dealer, Oran Gragson, to four terms despite his heavy stammer. It had fallen in and out of love with Jan Jones, who came to City Hall with credentials as an executive with a car dealership and cut commercials with cross-dressing Las Vegas entertainer Kenny Kerr.

In Bingham, Adamsen, and Fine, the public would be faced with yet another political paper doll who came to the race with the blessing of one or another interest group and was without a scintilla of charisma. They were motel art to Goodman's Leroy Neimanesque personality.

If Goodman managed to humanize himself and overcome the inevitable portrayal as a mob lawyer with blood on his hands, he'd have a chance. If he cracked jokes with enough jaded voters, especially politically active retirees at the upscale Sun City community, he might allay the fears of those believing his candidacy represented a return of gats-and-spats Las Vegas. Although he promised not to go negative in his upstart campaign, that didn't mean Goodman planned to say anything positive about his opponents.

¶ ¶ ¶

Most political insiders downplayed Goodman's importance. However, his endorsement of charging developers impact fees was sure to resound with stressed-out voters, though infuriate homebuilders accustomed to having free rein with their puppets in local government. Goodman didn't dwell on the fact that impact fees, which in other communities were used to build parks, fire stations, schools, and water and sewer infrastructure, would surely be passed on to new homebuyers. It was a populist message that rang true with voters and immediately set Bingham and Fine, the chosen candidates of some of Southern Nevada's largest developers, on the defensive.

Goodman didn't indict his developer-friendly opponents; he let the voters fill in the blanks.

Rattling Adamsen was easier still. All Goodman had to do was say, "Downtown stinks," which he did often, to raise the issue of Adamsen's competence during his 12-year tenure on the City Council. Although strides had been made in the area of downtown redevelopment under Jones' administration, the perception of the heart of Las Vegas as a dirty crime-riddled inner city remained.

And the city's redevelopment attempts had been far from sweeping successes. Although it would be unfair to lay those embarrassments at the feet of one person, the officials in power—and that included Adamsen—were held responsible by the public for the city's liberal and legally questionable use of eminent domain to grab long-held real estate and hand it to casino owners, juiced-in lawyers, and other friends of City Hall. The Jones administration had begun to take on a malodor of arrogance and irresponsibility, nothing unique in city government, but the effect was to make voters more willing than usual to try someone other than the list of usual political suspects.

Then, Goodman let it be known that he already had $200,000 in reserve and was willing to spend many times that to support his candidacy. This rendered the mob lawyer an immediate concern to the development community. Although

Goodman's tough talk was long on hyperbole and short on specifics — the fact was, only weeks earlier he didn't know an impact fee from a parking fee — his words gave water to thirsty Las Vegans who'd grown sick of the traffic congestion, worsening air, overwhelmed parks, and crowded classrooms that had accompanied Southern Nevada's economic prosperity. The boom was damaging their quality of life and only Goodman was consistent in his vilification of developers.

The early days of the short campaign weren't all speeches and one-liners. Controversies, such as they were, presented themselves. Goodman's first town-hall meeting went reasonably well until a question from the audience, offered by former newspaper reporter-turned-federal-investigator Al Tobin, an Adamsen supporter, sent the candidate off his game: Goodman was running for mayor, but how many City Council meetings had he ever bothered to attend? (The answer: One in three decades of representing clients. He'd appeared on behalf of wife Carolyn for a Meadows School zoning matter.) If he'd attended only one council meeting, what made Goodman think he was prepared to be mayor?

As Tobin returned to his seat, Goodman went Bugsy.

"Don't walk away from me, Mr. Tobin. I'm talking to you!" Goodman roared.

Tobin later recalled, "I think he was expecting me to ask a softball question. When that didn't happen, his true nature came out during that diatribe."

It was one of the few times during the campaign Goodman was thrown off. In the early going, Adamsen and his campaign manager Lindsay Lewis, an experienced Washington fundraiser who'd spent little time in Las Vegas, marginalized Goodman's chances. They clearly underestimated his appeal with common voters. Lewis refused to believe that the public, no matter how gullible or inured to the Las Vegas scene, would vote a notorious mob lawyer into the mayor's office.

"We need somebody who can hit the ground running," Adamsen propounded during the candidates' first debate March 18 before a group of developers and business owners. "I have something money can't buy: experience."

But he also lacked something no amount of money could buy: a colorful personality. Truth was, voters didn't want experience. They'd had it up to their ears with the experience of status-quo city government that was blindly pro-development.

The voters wanted someone who talked a different game, someone who didn't bore them. Goodman's opponents had lost the personality race in a matter of minutes. Furthermore, their takes on the issues such as impact fees and downtown redevelopment simply didn't reflect the feelings of a large number of Las Vegans.

While Fine and Adamsen said downtown was improving slowly but surely, as it appeared to be in some estimations, Goodman went scorched-earth. He called the downtown corridor "Honkytonkville" and in doing so made sport of the efforts of Mayor Jones, the City Council, and Fine's developer and casino friends.

While Adamsen relied on statistics and endorsed the concept of a $1.5 billion monorail system downtown, and Fine reminded those present of his experience in building quality planned communities, Goodman threw bombs and let fly one-liners. He jabbed Fine's role as a developer. He nipped at Adamsen by criticizing the state of affairs downtown.

While Fine relied on his experience as a businessman— "Nobody can bring a CEO business approach to Las Vegas the way I can"—he opposed impact fees, a stance sure to please his immediate audience, but sink him with voters. While Adamsen attempted to make much of his dozen years of political experience, he had too little to show for his time in office to bowl over the voters.

Goodman hammered the rhetorical themes he sensed would resonate with the public, including the unlikely prospect of bringing a professional sports franchise and stadium to the heart of Las Vegas. Forget that such thoughts were considered absurd by professional football insiders, and was sure to be crushed by opposition from the casino industry, which made millions from bookmaking on NFL games. Goodman had a dream that was bigger than filling neighborhood potholes and steady-as-she-goes mewling.

"Las Vegas is the entertainment capital of the world and unless downtown keeps up, it's going to be like the core of the apple rotting. ... If they don't like to hear that, screw 'em," Goodman blasted. "When people come to Las Vegas, they come to see glamor and glitz. I'm the man. I'm not going to be one of those [boring politicians]. If they want one of them, they can have one and I'll go fishing."

The man was clearly dangerous and wasn't playing by the conventional rules of local politics.

While the other candidates attacked each other, Oscar Goodman kept running from meeting to meeting, at one point taking to horseback to meet and greet a group of equestrians at nearby Red Rock Canyon, a stunning sandstone monument and national conservation area that the mayoral candidate, in 36 years in Southern Nevada, had never before visited. He'd been too busy working for clients who, ironically, were known to use the Red Rock area as a graveyard.

All he had to do was keep meeting voters, most of whom seemed to warm up to him immediately. They saw no devil's horns sticking up through his salt-and-pepper hair, no thick-necked thugs hanging around his entourage.

Carolyn Goodman noticed a change in her husband. The increasingly dour attorney who had lost his fire for running a full-time law office had transformed himself into the tireless candidate willing to work 14 hours a day and more to meet the people. Somehow, his formidable constitution still allowed him to knock down a pitcher of martinis after a long day of campaigning. Only near election time would the first signs of gout begin to appear in the form of a swollen ankle.

Goodman was still shaky in face-to-face interviews with the press. His knowledge of many of the issues on which he held forth with such gusto was marginal at best. He was also sensitive to being reminded of some of his past remarks on the "Closing Arguments" show, on which he had endorsed the legalization of prostitution and the decriminalization of marijuana, among other controversial blasts. As mid-April approached, Adamsen's camp scrambled to prepare commercials depicting Goodman as the champion of the criminal element whose philosophies were contrary to those held by the upstanding citizens of Southern Nevada.

In response, Goodman hired Mark Fierro, the television newsman-turned-campaign specialist, to craft image-enhancing television commercials that focused on humanizing the candidate in the face of the mounting name-calling and scare tactics. One showed Oscar and Carolyn with their four children with the message, "Our greatest accomplishments." Another, with soft music playing in the background and family photos on the screen, whispered, "We never missed a soccer game." In truth, even his worst courtroom adversaries knew Goodman as a man so devoted to his family that he flew home from major criminal trials on weekends.

On the heels of the soccer spots, which Carolyn Goodman gave credit for sinking her husband's critics, were TV endorsements from former FBI Agent Berk Smith, ex-U.S. Attorney Lamond Mills, and former Clark County District Attorney George Holt, all of whom extolled Goodman's virtues. "You were always aboveboard, ethical, and good for your word," Mills chimed. What they were really saying was, "Don't be afraid; he's not his clients." As the election drew close, Goodman's old FBI nemesis, Joe Yablonsky, ripped Smith for being charmed by the candidate and made plans to settle old scores by writing his memoir.

The soccer commercial became the image of the campaign. The effect was two-fold: to render Goodman a family man and calm voter concerns that they might be electing a Mafia *consigliere* mayor. Goodman was galvanized against increasingly nasty attacks on his character and client list.

"Two things were critical to making the entire thing work," Fierro said. "One was the idea that the acorn didn't fall far from the tree. We were sitting talking one day and Oscar said, 'My dad was a career prosecutor. He told me the system only worked when both sides were represented.' In our video, we leveraged the fact that Oscar's family was a reputable family, pillars of the community.

"The second goal was finding a way to establish a clear vehicle to show what was in this guy's heart, to humanize him. We came up with the spot about Oscar's Goodman's five greatest accomplishments: his four children and the fact he and Carolyn had never missed a soccer game. When the media asked us for the script, I faxed over a white piece of paper. There literally was no dialogue. These spots came together in about ten days and during that time Jay Bingham dropped out of the race.

"We knew they were going to come for Oscar, so we decided to beat them to the punch by creating a commercial using a dark black background and the theme, 'This is what a few of Oscar Goodman's courthouse adversaries think of him.' We quoted Dick Crane saying Goodman never crossed the line. And FBI Agent Berk Smith saying Oscar was always aboveboard. And finally, former U.S. Attorney LaMond Mills saying he was tough but fair with the last line, 'Imagine what his friends say about him.'

"We even used Oscar's mom, who wrote a letter telling the people why they should vote for her son.

"We had a spot where he was supposed to say that, if elected, he'd donate his salary, but he couldn't say the line. He has an issue with memorizing lines and at one point he gave up and said, 'I don't mind giving up my money, but my mom's Jewish and she'll never speak to me again.' Obviously, he never lost his sense of humor."

With Letizia running the downtown office, Fierro redefining the candidate, Ferrence ensuring day-to-day operations ran smoothly, and a small group of volunteers helping where needed, the upstart organization appeared bigger than it was.

The only man of mystery in Goodman's life was a diminutive California private investigator named William Cassidy, who specialized in intrigue and claimed to possess credentials ranging from philosophical studies with the Dali Lama to contract work with the Central Intelligence Agency. Whatever Cassidy was to Goodman, he was clearly his close friend and confidant.

As the May 4 primary approached, the opposition sputtered.

Although Adamsen's man Lindsay Lewis remained confident that Goodman would eventually scare away voters, as an outsider to Southern Nevada he still didn't understand that most locals were neither offended nor frightened by the mob mystique. The rhetoric of the Chamber of Commerce and a few sensitive casino bosses aside, it was what separated Las Vegas from most other communities. And many new residents were obviously enamored of Goodman's personality, shadowy celebrity, and unabashed confidence.

"My concern is, where has he been for thirty-four years?" Fine argued. "We've worked to create an image as family and entertainment-friendly. He hasn't made a civic contribution to Las Vegas and then he wakes up one day and wants to be mayor.

"Symbolically [having Goodman as mayor] would hurt the message we're trying to deliver around the country."

Added Adamsen, "I think it would devastate our image we've taken decades to build."

"Nobody has ever said I am my client," Goodman responded. At least, they hadn't said it on the record.

The primary poll numbers continued to improve for Goodman. Adamsen mounted what his camp believed was an all-out assault on the mob lawyer who favored legalizing prostitution and marijuana and had defended all manner of thugs. The negative advertisements came complete with a haunting sound track and such statements as "For the past thirty years, Oscar Goodman has made millions representing some of the worst drug dealers, mobsters, and corrupt politicians. Now he wants to be mayor. But Oscar Goodman has no experience and takes the side of criminals against the victims of crime." There was also a segment from the irreverent "Closing Arguments" series, quoting Goodman ranting, "I'm trying to show the American public that our government is a bunch of stinkin' Nazis trying to break us in half."

The ads even quoted Goodman's 1995 statement to a newspaper reporter that he "would have been the world's worst mayor."

The spots stung, but came weeks after Goodman had reminded everyone he met to expect him to be viciously attacked by his opponents. In effect, he'd already inoculated the public.

"We tried to prevent those clips from being released, but they'd been given to Tom Leen as a gift, so we couldn't stop them," Letizia said. "It was probably our toughest day of the campaign."

"They had a chance to do something with those spots," Fierro said. "But they ran them and then moved on. We recovered almost immediately because they didn't pound away."

Goodman, the street fighter who'd taken so many shots at the government over the years, managed to assume the high ground. "If people are so desperate as to resort to half-truths and mean-spiritedness, it has no place in my campaign. The public will see through this and reward those who are ethical and punish those who are deceitful."

What cynical laughter that must have brought from the countless prosecutors, FBI agents and cops he'd maligned while defending the likes of Anthony Spilotro, Nick Civella, and Frank Rosenthal.

After a week of attack ads, a Mason-Dixon poll of 418 registered voters showed Goodman favored by 36% of voters responding, compared to 21% by Fine and 20% by Adamsen, who only 90 days earlier had been considered a shoo-in for the job. Fine might have become a contender if he'd had another four weeks to campaign, but the election was in less than a week.

The city's key campaign contributors were finally beginning to wake up to the Goodman factor. By the late-April filing deadline for campaign contributions, Adamsen reported raising $664,685, spending nearly $300,000 on television ads that initially focused on Fine. Fine, meanwhile, had raised $595,152 and focused his campaign on Adamsen's ineffective record. Goodman reported raising $571,236, including personal contributions totaling $140,000, which he immediately reimbursed himself as he raised funds, and spent $248,020, mostly on warm, fuzzy, and positive advertisements for himself. Goodman had bragged about spending whatever it took, but despite his six-figure infusion, he was clearly receiving more support than skeptics had predicted.

"If you told me a month ago that Oscar would be ahead in all the polls a week before the election, I would have told you, 'I don't think so,'" veteran political consultant Kent Oram told a reporter. Oram had started the mayor's race backing Bingham, then offered his services to Adamsen, who refused them, before winding up at Goodman's doorstep." He is touching populist issues, talking about what people want to hear and what they care about."

Publicly, Goodman kept running as an underdog outsider who was being wrongly criticized for his positions, but privately he was growing ever more confident.

？ ？ ？

Political advisor Billy Vassiliadis recalled hearing Goodman's name associated with a possible City Council appointment, but initially laughed at the prospect of a mob lawyer crossing into politics. A few years later, he took no more seriously the talk that Goodman might run for lieutenant governor.

But as the end of the century approached and Goodman's name surfaced in connection with a possible mayoral run, Vassiliadis thought it at least possible.

"I told a reporter I thought that if Jesse the Body or Jesse the Mind [Ventura] could be successful, this could be the 'Big O' kind of campaign. He's different. He's a great communicator. Not in the statuesque Reagan sense, but more in the common man communicating. Arnie, who I think is a sweet man, was too establishment and not articulate and glib.

"They ran a really, really good campaign. He connected like crazy. It took off and he never looked back. I think the one thing that really surprised people at first is, I think there was an assumption that Oscar was a rich fat cat, and rich fat cats don't mix it up. I think he blew people away by working twelve hours a day, shaking I don't know how many hands, kissing I don't know how many babies. He didn't miss a public event. He was a hot dog-eating, gin-drinking, football-betting, trash-talking guy. I think the one thing Oscar showed that nobody would have guessed is he clearly looked like he wanted the job. I think there's a lot to be said for that passion."

❡ ❡ ❡

On primary night, Goodman's headquarters bustled with well-wishers, most of them either lawyers or long-time locals. As the results started to come in, it was obvious Goodman would crush his opponents. The only question was, would he win the race outright by collecting 50%-plus-one of the vote?

Adamsen's crowded headquarters appeared stunned as the results returned showing him barely holding on as Goodman pressed the 50% mark. There was no drama. It was a rout. Goodman finished with 49.4% of the vote to Adamsen's 29%. Fine faded with 16%. The rest of the field garnered 6%.

Although Adamsen kept his Custer-like composure — "We

stopped the momentum and wiped the slate clean" — he was scalped. With Goodman missing outright election by half a percentage point, Adamsen's campaign was dead. It began to smell the morning after the primary. Major contributions to his cause ceased. Adamsen failed to collect enough cash to air a single TV commercial after the primary. The *Review-Journal* attempted to soften the impact of the Goodman victory with an editorial titled, "City Hall Squeaker." But all Goodman had to do was keep from getting his picture taken with the ghost of Tony Spilotro to ensure victory.

Adamsen had a few short weeks to come up with dirt so devastating the public would be soured on a Goodman victory. But instead of digging deeper by hiring skilled researchers, his camp stuck with the oft-repeated sound bites about having a friend of mobsters on their hands. It made barely a dent in the public's perception of its new favorite candidate.

Questions were raised in the press, rather than by Adamsen's team of experts, about Goodman's personal finances and business partnerships. Goodman had spoken often and articulately about open government, but refused to reveal the names of his business partners until after the election. State law didn't require candidates to do so, only elected officials.

Although he was technically not in violation, his unwillingness to open his personal financial files beyond the cursory disclosure forms required by law made him appear hypocritical. After the election he complied to the letter of the law but not beyond, leaving questions as to the identity of some of his partners.

One of those unnamed partners was Dennis Mastro, a former Las Vegas man convicted of skimming for the mob in the Jolly Trolley casino case in the late 1970s. Mastro had been associated with a variety of Mafia figures, including Genovese capo Anthony "Little Pussy" Russo. After serving his time, Mastro opened two restaurants in Arizona, in which Goodman invested as a nonparticipating partner — and dined on the house.

Goodman's estimated $10 million-plus net worth was not insubstantial, but did not include the holdings of his wife or children, who might have benefited from his generosity. He listed himself as at least part-owner of 240 acres of raw real estate, one-third partners of a medical building, and owner of pieces of other buildings, including the high-rise condominium on Coronado Island. He was listed as an officer, often minimally as merely a resident agent, for a number of other business partnerships, most of which were linked to his law firm. He also held an inactive partnership in a company with David Chesnoff and former heavyweight boxing contender Jorge Luis Gonzales called Cuba Libre, Inc.

And that was that.

Criticism mounted, but Goodman's lead was insurmountable. Days before the election, a Mason-Dixon poll reported that Goodman was a 19-point favorite over Adamsen, who was suffering one of the heaviest turns of political fortune in Las Vegas history — from favorite to blowout victim in fewer than 90 days.

Adamsen successfully called out friends from the corporate and development community who told reporters they felt a Goodman mayoral victory would be bad for business. He offered as proof a privately funded and scientifically questionable poll indicating that Las Vegas' important California tourism trade would be damaged if Goodman won the election.

But veteran Wall Street observers called the Goodman race a non-issue. If having a controversial mayor was enough to scare off business, such corporations were unlikely to find the rest of Las Vegas palatable, either.

Meanwhile, national newspapers and magazines were having a feeding frenzy.

"Is Las Vegas Remarrying the Mob?" asked a *San Francisco Chronicle* editorial.

Offered *Time* magazine, "A Lawyer to Wise Guys Would Rule Sin City."

And the *New York Times* asked, "Will a city linked to the mob turn to a defense lawyer as mayor?"

But none of the scare tactics was sticking. The numbers were too strong. Oscar Goodman was leading a political parade in his honor.

Although continuing to soften its stance, the *Review-Journal* still jabbed at Goodman, calling the June 8 election a race that gave voters "two bad choices."

"We believe it would be difficult, if not impossible, for Mr. Goodman to credibly represent Las Vegas on any number of national issues facing our city," one editorial stated. "Beyond that, though, Mr. Goodman appears to have no coherent political philosophy."

Regardless of the issues, polls, editorials, and politics over a largely figurehead position, the perennially bland Las Vegas mayoral race was, for once, worthy of the image of the city. Goodman at least had the attention of the public and the national media. Adamsen, meanwhile, failed to capture the attention of even long-time supporters.

As Election Day neared, there were a few last gasps of criticism. Southern Nevada public-relations-company owner Sydney Knott said, "In just a few short weeks since Oscar Goodman's candidacy for mayor, the specter of the mob is back and the nation's press is, once again, laughing at Las Vegas. ... We don't need this distraction. At the dawn of the 21st century, Las Vegas is on the verge of greatness. We don't need a notorious mayor. We need a serious mayor who will hit the ground running and lead us, not embarrass us, into the next decade."

But few were listening. There would be no miracles for Adamsen. The community wouldn't, as he privately hoped, snap to its senses and select the safe and sane candidate. Instead, he was slipping back into obscurity.

Goodman pummeled Adamsen, 64% to 36%. Adamsen was gracious, calling his own election night a celebration and wishing the mayor luck in public office, which he knew could be very unkind to even the most well-meaning of men. In his own words, Adamsen was making the transition from "Who's Who" to "Who's He?" He returned to private life, leaving his job at Stewart Title a short time after the election, turning to developing real estate in Southern Nevada.

"Las Vegas has sent a message to the rest of the world," Goodman told his campaign workers with television cameras lighting up the night outside his Third Street headquarters. The story of his election victory was on its way to circling the globe. "I'm going to paraphrase Lou Gehrig when he said, 'Today I consider myself the luckiest man in the world.'"

Privately, soon-to-be Mayor Goodman was in his element.

"He was so light on his feet," Fierro said. "He loved running, maybe more than he loves being mayor. After he won that night he turned to me and said, 'What did you get me into?' He embraced the race. He savored it every single day. He was made to be a candidate, he really was. He works differently than most people. He derives energy from meeting people."

Tom Letizia said, "I wish I had kept a diary, because every day was just a phenomenal experience. Everything went our way. I don't think we were geniuses. I think we had the kind of candidate who comes along once in a great while. We worked hard, but we were lucky."

Aside from Jay Bingham's timely heart murmur, luck had little to do with it. Next to Adamsen and Fine, Goodman shined. His poor knowledge of the issues was far outweighed by his personality. He was no drone bureaucrat or builder; he was the mob lawyer-become-human, the populist government-basher who would be mayor of Las Vegas.

Goodman had also benefitted from a loyal team of under-rated campaign managers and more than a million bucks in contributions. Adamsen raised $947,400 and spent nearly $1.1 million in the most expensive mayor's race in city history. Less than $105,000 came in for Adamsen after the primary debacle. He'd been hung out to dry.

Now that he'd been elected, Goodman would have no shortage of political consultants volunteering their services. Many of those were the same insiders who'd privately derided his entry into the race only weeks earlier. But he would remain loyal to Ferrence, Fierro, and Letizia.

As news photographers captured the moment, Goodman's small team of political insiders, including Fierro, Letizia, and Cassidy, basked in the glow of victory. Within weeks of that night, however, Fierro was accused of attempting to broker a council appointment for Goodman mayoral opponent Mark Fine, an accusation he denied and that was never found credible. Letizia was criticized for almost immediately attempting to lobby City Hall, criticism he shook off as his advertising and political-consulting interests grew.

And Cassidy, well, he became a walking lightning rod of criticism over his personal and business comportment not long after being appointed Goodman's chief liaison. As a paid "trial consultant" for accused killer Sandy Murphy, Cassidy was accused of threatening the life of private investigator Tom Dillard and suspected of acting as the eyes and ears of Goodman, a suspicion that never rose to the level of fact. He was ultimately suspended by the mayor for failing to properly fill out his leave-of-absence paperwork during Murphy's murder trial. By the spring of 2001, following more than a year of acting as the mayor's City Hall operative, Cassidy was asked to resign his position after being arrested on charges of spouse battery.

In addition, Goodman immediately put his lucrative law practice on hold, taking a huge cut in pay. But for the moment, the new mayor and his team of underdogs were on top of the world.

24

The Happiest Mayor

Not long after the election, Oscar Goodman sat behind his desk at his law office when a secretary rang his phone. An old friend was calling to congratulate him. It was long-time client, reputed West Side heroin kingpin Manny Baker.

Baker had pulled up stakes after a final latest brush with infamy and relocated to Texas, where he kept a ranch near the Mexican border. Goodman and David Chesnoff had doubtlessly saved Baker from a long stretch in the penitentiary, and a rise in violence in the local drug scene, along with some medical ailments, had persuaded Baker to retire.

Baker graciously heaped praise on Goodman. The two exchanged pleasantries.

Moments later, the office phone rang again. It was another call of congratulations for the newly elected mayor of Las Vegas, this time from President Clinton.

"At first I thought it was a joke," Goodman recalled. "Manny Baker one minute and Bill Clinton the next. Now that's casting a wide net."

Only in the crazy life of Oscar Goodman did so many worlds brush so closely together.

In his first year in office, with a few exceptions, Goodman enjoyed the standard press honeymoon given a new mayor. For the moment, even the *Review-Journal*'s recalcitrant editorials grew warmer and fuzzier as he embarked on his quest to revitalize downtown and show the city and the world that Las Vegas voters hadn't made the biggest mistake of their lives.

He'd learned how to attract attention by the time he'd turned 10 years old. He'd mastered the art of the candidacy in a few short weeks. But learning to govern from the odd and overrated political perch of the mayor's seat would take time.

_ _ _

During Goodman's hectic transition from lawyer to mayor, he was accompanied by the ubiquitous Bill Cassidy and a handsome woman who at first appeared to be a member of his burgeoning entourage. But Connie Bruck was no liaison or lackey. She was one of the most gifted investigative reporters in the country. On assignment for *The New Yorker* to write a profile of the new mayor, Bruck easily charmed her way into Goodman's inner circle after first developing a lengthy background on him. As she had in her brilliant books — *Master of the Game* about controversial business tycoon Steve Ross and *The Predators' Ball* about Michael Milken and the junk-bond era, along with her award-winning profiles of Ivan Boesky and Newt Gingrich — Bruck laid Goodman open, warts and all. Although few in his inner circle of poised-to-please assistants appeared to fully appreciate Bruck's expertise, Goodman was warned to watch his language with Bruck. But it was like warning a gourmand to stay away from the foie gras. The bottomless hunger of his ego was too great. He gorged himself on the prospect of having a story written about him in *The New Yorker*. How urbane he would be. With a single article he'd vault to the national stage.

The results, to say the least, did not fit his fantasy. The man known as a wily rhetorician in the courtroom looked like an overrated lout in print. His one-liners about his mob-lawyer days were written down without a grain of salt and served up in a 7,000-word piece titled, "They Love Me!"

The voters of Las Vegas, yes.

Connie Bruck, no.

The profile told of a Goodman who beneath his cheerful populist veneer was a beady-eyed vindictive former mob mouthpiece who talked more like his clients than a respected member of the bar. Bruck recorded him joking about loving his job as much as former Philadelphia mob boss Nicky Scarfo, when he uttered his infamous "I love this" after murdering his friend and associate Vince Falcone. Although much of the material in the profile was well-known and Goodman's remark about preferring that his daughter date Tony Spilotro over an FBI agent resurfaced, Bruck noted from a mayor's aide that His Honor was already considering a run in 2002 against Nevada Governor Kenny Guinn, speculation Goodman was later forced to disavow. She'd even reported that Spilotro and other associates of his gang had attended Cara Goodman's bat mitzvah at a lodge in Kyle Canyon, a fact not widely circulated but evidenced by a small photograph on the wall of his office rogue's gallery.

Far worse was Goodman's printed admission that he kept a "hit list" of political enemies and those who'd failed to support his candidacy. Many politicians did, but few admitted it in a national magazine. Among those on his list: MGM Grand president Terry Lanni and *Review-Journal* publisher Sherman Frederick.

"All I care about is being a good mayor now," Goodman told Bruck. "But I'm keeping a list of those who were never for me, who spoke out against me as though I were the Antichrist. It's not a long list, but it's a list. And I don't care how long it takes, but I will get them."

Suddenly, the charming self-described "happiest mayor" looked like just another rank political animal. A *Review-Journal* editorial snorted, "In the campaign, Mr. Goodman downplayed concerns that his ascension to mayor could embarrass Las Vegas. He said outright that he'd never do anything to cast the city in a bad light. But an enemies list? Idolizing vicious killers? It didn't take long, did it?"

Another editorial jabbed, "It is in fact not better to be a killer than to be a 'rat.' And it's time for Mayor Goodman to finally say so." Pundits and editorial boards would wait a long time before those words crossed Goodman's lips.

Goodman did not react well. The article had been rigorously fact-checked, but despite this Goodman said he'd been misunderstood and even quoted out of context. But in future dealings with the national press, Goodman began to rein in his Youngmanesque shtick. The result would be less inflammatory but no less compelling, as evidenced by a December 1999 appearance on "60 Minutes," in which he charmed his long-time acquaintance Mike Wallace and the theme remained one of the mob lawyer making the successful transition to Las Vegas mayor.

His own denials and those of his seconds aside, Goodman's name never stopped floating as a possible candidate for governor against Kenny Guinn on the Democratic ticket in 2002. In terms of policy experience, Goodman was overmatched. But when it came to pure charm and public presence, Goodman cast a long shadow over the sitting governor.

"No one is sure whether he would win a race for a different office," said campaign adviser Jim Ferrence, "but Oscar has uncommon charisma and celebrity status that allows him to overcome his policy shortcomings. The mayor's job is, to some extent, style over substance, and that's what the voters of Las Vegas have decided they want the position to be. People are ecstatic with approval ratings of 70% or 75%, and he's not happy with 85%. He's the perfect match for mayor of Las Vegas. People couldn't care less what his political philosophy is."

By 1999, few knew and fewer cared that Carolyn and Oscar Goodman had once been Republicans who'd changed parties in order to vote for then-law-partner and State Assembly candidate Richard Bryan. For Bryan, who went on to serve six years as governor and two six-year terms as U.S. Senator, his stint in private practice with Goodman didn't appear high on his lengthy list of career credentials. Throughout the heart of Bryan's political career, at no time did he mention in his biographical material that he had once been law partners with a notorious legal representative of the mob. It was the kind of arms-length relationship that Goodman had come to accept with the passage of time.

But now that Goodman had gone "mainstream," how would the establishment react to rumors of his larger political aspirations?

※ ※ ※

The Happiest Mayor

The first thing City Hall veterans noticed about Mayor Goodman was his friendliness, work ethic, and apparently unlimited energy. Early arriving janitors found Goodman rattling around his office. Employees on the lower nine floors at City Hall—everyone from the building-maintenance crew to the clerks in the Department of Business Licenses—were surprised to find Goodman greeting them and asking them how they liked their jobs and, occasionally, how their duties fit into the bigger picture. Goodman wasn't just apple-polishing; he was soaking in a bureaucratic system about which he'd been blissfully ignorant only weeks earlier.

Privately, Goodman chafed under the lack of mandated clout his newly won position held. Was the mayor's job, in a model dominated by the city manager, really no stronger than a city councilman with glorified ribbon-cutting privileges?

Which is why, in the early days, Goodman made an effort to meet everyone in the building. If he acted like a strong mayor, like the man in charge, then he thought it was possible that they would treat him accordingly. The new mayor was a curiosity to some, a breath of fresh air to others, but remained a threat to many of the deeply entrenched staff, who looked on most changes of the guard with fear and loathing. Unlike some previous mayoral regimes, which carried with them the broad threat of job changes while the new boss used his elected clout to fill positions through patronage, Goodman didn't have a lot of political debts to pay. His circle of liaisons was small and included former Senator Bryan aide Chris Castro, former R&R Partners employee Stephanie Boixo, and his private-investigator-cum-guru and drinking buddy Bill Cassidy. He didn't bother to immediately replace Jan Jones' executive secretary, Carla Balzano, even though the paranoid Cassidy suspected her of acting as a "double agent" for the former mayor. Nor did Goodman initially attempt to replace his Mayor Pro-Tem, former Metro police officer-turned-City Councilman Michael McDonald, who'd supported Adamsen and was an intimate of former Mayor Jones.

In fact, Goodman appeared ill-prepared even for some initial petty political intrigue as candidates for a pair of newly created City Council seats jockeyed for position and attempted to curry the favor of McDonald, the man the local political press had dubbed, "The Shadow Mayor." It was a title that privately made Goodman's blood boil.

For his part, McDonald had left the police department after 10 years and was known as a political climber with aspirations that far exceeded his education and elocution issues. With his loyal assistant Rick Henry at his side, McDonald was fond of double-breasted suits and kept company with local topless-cabaret mogul and generous political contributor Rick Rizzolo, whose Crazy Horse Too club on Industrial Road was one of the most profitable skin joints in the country. For all McDonald's wiseguy affectations, he was known as a hard-working and effective councilman whose Ward One constituents were often the first to receive the sort of neighborhood services that make up the lion's share of a local politician's duties. He liked being known as a Chicago-style alderman who was effective and accessible.

He was also Goodman's mayor pro-tem, the largely ceremonial second-in-command position traditionally reserved for either the senior member of the City Council or the mayor's pet. Goodman took office with neither the trust of McDonald nor clout to get rid of him, so he was reduced to smiling, biding his time, and studying the script of the City Hall "Peyton Place." He immediately set to work building his relationship with City Manager Virginia Valentine, who began telling her associates that the new mayor was a quick study.

But Goodman also continued to shoot from the lip, getting so far ahead of himself with downtown redevelopment plans that at times he sounded more like a giddy dreamer than a man capable of winning hard-fought negotiations and building the sort of brick-and-mortar infrastructure it would take to put his campaign promise to "save downtown" into effect.

≀ ≀ ≀

Since childhood Oscar Goodman had been a sports fan. He was fond of stickball in the streets of Philadelphia and even pickup basketball games that once featured a young Wilt Chamberlain. He often reminded those skeptical of his physical prowess that he'd played football in high school and college.

As an adult he reserved his greatest affection for sports betting, putting down thousands a day with his bookmaker on anything that moved. And yet when he blithely promoted the idea of bringing a professional sports franchise to Southern Nevada, in part on the encouragement of casino man Steve Wynn who briefly entertained thoughts of owning his own National Basketball Association club, Oscar Goodman was once again the neophyte politician.

A survey of public opinion found, unsurprisingly, that Southern Nevadans liked the idea of having a big-league sports team of their own. They just didn't want to pay to build a place for the team to play. The local elite coveted an NBA franchise. A few movers and shakers believed a professional hockey team was a more realistic plan. But the survey suggested that a National Football League team, with its eight regular-season home games, would have the best possibility of succeeding in the growing but extremely competitive market. What the surveys didn't measure was the gaming industry's refusal to accept the possible sports-wagering restrictions that would accompany winning such a professional franchise.

From the Houston Rockets, Denver Nuggets, and Vancouver Grizzlies of the NBA to the Oakland Athletics and Montreal Expos of Major League Baseball, names of teams regularly floated on the hot air of the 10th floor. But Goodman gradually learned that there were issues far larger than any one team's desire to rush into what would be one of the smallest markets in any professional league, a market that had rarely supported even its own college teams with any consistency.

For example, Goodman was immediately criticized by casino-industry representatives and political insiders for not doing his homework and laying sufficient ground fire through the lobbying process. Although he was reluctant to admit as much publicly, he knew their points had validity and was determined to meet with casino bosses, gaming regulators, and commissioners for the NBA and NHL to get answers to his questions.

He didn't like the answers.

Goodman flew to New York to meet with NBA Commissioner David Stern and NHL boss Gary Bettman, with hopes of ironing out a few differences and presenting a sunny Wall-Street-friendly side of Las Vegas. The commissioners were polite, but Stern was adamant: There would never be an NBA team in Las Vegas unless the casinos took the professional games off the board in the sports books. Goodman reported that Bettman's reception was warmer, but the fact was no NHL franchises figured to become available for years.

In short, Las Vegas, with its stigma as the only place in America where sports betting is legal, was a radioactive wasteland for professional sports. Goodman's dream appeared dashed, but he simply refused to quit, admit defeat, and move on.

Within weeks of goading Goodman into going out front on the issue, Wynn had given in to the slender odds of bringing his own NBA team to Las Vegas and turned his attention to other projects. Goodman, who as ever took the rebukes personally, insisted on fighting.

The Las Vegas sports press didn't know quite what to make of the mayor's insistence. Although many supported the idea of bringing a professional team to the valley, experienced reporters had seen too many minor-league and underfunded franchises come and go. Las Vegas kept a Canadian Football League team fewer than two years. Its XFL football team folded along with the league at the end of the first season. Goodman had everything but his indefatigable energy working against him.

? ? ?

Las Vegas' booming population flooded the City Council's four wards, necessitating by law reapportionment and the creation of two additional Council seats. Replacements would be nominated and voted on by the mayor and the four Council members.

It was a simple matter in theory, but the question of whose nominees would emerge victorious provided a defining moment in the first half of Goodman's term. True to his straight-ahead nature, Goodman nearly strolled into what would have been a disaster for a mayor who dreamed of redeveloping downtown and carving out a positive legacy.

City Councilman Michael McDonald, who entertained visions of higher office and had even considered running for mayor, imprudently bragged that he had the votes he needed to secure the appointments of his two hand-picked candidates, Lawrence Weekly and Orlando Sanchez. If successful, he would further consolidate his growing political power and image as the self-appointed "shadow mayor." For their part, the African-American Weekly and Latino Sanchez were experienced city employees who understood the workings of the Council and its role as a facilitator of constituent services. They fit the ethnic demographics of their respective areas and had reputations as solid family men.

Goodman took office with no one in mind, but clearly saw McDonald's fullback-style rush for power as a threat. So he began interviewing prospective Council appointees, eventually settling on handsome pawnbroker Michael Mack and young African-American attorney Uri Clinton. Goodman privately admitted he wasn't overwhelmed by the interviews of either man, but he also wasn't about to let McDonald bring in his favorites and, in doing so, control the council for the next four years. If Goodman was going to establish himself, even unofficially, as a strong mayor — wording of the city charter to the contrary — he would have to win at least one seat.

He began lobbying newly appointed Councilwoman Lynette Boggs McDonald, who had enjoyed the support of Michael McDonald, but was clearly concerned about being marginalized by his political ambitions. She also needed the sort of fundraising help McDonald was incapable of providing. When she put a toe into Goodman's camp and at least considered Mack as an alternative to Sanchez, the mayor's chances improved.

On October 20, 1999, the City Council chambers were jammed with placard-waving supporters of the prospective appointees, especially McDonald's favorites, Sanchez and Weekly. But their victory party was abruptly aborted when Goodman questioned whether appointing city staffers to the Council violated a rule against former employees lobbying for two years after leaving office. Weekly and Sanchez weren't lobbying for third parties, of course. They were, in effect, auditioning for their own new jobs. But Goodman used the skills of legerdemain he'd honed in so many courtrooms to prevent a vote and gain a 30-day delay while the city's Ethics Commission sorted out the question. It was a calculated ploy transparent to all present, but it worked.

The *Review-Journal*, gradually warming up to Goodman's mayoral act, wondered in an editorial headline, "Will Mayor's Stall Work?"

"It's doubtful the mayor expected to prevail, but that wasn't the point anyway. In challenging the legality of appointing city employees to the two new City Council seats, Mayor Oscar Goodman sought to add time to the clock in a game he was about to lose."

The Ethics Commission returned with the expected rejection of Goodman's question. Its chairman, former District Judge Earle White, said, "It does not appear this [law] has anything to do with the set of facts presented." Goodman's acting job was laughed out of court, but by then McDonald wasn't in the mood to smile.

In the interim, Goodman was busy bonding with plainspoken Councilman Gary Reese, a local barber, and Councilman Larry Brown, an Ivy Leaguer who had settled in Las Vegas after Harvard to pitch for the local minor-league baseball team. Brown appeared to appreciate Goodman's intellect, endless stories, and straight-shooting style.

When the votes were cast, Weekly won one appointment, but Sanchez lost out to Mack. In addition to Goodman's persuasive rhetoric, Boggs McDonald enjoyed the generosity of a fundraiser at the home of his law partner Marty Keach. But the biggest winner that day was Goodman, who now had a foothold at City Hall and had prevented his newfound nemesis from winning the day.

≀ ≀ ≀

As fate and the suspected hijinks of the mayor's man Bill Cassidy would have it, within weeks of the split decision, Michael McDonald found himself fighting for his political life after being accused of multiple ethical breaches. Local political gadflies were raising the specter of the councilman's relationship with the topless bar owner, Rizzolo. Gradually, it was revealed that such diverse law-enforcement agencies as the FBI, State Gaming Control Board, and Metro police were also curious about the relationship. McDonald defended their friendship as longstanding and innocent. Rizzolo's eclectic circle of friends ranged from former Mayor Jan Jones and numerous local judges to reputed mob figures Vinny Faraci and Joey Cusumano. His topless club employed Rocco Lombardo, brother of Chicago Outfit underboss "Joey the Clown" Lombardo and Metro cop and Spilotro sympathizer Joe Blasko.

Ironically, Rizzolo was a former Goodman client; McDonald was being scrutinized for possible associations with men Goodman and his law firm had represented. The proximity of the relationships gave off an air of incestuousness, but it was lost on much of the Las Vegas press. Goodman had successfully made the transition from mob lawyer to mayor.

McDonald suspected the mayor's mysterious but loyal liaison Cassidy of playing a role in the damaging speculation and rumor-mongering. Cassidy denied fueling the fires, but made it clear he believed McDonald had attempted to ruin Goodman's first six months in office. Time would reveal that McDonald's problems had not been concocted by Cassidy, but created by the councilman himself.

In the end, a chastened McDonald was sanctioned, but survived his ethics entanglement. And later, Goodman's hand-picked councilman, Mack, became embroiled in still another ethics inquiry, this one over his bankruptcy business and personal finances. Mack's personal problems hobbled his efforts at City Hall and gave Goodman's critics grist. They claimed that the mayor had been more interested in turning back McDonald than in placing the best person in a position of authority.

§ § §

Goodman may have put his lucrative law practice on hold, but he wasn't above attempting to make a shrewd business deal through client contacts. When it came to deal-making, client Kerry Rogers was in constant motion. Goodman said he received $112,500 in stock in an Internet startup company named e.Volve in exchange for representing Rogers. By the time the stock matured, he said it was worthless. According to records filed with the Securities and Exchange Commission, however, Goodman was one of a group of investors, including New Jersey Senator Robert Torricelli, who in January 2000 stood to reap a windfall from an insider deal. Goodman's 1999 purchase came just days before e.Volve was purchased by eVentures, a publicly traded high-tech Internet company.

In a matter of months in 1998, former Bear Stearns executive Steve Loglisci brought e.Volve from the brink of bankruptcy. Loglisci was Senator Torricelli's investment counselor. While Torricelli's financial transactions would be widely criticized after allegations were raised in 1996 of illegal campaign contributions, allegations that eventually led to the conviction of Lawrence Penna of Investor Associates, Goodman's investment generated not a line in the Las Vegas press.

Although he said the deal was a loss, as of 2000 Goodman's potential profit was a cool $4.8 million.

"Not a bad deal, if you can get it," commented Peter Eisner of the Center for Public Integrity. "The problem is, you can only get it if you're in the club of politicians, special interests, and lobbyists who scratch each other's backs and make sweetheart deals. You and I could not get that deal."

Goodman's potential profit was glorified tip money compared to Rogers' score: $64 million on a $1.35 million investment. But Goodman's potential multimillion-dollar profit held the promise of softening any economic blow he figured to take during his four years as mayor. That is, until East Coast reporters got wind of it and negative press accounts helped send the share price plummeting.

Other rumors circulated that not long after he was elected, Goodman's attorney sons Eric and Ross began to land lucrative real-estate and business deals through the generosity of enigmatic Las Vegas attorney Jay Brown. Brown's career had ranged from being named as a key player in a casino deal tied to the mob to acting as the ultimate insider with U.S. Senator and former Gaming Commissioner Harry Reid.

But by far the most entertaining business deal cut by Mayor Oscar Goodman came when he agreed to switch brands of gin, forsaking Beefeater to "endorse" Bombay Sapphire. With assistance from his friend, Southern Wine and Spirits executive Larry Ruvo, Goodman agreed to make himself available for commercial purposes in exchange for $100,000: $50,000 to the city for an alcohol-abuse program targeted at the homeless and $50,000 to the Meadows School, of which his wife Carolyn was a co-founder and president. Instead of winding up an entertaining bit of trivia starring the party-animal mayor of Sin City, Goodman was shellacked by columnists for daring to sully Las Vegas with a celebration of demon gin.

This time, he didn't flinch. Instead, he let the critics gnash about the seriousness of alcohol abuse and the potential for tragedy from intoxicated partygoers who climbed behind the wheel. While he was being nipped at for running dangerously close to selling out the city, his "Martinis with the Mayor" parties brought attention to downtown and he reveled in the boozy movable feast on Fremont Street. Politicians love parades and Goodman wasn't shy about leading his own, at various times flanked by "Coochie-Coochie" girl Charo, "Lifestyles of the Rich and Famous" rake Robin Leach, Strip entertainers, and showgirls. Although it fed his critics material to portray him as a lovable lush buffoon, Goodman in the role of the Dean of Martinis parlayed the event into national news coverage for the city, the sponsor and, no less importantly, the "Happiest Mayor."

❦ ❦ ❦

On North Seventh Street, new homeowners were attempting to reclaim the once-proud area by remodeling houses more than 50 years old in a city known for imploding and bulldozing its short history.

Near Charleston and Las Vegas boulevards, lawyers, artists, university professors, and writers have found refuge, inspiration, and value in older homes on half-acre lots located a short stroll from the noisy grind.

When Goodman and Councilman Gary Reese led a concerted effort to prevent billionaire Carl Icahn from adding a roller-coaster thrill ride that would have crossed Las Vegas Boulevard and possibly invaded the neighborhood's sound space, it ranked as one of the only times in the city's history that a major developer—one who'd hired classic juice attorneys and had threatened the political future of the area's councilman—had been denied a zoning change. Icahn's attorneys vowed to sue, but the council held firm.

During a meeting at City Hall, Icahn was flabbergasted by the lack of cooperation he was receiving. At one point, Goodman recalled, the billionaire mumbled, "This would never happen in New York."

"This isn't New York, Mr. Icahn," Goodman responded.

He might have been the only mayor in America to casually rebuff the king of the corporate raiders.

Goodman's army of downtown believers was growing. He gave some optimists reason for hope by ushering into being the "Little River" walk and City Hall park near the old courthouse. The additions were sights for sore eyes in the tattered corridor.

⁊ ⁊ ⁊

Goodman's dynamic personality worked overtime to keep up with his insatiable appetite for outrageous public comment. Not long after winning election, he noticed that downtown Las Vegas was awash in the unwashed. From homeless newcomers to long-time winos and the mentally ill, the declining street scene was one of several factors standing in the way of a downtown renaissance. The mayor wanted to do something about it, but like others before him was challenged for a fresh idea to address an age-old problem.

On weekends at Coronado, he'd noticed a distinct lack of homeless people, even in the city parks and on the public beaches. How, he wondered, had the police and local officials enjoyed such success? So he asked a police officer and was told candidly that anyone found loitering was asked to leave the idyllic island community that lies across a bridge from San Diego. Those who lingered, he was told, received "very special treatment." That meant they were given free transportation back to the city. In short, the proverbial bum's rush. There were no soup kitchens or social services available on Coronado and with the chilly law-enforcement climate, the indigents got the message.

But Las Vegas was not an island paradise; it was an asphalt jungle. And Goodman had inherited a tangled mess of buildings and services designed to meet the needs of the entire community's transient population. Downtown might have been in decline in many ways, but for the homeless, all roads led there. Once the picture began to crystallize for Goodman, he was privately offended and vowed to change it.

For a while, he kept his hard-line philosophy confidential. In public speeches and news conferences, he began dropping hints of his interest in addressing homeless issues.

Suddenly, the mayor was embroiled in a power struggle between his dream of redevelopment and the army of street people and their private and professional advocates. While Goodman called for other local government entities to do more to assist the City of Las Vegas in its caretaker role, he also announced that he was considering using the vacant state prison at Jean, 30 miles south of the city, to house downtown's homeless. The plan was met with a roar of umbrage from the social-service community.

"The homeless are not criminals," many said.

"No, but they're an eyesore and a nuisance," Goodman replied.

Goodman talked of cutting the city's $500,000 funding of the MASH Village homeless center and complained to the press that other local entities weren't doing their fair share. His blunt criticisms of Clark County agencies sent their advocates to battle stations. Meanwhile, Father Joe Carroll of MASH Village immediately set to work against him. Within days, other representatives of private homeless programs began questioning Goodman's methods. He was losing the image war to Father Joe and Brother Dave, a cassock-wearing Franciscan who ministered to the poor and wasn't shy about challenging Goodman's motives in the press.

Goodman had made a silly political mistake by taking on men affiliated with religions — even if, in Carroll's case, one of them was clearly playing political games in an effort to protect a $500,000 handout that had been set up by Goodman's predecessor, Jan Jones.

The plan had been simple enough. After giving the center $500,000 for five straight years, the city and county were going to each contribute $175,000 with the shelter raising the rest. Trouble was, by late 2001, the festering problem on the street was only getting worse.

In February 2002, the Council voted four to three to transfer ownership of 10 acres north of downtown to MASH. Goodman and the area's councilmen, Lawrence Weekly and Gary

Reese, voted against the transfer, but were on the short end of a four-to-three decision.

Goodman lamented privately to associates, "How am I going to win a fight with a man in a collar? Forget that he's wrong and has been disingenuous and that the city has been more than generous to his group over the years. Forget all that. I can't win a fight with a guy who wears his collar backward. But you know what? I don't care. I'm right. If something isn't done to keep the homeless out of the downtown area, redevelopment is sunk before it begins. It's doomed. That's why I'll take these hits. I'm right and eventually I'll win."

In the meantime, the hits were raising welts.

Instead of allowing staff to negotiate privately, Goodman's insatiable need to lead in the public eye had gotten the better of him. When the day neared that MASH would close, Goodman received death threats and began to travel in the company of city marshals in plain clothes. "Someone called up and said if one person was put on the street they were going to kill me," Goodman told *Review-Journal* reporter Jan Moller.

What some residents of the MASH shelter believed Goodman failed to see was the fact that—no matter who was at fault when it came to funding such programs—many families would be forced back onto the street without the center's help.

Weeks later, Metro and city officials were called in to remove a homeless squatters' camp that had been set up near the transient corridor one mile north of Fremont Street. Although the land used was adjacent to the Union Pacific Railroad tracks and in the heart of an industrial warehouse district, city officials said they were acting at the request of a property owner and in an effort to clean up an unsanitary area.

By March, nearly 200 homeless people—some drunk, some mentally ill, some committing criminal acts, but all relieving themselves in public—lined the sides of Foremaster Lane not far from the overwhelmed MASH Village tent. On a miserably cold and rainy Sunday morning, police converged on the area and the squatters were moved once more. Homeless advocates and local American Civil Liberties Union lawyers Gary Peck and Allen Lichtenstein raised objections in the rain, but that didn't stop the police and sanitation crews from clearing out the area. A few dozen transients filled the limited shelter space available, but others refused to give up their booze or put their only worldly belongings in storage and enter a temporary shelter. Goodman was driven to the scene by a city staffer and conducted an impromptu press conference with reporters who stood in the rain while he remained inside the car. Despite the work he'd done, the hours he'd spent meeting with homeless advocates and concerned citizens, the image he managed to project was one of a mayor who was more interested in making a blighted area more inviting for neighborhood shopkeepers than in finding a reasonable solution to a complex problem.

Only a man as naively confident and popular as Oscar Goodman would make the foolish promise to fix the homeless dilemma in Southern Nevada.

"Oscar's not all wrong about the issue, but no matter how he tries to explain it, his stance on the homeless issue made him look bad," veteran journalist Al Tobin observed. "The Jedi Warrior for constitutional rights wants to house the homeless in the Jean prison. Then he wants to sweep them up and clear them out. It's a little hard to spin that into something positive."

Although he took criticism for his steamroller approach — one County Commissioner sniped, "In the short-term it's nice to see that area cleaned up, but you can't just chase people from place to place" — the action appeared to do little to diminish his 80% popularity with voters. Truth told, not many of them had much sympathy for the community of down-and-outers that existed just beyond the lights of Fremont Street.

By November 2002, the public resoundingly rejected a plan to levy a minuscule property tax to aid the region's homeless. Although he'd taken plenty of criticism in the press, Goodman's hard line on the issue reflected a majority of the voting public's own sentiments.

？ ？ ？

Meanwhile, Goodman continued to stump on the national stage for his downtown revitalization plan. Reporters from across the nation interviewed the former mob lawyer and listened as he extolled the virtues of his vision of the future of Las Vegas. He was depicted favorably by a variety of major newspapers and television news magazines. Few failed to mention former criminal clients Meyer Lansky and Tony Spilotro, but they also took Goodman seriously on the subject of the development of the 61 vacant downtown acres, as well as a variety of other projects ranging from new apartment buildings to a behemoth Furniture Mart, which received approval for juicy tax breaks from a city itching to show a spark of urban vitality.

"For the rest of our lives, we're going to have to live with the decisions that are going to be made within the next couple of months," Goodman told Denise Becker of the *Greensboro News & Record*. "If we blow this, shame on us."

For a man who prior to winning election hadn't shown the least interest in the development of even his own real-estate holdings, much less the city's, he made a quick turnaround. Various public-opinion surveys continued to measure his approval ratings in the 80% range. The public appeared to like his candid one-liners and unabashed energy and he managed to remain popular despite issuing daily opinions on just about everything: the future of downtown's Neonopolis, a Jones-administration project which he panned at every opportunity; to the aggressive rhetoric of Southern Nevada's wobbly chapter of the Black Panther Party, whose hollow threats he brushed aside in a fashion that would have made Philadelphia Mayor Frank Rizzo proud; and leading the fight to add regulations to the city's outcall entertainment businesses.

The *Review-Journal's* Jan Moller described Goodman's outcall-service agenda: "With a wink, he says he won't try to legalize the world's oldest profession until his second term — hinting that such an effort might be in store in the future. It's vintage Goodman, spoken like a lawyer who spent three decades defending characters who made a lucrative living exploiting the darker side of human desire. Yet on the City Council dais, he's championed efforts to tighten regulations on escort and outcall services — businesses widely viewed by police as fronts for prostitution."

If one day, as the mayor and Council theorized, the city passed ordinances limiting the locations of escort businesses and introduced bills requiring outcall entertainers to get health cards, it did nothing to hurt Goodman's image with the voters. Only those who understood the inner workings of the racket saw it as opening a door that led to a future in which prostitution would be decriminalized and regulated.

Residents who wondered even briefly whether Goodman was becoming slightly conservative in his 60s were reminded of the mayor's true feelings after Clark County officials passed a controversial plan to regulate topless dancing and raise the minimum age requirement from 18 to 21. Goodman dropped jaws by suggesting that all those under-21 dancers were more than welcome in the City of Las Vegas, which is administered separately from the county. It was the sort of rhetoric he'd later soften.

Somehow, no matter how inflammatory his rhetoric, Goodman's popularity with the voting public continued to climb. By the fall of 2002, some surveys measured his approval rating as high as 90%.

§ § §

As he neared the end of his first term in office, Goodman had gained the respect of a number of the city's senior staff.

One top city official, speaking on the condition of anonymity, viewed Goodman's first four years this way: "I think, effective or not, he's certainly put the spotlight on the city. In this valley, politically, the city is the dominating force by far and that is directly attributable to Oscar's energy and effort. He's not my favorite person, but he's made more of a difference than I thought he would."

Another senior official added, "I was more skeptical than most and was among those less than enthused by him becoming mayor. But the fact is he's taking a shot at making some real differences downtown. There's a significant amount of stuff that we're doing and some of it will be successful. It just takes time."

Patience, however, is not among Goodman's virtues.

"Oscar has to learn that nothing moves quickly in city government but the line out of the parking lot at quitting time," a senior official said. "If he can master that, he'll be more successful. He's a catalyst, at least to put people's feet to the fire."

§ § §

Goodman called the Neonopolis retail project on Fremont Street "the worry of my life. It wasn't my project, but it has cost taxpayers millions of dollars, so we have an investment that the city needs to protect. We need to do what we can to protect it."

With more than $30 million in the Neonopolis mall, $70 million in the construction of the Fremont Street Experience light canopy, and another $1 million in annual upgrades and maintenance, the investment in salvaging the old heart of Las Vegas shows no signs of slowing.

In the end, the question is not whether the money is well spent, but whether city officials — its flamboyant mayor most — can attract enough outside interest to turn the tide from decay toward the true renaissance Goodman dreams about.

With most members of the powerful casino industry long ago having written off the area, it would be up to Goodman and the city's Business Development office to stir the interest of potential investors. The sale of Fitzgeralds and the casino properties of long-time downtown owner Jackie Gaughan to outside investors were taken by some as signs of life and hope on Fremont Street.

Dealing with the local office of the FBI tested Goodman's political maturity. The man who'd been so quick to vilify agents now had a problem: The local office was preparing to pack up and leave the downtown area.

Goodman scrambled to negotiate with Special Agent in Charge Grant Ashley. The hasty courtship paid dividends when Ashley, who was later promoted to Assistant Director of the FBI, announced that his troops would remain in the downtown corridor on land provided by the city.

"I remember our past conversation," Ashley said in a letter. "You telephoned me and asked, 'What would it take for the FBI not to move out of the city limits?'

"Well, you delivered 5.3 acres to the U.S. Government at no charge and we are staying in your fine city!

"Thank you very much for your personal interest in this project and tenacity in culling through the bureaucratic quagmire, which has essentially held this project in limbo for over three and one-half years."

But Ashley, known for his pugnacity and biting sense of humor, couldn't resist a little dig at the Bureau's former nemesis.

"On an unrelated matter, I have a question," he wrote. "A comment was attributed to you in the early 1980s that you would rather have your daughter date one of your former clients (who I believe met with an unfortunate demise) rather than an FBI agent. In that we are essentially neighbors, how do you now feel about her dating one of my fine, young, and single Special Agents?"

Despite a falling out with Councilwoman Lynette Boggs McDonald and his at times prickly relationship with Councilman Michael McDonald, as he neared the end of his first term, Goodman confidentially observed, "I've got a council that, for all intents and purposes, is completely supportive." And he clearly understood that, as long as his popularity remained high—up to 90% in some election-year surveys—the council, for the most part, would remain in his corner on major issues of redevelopment.

The raw political rookie had learned to play the game at City Hall. He was trying to remain focused on a few attainable goals, while helping to plan legislative strategies and prepare for his own re-election.

There could be no reasonable expectation of a competitive challenger. In March 2002, Goodman all but assured he would run unopposed by holding an event at former Computer Group client Billy Walters' Bali Hai country club that raised $400,000 in a few hours from well-wishers ranging from District Court judges to topless cabaret moguls. That figure was as much and more than some presidential candidates had generated during trips through Las Vegas. The mayor was flexing his muscles, as if to remind pundits and powerbrokers that he was capable of wreaking havoc even at the state level if he really wanted to.

Ironically, after so many years of playing the role of the snarling pugnacious criminal mouthpiece, Goodman thrived in his new role as the consummate defender of and ace public-relations man for Las Vegas.

"I think I've given Las Vegas an awful lot of publicity, and of course I love the adulation," Goodman said. "I've said it from the first day I took office that Las Vegas must not forget its roots. It's not simply for reasons of nostalgia or because people think the mayor has a thing about the mob, but because it's what gives us our mystique. It's what separates us from all the other cities that have gambling. It's what differentiates us from everyone else. It's a rich history. These are romantic characters, fascinating and intriguing characters."

The mouthpiece-turned-mayor not least.

As Goodman piled up the press, generating feature stories in every major newspaper in America and several in Europe and Asia and appearing on an eclectic array of television programs such as "Crossfire" with his new pal James Carville, "Money Line" with Lou Dobbs, and the Discovery and Travel Channels, he appeared to be receiving all the adulation, as his wife would put it, that a man could want.

And still, on some slow Saturday mornings when there wasn't a seniors group to address, a parade to lead, or a ribbon to cut, he would lace up his sneakers and go to the local Costco discount store, browse for a few nonessential items, and introduce himself to shoppers and clerks, most of whom already recognized him and greeted him with "Hey, Oscar" and "How's it going, Mayor?"

It was going fine. The life of the overachieving Jewish kid from West Philadelphia, who'd lived so long so close to organized-crime infamy, had never been better. He had a beautiful intelligent wife who loved him, four successful children who adored him, all the material possessions a reasonable man would need, the morning sports betting line delivered, an actual sponsor for his copious gin consumption, and an enormous stage on which to perform his one-man act — not to mention that the judges and FBI types who'd once dreamed of throwing him in jail were now singing his praises.

All in all, not a bad life.

؟ ؟ ؟

Not everyone was sold on Goodman. Authors Sally Denton and Roger Morris panned him in their book, *The Money and the Power: The Making of Las Vegas and Its Grip on America*. Denton and Morris expected plenty of fallout from their thoroughly researched study of the city as a metaphor for a nation riddled with corruption. Its unsparing depiction of Las Vegas as a gaudy curtain behind which the Mafia maneuvered, millions in drug profits were laundered through casinos, and even U.S. presidents were manipulated caused an uproar from many established residents who'd known and loved some of the racketeers who'd built the town from sand and mesquite.

About Goodman they wrote, "In June 1999, Las Vegas elected its last mayor of the twentieth century and its first of the new millennium. Richly symbolic of what the city was and would become, the landslide winner would be the lawyer Oscar Goodman. Apologist for the worst of the Strip's past and present, the fifty-nine-year-old Philadelphian had been 'juiced in' since his arrival in 1964. Since then, as lawyer, spokesman, and social friend of a retinue of some of the vilest clients in organized crime, he had won local fame and fortune not simply as a constitutional defense lawyer but as the Syndicate's on-call publicist and legal manipulator."

On the subject of Las Vegas and its relationship with the international drug and money-laundering trades:

"As if to span it all from the seventies to the end of the century, there was Jimmy Chagra's lawyer, Oscar Goodman. Drug and other mob money paid Goodman's fees, and his reputation was made when Jimmy Chagra was acquitted in the murder of a federal judge. Goodman would go on to become mayor of Las Vegas on the eve of the twenty-first century, with his own ambitions for Carson City or Washington beyond."

Predictably, Goodman registered his objections. He responded in part, "Because of the deep respect I have for you as a result of our past conversations, I have to express how sorely disappointed I am in your characterization of me in *The Money and the Power*. It appears that you have adopted Joe Yablonsky's pablum completely. That, of course, is your prerogative."

His chief lament focused on the "juiced-in" reference. Goodman dusted off his well-worn tale of how he and Carolyn had come to this strange place with just $87 between them. The rest was the result of luck and hard work, not some darker connections from Philadelphia or, as his federal critics had long whispered, Miami Beach or Chicago. At the height of his legal career, of course, Goodman had more juice than a Florida orange grove. But despite the presence of Meyer Lansky and Al Malnik in his life, no indictable evidence ever surfaced linking him as a pawn of organized crime. He had seen kept men throughout his career and he was proud not to be one of them.

"With whom was I supposed to be 'juiced in' since my arrival to the city I love, I have no idea," Goodman wrote. "Knowing your pedigree, I truly believe I am entitled to an apology."

He didn't get one.

❧ ❧ ❧

In October 2002, KLAS-TV 8 investigative reporter George Knapp interviewed Frank Cullotta, the street soldier and hitman who had turned on Tony Spilotro and the rest of his Las Vegas outfit. While Goodman had never had a kind word for Cullotta, the informant was almost kind to the former mob mouthpiece.

"Let me give you my take on Oscar," Cullotta said. "Let me get this out on the table once and for all. He's never going to admit they were criminals, rightfully so. He's not supposed to. He's done his job there. Oscar was well aware of what we were doing, I believe. I've sat in his conference room with my guys. He set up his conference room with Tony and them and we'd discuss cases. Oscar knew what was going on. But he's a lawyer, with lawyer confidentiality, so he did his job."

But did Goodman have anything to fear from Cullotta?

"Absolutely not," the aging hitman said. "I'm not gonna hurt him."

And unlike Joe Yablonsky, who believed Goodman had been a part of Spilotro's criminal web, Cullotta held a higher opinion of the lawyer-turned-mayor. Cullotta, for instance, had never believed Goodman was associated with any of what the FBI privately contended were key-witness assassinations.

"I never heard any of that," Cullotta said flatly.

❧ ❧ ❧

Goodman's ambitions, such as they were at the moment, were sated for the most part by a daily dose of adoration from the citizens of Las Vegas, national notice in the press, and an unhealthy dose of after-five o'clock gin. But he was beginning

to miss some of his old clients, who to him were more honorable than many of the people he'd met in politics.

Although few former clients took time to wish him well at
City Hall, Goodman remained respectful and kept in touch
with a few of his special cases.

One was Gambino dinosaur Natale Richichi.

"Richichi was dying. He hadn't been convicted of a violent crime. In my opinion he was well-qualified for a compassionate release by the government, but no one was going to let
a notorious mobster, even one who was clearly gravely ill, out
of prison. They had cast him in a role, one that he probably fit
at one time in his life, but they were making him play it to the
bitter end."

Attempts by Goodman's law partner David Chesnoff to
win a compassionate release for Richichi were unsuccessful
and in January 2001 at age 84, the old bear of a man died in a
cage at the Medical Center for Federal Prisoners at Springfield,
Missouri. Although he was born in New York City, Richichi
had been a 16-year resident of Las Vegas and his family chose
to hold the funeral service in his adopted home.

The Southern Nevada service raised a question: Would
Mayor Oscar Goodman be attending?

"With me, he was honorable in his word and deed and
that's all I care about. I don't care how other people perceived
him. I care about how he treated me. With me, he was a gentleman. He was a friend, period. I took what some people said
about him with a grain of salt."

Goodman's presence so close to a Mafia funeral would
surely be noticed by reporters and might be picked up on in
the national press, bringing just the kind of focus on Las Vegas that many local leaders feared when they attempted to keep
him from winning office. In the end, Goodman attended
Richichi's funeral.

But it attracted sparse newspaper commentary. Only television reporter Glen Meek raised the issue of the mayor's presence at the mobster's sendoff. Goodman's and Richichi's friend,
the Colombo family's Charlie Panarella, anonymously shuffled
into the service with his walker to pay his respects.

More problematic for Goodman was law partner David
Chesnoff's propensity for inviting criticism by escorting noto-

rious clients to pay their respects to the mayor. One of them was gangster-rap record mogul Marion "Suge" Knight, whose visit to City Hall brought into question Goodman's stated willingness to keep the felons off the 10th floor. Another controversial visitor was mobster-turned-Hollywood dealmaker Bill Bonanno, son of crime-family legend Joe Bonanno. Bill Bonanno came to the mayor's office on more than one occasion in 2002 to attempt to persuade Goodman to cut a book and movie deal about his life. Goodman politely declined.

But gentlemanly Joey Cusumano was a fellow Goodman could never resist. He'd known Oscar more than 30 years, had raved about him in the documentary *Mob Law*, and had relied on Goodman's counsel after assassins attempted to murder him in 1990. More than anything, Goodman liked Cusumano as a man and a character. To Goodman's way of thinking, the fact that Cusumano was a convicted felon, a member of Nevada's casino Black Book, and considered by law enforcement to be a long-time mob associate was no reason not to admire the guy.

Even if it was sure to be criticized by outsiders, it was a sure bet that sooner or later the two would get together as friends. On February 3, 2002, Cusumano and his wife Sharon joined Catholic Bishop Joseph Pepe at the Goodman's Bannie Lane home to watch the Super Bowl. Goodman lightheartedly kept Pepe by his side as an impromptu handicapper with otherworldly connections and won all his bets that day, cutting in the church on a piece of the action.

It was a quiet afternoon spent among friends without a controversial word spoken, but how would such a gathering be perceived if it became known publicly and Goodman decided to run for higher office?

(A year later Goodman found out when word circulated that Cusumano was among more than 100 guests in attendance at Cara Goodman's backyard engagement party at the Bannie Lane house. Cusumano, who had also been present at Cara's bat mitzvah, was publicly linked to Goodman in the press and allowed an opportunity for Gaming Control Board Member Bobby Siller, an ex-FBI agent with a career spent battling mob figures, to offer to reporter Jane Ann Morrison, "You know, it would be questionable whether I could support Oscar Goodman for a work card. I'm offended. It truly is an embarrassment to us."

Goodman bristled at the criticism and reminded anyone willing to listen that Siller and he had never exactly been on speaking terms. But as he'd done so often during his legal career, Goodman illustrated his argument that what he did in the privacy of his own home was his business by using a hyperbolic hypothetical scenario to stun his skeptics: Not only would Goodman invite his friend Cusumano to his home, but were Tony Spilotro living, he'd also add him to the guest list.

Such comments would cripple a score of political careers, but the brazenly candid Goodman's popularity remained higher than any elected official in the state.)

Goodman simply refused to stop associating privately with his few favorite old clients. He'd attended Natale Richichi's funeral, made no secret of his affection for Moose Panarella, and was warmest of all toward Cusumano, who was rumored to have brokered peace between the mayor and Councilman McDonald. It was clear that although he took his new duty at City Hall seriously, he hadn't changed his independent nature or abandoned his romance with the wiseguys.

§ § §

The city's spring 2001 election provided Goodman an opportunity to share his political popularity. He made it clear who his favorites were by lending his name to campaign mailers and phone-bank messages. His support helped make winning election easy for political appointees Michael Mack, Lynette Boggs McDonald, and Lawrence Weekly. The peripatetic mayor managed to be captured by news photographers with two of the three candidates at their separate headquarters on election night.

A year later, Goodman's magic couldn't save Congressional candidate Dario Herrera, who lost in a landslide despite the mayor's endorsement. Goodman also gushed on behalf of Congresswoman Shelley Berkley in a race the Democrat easily won against Boggs McDonald. Goodman's embrace of Berkley, after initially stating publicly that he would stay out of the race entirely, caused a rift between him and Boggs McDonald, who returned to her City Hall duties and was rumored to be contemplating an ill-advised run for mayor herself.

But what of Goodman's own political future?

He was easily the biggest story in Nevada politics, and the state's senior Democrats, U.S. Senator Harry Reid among them, quietly lobbied Goodman to take a shot at the governor's office. Goodman, ever the competitive overachiever, was sorely tempted to take on Republican Kenny Guinn, a former Clark County School District Superintendent and gas company executive who'd risen to the state's highest office on the strength of his long relationships with Nevada's casino and business executives and power-brokers. In keeping with a longstanding Nevada tradition bucked only a handful of times in the state's history, Guinn was a machine candidate.

Goodman, who saw himself as the ideal wrench in the machine, was intrigued.

After a long day, when the martinis kicked in at Fellini's restaurant, he'd confess to Carolyn how he knew he'd win if he ran. He could feel it. The people liked him. They didn't care that he didn't know all the issues. They didn't know the issues themselves. And even some of Guinn's staunchest Republican supporters were disappointed in the image he was projecting from Carson City. They suspected he'd used his knowledge of economic policy to shield himself from other issues. They suspected he'd allowed political advisors Pete Ernaut and Sig Rogich to rule his thoughts and run his administration. Guinn was a likable plodder. Goodman was a lovable dreamer.

The trouble was, even in a slightly sloshed state, Goodman could still read the writing on the wall. For as long as he'd known his fast friends in politics, Senator Harry Reid chief among them, they'd looked out for themselves first and foremost. And they hadn't exactly shown up on the front lines of his upstart mayoral campaign less than three years earlier. Despite his windfall investments and personal wealth of several million dollars, he couldn't prudently self-fund a gubernatorial campaign even in Nevada, where Guinn would be able to amass millions if need be. And as for the whisperers? Former Mayor Jan Jones had heard those same promises on her way to the slaughter in two runs for governor after allowing her dreams to get in the way of her good sense.

He might play the stand-up vaudevillian for the press and public, but Oscar Goodman wasn't a fool. That he made a good candidate and had obviously alarmed Guinn's insiders with the possibility he'd run was flattering. Guinn had the formidable financial strength and ruthlessness of Nevada's political machine behind him and that meant a vicious dogfight, one that would not only attempt to characterize him as an evil mob lawyer, but would make much out of his business investments, including the small piece of mob associate Dennis Mastro's restaurant.

For her part, Carolyn never wavered. She was happy as long as Oscar was happy. Running a statewide race would put their lives on hold and make those weekend getaways to their condo on Coronado a thing of the past. She would be able to help him on the stump in Nevada's rural counties, since despite her New York upbringing, she had distant relatives who'd helped settle the region more than a century earlier. And his well-established distrust of the federal government and strong libertarian streak would give him at least some common ground with voters in the state's conservative "cow counties." Plus, Goodman had money and was a member of the majority party in Clark County, where only Guinn's popularity rivaled his own.

It might have been a dogfight, but the underdog had a chance.

It was almost irresistible.

At heart Oscar Goodman was still that supremely competitive overachieving kid from Philadelphia who wasn't afraid to square against bigger players and launch his set shots over the taller boys, whatever the odds. He was still Allan and Laura Goodman's tough little charmer. His friend Congresswoman Shelley Berkley said he was destined to become the first Jewish governor of the state of Nevada. And he still loved a good fight.

Finally, it was time to decide.

On Tuesday October 9, 2001, he called a press conference at City Hall. Although he sounded like a candidate for governor and City Hall reporter Jan Moller briefly winced at the prospect of covering local government without the flamboyant mayor leading the parade, Goodman declared he would not seek higher office. His eyes brightened only when he toyed with Guinn without naming him.

"I believe the state of Nevada is in need of strong leadership," he said, managing to sound like a candidate even in concession. "If I were governor, I'd be a strong leader."

But the tweaking of the establishment was little more than a love tap. He spoke of having unfinished work and he was right as far as it went. The redevelopment of the 61 acres and a host of other important downtown projects were still on the drawing board. There were the issues of homelessness, regional planning, pollution, tourism, water usage, and more. He would remain mayor of Las Vegas.

§ § §

Why didn't Goodman run for governor?

Because he didn't want to work a smaller room under a smaller spotlight.

He would have gone out of his mind in Carson City, where his nightlife activities of betting and Beefeater might not have been fully appreciated. For a consummate showman, giving up his starring role as Las Vegas mayor to run for governor would have been like leaving Broadway to pursue summer stock in Winnemucca. In terms of a national profile, there was no comparison. The mayor in Las Vegas is far more visible than the governor in Carson City. It also better fit his personality. At heart, he was more of a showman than a statesman.

Beyond the sheer ego gratification, Oscar said he realized that although he wanted to win the governor's race, if only to prove he was good enough, in the end he didn't want to serve. On a larger scale, it was reminiscent of his lobbying to become the president of the National Association of Criminal Defense Lawyers, then hustling overtime to shirk meetings and avoid any overly meaningful work. The title was an honor, the toil a headache.

Several key Democrats lamented Goodman's decision, even if he was comfortable with it. But the *Las Vegas Review-Journal*, which had published its first observation of Goodman-as-politician by proclaiming "Anyone but Oscar," was more generous after he decided against running for governor before the end of his first term. After noting the obvious — that Goodman's candidacy would have infused excitement into an otherwise bland campaign — the newspaper gave the mayor credit: "Mr. Goodman deserves a pat on the back for keeping his promise to Las Vegans and channeling his energies into his current job. Unlike his predecessor, Jan Jones, who spent nearly one-third of her eight years as mayor seeking the governorship, Mr. Goodman's focus has never wavered from the city and its welfare."

Campaign adviser Jim Ferrence said, "I would have loved to have seen Oscar run in 2002. I would have loved to see that race. I think he would have had a very good chance to win. I think one thing Kenny Guinn has on Oscar is that he looks like the governor. Beyond that, I think even the governor's advisers would admit that a debate would have gone Oscar's way.

"Now I don't think there would be anything that would interest him other than the U.S. Senate. I think the Senate has piqued his interest, but other than that, I think he might be out of politics after his second term."

It wasn't all roses and warm wishes, of course. Political columnist Jon Ralston observed, "He was like a man who was desperate to let people know he could do the job, just that he didn't want to do it. His insistence, after he listed a slew of areas where the state was failing, that he was 'not being critical of anybody' was embarrassing."

Behind the scenes, Ralston and Goodman, who kept a photograph of the columnist on his office wall, had had a falling out. After Goodman refused to appear on Ralston's cable-television interview show, the political pundit began to criticize even Goodman's most trivial public statements. But even a thorough shellacking from the state's senior political analyst and the shunning by the state's political machine that accompanied it, did little to diminish Goodman's appeal with the public.

As the weeks passed, Ralston mounted a daily assault on Goodman in his political-insider e-mail and rarely passed up an opportunity to vilify the man he called "Mayor Bobblehead." Goodman was incensed initially and had legal ally Marty Keach pen an ill-advised letter to Ralston's superiors threatening legal action. After he calmed down, Goodman realized the sniping was having zero effect on his popularity and only made Ralston appear increasingly obsessed. "I'm in his head," Goodman told a City Hall colleague. "I'm driving him crazy like I did Joe Yablonsky." But as with Yobo Joe years earlier, it was also true that at times Ralston was in Goodman's head.

Reporters dwelled on such trivialities as whether Goodman would endorse another's candidacy and whether he believed Guinn was providing sufficient leadership during difficult economic times. What they should have done was drop to one knee and beg him to reconsider, for without the Flamboyant One in the race, there would, in effect, be no race at all.

Guinn, who'd already lined up a wide spectrum of support, $3 million in contributions, was re-elected in a landslide over veteran state Senator Joe Neal. The state's tightly controlled political system remained so snug that little air, and less light, could penetrate it.

Although they feigned indifference, Guinn's top advisors were relieved. They managed to keep their remarks civil. Perhaps they could read between the lines: If they pissed him off, Goodman would run out of spite. His professional life was full of cases in which his spite for arrogant government prosecutors had carried the day. Guinn's chief political advisor Pete Ernaut told *Review-Journal* political columnist Steve Sebelius simply, "I don't see someone on the horizon who gives us great concern."

§ § §

As he approached the end of his first term in office, Goodman betrayed no sign of losing his zest for the spotlight and potential, no matter how frustrating the mayor's job. He'd made plenty of mistakes, most out of a lack of political experience and his insistence on speaking his mind whatever the cost. But he could also point to his share of successes, greatest of which was his work to secure those coveted 61 acres of undeveloped real estate that held the long-term promise of large-scale redevelopment for downtown. There was also the development of a sprawling outlet mall on vacant land downtown and the acquisition of the historic former Federal Courthouse, which he only half-joked might become the city's first mob museum.

And, always, there were the resounding applause and

standing ovations at speaking engagements and public pro-
nouncements. Wherever Goodman went, his insatiable ego and
larger-than-life public persona floated above him like a Macy's-
parade balloon. He was establishing himself as a Las Vegas
entertainment legend right up there with Wayne Newton and
Siegfried & Roy. And he was having the time of his life.

"I know him like I know my left arm," Carolyn Goodman
said. "He thrives on applause. He's been that way since I met
him forty years ago. When he says he loves being mayor, he
absolutely adores it. It's like he's been given a whole second
life. And he genuinely feels he can make a difference and is
trying very hard to make the difference here in Las Vegas."

"I'm like a folk hero, I really am," Goodman said without
an ounce of modesty. "Carolyn calls it my adulation. She says
when she wakes up she has to go to my side of the bed and
start applauding and she's only half kidding.

"I like the fact the little kids know me. I saw two children
today who had been in the school system with behavior problems, but recently made strides and were going back into the
mainstream. When their teacher asked them how they could
be rewarded, they said they wanted to come down and meet
the mayor. They were genuinely ecstatic, which makes me
genuinely ecstatic.

"People make fun of me because I say I love it, but I don't
care what they think. I do love it. I haven't gotten tired of it.
It's almost like a narcotic."

Observed long-time Las Vegas journalist Al Tobin, "I think
the guy is the best mayor we've ever had. He's a great mayor
who certainly represents the city well. And I say that having
supported the other guy." He paused and added, "However,
Oscar doesn't take criticism very well. He wants to be worshiped. He wants to be applauded. He wants to be commended.
And if you don't do those things, he takes it as an attack. He
hasn't always surrounded himself with the best people and
that could hurt him in the long run."

Although polls show that Goodman continues to enjoy his
astronomical popularity rating, he'll never win points or plau-
dits from his political enemies.

"He hasn't done anything for Las Vegas," Republican Party
activist Steve Wark told *Las Vegas Sun* political reporter Erin

Neff. "He's been a great cheerleader outside Las Vegas, but he's achieved very little as far as redeveloping the city or solving the city's problems."

Former Mayor Jan Jones: "It's different when you're coming from the private sector; you overestimate the speed at which you can move. I think he needs to be more of a political realist with respect to what he can get accomplished, then work to make those things a reality. Probably the most significant thing he's done is solidify his control of the Council. It remains to be seen if he can use that control to actually make things happen."

Adds Goodman's ally and campaign consultant Jim Ferrence, "The one thing that has surprised me is just how quickly he's latched on to the policy side of things. The critics thought he'd get bored within weeks of taking office and wouldn't like the policy side and he'd just be a ribbon-cutter. Nothing could be further from the truth."

So, as a mayor he remains a work in progress. But what about the man?

As he rolled toward a sure landslide re-election in 2003, the mob's last outlaw defense attorney appeared to have found a job for life as mayor of Sin City — if only this hard-drinking sports-betting anarchist in a Brioni suit can accept his role as an unconventional, but largely adored, member of the Establishment. For an aging courtroom bomb-thrower, at times it remained almost too much to handle.

"Sometimes I get up in the morning and feel like I've gone over to the other side," Oscar Goodman said, smiling wistfully. "I almost feel guilty about it, like I've betrayed something, like I have a little rat in me now. But then the feeling passes, and I know I'm in it for the right reasons. I love Las Vegas."

And who better to represent an old mob city than an old mob lawyer?

Doing It His Way:
An Epilogue in Motion

Placing a coda on the break-neck life of Oscar Goodman is impossible. Keeping up with Goodman is like trying to catch a bullet train, albeit one that sometimes appears dangerously close to jumping its track. As he reached the end of his first term in office, more than ever Goodman came to embody the city he represents: simultaneous shadow and light.

While his political popularity remained unrivaled and even some of his staunchest critics appeared to have been won over by his boundless energy and roguish charm, Goodman simply refused to step away from the edge and settle into the political mainstream. By doing so, he sometimes courted calamity.

He remained loyal to his old mob friends and — his occasional protests to the contrary — didn't hesitate to embrace them and show them the respect he believed they deserved. Attending Gambino crime-family-capo Natale Richichi's funeral was one thing; it was something else to invite Bill Bonanno — whose father Joseph Bonanno rose so high in La Cosa Nostra that he had a family named after him — to his City Hall office for a meeting about a possible movie based on his life as a mob lawyer.

Then there was the engagement party of daughter Cara, at which Goodman's long-time client and friend Joey Cusumano was among the more than 100 in attendance. Cusumano's casino Black Book status made him persona non grata in Nevada resorts, but not at the House of Goodman. The mayor took heat from a previous-life nemesis, Bobby Siller, the former FBI Special Agent in Charge who had become a member of the Gaming Control Board, but refused to flinch. And the voting public cared not a bit.

Then there was old Charlie Panarella, the ancient Colombo street boss whose 1999 visit to City Hall surfaced first in a *New York Daily News* story recounting assertions made by mob turncoat Vincent "Vinnie Ocean" Palermo that, as a candidate, Goodman had accepted a $10,000 donation from the hoodlum. Goodman denied the allegation and retorted that he'd never heard of Palermo, the one-time boss of New Jersey's DeCavalcante crime group.

"I don't know anyone named Vinnie Ocean and that's a name I'd certainly remember," Goodman said. He did, however, say he'd made an unsuccessful attempt to land a job for Panarella's son. The meeting appeared harmless enough, but it was yet another example of Goodman's past haunting his present. As ever, he exacerbated the issue by getting testy with a reporter, at one point threatening to ban him from City Hall. Coming from the media darling who bragged about opening government to unprecedented levels, it sounded petulant. A UNLV professor called the mayor's ongoing relationship with old mobsters "a blight on everyone," but Goodman showed no remorse and the masses didn't seem to mind. He was as proud of his friendships with the infamous as he was of his associations with legitimate society.

But of all his notorious contacts, it was his old friend Bill Cassidy's arrest for arson and sexual assault that threatened to tar him the worst.

"Oscar's always had trouble with his associations," said one long-time courtroom combatant. "Look at this Cassidy clown. Anybody who ever met him could tell he was a phony, but he latched onto Oscar. And Cassidy would constantly shoot his mouth off about how tight he was with the mayor. Sometimes Oscar is his own worst enemy.

Doing It His Way

"The man is like a magnet. He's got two polar ends. There must be something very good about him innately to be so loved by his family. I don't like him, but I think he's a super dad whose family has always come first."

But there were scads of high-profile contacts to balance the scale. One of those was Los Angeles Police Chief Bill Bratton, who dined with Goodman in a meeting arranged through David Chesnoff. Celebrities ranging from Muhammad Ali and Sir Anthony Hopkins to Charo and Joe Pesci also sought his company. Pesci even discussed the possibility of teaming with Goodman to open a "speakeasy" in the downtown redevelopment area. "The problem is," the mayor told columnist Norm Clarke, "he probably wants to call it Pesci's, and I want to call it Oscar's. We might have to settle it in the desert."

During an earlier visit with Muhammad Ali, Goodman embraced the Greatest and listened as he whispered, "I'm just a niggah who tried to be biggah."

Goodman replied, "I'm just a Jew who's trying to stay true."

The same man who'd been given little chance to win the 1999 mayor's race had by 2003 emerged as a semi-regular guest on "Crossfire," the political television program with hosts James Carville and Paul Begala raving about their "favorite mayor in America." Goodman had gained entrée into political circles he hadn't dreamed of even a few years earlier.

Goodman also managed to enjoy more mainstream pursuits, rarely outside the eye of a television camera. His weight-loss program, which apparently still allowed him to drink copious quantities of Bombay gin after 5 p.m., was a regular feature on the local NBC affiliate and he appeared to be successfully fighting his battle of the bulge. He made light of his prolific sports-betting habit by betting he'd sing the Village People's "YMCA" on a busy street corner if he lost his Super Bowl wager. He lost and was joined by several Council members in the buffoonery.

Goodman set aside his animus toward the Neonopolis mall project to become one of its few vocal supporters, even endorsing a plan to outfit it with slot machines in order to improve flagging business.

He pleaded for donations to local homeless shelters even

as he fought for tougher treatment of recalcitrant winos and street people in the downtown corridor. He was vilified as a key reason a national homeless group called Las Vegas the most dangerous city for the downtrodden, but continued his double-edged crusade to make downtown cleaner and safer without violating anyone's civil rights. To some observers, it was the most troubled part of his first four years. Columnist Steve Sebelius called it "his callous treatment of the chronically homeless and the down-and-out of downtown, people to whom he generally refers to as 'cockroaches.' Goodman has spearheaded almost-anything-goes efforts to get both groups moved out of the area, saying they interfere with his vision."

Las Vegas ACLU official Gary Peck observed, "Personally, I like Oscar a lot and have enormous respect for his long-standing professional commitment to defending the Constitution and the legal rights of his clients. That's why I am so deeply disappointed in the way he has conducted himself since becoming mayor. Certainly he has done some good things and on balance has been a great ambassador for the City. But in other regards, particularly with respect to the homeless, his words and actions have been unpardonable and anathema to everything he claimed to believe in when he was a criminal defense lawyer."

Attorney Dominic Gentile, one of Southern Nevada's most active First Amendment lawyers, offered a different take on Goodman as the ogre of the homeless.

"I think it took a lot of courage for a guy who's basically a civil libertarian to take a tough position on the homeless," Gentile said. "There are many things he does not lack, and courage is certainly on that list. I think he presents a wonderful image for a city that has its economy based on unabashed hedonism and entertainment. I don't think a person exists who could match him for being the mayor of the city of Las Vegas. I think they're going to have a hard time when he decides to leave."

A major Southern Nevada developer snorted, "You've got to be joking. Oscar Goodman is a man who's always on the verge of embarrassing the community."

Ever the salesman, Goodman was at his best when he was closing a deal or defending the city. After the National Football League rejected Las Vegas Convention and Visitors Authority advertisements for the Super Bowl because the city was deemed too synonymous with gambling, Goodman responded with rhetorical guns blazing. He blasted NFL Commissioner Paul Tagliabue, appeared nightly on national television, and was quoted widely in major newspapers. Goodman turned the teapot tempest into a cause célèbre that resulted in approximately $12 million in free advertising for Las Vegas. He was keenly aware of the hucksterism involved and loved every minute of the fight.

So did political advisor Billy Vassiliadis, whose company has the Las Vegas Convention Authority's advertising contract.

"We have to think hard to try to categorize or classify Oscar, because he so defies the categories. Being mayor of Las Vegas, I think he wears two hats. The first is the tourism hat, the public image of Las Vegas to the world. As a guy who gets paid a lot of money to market Las Vegas, I love Oscar as mayor. Vegas has to have a swagger. Vegas has to have an attitude, a little bit of naughtiness. Vegas has to have a strut that other towns can never match. Oscar fits it. Not only does he fit it. He loves it. Whether assailing Tagliabue or defending the Fremont Street Experience or whatever it might be, there's a certain magic there when it comes to being a Las Vegas mayor."

Goodman has the Vegas style down solid. It's the substance that is the real challenge.

"The second is the manager's hat. One thing Oscar still has to prove is that he has the persistence, the follow-through, and the concentration to get some important things done," Vassiliadis said. "He needs to learn how to partner, which I think he's getting better at. If he continues to sell the vision and he works with staff to get it done, if he nails down a medical research center or a theater or some downtown redevelopment, I think people will say he's been successful."

But by partnering with gaming bosses and entrenched political insiders, Goodman risked losing that special pugnacity that had endeared him to many and excluded him from legitimate society.

"I'm pissed at him for falling in line with the Nevada Resort Association and all the gaming people," said one longtime confidant. "He's sort of given up and has decided to go with the flow. They got to him. He knows the only way he can get anything done is by working with some of the same people he's despised for years."

Although some allies would demur, Goodman's political ground game was improving. He was comfortable working the halls of the Nevada Legislature to lobby on behalf of the city. After taking personal control of the destiny of the 61-acre vacant parcel downtown, he worked with staff on his redevelopment and Cleveland Clinic projects and even warmed up to the importance of selling Neonopolis to the public, the handsome white elephant left from the previous administration.

Las Vegas attorney Marvin Longabaugh tracks political trends through his Magellan Research polling company. After many years of watching politicians of every stripe, he marvels at Goodman's popularity.

"He's the Colombo of politics," Longabaugh said. "Out front he's got all these bombastic outlandish statements, but behind the scenes he's carefully crafting and formulating smart strategy.

"Not being like everyone else is what gets him eighty-five-percent approval ratings. He's the living embodiment of the populist. He is what everyone wishes the town still was: the old-fashion mob town where certain laws could be broken and other laws, if you broke them, you paid dearly."

In the end, none of his controversies meant a thing to the public, which retained him by a record margin in April 2003. Goodman shattered known local records by receiving 86% of the vote. His closest challenger, a retired piano player who moved with the aid of a walker, managed to scrape up 6%. Rumors circulated that Goodman had placed a large bet on himself to win by 90% of the vote. The story was never confirmed — it did, however, fit his image.

After raising more than $1 million, the mayor had proven an effective fundraiser, which gave rise to more speculation that he might one day run for higher office. He denied interest in leaving City Hall, but loved the agitation such talk generated in the systems of his political enemies.

"Our research shows that Oscar has stronger numbers than either of the Daleys would ever hope to have," Goodman's spin doctor Jim Ferrence said, comparing Goodman to the

Chicago political dynasty. But it was just as clear the job remained light-years behind those found in major cities. Goodman was the undisputed big fish in his relatively small pond.

§ § §

Meanwhile, there was talk that Goodman would return to the practice of law at some point in his second term. At the House the Mob Built, David Chesnoff had moved into his mentor's office. But things just weren't the same.

"I represent Vinny Ferrara in his appeal in the Boston case and he still asks for Oscar in every conversation we have," Chesnoff said. "While Oscar was here at the law office, he was like the guru. Obviously, he had this kind of effect with the people who were around here. He was the Big O. That's missing now."

The law office and Las Vegas may never be the same.

"At some point," Billy Vassiliadis said, "you're going to have to write an actual conclusion. Frankly, I would not make book on how it concludes."

The only certainty is that Oscar Goodman will do it his way.

Selected Bibliography

Books

Balboni, Alan. *Beyond the Mafia: Italian Americans and the Development of Las Vegas.* Reno, Nevada: University of Nevada Press, 1996.

Becker, Ed and Charles Rappleye. *All-American Mafioso: The Johnny Rosselli Story.* New York: Barricade Books, 1995.

Birmingham, Stephen. *"Our Crowd": The Great Jewish Families of New York.* Syracuse, New York: Syracuse University Press, 1967.

Burbank, Jeff. *License to Steal: Nevada's Gaming Control System in the Megaresort Age.* Reno, Nevada: University of Nevada Press, 2000.

Capeci, Jerry and Gene Mustain. *Gotti: Rise and Fall.* New York: Onyx Books, 1996.

Cartwright, Gary. *Dirty Dealing: Drug Smuggling on the Mexican Border and the Assassination of a Federal Judge: An American Parable.* El Paso, Texas: Cinco Puntos Press, 1998.

Castleman, Deke. *Nevada*. Oakland, California: Compass American Guides, 2000.

Cox, Donald. *Mafia Wipeout: How the Feds Put Away An Entire Mob Family*. New York: Shapolsky Books, 1989.

Cummings, John and Ernest Volkman. *Goombata: The Improbable Rise and Fall of John Gotti and His Gang*. New York: Avon, 1990.

Demaris, Ovid. *Captive City*. Secaucus, New Jersey: Lyle Stuart Books, 1969.
The Last Mafioso. New York: Bantam Books, 1981.
The Boardwalk Jungle. New York: Bantam Books, 1986.

Denton, Sally. *The Bluegrass Conspiracy: An Inside Story of Power, Greed, Drugs, and Murder*. New York: Doubleday, 1990.

Denton, Sally and Roger Morris. *The Money and the Power: The Making of Las Vegas and Its Hold on America, 1947-2000*. New York: Alfred A. Knopf, 2001.

Drosnin, Michael. *Citizen Hughes*. New York: Bantam Books, 1986.

Farrell, Ronald A. and Carole Case. *The Black Book and the Mob: The Untold Story of the Control of Nevada's Casinos*. Madison, Wisconsin: University of Wisconsin Press, 1995.

Fopiano, Willie and John Harney. *The Godson*. New York, St. Martin's Press: 1993.

Foreman, Laura (Editor). *Mafia*. Alexandria, Virginia: Time-Life Books, 1993.

Franzese, Michael and Dary Matera. *Quitting the Mob: How the 'Yuppie Don' Left the Mafia and Lived to Tell His Story*. New York: HarperCollins, 1992

Selected Bibliography

Gentry, Curt. *J. Edgar Hoover: The Man and His Secrets*. New York: Plume, 1991.

Giancana, Antoinette and Thomas C. Renner. *Mafia Princess: Growing Up in Sam Giancana's Family*. New York: Avon Books, 1984.

Greenspun, Hank and Alex Pelle. *Where I Stand*. New York: David McKay, 1966.

Hulse, James W. *The Nevada Adventure: A History*. Reno, Nevada: University of Nevada Press, 1966.

Jeffreys, Diarmund. *The Bureau: Inside the Modern FBI*. Boston, Massachusetts: Houghton Mifflin, 1995.

Johnston, David. *Temples of Chance: How America Inc. Bought Out Murder Inc. to Win Control of the Casino Business*. New York: Doubleday, 1992.

Lacey, Robert. *Little Man: Meyer Lansky and the Gangster Life*. New York: Warner, 1995.

Land, Barbara and Myrick Land. *A Short History of Las Vegas*. Reno, Nevada: University of Nevada Press, 1999.

Lane, Mills and Jedwin Smith. *Let's Get It On: Tough Talk From Boxing's Top Ref and Nevada's Most Outspoken Judge*. New York: Crown Books, 1998.

Lehr, Dick and Gerard O'Neill. *Black Mass: The Irish Mob, the FBI, and a Devil's Deal*. New York: PublicAffairs, 2000.

Lehr and O'Neill. *The Underboss: The Rise and Fall of a Mafia Family*. New York: PublicAffairs, 2002.

Lopez, Steve. *Land of Giants: Where No Good Deed Goes Unpunished*. Philadelphia, Pennsylvania: Camino Books, 1995.

Maas, Peter. *Underboss: Sammy the Bull Gravano's Story of Life in the Mafia*. New York: HarperCollins, 1997.

Manteris, Art and Rick Talley. *SuperBookie: Inside Las Vegas Sports Gambling*. Chicago: Contemporary Books, 1991.

McManus, James. *Positively Fifth Street: Murderers, Cheetahs, and Binion's World Series of Poker*. New York: Farrar Straus & Giroux, 2003.

Messick, Hank and Joseph L. Nellis. *The Private Lives of Public Enemies*. New York: Dell, 1974.

O'Brien, Joseph F. and Andris Kurins. *Boss of Bosses: The FBI and Paul Castellano*. New York: Island Books, 1991.

Odessky, Dick. *Fly on the Wall: Las Vegas' Good Old, Bad Old Days*. Las Vegas, Nevada: Huntington Press, 1999.

Pileggi, Nicholas. *Wiseguy: Life in a Mafia Family*. New York: Pocket Books, 1987.
Casino: Love and Honor in Las Vegas. New York: Simon & Schuster, 1995.

Porter, David. *Fixed: How Goodfellas Bought Boston College Basketball*. Dallas, Texas: Taylor Publishing, 2001.

Ranalli, Ralph. *Deadly Alliance: The FBI's Secret Partnership With the Mob*. New York: HarperCollins, 2001.

Reid, Ed and Ovid Demaris. *The Green Felt Jungle*. New York: Buccaneer Books, 1963.

Roemer, William F. *Man Against the Mob*. New York: Donald Fine, 1989.
The Enforcer: Spilotro — The Chicago Mob's Man Over Las Vegas. New York: Ivy, 1995.
Accardo: The Genuine Godfather. New York: Ivy, 1996.

Selected Bibliography

Salerno, Joseph and Stephen J. Rivele. *The Plumber: The True Story of How One Good Man Helped Bring Down the Entire Philadelphia Mob*. New York: Knightsbridge, 1991.

Simone, Robert. *The Last Mouthpiece*. Philadelphia: Camino Books, 2001.

Smith, John L. *Running Scared: The Life and Treacherous Times of Las Vegas Casino King Steve Wynn*. New York: Barricade Books, 1995.
The Animal in Hollywood: Anthony Fiato's Life in the Mafia. New York: Barricade Books, 1998.
On the Boulevard: The Best of John L. Smith. Las Vegas, Nevada: Huntington Press, 2000.

Smith, John L., and Jeff Scheid (photographer). *Quicksilver: The Ted Binion Murder Case*. Las Vegas, Nevada: Huntington Press, 2001.

Torgerson, Dial. *Kerkorian: An American Success Story*. New York: Dial Press, 1974.

Turkus, Burton B. and Sid Feder. *Murder, Inc.: The Inside Story of the Mob*. New York: Manor Books, 1951. (This work has been retitled as *Murder, Inc. The Story of the Syndicate*. New York: DeCapo Press, 1992.)

Valenti, John and Ron Naclerio. *Swee'Pea and Other Playground Legends: Tales of Drugs, Violence and Basketball*. New York: Kesend Publishing Ltd., 1990.

Wilmshurst, Paul. *Mob Law: The True Story of Oscar Goodman*. New York: WinStar Home Entertainment, 1998.

Yaeger, Don. *Shark Attack: Jerry Tarkanian and His Battle with the NCAA and UNLV*. New York: HarperCollins, 1992.

Newspapers

Albuquerque Journal
Arizona Republic
The Record of Bergen County
Boston Globe
Boston Herald
Chicago Sun-Times
Chicago Tribune
Las Vegas CityLife
Daily Oklahoman
Dallas Morning News
Kansas City Star
Las Vegas Israelite
Las Vegas Mercury
Las Vegas Review-Journal
Las Vegas Sun
Las Vegas Weekly
Los Angeles Times
Miami Herald
Newsday
New York Daily News
New York Post
New York Times
Philadelphia Daily News
Philadelphia Inquirer
Philadelphia Weekly
Press of Atlantic City
Reno Gazette-Journal
San Diego Tribune
San Diego Union
Statesboro Herald
The Wall Street Journal
Washington Post

Government and Legal Documents

(A representative list of federal court and federal appeals court documents only.)

Freedom of Information File: Federal Bureau of Investigation File No. 166-7268. Subject: Anthony Spilotro. 11 Volumes.

In Re: Special Grand Jury Proceedings Subpoena Served on Goodman & Chesnoff. CV-S-94-PMP.

In Re: Special Grand Jury Proceedings, Subpoena Served on Goodman & Chesnoff. Document 12. Contempt of Court Hearing. CV-S-94-PMP.

In Re: Special Grand Jury Proceedings, Subpoena Served on Goodman & Chesnoff. Document 32. Contempt of Court Hearing. CV-S-94-PMP.

U.S. v. Witten, Fechser, Cofield. 1992. WL 114663 (9th Circuit) No. 91-10529.

U.S. v. Chagra, 1992. 957 F. 2d. 5th Circuit. No. 90-50604.

U.S. v. Taketa 1991, 9th Circuit. No. 88-1022.

U.S. v. Goff, 1988, 5th Circuit, No. 87-1183.

U.S. v. Spilotro, 1986, 9th Circuit. No. 84-1245.

U.S. v. Claiborne, 1986, 9th Circuit, No. 86-2018.

U.S. v. Claiborne, 1985, 9th Circuit, No. 84-1294.

U.S. v. DeLuna, 1985, 8th Circuit, No. 83-2408.

U.S. v. Thomas, 1985, 8th Circuit, 84-2286.

U.S. v. Chagra, 1985, 5th Circuit, No. 83-1202.

U.S. v. Chagra, 1985, 5th Circuit, No. 83-1278.

U.S. v. Chagra, 1984, 5th Cicuit, No. 83-1807.

U.S. v. Claiborne, 1984, 9th Circuit, 84-1009.

U.S. v. Offices Known to 50 State Distributing Co., 1983, 9th Circuit, No. 82-5671.

U.S. v. Spilotro, 1983, 563 F. Supp., No. CR-R-80-57-ECR.

U.S. v. Spilotro, 1982, 9th Circuit, No. 81-5670.

U.S. v. Chagra, 1982, 5th Circuit, No. 80-1377.

U.S. v. Chagra, 1981, 1st Circuit, No. 80-1708.

U.S. v. Civella, 1981, 8th Circuit, No. 80-1828.

U.S. v. Calabrese, 1981, 10th Circuit, No. 79-1388.

U.S. v. Linton, 1980, 9th Circuit, No. 80-1548.

Of Rats and Men

U.S. v. Conforte, 1980, 9th Circuit, No. 77-3956.

Rosenthal V. State of Nev., 1981, 514 F. Supp., No. 79-39-RDF.

U.S. v. Bendetti, 1980, F. Supp. New Jersey, C-79-321.

U.S. v. Chagra, 1980, F. Supp. Mass., 80-00165-S.

U.S. v. Linton, 1980, F. Supp. Nev., CR-R—24 ECR.

U.S. v. Civella, 1980 F. Supp. Mo., 80-0023-01-W5.

U.S. v. Conforte, 1978, CR 77-00024-BRT.

Uston v. Hilton Hotels Corp., 1978, F. Supp Nev., 76-108-RDF.

U.S. v. Swanson, 1975, F. Supp. Nev. R-74-79- BRT.

U.S. v. Garramone, 1974, Penn., C-73-648.

U.S. v. Sklaroff, 1973, F. Supp, Fla., C-71-614

Proceedings of the U.S. Senate in the Impeachment Trial of Harry E. Claiborne, A Judge of the United States District Court for the District of Nevada. October, 1986.

Notes

Prologue

Oscar Goodman's name has been synonymous with the law in Southern Nevada for more than 35 years, but it was representation of members and associates of organized crime that led to his national reputation as a mob mouthpiece. Though he reveled in the role as the fearless legal protector of the Chicago Outfit's Las Vegas street boss Anthony Spilotro, the fact is Goodman managed to combine his representation of a wide array of accused mob figures with a full slate of more conventional clients. But after sitting in Goodman's office and experiencing the phone calls from representatives of a number of the nation's La Cosa Nostra families, it was obvious even to the casual observer that Oscar was one of the last of the great mob lawyers. In the early stages of the research process, Goodman sat for many hours of interviews and allowed access to his family, friends, and files. Seldom shy of the spotlight, he was happy to set aside time for early-morning interviews — until he decided to file for the office of Mayor of Las Vegas. At that point, Goodman's already busy schedule stretched to up to 14 hours a day and that kept him too busy to be bothered by my endless questions.

Around that time, I began working on the memoirs of Goodman's archrival during the Spilotro era, former FBI Special Agent in Charge Joe Yablonsky. My hope was to have both men's views of the world be published at approximately the same time. After many months of effort, the Yablonsky project fell through. But Goodman continued to make himself available even after taking office at City Hall. His candor and help—even in the face of the criticism found in this book—is greatly appreciated.

Chapter One

Images of Goodman's youth came courtesy of Laura Baylin Goodman, Lona (Goodman) Livingston, Hank Gladstone, Edward Glickman, Edward Pollock, and the subject. Pollock, his former grade-school teacher, contacted Goodman after he was elected mayor. Some 50 years after having young Oscar in his class, Pollock recalled in detail his favorite student's sense of humor and personal style. Stephen Birmingham's *Our Crowd: The Great Jewish Families of New York* was not only a compelling read, but provided insight into the mindset of the Goldmark family. Special thanks to legendary Las Vegas sports bettor Lem Banker, whose memory of the early days of Caesars remains impeccable.

Chapter Two

The "$87" story is now part of the growing Goodman legend. He has less success explaining how a man of so modest means could bet so prolifically from such an early age, but that is the nature of legends. The late attorney Morton Galane, who was interviewed briefly for this book, remained an admirer of Goodman. It is difficult to say the same for impeached U.S. District Judge Harry Claiborne, who was interviewed but declined to go into detail when asked about his current relationship with the lawyer who tried unsuccessfully to save his career and freedom. It was clear the friendship had gone cold, and multiple sources seeking anonymity said that Claiborne privately had questioned whether Goodman had been the right man for the job. Carolyn Goodman's insights were used in this chapter and throughout the book. Her role as Oscar's rock of personal strength was ever evident. Former Strike Force Attorney Dick Crane was helpful in clarifying Goodman's image among federal prosecutors.

Chapter Three

In my two decades in the newspaper business, few street characters rivaled Bob Martin and Marty Kane in the story-telling department. Both had been mob bookmakers at one level or another and each had had his scrapes with the law, but they defined "colorful" in a sports book industry that was rapidly being bled white by corporate control. They admired Goodman and, not incidentally, each took credit for making his career. An interview with Frank Rosenthal was also helpful on this subject. Rosenthal remains one of the last of the hall-of-fame handicappers from a bygone era. I also interviewed "Bobby the Midget" Kaye for this project. Thankfully, he did not plead "the two-and-a-half."

Chapter Four

Goodman's representation of Lansky played a big role in cementing his reputation as a "mob mouthpiece," but in reality he did more work for Flamingo casino-skim defendants Sammy Cohen and Morris Lansburgh. Goodman clearly did not object to the media using the Lansky representation as a marketing tool. An enigmatic aspect of this story is Goodman's relationship with Alvin Malnik, a Miami man once known as Lansky's heir apparent. Malnik's relationship with the Perlman casino family is well-documented (it was stated as a key reason the Perlmans were unfit for licensure in Atlantic City). The Perlmans also have a tie to Philadelphia, Goodman's hometown. But more intriguing is Goodman's own apparent admiration for Malnik, whom he called "my man Malnik" in one interview. Attorney Dominic Gentile offered insight into the importance of the Lansky representation to Goodman's growing reputation. Also, two former federal prosecutors contributed to this section.

Chapter Five

The Chicago Crime Commission remains an important source of historical perspective on all things related to the Outfit. The Rosenthal and Spilotro story is recounted in the greatest and most readable detail in Nicholas Pileggi's *Casino: Love and Honor in Las Vegas*, but the late FBI man Bill Roemer's book, *The Enforcer*, was also helpful. Stories from

The Las Vegas Review-Journal, Las Vegas Sun, Valley Times, Chicago Tribune, Chicago Sun-Times, and *Los Angeles Times* helped to flesh out the picture. Interviews with the late Marty Kane and Joey Boston were insightful, candid, and, until their deaths, off the record. Thanks also to Lem Banker and Frank LaPena. A note on LaPena: In a lengthy penitentiary interview with him, it became clear that he was a changed man. It also was clear that he was obsessed with receiving a pardon or having his case overturned, for he'd turned down more than one opportunity to gain an early release. He remains one of Nevada's most enigmatic criminal characters. An interview with Harry Claiborne was useful in this chapter, but it was just as interesting to see who among Goodman's defense bar peers declined to be interviewed for this project. Their names will remain anonymous, but some will be conspicuous by their absence.

Chapter 6

History professor Alan Balboni's *Beyond the Mafia* was useful in clarifying a time of great change in the Las Vegas casino business. Interviews with Gentile and others in the defense bar were also helpful. Allen Glick's house of cards tumbled and appeared to hurt everyone but himself. He somehow saved his freedom, but it's clear many years later that Goodman knows far more about the man than he is willing to share. Dick Odessky's remembrance of his tenure at the Stardust, recounted in entertaining style in his *Fly on the Wall*, was illuminating. For his part, Rosenthal remains as hard-edged as ever when the subject of Glick and the Stardust is raised. He clearly believes he should have been able to remain a man in good standing in the Nevada casino game. Instead, he is a member of the state's Black Book.

Chapter Seven

Perspective in this chapter was gained through several conversations with retired FBI undercover agent Rick Baken, whose own life story is nothing short of amazing. A background interview with the late Herbie Blitzstein added to the picture. And a special thanks to Goodman insider and all-around sports betting expert Vinny Montalto.

Notes

Chapter Eight

No research into the incredible life and crimes of Jamiel "Jimmy" Chagra is complete without consulting Gary Cartwright's *Dirty Dealing: Drug Smuggling on the Mexican Border and the Assassination of a Federal Judge – an American Parable.* Beyond that, Goodman made available substantial amounts of case material and transcripts associated with the case. As an aside, there was no shortage of Las Vegas casino employees and street gamblers who knew Jimmy Chagra and enjoyed the run of luck that invariably accompanied his arrival in the city. He was a boorish fellow to many, but he threw around a fortune in cash wherever he went. He also heaped piles of greenbacks on his favorite attorney. Stories from the *Dallas Morning News* were helpful in developing this chapter.

Chapter Nine

The Wood murder investigation was not only one of the most expensive in FBI history, but was also written about extensively in the press. Impressions and descriptions used in this chapter come from press accounts, Goodman's memory of the facts of the case, appeal documents, and, again, Cartwright's work. For those wishing to further their understanding of the battle between the defense bar and the Maximum Johns of the federal judiciary, I suggest the second edition of Cartwright's *Dirty Dealing*, published in 1998 by Cinco Puntos Press of Texas. It contains an illuminating essay by criminal defense attorney Frank Caballero, which shines a credible light on tough-sentencing judges who sometimes sacrifice justice to feed their own egos and please their friends in law enforcement.

Chapter Ten

The victory on behalf of Jimmy Chagra in the Wood assassination case remains one of the more incredible courtroom wins of the 20th century. Rarely, if ever, has one client had the entire weight of the federal government against him—along with seemingly overwhelming evidence and witness testimony— only to wriggle off the hook thanks to the dramatic display of his attorney. Chagra will be up for parole soon, but few observers of the system can possibly believe he will gain his freedom on the first pass. The Chagra family, meanwhile, was devastated by the curse wrought by its participation in the drug trade. Interviews with Goodman and a lengthy reading of court documents helped to clarify the case's complexities. I also interviewed an FBI informant who continues to maintain a letter-writing relationship with convicted killer Charles Harrelson, who has been suspected by some conspiracy theorists of being one of the three "bums" on the grassy knoll in Dallas on the day President John F. Kennedy was assassinated. Harrelson's contacts with the Texas and Louisiana underworld, combined with his life-long personal criminal history and connections to the Binion family, make him an ideal candidate to fill the role of secret assassin. To date, however, no credible evidence has been produced linking Harrelson to the Kennedy assassination.

Chapter Eleven

The 11-volume FBI file on Tony Spilotro, obtained through the Freedom of Information Act, was helpful in several ways: First, it showed the depth of the government's interest in the man from an early age. Second, it showed the increasing sophistication of law enforcement in investigating complex criminal enterprises and street hoodlums of Spilotro's status and prolific appetites. The *Chicago Tribune*'s and *Sun-Times*' veteran mob reporters did a number on Spilotro. Pileggi's *Casino* and Roemer's *Enforcer* provided factual background and Goodman and several retired FBI agents and Metro officers, all of whom requested and received my word that their identities not be revealed, helped to flesh out the picture of Tony and his lawyer. Thanks also to former Chicago attorney Jerry Werksman, whose insights into the era and Goodman's place in it were some of the most candid of anyone I interviewed for this project. Thanks also to Lem Banker and Kathy Buccieri Laughlan for their perspectives on some of Tough Tony's alleged victims. People tend to forget that, while Spilotro was never convicted of murder in his lifetime, many of his alleged victims left grieving families behind.

Chapter Twelve

An argument can be made that *Review-Journal* columnist and KLAS-TV 8 reporter Ned Day, who died in 1987, invented Tony Spilotro—or at least made him an underworld star. For what was Spilotro, really, but a soldier trusted with enforcing a racket that was far beyond his criminal expertise? Day rarely missed an opportunity to pummel Spilotro, occasionally risking his health by doing so. Ned's work in this area was unbeatable and invaluable. Ron Farrell and Carole Case's *The Black Book and the Mob: The Untold Story of the Control of Nevada's Casinos* and Pileggi's *Casino* were excellent research tools, but nothing beat an interview with Rosenthal and the perspective gained by many long conversations with Marty Kane, Joey Boston, and Bob Martin.

Chapter Thirteen

Nick Civella was clearly one of the most underrated mob figures of the latter half of the 20th century, just as his Kansas City family was overshadowed by its fellow *brugads* in larger media markets. Goodman, as in few times during our many interviews, held back little when declaring his admiration for Civella. Clearly, in Goodman's opinion, here was a man's man. Stories in the *Kansas City Star* contributed to the Civella family story, as did the substantial appeals documents produced by their various legal entanglements. One strong rumor circulating out of Kansas City at press time had several remnants of the Civella clan no longer enamored of Goodman and at least one accusing him of not giving his best effort to remain on the family's withering casino-rackets cases in the early 1980s. It should be noted that Goodman was disqualified by a federal judge in no small part because he had been arguably the most active criminal defense attorney representing mob figures in the nation. By the time the Civellas needed him most, he was a walking conflict.

Chapter Fourteen

Harry Claiborne is unquestionably among the most intriguing legal figures in Nevada history. Unfortunately, there is no definitive biography of the man, who in 2003 continued to practice his profession and maintain a low profile after decades in the public spotlight. Attorney Michael Stuhff, who was part of the Claiborne defense team, provided his insight into the judge's character, as did other Las Vegas lawyers and private investigators who spoke on the condition that they not be identified. In June 2003, Joe Schoenmann conducted an in-depth

interview with exiled brothel baron Joe Conforte that was published in *Las Vegas Life* magazine. Although Conforte was described as living comfortably in Brazil in a kind of pimp's penthouse paradise, it was clear from the interview that he was
still trying to make excuses for selling out his long-time friend
and personal lawyer, Claiborne. Conforte mewled about be
ing betrayed by Claiborne, when even the most damning facts
associated with the case revealed that the judge had never
promised Conforte anything as dramatic as an overturned
appeal at the Ninth Circuit. The Claiborne affair is one of the
most compelling case studies in the vast differences in the coverage of a news event by competing news organizations — in
this case, the *Las Vegas Sun* and *Las Vegas Review-Journal*. In
keeping with its status as the locals' servant, the *Sun* came out
early in support of Claiborne. In editorials by the firebrand
publisher Hank Greenspun and in investigative reports by Jeff
German and Gary Thompson, the *Sun* set the tone for the Clai-
borne-as-victim camp. The *Review-Journal*, meanwhile, followed developments in the case through a series of contacts
inside the FBI and Justice Department. Those reports appear
to have been fed in no small part by federal agents aligned
with Las Vegas Special Agent in Charge Joseph Yablonsky.
The Claiborne case eventually produced Yablonsky's biggest
scalp, but it also illustrated the lengths to which the government was willing to go to get its man and prove its case.

Chapter Fifteen

A study of Oscar Goodman's career is incomplete without
an appreciation of his juggling of clients Claiborne and Spilotro. Although federal law enforcement saw the representation as more than coincidental — Claiborne maintained a life-
long friendship with former Dallas racket boss Benny Binion,
whose associations with organized crime were well-documented — the real story was how Goodman managed to maintain a balance of representation along with his lesser cases and
weekend transformation into a family man. Columns by Ned
Day and reporting in the *Review-Journal*, *Sun*, *Chicago Tribune*,
and *Chicago Sun-Times* were augmented by court documents,
an interview with Claiborne, and an interview with a former
Strike Force attorney. Thanks also to *San Diego Union-Tribune*

reporter Phil LaVelle, a former *Review-Journal* staffer, who shared his memories of Spilotro at the courthouse. KLAS TV-8 Reporter George Knapp's interview with mob killer-turned-informant Frank Cullotta was also illuminating. Thanks also are due to Carolyn Goodman for sharing her memories of that time and of Geri Rosenthal and her family. The Freedom of Information Act was used to augment FBI background material on Spilotro.

Chapter Sixteen

Material for this chapter is rooted in the Congressional transcripts of the Claiborne impeachment trial, printed in October 1986. The document provides insight not only into the historic nature of the proceedings, but also into the lack of a level playing field. The judge, once convicted of felonies in a federal court, had no reasonable chance to convince Congress that he'd been railroaded. In its way, it was one of the great congressional dog-and-pony shows of the post-Watergate era.

Chapter Seventeen

Although the Beloff corruption trial was not Goodman's first return trip to Philadelphia—he'd been there years earlier on a bookmaking case that ended up in the recruitment of future law partner Steve Stein—the Scarfo-Leonetti family affairs were a clear point of departure from his past as a man considered to be tied with all things Chicago. Goodman's relationship with former Haverford classmate Robert Simone, Scarfo's attorney, remains somewhat murky to this day. Although in interviews Goodman claimed no great friendship with Simone, he did visit him in federal prison at Nellis after Simone's conviction on tax charges. When Simone finished his readable, though unabashedly biased, memoir on his career as a mob attorney, he sent his friend Goodman a loose-bound galley. Reports from the *Philadelphia Inquirer, Philadelphia Daily News, Philadelphia Weekly,* and *Press of Atlantic City* were especially helpful in capturing the scale of the Scarfo trials.

Chapter Eighteen

Donald Cox's *Mafia Wipeout: How the Feds Put Away An Entire Mob Family* provided excellent background on the Scarfo era. It was augmented by Ovid Demaris' *The Boardwalk Jungle* and columnist Steve Lopez's *Land of Giants*. Lopez has since left his post with the *Inquirer* and is now a columnist with the *Los Angeles Times*. Simone's *The Last Mouthpiece* provided endless color, most of it blood red.

Chapter Nineteen

The FBI helped make Goodman a prophet by its sinful handling of Boston gangster James "Whitey" Bulger. *Boston Globe* reporters Gerard O'Neill and Dick Lehr produced a pair of extremely readable works that illustrate the deceptive nature of the feds in the Bulger affair. Their first, *The Underboss: The Rise and Fall of a Mafia Family*, tears apart the Angiulo clan and uses FBI Agent John Connolly as a key, even heroic, source. It's the same Connolly who helps protect his deep source, Bulger, in their *Black Mass: The Irish Mob, the FBI, and a Devil's Deal*. Read together, they show the arc of ends-justify-the-means tactics that was present in the Boston office. *Boston Herald* reporter Ralph Ranalli's *Deadly Alliance*, Willie Fopiano and Jon Harney's *The Godson* and more than one hundred hours of conversations with mobster-turned-informant Anthony Fiato helped to flesh out the picture of Southie and the New England mob generally.

Chapter Twenty

Natale "Big Chris" Richichi was indeed one of Goodman's favorite clients. Although he says he misses his time with Spilotro, it's safe to say he misses Richichi even more, despite the Gambino capo's lengthy criminal history and air-tight association with mob boss John Gotti. Richichi and, to a slightly lesser extent, Charles Panarella are proof of Goodman's fascination and identification with strong men of notorious pedigree. A series of excellent books have been written about the Gotti era, in which Richichi played a substantial role. Among them: John Cummings' and Ernest Volkman's *Goombata* and Jerry Capeci's and Gene Mustain's *Gotti: Rise and Fall*. *Underboss: Sammy the Bull Gravano's Story of Life in the Mafia* by Peter Maas was also instructive.

Chapter Twenty-One

Goodman's post-mob cases are some of his most colorful and there's a clear trend toward high-profile banner-headline clients. Goodman himself admitted that he preferred the big-splash cases, if not only for the big paydays and headlines, then for the electricity associated with representing clients who commonly find themselves the subject of sports-page rumor and tabloid fodder. It's one of his mob clients, Carl DeLuna, however, who provides one of the last great riddles in Goodman's life. DeLuna, clearly, possesses a world of information about the time of transition in the Nevada gaming fraternity in which a substantial number of licensees kept close contact with their mob benefactors. What secrets could DeLuna reveal? If he has them, thus far he's keeping them to himself. Meanwhile, some of Civella's allies in Kansas City continue to grouse about Goodman's representation of the highly respected elder, Nick Civella. Thanks are due to Ed Becker, intrepid reporter, Las Vegas insider, and author, for his perspective on oral surgeon Gregory Minton. Ed stole the show in the documentary *Mob Law* and is one of the last great resources for those seeking perspective from the first-generation of Las Vegas mob-casino connections. His book with Charles Rappleye, *All American Mafioso: The John Rosselli Story* remains must reading for any serious student of the era. FBI SAC Joe Yablonsky's comments are drawn from his interview for *Mob Law*. I used none of the material developed in helping him write his abortive memoir.

Chapter Twenty-Two

Marty Keach was extremely helpful in putting the Tommy Allison story into perspective. Although Keach worked arduously on the case, he readily acknowledged Goodman's key role securing the settlement by appearing in person before the Nevada Supreme Court. Keach later alienated himself, possibly for the remainder of his career, by lambasting the high court in the Canterino beating case. A brave man, that Keach. The work of Jack Newfield remains the last word in Don King investigative criticism. Mr. Newfield got in King's kitchen and stayed there with *Only in America*, which remains one of the best shorter works of investigative journalism of the last decade. Goodman's relationship with the Spilotro family was changed forever by his appearance in Martin Scorsese's *Casino*. Goodman, in my opinion, truly regretted portraying himself in the movie and said so in several conversations. To the author's knowledge, Goodman has not maintained contact with Spilotro's family since the film.

Chapter Twenty-Three

Oscar Goodman was considered for a judgeship in 1973. The remark made by political consultant Sig Rogich was uttered in the hallway of the Cashman Field Center in front of the author and two other witnesses. Long-time Las Vegas Mayor Oran Gragson was an exceedingly pleasant man who laughed as he reminisced about his early days selling furniture to, among many customers, Roxie and Eddie Clippinger of Roxie's whorehouse. Interviews with Billy Vassiliadis, Mark Fierro, Tom Letizia, Jim Ferrence, Vinny Montalto, David Chesnoff, Marty Keach, William Cassidy, Carolyn Goodman, and Cara Goodman were extremely helpful in rounding out this chapter. Former County Commissioner Jay Bingham's heart ailment prevented him from continuing in the mayor's race, but he continued to maintain an active business life as the head of a major contracting company. I spent ample time in the presence of Arnie Adamsen and Lindsay Lewis during the campaign to see just how much they underestimated their opponent. During that time, they dwelled on Goodman's obvious attorney-client association with Anthony Spilotro, but did not seem to fully appreciate that nearly a dozen years had passed since Spilotro's death. In a rapidly growing place like Las Vegas, that meant the population had more than doubled and likely as not most Southern Nevadans were unaware of Spilotro's bloody reputation. Thanks to *Review-Journal* reporters Mike Zapler and Jan Moller and *Sun* reporters Erin Neff and Ed Koch, as well as former *Sun* reporter Diana Sahagun, for their wide-ranging coverage. A note on Dennis Mastro: He had been a player in Las Vegas at a pivotal time in the community's history, going from part-owner of the Jolly Trolley casino to an outcast due to alleged organized-crime connections. The Jolly Trolley was transformed into a sprawling souvenir superstore.

"I've always believed Oscar was a natural," Marty Keach

recalled. "For five or six years we'd been trying to get Oscar to run. He took a serious look at challenging Sue Wagner for lieutenant governor, but decided against it. Financially, he didn't need to work. Professionally, there was nothing left to prove. He does love this town. He does love to be in the public eye. And he does love the press. For him I think it was a natural progression."

Chapter Twenty-Four

Manny Baker, now deceased, was the subject of one of Goodman's most dramatic federal battles, in which he and law partner David Chesnoff proved a gang of federal agents had likely misled the court when arresting Baker on alleged drug charges. Those charges were later dropped after Federal Magistrate Lawrence Leavitt, himself a former prosecutor, dismissed the case on misconduct grounds. In an interview, Goodman said he'd been dazzled by casino man Steve Wynn's hyperbolic chatter about bringing an NBA franchise to Las Vegas. City Councilman Michael McDonald survived his problems with Goodman, but could not survive a 2003 challenge by trauma-center nurse and neophyte candidate Janet Moncrief. Moncrief, a close friend of casino maverick Bob Stupak, easily defeated McDonald and Goodman met with her even before she was sworn into office. On the subject of controversial businessman Kerry Rogers, Goodman remains consistent: Contrary to published reports, he insists he made no money off his e.Volve investment. Goodman's stance on clearing the homeless out of the heart of the downtown corridor remains the most controversial decision of his first four and a half years in office. ACLU official Gary Peck has been perhaps his fiercest critic. "Given my own commitments to certain core values, I cannot understand, let alone excuse, the way the Mayor has brazenly disregarded the rights of people who are least able to defend themselves and who can't hire the kind of high-priced legal talent he provided to his clients all those years he was proclaiming the importance of the Bill of Rights for everyone — especially those who are unpopular." But the Goodman who so offended the ACLU official is the same fellow who won over Peck's friends and associates by encouraging the redevelopment of downtown's long-neglected but historic neighborhoods, and the same fellow who stuck up for those neighbors when Stratosphere owner Carl Icahn attempted to win approval to place an enormous roller-coaster-type amusement ride at the resort. The City Hall official anonymously quoted is a member of senior management who has intimate knowledge of the day-to-day grind. Thanks to television reporter and newspaper columnist George Knapp for allowing access to his interview with mob hitman-turned-informant Frank Cullotta. The consensus on Goodman's decision not to run for governor is that it not only took the sizzle out of the race, but it also hurt the Democratic turnout on Election Day.

Doing It His Way: An Epilogue in Motion

Although Goodman flatly denied even a passing association with Vinnie Palermo, he remained respectful of his cordial relationship with Charles Panarella. A note about the Cara Goodman engagement party: The author and his wife were also in attendance. Despite his own rising celebrity, Goodman remains unbashful about his own fascination with celebrities from the world of sports, politics, film, and entertainment. He makes regular weekly appearances on local radio and television shows, has his own weekly call-in program on the city's TV station, still holds monthly town-hall-style meetings at City Hall, and managed to find time for his occasional "Martinis with the Mayor" happy-hour events. Goodman appeared to genuinely get a kick out of the three bobblehead dolls that were created in his likeness for various sporting events and casino promotions and he kept a mayor's commemorative gaming chip on his desk in an office whose walls had already grown cluttered with glossy photographs of hizzoner and everyone from President Clinton to the cast of "The Sopranos" — but not one of his old clients. Interviews with Vassiliadis and attorneys Dominic Gentile, Ferrence, and Chesnoff were helpful in bringing to a close an epilogue that promises to change, even as this book is being printed.

Index

Index

Index

Index

Index

About Huntington Press

Huntington Press is a specialty publisher of Las Vegas- and gambling-related books and periodicals. Contact:

Huntington Press
3687 South Procyon Avenue
Las Vegas, Nevada 89103
702-252-0655
www.huntingtonpress.com